The New Women's Theatre

Ten Plays by Contemporary American Women

Edited and
with an Introduction by

HONOR MOORE

VINTAGE BOOKS
A Division of Random House
New York

VINTAGE BOOKS EDITION May, 1977
First Edition
Copyright © 1977 by Honor Moore

Library of Congress Cataloging in Publication Data
Main entry under title:

The New women's theatre.

Includes bibliographical references.
CONTENTS: Jacker, C. Bits and pieces.—Russ, J. Window Dressing.
—Molinaro, U. Breakfast past noon. [etc.]
1. American drama—Women authors. 2. American drama—20th century.
I. Moore, Honor, 1945–
PS628.W6N4   812'.5'408   76–58261
ISBN 0–394–72206–X

Manufactured in the United States of America
9 8 7 6 5 4 3 2

For Kathryn, Leora, Lyn and Mary

Editor's Note

I would like to thank women in the theatre for inspiring me to do this book, especially the nearly two hundred playwrights across the country who sent me scripts of their produced plays. For help, enthusiasm, and the example of their work, I especially thank Louise Bernikow, Ellen Hawkes, Kirsten Grimstad, Susan Rennie, Avra Petrides, Deena Metzger, Barbara Babcock and Adrienne Rich. For putting me in touch with playwrights, I am grateful to Marilyn Hacker, Flora Roberts, Audrey Wood, Judith Katz, Julia Miles and Arthur Ballet. For her support at the beginning and throughout the project, I thank my agent, Wendy Weil. For her important help and the opportunity to do this book, I thank Anne Freedgood, my editor; for her support and hard work, Sarah Leslie; and for their help with a difficult project I am grateful to copy editors Nancy Inglis and Cordelia Jason. Last, I thank Venable Herndon for his inestimable encouragement at every stage of this anthology.

I have chosen plays that express the spirit of the new women's theatre for excellence, variety and readability. I include works by women who are not widely published, leaving out playwrights whose works are readily available elsewhere. I regret that I was unable to get permission to include *For Colored Girls Who Have Considered Suicide/When the Rainbow Is Enuf* by Ntozake Shange and *Voices* by Susan Griffin.

Contents

Introduction

As a student of theatre history, I learned that drama during its golden ages in ancient Greece and Tudor England employed no women. With the introduction of actresses, the quality of theatre apparently declined. When in the late 1960's Britain's National Theatre produced an all-male *As You Like It*,[1] I suppressed a "What about us?" assuming my services as a stage manager and factotum would still be welcome, and uneasily joined my male colleagues' rejoicing: perhaps John Dexter's experiment signaled a return to womanless theatre and the coming of a third golden age. It didn't. The actress retained her begrudged place in the theatre as the theatre did hers in society.

But what of the woman playwright? Virginia Woolf provides the most famous myth. "Let me imagine," she writes, "since facts are so hard to come by, what would have happened had Shakespeare had a wonderfully gifted sister, called Judith. . . . Like him, she had a taste for the theatre. She stood at the stage door; she wanted to act, she said. . . . The manager—a fat loose-lipped man—guffawed. . . . To have lived a free life in London in the sixteenth century would have meant for a woman who was poet and playwright a nervous stress and dilemma which might well have killed her. . . ." This Judith, writes Woolf, "had the quickest fancy, a gift like her brother's, for the tune of words." This Judith, she continues, was befriended by Nick Greene, the actor-manager, and "found herself with child by that gentleman and so . . . killed herself one winter's night and lies buried at some cross-roads where the omnibuses now stop outside the Elephant and Castle."[2]

[1] *As You Like It* was produced by the National Theatre at the Old Vic in 1967; the all-male cast was directed by John Dexter.
[2] Virginia Woolf, *A Room of One's Own*, New York, 1929, pp. 49–50, 51–52.

I had not read *A Room of One's Own* in college, but I had internalized the myth of Shakespeare's sister. One aspiring female dramatist was a classmate. I remember watching her walk through the theatre library on her way to a playwrighting seminar in which she was the only woman. My male cohorts, also in the class, said her writing was "pretty good"—a high compliment—but none of them produced her plays. I never even had a conversation with her. Women should not be playwrights, I theorized from my vantage point in the drama club office where I typed rehearsal schedules. Now I admire her guts.

After graduation, I went to the Yale School of Drama in theatre administration, and during my second year, a woman playwright asked me to direct her play. I was flattered enough to get up the courage to do it, and was pleased with the results. It was before the women's movement, but I felt a connection with the woman playwright and her central character. For the first time I believed the theatre could express me. At the end of the year, 1969, I quit the school and moved to New York City, where my first work was co-producing *The Nest* by Tina Howe. The play was a comic surreal treatment of the lives of three archetypal female roommates whose apartment on the 150th floor of an anonymous building had "a view of heaven." The stage doorman had let us in, but the critics pushed us out. Their monolithic rejection of this female vision convinced me the professional theatre was no context for a woman's expression. I turned my full energy to writing poetry, sensing there more flexibility for the woman artist.

I soon began to read my work around the country, and in early 1974, gave a reading in New York of work in progress, poems I'd begun about my mother's recent death from cancer. Mary Silverman, a producer, was in the audience and afterward suggested I create a theatre piece based on the poems. Six months later, *Mourning Pictures* opened at the Lenox Arts Center in western Massachusetts. The play puts scenes of the mother's dying in counterpoint to the story, told in poems and songs, of the daughter's acceptance of her mother's (and her own) mortality. It was well-received at Lenox and moved three months later to Broadway. The New York critics, with a few significant exceptions, were moved to hostility by *Mourning Pictures,* but many other people who saw the play were as disturbed as I was by the denial of death and of female experience implicit in the reviews. "It's so unfair!" I remember screaming; "they all write from one point of view!"

Another play in which a woman has cancer—Anne Burr's *Mert & Phil,* produced in New York City the same month as *Mourning Pictures*—provoked a similar response from the critics. Mert's mastectomy puts pressure on her relationship with Phil, her husband, and forces her, an inarticulate middle-aged woman, to face her separateness. Like *Mourning Pictures,* it is a play about identity and autonomy, but it was reviewed as a play about mastectomy. Clearly the critics, most of whom are men, were not ready to see the central events of women's lives as metaphors for their own experience. But these woman-centered plays and others, like Corinne Jacker's *Bits and Pieces* and Myrna Lamb's opera *Apple Pie,* were being produced, and people were seeing them and being moved. Susan Braudy wrote a sympathetic review of *Mourning Pictures,* and Marilyn Stasio analyzed the critics' response to *Mert & Phil,* both in *Ms.* magazine.[3]

Were there precedents? Or were we pioneering? I wanted to find out what had happened to women playwrights in the past. It was time to place these new plays in proper historical context, to bring them together, to name them.

Much of the energy of contemporary feminist scholarship has gone toward separating women's work from men's in order to identify independent female traditions and histories. Ellen Moers' *Literary Women*[4] reveals that women have a distinct literary tradition, that women writers have, since the eighteenth century, communicated with each other and, more important, read and learned from each other's work. Louise Bernikow's anthology, *The World Split Open,*[5] shows that, for four hundred years, women

[3]Susan Braudy, "Ladies and Gentlemen, My Mother Is Dying," *Ms.,* November 1974; Marilyn Stasio, "The Nights the Critics Lost Their Cool," *Ms.,* September 1975.

[4]Ellen Moers, *Literary Women: The Great Writers,* New York, 1976.

[5]Louise Bernikow, *The World Split Open: Four Centuries of Women Poets in England and America, 1552–1950,* New York, 1974.

poets in England and America have participated in a history of shared subjects and concerns. In short, women's literature has a coherence not previously suspected.

One appeal of the theatre to writers has been the relative camaraderie it provides; the playwright puts words on paper alone, but the work is brought to fruition in company, with the help of actors and directors. Male exclusion of women from this camaraderie, perhaps more than any other single factor, has been responsible for the lack of a female tradition in playwrighting similar to that which exists in both fiction and poetry. Woolf's story, though fiction, paints a true picture of the brutal form this exclusion has always taken—during Elizabethan days and throughout history. In the Roman era, a woman mime could be forced to take her clothes off or to grant sexual favors on demand. Her oppression, though more violent, was no more destructive of self-expression than her twelfth-century sister's who, swathed in white and crowned with flowers, decorated village mystery plays as Virgin Mary or virgin martyr and spoke no lines. Western theatre has mostly been a man's world in which women are violated or adulated, depending on the historical moment, but never allowed to express their whole selves. Women playwrights with important careers, few though they are, appear at times when a prosperous theatre is accompanied by relative freedom for women, expecially women of the middle class.

The first woman playwright was a rule-proving exception who escaped the leer of the stage doorman because she lived in a world of women. Hrotsvitha of Gandersheim, a tenth-century Saxon nun, wrote six comedies and much poetry (all in Latin) during her lifetime. She was a woman with intellectual aspirations who, like many others in her era, chose convent life as an alternative to the chattel existence of marriage. In the preface to her first book, poems in praise of the Virgin Mary, she recounts writing in secret, not telling "any experts for fear that the roughness of style would make them discourage me to such an extent that I might give up writing altogether."[6] She kept writing, with the support of her convent sisters, and her fame soon spread outside the convent and came to the attention of the imperial court of Saxony. Eventually she wrote a verse history of the reign of Emperor Otto II, which survives as an important document.

Apparently her success gave Hrotsvitha the freedom to write what she wanted to; she turned to plays toward the end of her life, a fact which has confused scholars, since she is the only person, of either sex, known to have written plays between the end of Latin tragedy (65 A.D.) and the beginning of the mystery play (twelfth century). But "The Strong Voice of Gandersheim," as she called herself, has survived caprices of scholarship that have written her off as, among other things, a literary hoax perpetrated by Conrad Celtes, the sixteenth-century discoverer and publisher of her manuscripts.

Even with her existence secure, Hrotsvitha is presented as a puritanical nun who wrote comedies in the Roman style to combat the sinful worldliness of the pagan originals. It is true that her plays celebrate Christian good, but the hijinks en route reveal an original comic mind and a dramatist obsessed with rape as a metaphor for male sin and the oppression of women. In *Dulcitus*, for instance, the title character, a grotesque Roman governor, goes to his palace kitchen, where he hopes to ravish the three young Christian maidens he thinks are imprisoned there. He is so overcome with sexual anticipation that he mistakes the pots and pans for the three virgins and fondles them the whole night through. The playwright shows us the three girls peeking into the kitchen, struggling to keep giggles under control as they describe Dulcitus' pathetic antics, kitchen equipment crashing and clanking offstage.

But where would a lone nun's plays have been performed in the tenth century when there were probably no theatres in Europe? It has been suggested that they were written as exercises or to be sung by the nuns. Rosamond Gilder, however, in her excellent

---

[6]Quoted by Rosamond Gilder in her book *Enter the Actress: The First Women in the Theatre,* New York, 1960, pp. 23–24.

history of women in the theatre, *Enter the Actress,* concludes that Hrotsvitha's plays, with their ribald humor and visual effects, would never have been primly chanted. She theorizes that Theophano, Otto II's Greek wife, told the nuns homesick tales of Constantinople's burgeoning theatre when she visited her daughter Sophia, a novice at Gandersheim, and that these stories inspired Hrotsvitha. "It does not require too wild a flight of imagination," Gilder writes, "to picture the nuns of Gandersheim eagerly preparing to welcome their royal guest with a form of entertainment particularly dear to her heart, and one of which she had been completely deprived since her departure from Constantinople. . . ."[7]

The story of Hrotsvitha—a woman who successfully wrote plays and probably directed and acted in them—counters the myth of Shakespeare's sister. One wonders if "The Strong Voice of Gandersheim" passed her craft along to younger nuns whose work has not survived, grieves that this first woman playwright did not found a tradition, and returns to the story of Judith Shakespeare reminded that Hrotsvitha's voice was strong because it issued from a world of women that supported a woman in the expression of her vision. The European theatre had to wait six hundred years before another woman was allowed to speak for herself.

The *commedia dell'arte,* which reached its height in Italy in the late sixteenth century, always included women. This form developed when the craft of the mime fused with the influence of Roman comedies, rediscovered in Italy in the fifteenth century. Performances of the comedies were controlled by the Church, which considered the theatre competition and women vessels of sin; in keeping with "historical accuracy," the plays were revived in Latin with all-boy casts. But the theatre was too popular to remain under ecclesiastical wraps for long; while monks and priests performed their all-male versions in church precincts, women of the nobility acted all-female productions in the privacy of their castles. Eventually secular Italians began to write and perform new plays and called on women to sing and dance during intermissions;

[7]Rosamond Gilder, *op. cit.,* p. 31.

those who weren't content to be merely decorative became min-
strels and jugglers and performed in the streets. Italian women
probably made their first public appearances as actresses in Il
Ruzzante's rustic street comedies in the early 1500's, but it was
the *commedia dell'arte all'improvizzo* that assured them a permanent place as professionals and provided women with the next
opportunity to express themselves as authors in the theatre.

Among the urges that inspire people to seek a theatre career are
the desire to perform and the desire to create a world and see it
come to life. The latter produces directors and managers as well
as playwrights. Important in the history of the *commedia* are two
actresses who combined these impulses, Vittoria Piisimi and Isabella Andreini. Piisimi was an early star of the Gelosi, the most
famous of the many *commedia* troupes that toured Europe, setting up their portable stages and playing to enthusiastic audiences
in marketplaces and town squares. Although being a manager
involves nourishing other people's talents, an actress who becomes
a manager controls her repertory and chooses plays to express her
own talent and vision; perhaps the Gelosi weren't playing *The
Portrait,* written by Scala especially for Piisimi, often enough.
Whatever the reason, during their 1562 Florence engagement,
Piisimi left the Gelosi, started her own troupe and became the first
actress-manager. The tradition she began survives today, in movies
and theatre, when female stars purchase properties and become
producers, casting themselves in leading roles.

It was Isabella Andreini, the most celebrated *commediante* of
all, who made her debut as a replacement for Piisimi. The Floren-
tines who were there that evening saw a new sixteen-year-old face
—leading ladies were not masked like other characters—and
heard new words as well. *Commedia* plays were improvised each
evening from scenarios that outlined comic situations for stock
characters. Even when a company repeated a play, lines were
added and cut each evening; characters became the creations of
the actors who portrayed them. Andreini performed with the
Gelosi her whole life; the character she played, *la prima donna
innamorata,* continued to be called Isabella after her death. Her
example improved the morally suspect image of women in the

theatre: Andreini personified a Renaissance ideal—not only was she talented, beautiful and witty, but she was virtuous, happily married, the mother of seven, a scholar and a poet. And she was a playwright: as a scenarist, with her husband, Francesco, and the famous Scala, she helped the rough-and-tumble *commedia* develop into an intricate and sophisticated form.

The Gelosi and other *commedia* troupes toured Europe in the sixteenth and seventeenth centuries and had an impact on native theatre everywhere. In France, the *commedia*'s stock characters formed the basis for Molière's comedies and brought actresses into his company. In England, plots of Elizabethan comedy show traces of *commedia* conventions—mistaken identities, romantic intrigue—but the casts remained all-male. According to most sources, this did not change until 1660, when the theatre and the monarchy were triumphantly restored after eighteen years of Puritan rule. Rosamond Gilder dates the appearance of the first woman on the English stage somewhat earlier. In John Webb's *The Siege of Rhodes,* which Sir William D'Avenant produced in 1656 with Puritan permission, as a "moral presentation," a woman called Ianthe played a heroic role. This woman, whose real name is not known, began the first era of great English actresses. These were the women—Mary Betterton, Nell Gwyn, Anne Marshall among them—who played the witty and brilliant women in the comedies of the Restoration. It was the presence of these actresses that enabled the first English women to write for the stage. Chief among them was Aphra Behn, the first woman to earn her living writing.

In 1681, eight years before her death, Aphra Behn expressed a sentiment which I am sure many women writing for the theatre have felt, although few have dared express it in a preface to a published play:

> This one thing I venture to say, though against my Nature because it has a Vanity in it: That had the Plays I have writ come forth under any Man's Name and never known to have been mine, I appeal to all unbyast Judges of Sense if they had not said that Person had

made as many good Comedies as any one Man that has writ in our
Age, but a Devil on't the Woman damns the Poet. . . .[8]

In an age of daring, Aphra Behn dared with the best; she wrote
thirteen novels, many poems, translations and dedications, and
was one of the most popular and prolific dramatists of her day. She
wrote eighteen plays, including comedies of romantic intrigue,
political plays (she was a Royalist), and verse tragedies.

When asked once why she started to write plays, Lillian Hellman answered, "Desperation, I guess."[9] Aphra Behn might have
answered similarly. Widowed in her middle twenties, she first
tried to support her mother and herself with a career in espionage;
she spent six months in Holland in 1666 on a secret mission for
King Charles. The government ignored her intelligence (which
later proved correct) and refused to remunerate her—she had to
borrow £150 to pay off debts and return to London, where she
tried unsuccessfully to get her money and was thrown in debtors'
prison. She somehow managed to obtain her release, probably with
the help of influential literary friends like Killigrew and Dryden,
and began to write herself out of debt, choosing the theatre perhaps because of the recognition another woman, Catherine Phil-
lips, had gained with her translation of Corneille's *Pompée* in
1663.

Her first play, *The Forc'd Marriage, or, The Jealous Bridegroom*,
was a solid hit in 1670, running at D'Avenant's Lincoln's Inn
Fields Theatre an astounding (for the period) six nights. She
followed it with *The Dutch Lover*, which failed, apparently because the actors hadn't sufficiently memorized their lines. Behn
held back before her next theatrical endeavor (Lillian Hellman
rewrote *The Little Foxes* nine times because the play before it
failed),[10] and was rewarded when one of her four plays produced
in 1671, *The Rover, or, The Banish't Cavaliers*, was a big enough
hit to make its author famous. Its hero, Willmore the Rover, was

[8]Quoted by Rosamond Gilder, *op. cit.*, p. 195.
[9]In conversation, August 1974.
[10]Lillian Hellman, *Pentimento*, Boston, 1973, p. 162.

such a perfect fop, so the quintessential Cavalier, that Behn was able to pass the play off at first as the work of a man. Eventually she revealed the playwright's true identity, and for a while her name on a book cover or outside a theatre insured the publisher or manager instant success.

Aphra Behn's brilliant reputation dimmed during the Victorian era, whose critics overemphasized the ribaldry of her plays; actually, they weren't any more risqué than those men wrote during the Restoration. Perhaps the assault on Behn was provoked more by her life as an independent woman (she was widowed and never remarried) connected with the questionable theatre than by the content or quality of her plays, which rank with others of the period. For us the tragedy of her life is that this mistaken valuation of her talents survives: she is left out of anthologies of Restoration plays, and comes to us more as a literary curiosity—considered less than her peers merely because of sex—than as one of the important writers of her age. She died April 16, 1689, at forty-nine and was buried in Westminster Abbey with the epitaph: "Here lies a Proof that Wit can never be/Defence enough against Mortality." In spite of Aphra Behn, the English theatre remained a male institution for the male voice. There are occasional comets, but no woman playwright with a career as sustained and serious as hers.

While the theatre in the late eighteenth and early nineteenth centuries was trying to bear up under the weight of neo-Shakespearean verse tragedy, women were developing the novel. Fanny Burney (1752–1840), best known to us as a diarist, wrote *Evelina*, an epistolary novel, when she was twenty-six. Because of its success, she came to the attention of playwright-manager Richard Brinsley Sheridan, who asked her to write a comedy for his Drury Lane Theatre. She did the next year and called it *The Witlings. A Comedy. By a Sister of the Order.* It is, according to Ellen Moers,[11] a funny and stageworthy satire of the bluestockings. Burney's father prevented its production, not, according to Moers, because he didn't want his daughter in the theatre, but because he feared the play would offend that sisterly order of literary

[11]Ellen Moers, *op. cit.*, p. 117.

women most responsible for *Evelina*'s success, the bluestockings. Fanny Burney wrote seven plays altogether (four verse tragedies and three comedies), none of which was ever published or produced. "I can't help speculating," Ellen Moers writes, "what might have happened to the English theatre had Jane Austen followed in Fanny Burney's footsteps as a playwright rather than a novelist."[12] And to the history of women playwrights!

Though she didn't write plays, Jane Austen must have gone to the theatre; her characters in *Mansfield Park* produce Mrs. Inchbald's *Lovers' Vows*. Elizabeth Inchbald (1730–1821) was a very beautiful woman who became an actress to get rid of a speech impediment. She had moderate success but, dissatisfied, turned to playwrighting, at which she hoped to make more money. She had popular success writing comedies and adapting others from French and German models. These plays, which have titles like *Wives as They Were, and Maids as They Are* (1797) and *To Marry or Not to Marry* (1805), are said to have been "spoilt by an obvious moral purpose and too much sentiment."[13] Mrs. Inchbald's less commercially successful contemporaries, Hannah More and Joanna Baillie, wrote verse tragedies.

The history of American theatre in the nineteenth century is the history of a new country fighting to build a drama independent of Britain. Although the rivalry between American plays and British imports continues today on Broadway, it is hard to believe that in 1849 twenty-two people were killed and fourteen wounded in a theatre riot stirred up by an American actor's jealousy of an English actor's season at the Astor Place Theatre in New York City. Edwin Forrest's fans fought William Macready's and had to be subdued by the militia. During the 1800's, acting companies, British and American, toured the United States with great success; it was the time when America was producing her first native tragedians like Forrest and tragediennes like Charlotte Cushman, a time when great fortunes could be made. American women playwrights, like their British sisters, often began as performers:

[12]*Ibid.*, p. 118.
[13]*Oxford Companion to the Theatre*, London, 1967, p. 463.

Charlotte Barnes, who wrote *The Forest Princess* (one of the many dramatizations of Pocahontas' life), started out as an actress in her parents' troupe. Her assignments included playing Juliet to her mother's Romeo. The most famous woman playwright of her era, however, was Anna Cora Mowatt, whose versatility rivals Isabella Andreini's.

Mowatt was born in 1819, one of twelve children. At age ten, she was reading Shakespeare's plays a second time; at fifteen, she married a rich lawyer; at seventeen, she published an epic poem and refuted its bad reviews in heroic couplets. At eighteen, she was off to Europe to recover from consumption, and during her convalescence wrote magazine articles, went to the theatre, took Italian lessons and wrote a play in blank verse. Her husband lost most of his money when she was twenty-one, so she began to tour, doing public readings, but her health failed again, so she left the platform and wrote a life of Goethe, novels and books on cookery, etiquette and marriage. When she was twenty-five, a friend suggested she try plays, and she wrote her famous and still-produced satiric comedy *Fashion* (1845), following it with another play, *Armand, the Child of the People.* In spite of her theatrical success, her husband's finances did not improve, so she capitalized on her literary reputation to launch herself as an actress. It turned out she had real talent, and she pursued an acting career with enormous success, stopping after nine years as impulsively as she'd begun.

American playwrighting had a number of commercially successful women writers after Mowatt. Alice Hegan Rice wrote a stage version of *Mrs. Wiggs of the Cabbage Patch* in 1903, and Margaret Mayo, a comedy-melodrama, *Baby Mine,* about a wife who dupes her husband into believing he is the father of a series of twins and triplets. One of the longest-running plays in history, *Abie's Irish Rose,* was written by a woman, Anne Nichols. Rachel Crothers (1878–1958) wrote commercially successful social comedies and was considered, as one critic puts it, a worthy successor to Mowatt. Crothers wrote many more plays than her predecessor; the first, *The Three of Us,* was produced in 1906 and was followed, in 1909, by *A Man's World,* a theatrical examination of the double standard. Although it was said that she "never allowed her feminist viewpoint to weaken the theatrical effectiveness of her writing,"[14] her 1912 play, *He and She*, reveals a pessimistic feminism. It is the story of a man and wife, both sculptors, who enter a competition for a $100,000 commission. She wins the contest and is shocked to discover that he will not help her with the sculpture as she would have if he had won. In the end she gives up sculpting to devote full time to marriage and family. Crothers, also an actress, performed the lead in a revival of *He and She* in 1920; her last success, *Susan and God*, a play about the Oxford movement, was produced in 1937.

In the nooks and crannies of theatre history books are recorded the careers of several other American women playwrights. Zona Gale (1874–1938), a novelist and playwright, won the 1921 Pulitzer Prize for the dramatization of her novel *Miss Lulu Bett*. Zoë Akins (1886–1958), also a poet, wrote many plays—the first, *Déclassée*, was produced in 1919; the third, *The Greeks Had a Word for It*, was her first big success, and she won the Pulitzer Prize in 1935 for her play based on Edith Wharton's *The Old Maid*. Most interesting of these women is Susan Glaspell (1882–1948), also a novelist, who is best remembered for two stunning one-act plays, the chilling *Trifles*[15] and *Suppressed Desires*, and for *Alison's House*. Inspired by the life of Emily Dickinson, *Alison's House* is the story of a family's efforts to suppress the poems of one of its recently deceased members; it was produced by Eva Le Gallienne's Civic Repertory Theatre in 1930 and won the Pulitzer Prize.

Lillian Hellman's extraordinary career, then, is not the isolated phenomenon it might seem at first; she had predecessors, other women who achieved commercial and literary success as playwrights. In the early 1930's, she worked in producer Herman Shumlin's office, where she read scripts that were submitted. Perhaps among them there were plays by Glaspell, Crothers, Akins or Gale; perhaps, too, in the stacks of manuscripts she and other young playreaders read were works of women less gifted or less

[14]*Ibid.*, p. 222.
[15]Anthologized in *Women in Drama*, ed. Harriet Kriegel, New York, 1975.

understood, who have not survived, as Hellman has so triumphantly, the brutal winnowing to which commercial production and critical response subject playwrights of both sexes.

Lillian Hellman, though her skill is acknowledged, is often spoken of as a playwright too obsessed with human evil and too dependent on the well-made play. This view has been reinforced recently by critics who feel that her playwrighting is important now mainly because it prepared her for her true literary form, the memoir. This underrates her plays; I saw scenes from several performed at a benefit tribute in late 1975[16] and subsequently reread *The Children's Hour* and *The Little Foxes*. Her plots are tense, her themes resonate, and the wholeness of many of her characters, especially her female characters, is impressive. Although *The Children's Hour* dramatized oppressive attitudes toward lesbianism that are now dated and depends heavily on a "bad-seed" young girl, the relationship between Karen and Martha acknowledges a kind of friendship between women—trusting, conscious and intimate—that is rarely dramatized. *The Little Foxes,* most often seen as the battle between a rapacious sister and her evil brothers, is also the story of a woman, Regina, turned bitter by her impatience and despair with provincial life, and the identity drama of the young daughter Alexandra, who must choose among the different ways of being a woman that she sees: her mother's cruelty and cynicism, which seem strong; the compassionate and artistic nature of her Aunt Birdie, which seems like weakness; and the strength and practicality of Abby, the black servant.

Hellman was obsessed with evil in her plays, but she was also obsessed with goodness, and with the effect of evil on innocence and goodness. Her use of the well-made play is an effort to make this moral vision coherent, to place these forces in some kind of balance. There is never a distinctly autobiographical character, and the rhythm of a play's machinery is never broken by one character's expression of need. The well-made play worked as a

[16] *The Celebration of Lillian Hellman,* Circle in the Square Theatre, Sunday, November 9, 1975.

medium for Hellman's theatrical vision, but the form her sensibility created was the form of the speculative memoir. In describing what women are now writing for the theatre, playwright Corinne Jacker said, "Women don't feel they have to write well-made plays any more; they're writing to let their sensibilities come through."[17] Two of Hellman's older contemporaries were the first modern theatre women whose sensibilities created new dramatic forms.

Gertrude Stein wrote, "a landscape is such a natural arrangement for a battlefield or a play that one must write plays," suggesting not only that plays are preferable to battles, but also that her interest in the theatre was more in landscape—the word in space —than in characters in time. Even in her more traditional plays like *Yes Is for a Very Young Man,* she concentrated on delivering the intricacies of what is said, rather than why it's said. Her plays are most profoundly for the individual voice in monologue, undulating between the conscious and the less conscious; when the characters converse, they sound like musical themes responding to one another. When it doesn't make linear sense, Stein's dialogue makes sound sense or humor sense or most often a combination of kinds of sense, and even when she names no characters to speak it, her poetry delivers such an accurate tone of voice that a speaker's identity is immediately suggested to the reader who will play along. In *A Play of Pounds,* for instance, one of the Act II's reads, in its entirety, "She may be always tractable or able or welcome if she is able. To be welcome."[18] Such a line presents countless possibilities for the director or actor willing to experiment.

But for women now, Gertrude Stein is not as important as a reinventor of language and syntax as she is as a woman writer who knew women profoundly and expressed that knowledge; part of her experimentation with language was experimentation with transcribing the way women speak. When her dazzling individual-

[17]In conversation, August 1976.
[18]Gertrude Stein, *Last Operas and Plays,* ed. and with an introduction by Carl Van Vechten, New York, 1975, p. 265.

XXV

ity connected with her deep understanding of her sex, she did her best work. Her opera *The Mother of Us All* is ostensibly about the career of Susan B. Anthony, but Susan B. is really poet Stein's image of a modern, pioneering woman much like Stein herself. Susan B. is a constant in the opera's landscape, singing aphorisms like "it is easy to be right, everybody else is wrong, so it is easy to be right," while whimsical lesser characters like Indiana Elliot, John Adams, Jo the Loiterer and others wander through her life uttering their obsessions, opinions and needs, a compassionate choral representation of the conservatism of American political, sexual and social attitudes.

The Mother of Us All is structured to gather emotional momentum and show that Susan B. is gathering wisdom as her struggle to get votes for women and to educate them progresses. "There is a devil gets into men when their hands are strengthened," Susan B. sings. "Men want to be half slave half free. Women want to be all slave or all free, therefore men govern and women know, and yet. . . ." For Stein's feminist heroine, there is always an "and yet . . ." She is a modern woman, tormented with ambivalence— how "all" must a mother be?—and it is her destiny never to be entirely understood, a fate her creator knew intimately. In the last scene of the opera, after her death, Susan B., now a statue, towers over her suffragist followers and sings:

> Do you know because I tell you so, or do
> you know, do you know
>
> *(Silence)*
>
> My long life, my long life.[19]

Her long life. *The Mother of Us All* was written two years before Stein's death from cancer at the age of seventy-four (1948).

Martha Graham, perhaps the most important woman dramatist who has ever lived, is not a playwright but a choreographer. She invented a language—modern dance—and has spent her long life (she's eighty-two at this writing) choreographing the more than a hundred and fifty dance pieces that express her woman-centered

---

[19]The Mother of Us All," in *Last Operas and Plays*, pp. 61, 73, 88.

vision. She was born in 1894, twenty years after Stein, amazingly, in Allegheny, the same Pennsylvania town.[20] Graham's family moved to southern California, where Dr. Graham eventually took his fourteen-year-old daughter to see Ruth St. Denis dance. That was the beginning of Graham's obsession, an obsession she was able to pursue with a quality of parental and educational support rare in the history of women artists. After high school in Santa Barbara, she went to Cumnock, a junior college in Los Angeles which stressed self-expression in theatre, dance and film, and after graduation, was accepted as a student at the Denishawn School newly opened in the same city. Denishawn (as Ruth St. Denis and Ted Shawn called their company) was the bridge in America between ballet and modern dance. Like Isadora Duncan, St. Denis and Shawn saw expressive possibilities in dance which they felt classical ballet obstructed. Unlike Duncan and other soloists of the period, they provided, through their school, a line of succession. After formative years as a dancer with Denishawn, touring the United States and England, Graham struck out on her own and began to build a company and repertory to express her particular vision as a choreographer and dancer.

Her early works were influenced by the exoticism of Denishawn but gradually, inspired by the example of Mary Wigman, the German expressionist dancer, and Ronny Johansson, who choreographed movements for the body seated on the floor, Graham developed the angular, vigorous style of movement that identifies her. In 1929, her first New York concerts introduced her company, The Group, and a dance, *Heretic,* which was, like Graham's later important work, a drama rather than simple movement exploration. For *Heretic,* the all-woman company was dressed in black, and their faces were made up to show the real face and accentuate the face-as-mask, a stark departure from the kewpie-doll appearance of exotic dancers of the period. Graham, as the heretic, wore white and danced, for the first time, a woman alienated from society because of her strong nature. The heretic tries

[20]My major source for biographical information about Martha Graham is *Martha Graham: A Biography* by Don McDonagh, New York, 1973.

to break through the boundaries of a disapproving, puritanical society (the black-robed group forms a living wall); twice she almost breaks through; ultimately she is kept out, forced to go on alone.

"Movement never lies," Graham wrote.[21] The source of her self-expression was her own body, and she refused to translate the language in which it moved to fit established categories of dance movement or of femininity. Reading through her notebooks, I was struck by the references to women writers: Emily Brontë—a scribble that may have given birth to her piece inspired by the Brontës, *Deaths and Entrances*; Emily Dickinson, jottings about *Letter to the World*, Graham's 1940 piece in which she danced the poet, accompanied by a reading of Dickinson's work. There are also references to classical mythology, the source of some of her greatest works, *Clytemnestra* and *The Cave of the Heart* among them. In the latter, a retelling of the story of Medea and Jason, Graham danced the part of Medea, pulling a long red ribbon from her breast, a material representation of Medea's frenzied jealousy of her younger rival. The acknowledgment, in Medea's solo, of the violence of this rage and of its sexual origin—the dancer moves across the floor toward the audience on widespread knees, back arched, energy pelvis-centered—is an impressive example of this choreographer's honesty and courage. But Graham was not content to explore only the dark sides of female passion; the dances inspired by her sense of the spirit of America are distinguished by their extreme gentleness and delicacy. One of them, *Frontier*, a solo piece, celebrates the strength of the pioneer woman, an illuminated creative power that looks to the future. She stands, dressed in a ruffled pink gown, alone on the stage—the prairie—in front of a graceful fencelike structure. Her movements show her independence, her joy, and her vulnerability.

Although she has met with resistance of all kinds—financial, critical, administrative—during her career, Martha Graham has,

[21] *The Notebooks of Martha Graham*, ed. Nancy Wilson Ross, New York, 1973, p. xv.

for fifty years, been able, through the medium she invented, to express her whole self in the theatre. Although modern dance in general has greatly influenced the modern theatre, what is inspiring for the contemporary woman playwright is that Graham's creativity expressed itself in uniquely female terms. Women in the 1970's, freed by a movement that has validated the expression of female experience, may be able to bring to the theatre of words the depths of female feeling that Graham has brought to the dance.

During the 1950s a few women emerged as American playwrights: Carson McCullers's *A Member of the Wedding* was produced in 1950; Alice Childress' *Gold Through the Trees* in 1952; Jane Bowles's *In the Summerhouse* in 1953; and Lorraine Hansberry's *Raisin in the Sun* in 1959. The off- and off-off-Broadway movements of the next decade offered more frequent opportunities for the production of women's plays: Rosalyn Drexler, Irene Fornes, Adrienne Kennedy, Rochelle Owens and Megan Terry all began important careers. Terry, now co-director of a feminist theatre in Omaha, Nebraska, wrote the first major play protesting the Vietnam War: *Viet Rock,* performed by the Open Theatre to launch the Yale School of Drama's first professional season in 1966, is the acknowledged predecessor of *Hair* and other rock musicals. Rochelle Owens's *Futz,* about a man's obsessive love affair with a pig, began off-off-Broadway and eventually became a feature film. The playwright-poet introduced its published version[22] with this epigraph from Corinthians: "Now concerning the things whereof ye wrote unto me:/it is good for a man not to touch a woman."

During the sixties, much of the theatre did not touch real women in spite of the number of female dramatists. But in the seventies, with the shift in the theatre away from "absurdism" and back to a kind of realism, women have begun to write from their own experience. "First you had to write an Arthur Miller play," Eve Merriam has said, "then you had to write an absurd play. Now

[22]Rochelle Owens, *Futz & What Came After,* New York, 1968, p. 4.

there is a new freedom—you can write empathetic women characters."[23]

The women playwrights of the seventies are not part of a single
movement; they write in many different styles and come to the
theatre with many different life-histories. Some may not even be
conscious that, since its beginning, the present women's movement has had its own theatre. In the late sixties in New York City,
Anselma Dell' Ollio began the New Feminist Repertory, the first
political theatre in the new wave of feminism. Among other plays,
they produced *But What Have You Done for Me Lately?*, Myrna
Lamb's cautionary one-act about a pregnant man who comes to
a woman doctor for an abortion. After the movement's initial
educational stage, the consciousness-raising group became its major political form, and new women's theatre groups, utilizing im-
provisatory techniques, began to work with the material from
women's lives that CR brought to the surface. I remember a
performance of the It's All Right to Be a Woman Theatre at
Washington Square Methodist Church during which actresses
asked for dreams from the all-woman audience, then acted them
out: *It's all right to be a woman, it's all right to have that dream.*
In the following years many improvisational theatre groups like
Womanspace Theatre in New York and Circle of the Witch in
Minneapolis formed and continued to show women their lives in
dramatic form. Other women started theatres, like the Washington Area Feminist Theatre and New York's Interart Theatre, to
produce new works by women playwrights.

At first only a few plays written by women out of the concerns
of the women's movement were performed in the professional
theatre, and most had difficulty surviving the critics. In 1970,
Myrna Lamb's *Mod Donna* was produced at the Public Theatre
a few blocks from the Mercury, which had housed Tina Howe's
The Nest weeks before; and other strides were made. Eve Merriam
and Helen Miller's *Inner City* and Gretchen Cryer and Nancy
Ford's *Shelter* were the first Broadway musicals by women. But

[23]In conversation, August 1976.

you could still count the names in the *Arts and Leisure* section of the Sunday *New York Times*, as an actress friend and I did, and come up with a total in which men's names outnumbered women's five to one—when was the women's movement going to hit the theatre?

A year or so later I was writing the poems that became *Mourning Pictures*, and that actress friend called to say she had begun writing a play, she was sick of playing shallow female parts. While my play was in production, I met another poet, Susan Griffin from San Francisco, who had used poetry in her all-woman play, *Voices*. Corinne Jacker's *Bits and Pieces* was produced at the same time as *Mourning Pictures*, November 1974, and Jacker was a double Obie winner[24] the following spring for *Bits and Pieces* and *Harry Outside*, which the Circle Repertory had produced the same season. *Apple Pie*, with a feminist libretto by Myrna Lamb and music by Nick Meyers, was produced soon after as a workshop at the Public Theatre (and given a full production a year later), and that April (1975), I went to California on a reading tour and heard there that Ntozake Shange was performing the narrative poems from her book *For Colored Girls Who Have Considered Suicide/When the Rainbow Is Enuf* as theatre pieces. Months later *Ms.* and *The New Woman's Survival Sourcebook*[25] published lists of women's theatres: combined, there were more than thirty.

I decided to do an anthology to reflect this new energy of women in the theatre, and in response to solicitation letters, received manuscripts of nearly two hundred produced plays. As I was reading them during the spring of 1976, more plays by women than I was able to go to see were being performed in New York City. One of them, directed by Nancy Rhodes at the Good Shepherd Presbyterian Church, was a revival of *The Mother of Us All*.

---

[24]The "Obie" is the off-Broadway award for excellence; winners are chosen by a panel of New York theatre critics.

[25]Lillian Perinciolo, "Feminist Theater: They're Playing in Peoria," *Ms.*, October 1974; *The New Woman's Survival Sourcebook*, New York, 1975, p. 175. This book is also a good source of information about published women's theatre materials.

Another, Shange's poems, now a theatre piece, opened in June and became the first play, clearly influenced by the feminist movement, to be a Broadway hit.

Women are writing plays about female experience to an unprecedented extent; I have chosen plays that show some of the many different ways they have chosen to place that experience in the theatre. Some, like Corinne Jacker, Joanna Russ and Ursule Molinaro, view the contradictions of their characters' experience from a wry distance. Iris, the heroine of *Bits and Pieces*, puts herself through a rite of mourning which involves seeking out her dead husband's parts (he left his body to medicine) in other people's bodies all over the world. The journey is a striking theatrical metaphor for a woman's difficulties in accepting her autonomy. Marsha, the window dressing of Russ's title, finds real womanhood so much more complex and painful than mannequin-hood that she throws herself out of the apartment window of the man who "freed" her. The protagonists of Molinaro's *Breakfast Past Noon*, speak in the past tense because there is no way out of their stagnated mother-daughter relationship.

Some of the playwrights stand at no distance from their characters; their plays have a fierceness and immediacy and send us from the theatre not contemplative and calm but disturbed by vivid pictures of worlds where the real seems almost too absurd to be actual, and is much too painful to be absurd. Tina Howe's *Birth and After Birth* is "about" the fourth-birthday party two parents give their only son (played by an adult to emphasize his will), to which they invite their childless anthropologist friends whom they hope to persuade to become parents. In the arena this situation provides, the playwright dramatizes, with grotesque comic energy, the emotional push and pull of a young mother's situation and the rage and ambivalence it inspires. Even though the play is from the mother's point of view, she is drawn with merciless objectivity, a person shackled by the demands of her husband and son, unable to act even when she sees that her body is beginning to decay: "When I looked in the mirror this morning, I saw an old lady. Not old, old . . . just used up."

Toward the end of *Mourning Pictures*, close to her mother's death, twenty-seven-year-old Margaret asks:

> How do I
> know I am not her? I have always been her,
> and it's never mattered before who was
> who.

It is almost as if she is losing part of her own body. The action of the play is her struggle to express her love to her dying mother and to come to terms with her own survival as an adult—no longer a daughter. At the end of the play, Margaret, at the hospital, kisses her dead mother and says with surprise, "She is not cold," somehow realizing that as an influence her mother will never be dead.

Wedding Band, too, is a rite of autonomy, involving a woman's survival of a person she loves. Alice Childress' Julia and her white lover, Herman, live psychically apart from their respective claustrophobic societies in racist World War I South Carolina, where interracial marriage is against the law. On the tenth anniversary of their secret affair, Herman collapses from influenza, and Julia's neighbors (who become almost a chorus representing conventional Southern black values of the era) summon Herman's mother and sister. In his delirium and to placate his mother, an archetypally bigoted though compassionately drawn woman, Herman repeats the racist speech he recited as a child at the Knights of the Gold Carnation picnic. When his relatives take him away, Julia, ordinarily a soft-spoken person, explodes with an angry declaration of independence:

> When I die I'm gonna keep on hatin' . . . I don't want any whiteness in my house. Stay out . . . out . . . *(Dumps the things in the yard)* . . . out . . . out . . . out . . . and leave me to my black self!

But Herman knows he is going to die, and returns to Julia's house to do it. Childress writes in a stage direction:

> *(The weight has lifted, she is radiantly happy. She helps him gasp out each remaining breath. . . .)*

Like *Wedding Band*, Ruth Wolff's *The Abdication* is a play in which a woman's conflict with a man brings about a crisis which helps her define herself. The title refers to an actual historical event: Christina, a seventeenth-century Swedish queen, left her throne and traveled across Europe to Rome, where she hoped to be received into the Church by the Pope. Her marathon confession to Cardinal Azzolino (absolution must take place before she can see the Pope) becomes a debate between a passionate, expressive, rebellious woman and a man who has chosen the celibate existence of a priest. Confession of sin for a woman like Christina, it emerges, is synonymous with expression of her true self. People from her past, including two younger selves, appear to haunt, mock, contradict and move her to say things that are joltingly and provocatively honest like

> Me? Submit to that from a man? The Sovereign Queen of Sweden go down on her back and be ploughed like a field? Never!

Ruth Wolff's regal and very modern heroine ultimately accepts patriarchal reality without giving into it; her tortured "Why!" at the end of the play is one we have all felt.

Joanna Halpert Kraus's *The Ice Wolf* also asks, Why? It is a play for children. Kraus says she writes for children because she believes "you can reach a kid when you can't reach an adult,"[26] and that it is important for children to be exposed to profound feelings and issues. The play is the story of Anatou, a fair-haired girl who is rejected by the Eskimo tribe into which she was born because she is different. They believe she is the cause of their hardship:

> She will offend Nuliayuk, the goddess of the seals. Nuliayuk will stay at the bottom of the sea, and keep the seals beside her, and we will all go hungry. Put the child out into the snow or we will die of famine!

They do not put her out in the snow, but as she grows older, they never let her forget their suspicion. When her parents disappear searching for food, the tribe turns on Anatou, now unprotected.

[26]In conversation, September 1976.

She does not accept her alienation; she journeys into the forbidden forest and asks the Wood God to change her into a wolf. As a white wolf, she takes her revenge, killing many of the people in the town. Anatou dares to be different, dares to express her righteous anger, and dies for it. But her spirit lives on as a warning to the tribe:

> Tarto will tell your story tonight, the first time, and they will tell it for many nights. They will remember, for someone will always tell the story of Anatou, the Fair One.

The father-daughter relationship is less explored in the new women's plays than the mother-daughter relationship. Myrna Lamb's *I Lost a Pair of Gloves Yesterday* is an acknowledgment of the loss of a father, told with painful humor. How is Lamb's character to handle the world without the "gloves" her father's existence gave her? Her life in the present, her parents' relationship, and events in her past all feel different after this loss, and that is what she must tell us: "Anyway," she says, walking off the stage, "this pair of gloves. Yesterday. Yesterday." I first saw *I Lost a Pair of Gloves Yesterday* when the playwright performed it at the Manhattan Theatre Club in New York. There was, in her performance, a sense of testimony. The play came out with the urgency of something long unsaid, like contemporary women's poetry.

It has been said that women will not write great plays until they do more in the world, the genius of these women's plays is that they communicate the inner drama, the process of consciousness. The consciousness-raising group is an instrument for getting women to speak—only when they name their experience can they begin to grow. In the past, women have used journals and letters to express the things they could not say. *Out of Our Fathers' House*, a theatre-piece molded from the private writings of six American women, creates a sort of consciousness-raising group among women who probably never met one another: three actresses, onstage together for the whole play, portray six women whose life stories alternate and intertwine. In the theatre, the alienation of the actress is a particular oppression. *Out of Our*

Fathers' House came to be through the efforts of two theatre women to make meaningful work for each other. Eve Merriam saw Paula Wagner in a play in New York, and afterward the two talked. Wagner said what many contemporary actresses feel—that she was sick of playing anti-woman parts. In response, Merriam offered her anthology, *Growing Up Female in America: Ten Lives*, as the basis for a one-woman show. Wagner went to Jack Hoffsiss, a young director, with the idea, and he suggested that three actresses perform the piece In the summer of 1975, *Out of Our Fathers' House* was produced at the Lenox Arts Center, where music was added, and later it toured colleges. All over the country, women in the theatre are beginning to create plays, not only from their own lives, but that dramatize history, bring our foremothers to life. *Out of Our Fathers' House* combines the historical with the personal: we learn about the young womanhood of such women as Elizabeth Cady Stanton and Anna Howard Shaw, the preacher and doctor, and less-known women like Eliza Southgate, who died while still a schoolgirl in 1809. We hear women's voices testifying to struggles for maturity, independence, and relationships much like our own, reassuring us that the journey "out of our fathers' houses" is worth taking.

The theatre has never been taken away from the young male god to whom it has been dedicated since Greek drama evolved from rituals to Dionysus. Women in the theatre are now attempting a rededication by writing from their own points of view, in their own forms. The Dionysian rites had their origins in the earlier rites to Demeter, a woman god. Classical scholar Jane Harrison wrote that art and ritual "spring from the incomplete cycle, from unsatisfied desire, from perception and emotion that have somehow not found immediate outlet in practical action."[27] One goes to the theatre not only to find out what is real, to see a mirror of the world, but with a need for ritual, a desire to feel nurtured by the artist's vision—to be taken in, included, not pushed away. This winter I went to see a woman's opera, Myrna Lamb's *Apple Pie*. It was about another woman's life, but it was

[27]Jane Ellen Harrison, *Ancient Art and Ritual*, New York, 1913, p. 41.

also about my life. I could hardly bear the brutal history with which I was confronted, but I felt a connection, a dull pain. I left the theatre crying. The two women I'd come with were also crying. A need had been filled. This book expresses my hope that we will not turn back, that the new theatre women have begun out of their connection with other women's lives will last.

Bits
and Pieces

by
CORINNE JACKER

Corinne Jacker began writing *Bits and Pieces* because, while ill with a disease she was told was terminal, she "started thinking about death, and death seemed less important than the problem of leaving behind—what are the people you're close to going to do?" She began with the Egyptian Osiris myth (Osiris, a good king, is dismembered by his wicked brother Seth, who scatters the parts all over the world. Isis, his faithful wife, finds the fragments, burying each where she finds it.) Jacker named her heroine Iris to echo both Isis and Osiris. "As I was writing it, it became a play about life, not about death."

She wrote her first play at nine and at twelve adapted Chekov's *The Sea Gull* to life in the Chicago suburbs. She was educated at Stanford and Northwestern, where she received a master's degree in theatre. When she was twenty-five, her dramatization of Katherine Anne Porter's *Pale Horse, Pale Rider* was produced off-Broadway. Shortly after, she stopped writing plays for several years—"I lost my faith in it"—and earned a living writing popular books on scientific subjects like cybernetics, the use of the microscope and the new biology.

She returned to the theatre in the early seventies with great energy. *Bits and Pieces* was produced at the Manhattan Theatre Club and *Harry Outside* by the Circle Repertory; both won Obies. Her musical, *Travelers,* was produced at the Cincinnati Playhouse, and in the 1976–77 season, *My Life* was produced by Circle, and *Other People's Tables* (three one-acts) at the Billy Munk, both in New York City. Jacker also writes for movies and television and is collaborating with poet Janet Sternburg on a play based on the letters, journals and poems of Louise Bogan.

"It seems to me that what women are doing now is letting their own sensibilities come through—you don't write like a man any more, you write like yourself." Asked about her sense of an audience, she told a story of meeting a male playwright friend in the theatre lobby after a performance of one of her plays. He was shaken, very moved. It was, he told her, the first time he had seen a man through a woman's eyes. "I want to be able to do that," she says. "I write like a woman, but I don't write only for women."

CHARACTERS

PHILIP

DOCTOR

TECHNICIAN

IRIS

HELEN

FARLEY

MRS. EBERLY

ANTONIO

MONK

The DOCTOR, FARLEY, ANTONIO, and the MONK are to be played by the same actor. One actress should play both the TECHNICIAN and MRS. EBERLY.

AUTHOR'S NOTE

There are many scenes in this play; they happen in a number of places. Before each scene there is a title. The title should be shown to the audience by means of slide or projector. The scenery should be minimal. Most important is that the audience be helped in every way possible to understand when IRIS is on her journey and when she has returned to the past life from which she started.

SCENE 1
PHILIP AND THE PAST

PHILIP *is alone on stage. He is holding a picture of an ancient Greek vase.*

PHILIP

This vase was twenty-five hundred years old. It was made in Greece, when men knew gods and dark things moved beneath the earth. The painting on it has been evaluated in two ways. Some said it was the work of a master craftsman, one of the finest of the classical period. They pointed to the line of the shoulders, to the almost dancing movement of the figures . . . But others found the execution mediocre, the work of a hack. *(He puts the picture down, picks up a shard, a hunk of a vase)* Unfortunately, while it was on loan to a museum, the vase broke. Only a few shards were left. The state of the art is no longer in question. It has become the work of a master craftsman. And time is standing still now, for the vase, for the man who painted it. And this piece—it's something to pick up in the night when you can't sleep and rub your hands around. A little powder talcums the fingers, and they've become 2,500 years old.

SCENE 2
WHAT HAPPENS AFTER DEATH?

The DOCTOR *and the* TECHNICIAN *are working in a hospital "white room," adjacent to an operating room. They are surrounded by styrofoam boxes of various sizes. Each box is piled haphazardly on top of another. Each box contains one human organ; all the organs have been taken from* PHILIP'*s body just after his death. He was a donor, and now his parts are packed up and being made ready for shipment. The* DOCTOR *and* TECHNICIAN *have been working all day. They are tired. They have only a few more boxes to label and record.*

DOCTOR

(He is checking his records. He has lost track of one of the organs. He tries to get the attention of the TECHNICIAN*)* Hey . . . Hey, did you see the liver anywhere?

TECHNICIAN

Under the kidney.

DOCTOR

No. It's not there.

TECHNICIAN

Really? I'm sure I put it there. Look again.

DOCTOR

I have looked. Twice. *(She comes over, finds it for for him)* Thanks.

TECHNICIAN

When I label the eyes—the corneas—I mean, do I put left and right or what?

DOCTOR

Have you ever done this kind of work before?

TECHNICIAN

No. Usually they keep me down in obstetrics. I like it down there . . . So—do I put left and right, or what?

DOCTOR

It's optional . . . You know, this man—the guy who donated all this. He was incredible.

TECHNICIAN

All this stuff came from one body? *(The* DOCTOR *nods)* Well, how many more organs do we have to label? . . . I'm hungry.

DOCTOR

You just ate a Twinkie.

TECHNICIAN

Well, we've been locked up in here working for hours and hours.

DOCTOR

There's never been one like this. I'm sure of it. He gave away everything. He—you know—he thought about it, and he made a will, and he arranged to have himself cut up and—distributed.

TECHNICIAN

If they're going to have many more like this, there's going to have

6

to be some financial arrangement. I'm seventeen minutes into overtime.

DOCTOR

Listen . . . The thing is—suddenly—I have this irresistible urge to fuck you.

TECHNICIAN

Now? In the middle of all this?

DOCTOR

Why not?

TECHNICIAN

Forget it. His soul could be here right now. Floating all over his parts, trying to find a new host body. Please. Not here.

PHILIP

(He comes on, speaks quite matter-of-factly) At least death was instantaneous. It took me completely by surprise. Even though I'd been lying there, waiting for it.

SCENE 3

IRIS: THE MOURNING BEGINS

IRIS and HELEN are in the kitchen of what was PHILIP and IRIS's apartment. IRIS is his wife, HELEN, his sister. The two women are sitting at the table. They both wear dark clothes. They have been at PHILIP's funeral. Now, after the people have gone, they are sitting and drinking.

IRIS

He was the most important person in my life. I lived for him. I thought about him all the time. We were attached to one another by a thin invisible unbreakable—thing.

(HELEN looks at her. Short pause)

HELEN

Go ahead and cry. It would do you good.

IRIS

Would it? . . . We know he didn't give away the penis. He was very explicit about that.

HELEN

Would you like another drink?

IRIS

Why are you talking to me as if I'm retarded?

HELEN

Funerals are hard.

IRIS

David told me on the phone last night—he didn't want to come back for the funeral. It was no good, he said, if his father wasn't going to be there. That's pretty good for a nine-year-old . . . I didn't feel much like being there either . . . There wasn't anything to bury. A little heap of unwanted stuff. The bones. There was nothing to do with the bones.

HELEN

Stop it, please.

IRIS

So, when the undertaker called, you know, to ask me what to do, I said we'll burn it, the remains. Just a few ashes in a little box, put into a bigger box and buried in the ground . . . Did you know that ashes don't rot? He isn't even going to rot.

HELEN

Do you want me to leave, Iris?

IRIS

I will have another drink, thank you . . . I'm not a logical person, Helen. That's why I can't figure it out. You and Philip were raised on syllogisms. I grew up with the collected poems of Robert and Elizabeth Browning.

HELEN

There's nothing difficult about logic.

IRIS

Oh. I think there is. There's a logic attached to all this death and dying. And I'm going to figure out what it is. I'm going to be the most logical of us all . . . For instance—more scotch, please. I don't think you put any scotch at all in my last drink. For instance, take how we got to the cemetery. There we were. Up the avenue, down the main street, onto the throughway. We were following the hearse. Until—did you notice when it was we weren't following the hearse any more? I didn't. But all at once it wasn't there. But I figured it out. The hearse takes a short cut. Or we take a long cut—and it gets to the cemetery ahead of us. And the whole thing is out and on display before the mourners turn up.

HELEN

You're being morbid.

IRIS

That bastard your brother didn't leave me anything to bury. How could he do that if he loved me? What am I going to do?

HELEN

You'd better go to bed.

IRIS

Don't you try to manage me!

HELEN

I'm trying to be sensible. Philip would want me to be sensible.

IRIS

Echo, echo—I've got to figure out what he was paying me back for. Giving himself away like that. Like pieces of a saint . . . Please. Get the hell out of here, will you? This is no time for sister-in-laws—sisters-in-law . . . Stay. I'm sorry. Let's have a drink together.

HELEN

You don't want me here.

IRIS

What do you want to do? Move in?

HELEN

Should I? For a few weeks?

IRIS

No.

HELEN

He was my brother.

IRIS

That's right.

HELEN

I'm very tired.

IRIS

I'm not going to live. I know it. I'm going to develop a wasting disease and die slowly.

HELEN

We'll talk about that later.
(PHILIP *appears*)

IRIS

I tried turning on the radiator in the living room. There wasn't any heat. I'm cold.

HELEN

Do you have any aspirin? Or something stronger.
(IRIS *does not respond. She has been drawn to* PHILIP)

PHILIP

And save the Sunday *Times* till I've read it? . . . And don't use the business section for the garbage pail.

IRIS

I can't stand it when you're pompous.

PHILIP

You love me when I'm pompous. It makes me sexier.

IRIS

Go to hell.

PHILIP

Go to hell yourself.

IRIS

They don't have double beds in hell.

PHILIP

Then it must be heaven.

IRIS

(*Laughing*) You bastard.

PHILIP

Sexy bastard.
(*He leaves;* IRIS *is back with* HELEN *now*)

IRIS

Let's stay up all night and talk about love, Helen.

HELEN

You need your sleep.

IRIS

I thought I'd sleep out there. On the sofa.

HELEN

You slept in the bed when he was in the hospital.

10

IRIS

It's different now.

HELEN

You can't have a nervous breakdown. You have obligations.

IRIS

He's dead. He's gone.

HELEN

I know that.

IRIS

Not like I know it.

HELEN

Let's not argue. I'm trying to help you. *(She takes out a list)*

IRIS

Not now . . . Please. Put me to bed. Stay the night. Just one night more.

HELEN

You don't want me to move in here. You said so

IRIS

Just as a guest.

HELEN

I have a home of my own . . . You'll have to pack up the clothes. We should give them to the Salvation Army. It'll be a tax deduction. You can use it next year.

IRIS

Fine. You take care of it.

HELEN

No. You. And the books. You don't read French or German. You might as well give them away, too. Maybe to the university library. In his name . . . Oh, there's one—*A Child's Garden of Verses.* From when we were little. I'd like that, if you don't mind.

IRIS

All right. Go home. Leave me alone.

HELEN

Only a few more things. Did he leave a will?

IRIS

I'll kill myself. I'll jump out a window.

11

HELEN

Didn't he go over any of this with you?

IRIS

I won't be intimidated when I'm in mourning.

HELEN

Next week will be worse. You'll see.

IRIS

What's so important about the will? You want to know if you're
a beneficiary? What shall we do, Helen? Make an agreement now,
we'll split it all, fifty-fifty? My God, you want his, and mine, and
the whole family's. Well. The money stops here. I'll be sure you
don't get any of it.

HELEN

I thought you were going to kill yourself.

> (IRIS *reaches out to hit* HELEN, *who intercepts her fist and
> gets in a slap of her own.* IRIS *stands a moment, dazed, and
> then cries)*

IRIS

(She sits down, talks really to herself) He never explained that I'd
be all alone. Forever. He didn't go into that.

HELEN

I'm going to run a hot tub for you. Bubble bath. And then I'll
bring you a hot drink. Tea with rum. And you'll drink it and fall
asleep. Tomorrow you'll be thinking of other things.

IRIS

We really shouldn't argue.

HELEN

You'll put cream all over your body. Some good-smelling cream.
You'll sleep. You'll see.

> *(She leaves, for the bathroom, to fix* IRIS's *bath.* PHILIP
> *comes in with a book. He is the young* PHILIP, *in the early
> years of his teaching.* IRIS *has gone to a mirror. She looks
> carefully at herself)*

IRIS

Mirrors are absolutely fascinating. Look. There's something about
the eyes. There's something strange about that woman's eyes
. . . Phil! Phil! I need you.

PHILIP

(Now in the past with her) Come on! I just need five minutes more. I'll be there in five minutes.

IRIS

(Directly to PHILIP*)* I was afraid. I looked in the mirror and I was afraid. There was something so odd—and I wanted to go on looking until I figured it out.

PHILIP

(Into his book again) We'll talk about it at dinner.

IRIS

Dinner's been ready half an hour.

PHILIP

Heat it up.

IRIS

Why do you have to be such a damn scholar?

PHILIP

Because it's my business. To be a scholar.

IRIS

Well, you can think on your own time. Come eat your supper.

PHILIP

I'll be right there. I just want to finish this page.

IRIS

You just turned a page, you cheating bastard. You have sixty seconds to get to the table. If you don't, I'm picking up the phone and calling Howard Garfield. He's been trying to seduce me for three weeks.

PHILIP

Howard Garfield's a prick.
(She leaves him for the kitchen)

IRIS

(With her back to him) You haven't put the book down yet.

PHILIP

How do you know.

IRIS

I'm psychic. Twenty-seven seconds.

PHILIP

Are you at the phone?

IRIS

Come and see.

PHILIP

Howard Garfield? . . . Now I've forgotten why I was reading the damn dialogue.

IRIS

Then come eat your supper. You've got fifteen seconds.

PHILIP

Shit. Have your affair with the bastard, then.

IRIS

Phil . . . Phil . . . *(She goes to him)* I don't have a watch with a second hand.

PHILIP

(He is angry. Then he finds it funny. He laughs) My God. Think what I'd be like if I had original ideas.

IRIS

Come on. It's roast beef. I got a special price today.

PHILIP

I like my work, but oh you kid. *(He pulls her down onto his lap)*

IRIS

I love you despite your eccentricities.

PHILIP

Let's get married.

IRIS

Not again.

PHILIP

I want to marry you. I want to be the father of your children. Me Tarzan. You Jane.

IRIS

Why do you waste all that energy on books?

PHILIP

There's plenty for other things.

IRIS

I bet you're awful at touch football. The Kennedys are great at it.

PHILIP

They have more money than I do.

IRIS

Not much. I'll be very rich when we get married, won't I?

PHILIP

Very.

IRIS

That's good . . . I said I'd marry you.

PHILIP

I heard you.

IRIS

Good.

PHILIP

Good.

IRIS

I'm an idiot.

PHILIP

You'll be completely happy.

IRIS

Will I?

PHILIP

Now get the hell out of here and let me finish my work.

(He dumps her on the floor and starts to make notes. IRIS *runs out, back to the apartment area)*

IRIS

I hope the damn roast is burned to a crisp.

PHILIP

I like it that way.

(The DOCTOR *is in the apartment area, sitting on the sofa.* IRIS *hands him a drink)*

IRIS

I'm a very rich widow, you know.

DOCTOR

So I've heard. Most donors are—upper middle or upper.

IRIS

I want the names of all the donees. For each organ you gave away.

DOCTOR

I'm afraid not.

IRIS

It isn't like adoption, Doctor. I'm not going to try to get the pieces back.

DOCTOR

It's a question of medical ethics.

IRIS

Doctor, my husband was unique—and while he was dying—the two months it took—he continued to be unusual. I have tapes he made for me. Points of view. Philosophical recollections. He thought they would last me as long as I needed. Keep us connected while I was grieving. They may. (IRIS *takes out a cassette machine, puts in a cartridge, turns the machine on*)

PHILIP

(On the machine) What Osiris is, you see. He had a powerful magic. He gave the dead a drink of water, and that brought them back to life. Because the soul has to quench its thirst or die.

    (IRIS *turns the tape off*)

IRIS

All the tapes are like that. Not one personal remark. Not one intimate memory. When I've finished, I can donate them to a library.

DOCTOR

I was very moved by it.

IRIS

I have to have your list. It's—a kind of mission. It's crucial. He's dead. But his parts aren't. They aren't rotting away in the ground. They weren't burned to ashes. That was a present he gave me. Or a curse. He's somewhere, in someone's body. Alive, with blood running through him. Moving. A hand grasping some other woman's hand. And I could see that hand.

DOCTOR

All right. I'll do it. I'll try to get the list. If I fuck you. Right now. I have this thing about making it with strangers.

IRIS

I always seem to bring out definitions in people . . . All right, Doctor, let's, as you said, fuck. *(She abruptly begins to undress)* I

16

suppose you're blessed in your way. Hermes the messenger. I
forget what the Egyptians called him.

PHILIP

Where the hell's my pipe? Did you hide it again?

(IRIS *turns when he calls her, then she turns back to the*
DOCTOR. PHILIP *does not leave the room*)

IRIS

(To the DOCTOR*)* Don't worry, I'm not mad. Or if I am, it's
harmless. A death psychosis. Gone in a month or two.

DOCTOR

Don't you have a bedroom?

(IRIS *leads him into the bedroom. As they are going out of*
the room, PHILIP *comes down, takes the recorder, turns it*
on, speaks into it. He is making a recording for her)

PHILIP

I have it now. The clear, bright core. Here in my bed, waiting to
die, I see the perfection of my essence. I see myself shining,
phosphorescent in the darkness. Clear of mind, only functioning,
heart beating, blood moving, fingers curling with my breath and
moving out again, air coming in, sweat on my skin. This is what
I am. The body living. And all there will be. Well . . . The one
breath that is left is frozen. Suspended. The heart contracted,
about to beat. The diaphragm still stretched. The word not
spoken. I would say something to her. She would say something.
But, tranquil and quiet. The last second is about to flick by. The
swelled artery stretches, bursts, and I am dead.

SCENE 4
THE JOURNEY BEGINS. IRIS IN CALIFORNIA

IRIS *has changed her clothes. It is a week or so later. She is with*
a young man, FARLEY. *They are in Los Angeles, beside* FARLEY's
swimming pool. He is a plain but rather attractive person; FARLEY
is paralyzed from the waist down and in a wheelchair, but although
some of his movements are restricted, he is not a passive person.
He speaks with an exaggeratedly British accent.

17

IRIS

I don't know. I thought—just barging in. I had to see you.

FARLEY

My days are very free.

IRIS

(She has been waiting for him to talk. The pause has become very difficult) I'm not supposed to be here. I bought your name and address . . . I don't know how to— *(Another pause)* Helen—my sister-in-law—thinks I'm crazy.

FARLEY

Do you want some tea? . . . I can make some . . . I don't really care for it.

IRIS

I thought you were English.

FARLEY

Canadian . . . I came here to be in films. For God's sake, sit down. So he's in a variety of pieces, then—your husband.

IRIS

In a variety of places.

FARLEY

That must be unpleasant.

IRIS

Painful.

FARLEY

(He is having her on) You loved him.

IRIS

Intensely.

FARLEY

Why the hell didn't you stay home in your nice little house and mourn, like a sensible widow?

IRIS

I couldn't . . . We were very close. Extremely close, Philip and I. And. I really can't stand it, you know, not having him. He gave his parts away for a reason. He wanted me to know something. I'm sure of it. I'm sure I'll have a sense of him again—when I see it. Whatever you have—or touch it—or—that's why I'm here.

FARLEY

To find his little piece in me.

IRIS

I won't hurt you.

FARLEY

Do you know what piece I have, then?

IRIS

No. He just gave me a list.

FARLEY

Organ, organ, who's got the organ . . . I'm sorry.

IRIS

Please—won't you let me see it.

FARLEY

His eardrum? You must be joking.

IRIS

I don't make jokes.

FARLEY

They offered a leg first. It wasn't the first offer. But it has to be a pair of legs. It can't be just one, you see, it's got to be a matched set. But legs don't satisfy me. Not yet . . . But it was essential for me to hear. I needed his eardrum.

IRIS

Hear what?

FARLEY

You should be under guard.

IRIS

Look. I've got a light. Like the doctors use. It won't hurt. You'll turn to one side, and I'll put the light in your ear, and take a look. Just one look. *(She waits for a response)* Do you want money?

FARLEY

Don't try to buy me! I don't need your money! I don't need anything from any of you . . . I collected a great deal for this. *(He means being crippled)* I spend it, too. On books, and liquor, and clothes. I still like to wear good clothes.

IRIS

Please let me see it.

19

FARLEY

Suppose I showed you the wrong ear?

IRIS

I'd know.

FARLEY

Would you?

IRIS

Would you? *(That is, show the wrong ear)*

FARLEY

You're absolutely bananas.

   (He turns. IRIS *looks, then takes the light and puts it away)*

PHILIP

(Appearing as IRIS *looks in* FARLEY's *ear)* How do you do. My name is Philip Uberman. I teach assorted subjects at various universities.

FARLEY

Is it all right?

IRIS

(Happy at PHILIP's *presence)* Were you ever in a movie?

FARLEY

Three. I had no lines in the first two. They cut my scene out of the other one.

IRIS

I'm sorry.

FARLEY

I didn't want to be an actor—just to be in films. I thought it would make me handsome.

PHILIP

I'm a socialist. I inherited it from my father.

IRIS

I guess I'm an anarchist.

FARLEY

Really? I thought it was illegal.

IRIS

No. I'm the nonviolent kind.

PHILIP

There is no such thing as nonviolence.

20

FARLEY

I did it myself. I ran the bloody machine off the road. I was pissed. Just giving way to another cliché. Like the phony accent . . . It's all right, being a cripple. It's less demanding.

IRIS

(To PHILIP*)* Success is crucial to a man, isn't it?

FARLEY

(Sensing her separateness) Is it all right? The ear? What did it look like? It feels odd, you know, someone else living in my head.

> *(*IRIS *does not answer. A Mozart record is playing. It has grown louder as* FARLEY *talked, and* IRIS *leaves him, moving to* PHILIP*)*

PHILIP

We'll play music till dawn, and screw the neighbors.

IRIS

I love you.

PHILIP

Only because my book has been published today. And I will be a full professor, and short of moral turpitude or other failing of character our future is secure.

IRIS

Dionysius and the Moral Temper of the Athenians. It'll be a best seller.

PHILIP

A first printing of two thousand.

IRIS

And it's so relevant.

PHILIP

Let's dance.

IRIS

To Mozart?

PHILIP

Why not.

IRIS

You're drunk.

21

PHILIP

Not much. Thanks for the champagne . . . Listen to this part.
Right here. It's so damned personal.

IRIS

Mozart?

PHILIP

Why do you keep asking about Mozart?

IRIS

Okay. Let's dance . . . Let's toast the book. And the next one. And
the next one.

PHILIP

Let's hope one of them's original.

IRIS

I'll just slip into something more comfortable, as the mummy said
to the pharaoh.

(PHILIP *groans*)

PHILIP

Did you make that up?

IRIS

I've got a million of them.

PHILIP

Shut up and kiss me.

IRIS

Let's talk. All night. While the Mozart plays . . . Except at the
good parts. Tell me about Ricardo's economic principles. Or the
decline and fall of the Roman Empire. Anything. I just want to
hear you talk.

PHILIP

Like a waterfall, babbling in the distance. Well, in the beginning,
God made Karl Marx, and Karl Marx grew. On the first day, he
went to God and said, here is my thesis. I've got to publish in order
to become famous. On the second day, he went to God the Father
and said: Only bullshit and clichés are written down. That's my
antithesis.

SCENE 5
A Conversation Between Two Women

IRIS *and* HELEN *are in* HELEN*'s apartment. They have had lunch; now they are sitting, looking at* HELEN*'s photo albums, books of clippings, etc. All of it, mementos of* PHILIP. *The two women are just getting to know one another. This is just after* PHILIP *and* IRIS *were married.*

HELEN

Don't ever tell him I showed it to you.

IRIS

(Holding up a bronzed baby shoe) I think it's sweet.

HELEN

He'd kill me. He's forgotten about it, I'm sure.

IRIS

He was so little. Look at that little foot.

HELEN

Not so little. He must have been a year old. He didn't walk till then. And he didn't talk until he was two. I was sure he was retarded. But once he started, he didn't shut up. Sentence after sentence. Talking on and on . . . He loved spaghetti, the canned spaghetti. But he couldn't say it. Pisgetti, he'd say. I'd say it to him, spa-get-ti. And he'd repeat it, spa-get-ti. Okay, spaghetti. Pisgetti. Our father loved to do it with him over and over. *(She laughs with the memory)*

IRIS

Show me some more pictures.

HELEN

There aren't any more. You've seen everything.

IRIS

Tell me something else. Anything. Did you go to the movies together?

HELEN

A lot. When we saw *Hound of the Baskervilles,* we took turns looking at the screen. We were both scared.

23

IRIS

Tell me about when he was born.

HELEN

I don't remember that. I was so little myself.

IRIS

What did you do when they brought him home from the hospital?
Was it sibling rivalry at first sight?

HELEN

He was so quiet. I remember that. He was boring. Sleeping all the
time. Just laying there and grinning. He was too good-natured to
believe . . . Oh, and he liked beer. Dad used to give him little sips
of beer.

IRIS

I love it. Go on. I want to pump you dry.

HELEN

. . . I had such a bad complexion when I was a girl. I ate too many
starches.

IRIS

When he was in high school—was he a Romeo?

HELEN

. . . He's still my best friend. He always has been.

IRIS

I'm an only child . . .

HELEN

My first year in college. I was home over Christmas. And after
breakfast, while I was still drinking my coffee, he called me on the
phone. Where are you, I asked. We have to talk this way, he said.
I can't tell you this face to face. What can't you tell me? What's
so terrible? You tell me everything. I'm having a spiritual crisis,
he said. I've become an atheist. So of course, I burst out laughing.
God damn you, he said, and hung up on me. He never would talk
to me about it after that. Not at all. Right now, I still don't know
whether he's an atheist or not. You know, there are these subjects.
He gets so stubborn. Nothing's going to move him from A to B.
Nothing at all.

24

SCENE 6
Iris in Wisconsin

MRS. EBERLY's *kitchen. There is an old, often-painted table, and three straight-backed chairs.* MRS. EBERLY *is shelling peas.* IRIS *has just been let in to talk to her.*

MRS. EBERLY

I have to go on workin' while we talk. I have my living to earn You know how to shell peas? *(Iris nods)* Show me. *(*IRIS *takes a pea, shells it)* You have to work faster than that.

IRIS

What do you do with them?

MRS. EBERLY

The shells or the peas? The shells I throw out. I don't keep pigs on my property. *(Pause. They work)* And I don't have any sodas.

IRIS

I'm here because of my husband. He died recently.

MRS. EBERLY

People don't eat right. Not enough roughage.

IRIS

Your address was given to me by a doctor.

MRS. EBERLY

I don't do cures . . . If a doctor can't help you, I'm not going to try. I can tell by lookin' at you, though. Your kidneys don't flush proper. Nobody pays attention to that anymore. My father had a glass of hot water with lemon in it every morning of his life. And he died of a stroke, not one of your dirty diseases like cancer. You don't believe me. You think, that's what they all say . . . Things used to be different. When I was a girl, I used to swim all the time. I was going to swim the English Channel. First woman ever. I trained and trained. My father had me in the lake water soon as the ice thawed. I swam. For hours a day. The crawl, and the backstroke; my specialty was the butterfly. You know how that goes? Arms and legs together, then you push out. I was good. I had lots of power. And I was ready. My father was sure of it. And then that—bitch—that Gertrude Ederle got greased up and into

25

the water 'fore we'd even left for England. So there was nothing left for me to do. Oh, for years I was a very unhappy person.

IRIS

I'm sorry.

MRS. EBERLY

You'll have to speak up. I don't hear good . . . I'm a medical phenomenon. But I suppose you know that. I was rotting away inside. So they cut it out and put in new stuff.

IRIS

That's what I've come to see you about.

MRS. EBERLY

Last month, God saved me. While I was on the operatin' table, when they were givin' me the ether, he came to me in the form of Gabriel the archangel. And he said, "Gertrude, you will be saved. You will live and be fruitful." Since we was talkin' I asked him about my investments. "Should I buy or sell, God," I said. He paused a minute. Then he said, "Buy industrials and hold." . . . So I did . . . I put all my cash into stocks. Now I'm goin' to be rich. When I die, I'm leavin' the money back to God. He'll know what to do with it.

IRIS

My husband was your donor.

MRS. EBERLY

He gave me his lung? I trust in God. I take his advice. If more people listened to God, there'd be less divorce.

IRIS

I'm sorry, you're confusing me.

MRS. EBERLY

Oh, yes. That's what they all say . . . You want to see the scar? It's seventeen inches long. I charge, though. And then I invest the money. It's small investors like me that keep American business running. Did you know that?

IRIS

Yes. I want to see the scar. He'll come then. He won't leave me alone.

MRS. EBERLY

Jesus Christ the savior is always with us . . . Give me five dollars

26

and I'll open up for you. *(IRIS opens her purse, takes out five dollars and puts it on the table. MRS. EBERLY picks it up, makes sure it's money, and opens her dress. The scar is huge, diagonal across her chest. It is suppurating and very ugly. IRIS can't look at it)* You have to kiss it. Because you could be Christ in disguise. There's no point in letting opportunity go by. If it turned out you were, I'd refund your money . . . All right, now. Kiss it, like a good girl. *(It takes a moment, but then IRIS does kiss the scar)* No. You aren't God. I thought not. *(MRS. EBERLY closes up the dress, buttons it up again. She is disappointed)* You want your money back? No chance. You're a nice girl, though, you can live here with me if you want. I need someone to strain the fruit. My hands are stiffening up. You want the job?

PHILIP

(Suddenly appearing) I don't feel like talking.

IRIS

Did I invent you?

MRS. EBERLY

(Laughs) That all depends on how you look at it, don't it, dear. What's your name?

IRIS

Iris.

MRS. EBERLY

You ought to be married.

IRIS

My husband died.

MRS. EBERLY

Good for him.

(PHILIP has only passed through the stage. Now MRS. EBERLY leaves IRIS alone. She hesitates, is lost without PHILIP. Then, she moves down to his chair as there is the sound of a key in the lock. IRIS sits in the chair, afraid and angry. PHILIP walks into the light. It is eight years before he died. They have been married two years)

IRIS

Phil? Phil? Is that you? . . . Who is it?

27

PHILIP

It's me. I still have my key . . . I hope I didn't frighten you.

IRIS

Give me the key.

PHILIP

Sure. *(He tosses the key down)* I've got to get to school.

IRIS

What did you come for?

PHILIP

Books. I need some books.

IRIS

Do you want breakfast? I could make some eggs.

PHILIP

I don't like eggs.

IRIS

I've already eaten.

(Short pause. They look warily at one another)

PHILIP

Did you talk to your uncle?

IRIS

Did you see your cousin?

PHILIP

Not yet. I thought I'd let you go first.

IRIS

I've been busy.

PHILIP

Well, I'll come back next week for the rest of my clothes.

IRIS

I'd rather know in advance. So someone else can be here.

PHILIP

Anything you say.

IRIS

I'm trying to make a list. Of what we should each have.

PHILIP

You keep the china, all that stuff.

IRIS

And I suppose you want the *Britannica?*

28

PHILIP

That's right, Iris.

IRIS

Anything you say, Philip.

PHILIP

Philip?

IRIS

I don't have to call you Phil any more.

PHILIP

Most people do.

IRIS

Phil's a little boy's name. Now that you're getting a divorce, you're a big grown man.

PHILIP

(He starts to leave) I'll have a lawyer call you in the morning.

IRIS

I'm sorry. I just get these trolls.

PHILIP

You sure as hell do.

IRIS

I had a migraine this morning when I woke up. About five in the morning. It was all grey and ugly. There was soot on the window sill in the bedroom.

PHILIP

You should see a doctor.

IRIS

I'll call you Phil if you want.

PHILIP

What is this with names? You want me to call you I—I love you I, or give us a kiss, Ris?

IRIS

You made your point.

PHILIP

Damn it. Why did I come back here. I could have sent one of the grad students. Or had my secretary call.

IRIS

(After a moment) There's no reason we can't be orderly about this.

PHILIP

Have you been sleeping all right?

IRIS

I'm going to apply to law school.

PHILIP

You look like you were up all night.

IRIS

The fact is, I want the *Britannica* myself. I'll need it in school.

PHILIP

In law school?

IRIS

I may get my doctorate in English instead. I'm not sure.

PHILIP

Let's toss for it.

IRIS

You can buy another. *(*PHILIP *takes out a coin, tosses it)* Tails.

PHILIP

Heads. You have any paper. I'll keep a list.

IRIS

Now the unabridged. *(He tosses again)* Tails.

PHILIP

Heads again.

IRIS

You call the next one.

PHILIP

This is childish.

IRIS

Make it the Grote.

PHILIP

I don't want the Grote. You keep it.

IRIS

All right. You give me the dictionary and I'll take the Grote.

PHILIP

I *need* the dictionary.

IRIS

All right. I'll take the Grote and you take the bar glasses.

PHILIP

I don't want the fucking bar glasses . . . That's the whole thing. You manipulate me. From beginning to end. You're a fucking psychologist. That's what you are. *(He pounds his fist into the table)*

IRIS

You wanted to beat me, didn't you?

PHILIP

All the time. And I should have. You needed it.

IRIS

Hit me now if it helps you.

PHILIP

No.

IRIS

Go ahead. Maybe then we can talk to one another.

PHILIP

Jesus. Manipulation.

IRIS

I'd like to indulge in an act of rage myself. I'd like to take my coffee cup and break it over your head. I'd like to scald you with boiling coffee, all over your face and in your eyes. And rip your clothes apart with my nails. I'd like to take the fucking bar glasses and shatter them and grind the fragments up and feed them to you with a sterling silver spoon, so you'd writhe on the floor with your intestines bleeding . . . I'm not ready to live alone. Not at all.

(Pause)

PHILIP

I'd better leave.

IRIS

(Going on) I know. We're not good for one another. We just— it's chemical or something. We fight all the time. You were a fool for marrying me.

PHILIP

I'm a fool to put up with all this nonsense. Come on. Go wash your face and comb your hair. Do what I told you, for Christ's sake, or I'll start socking you around.

(She looks at him, leaves. He pauses, sits in his chair, lights out)

SCENE 7
ANOTHER CONVERSATION BETWEEN TWO WOMEN

IRIS's *living room. She is with* HELEN. *It is long before* PHILIP's *illness.*

IRIS

I wish you'd stay. At least till Phil gets home . . . At least for some dinner.

HELEN

No. Thank you.

IRIS

Why just drop in for five minutes at a time, Helen? You could do that on the phone. You should stay with us. Spend time with us.

HELEN

I'm sorry.

IRIS

Have I done something? Are you angry with me?

HELEN

Well then, I'll be going.

IRIS

What's wrong, Helen?

HELEN

Nothing.

IRIS

You sit there and you stare at me. What're you trying to tell me?

HELEN

Philip told me you're going to have a baby.

IRIS

That's right.

HELEN

I'm glad.

IRIS

Good.

HELEN

When?

IRIS

About six months . . . nothing shows yet.

HELEN

(Brightly) Do you want a boy or a girl?

IRIS

I don't care. Both . . . Maybe it'll be twins.

HELEN

It's a good thing you're not a career girl like me.

IRIS

Come on, hang around, Helen. We'll have a drink. Maybe some wine. I feel like celebrating . . . Maybe on Saturday we can go shopping, get started with the layette . . . I guess people still buy layettes. *(She laughs)* I'm going to feel so odd, being a mother. *(She hugs* HELEN*)*

HELEN

I'm sure you'll adjust to it.

IRIS

We want you to be part of it—of everything—of—you know, what the hell.

HELEN

I know. *(She smiles)*

IRIS

I like you, Helen.

HELEN

I know.

IRIS

Well? Don't you like me?

HELEN

Of course. Of course I do. You've been good for him, too. For Phil . . . And I'm certainly very happy you're going to have a baby. *(She reaches for a cup of coffee, spills it, starts to cry)* Oh, damn it. Damn it!

IRIS

I'll get something to clean it up.

HELEN

Don't bother. I'm fine. I'm fine. I just—it's all over the floor.
(She gets Kleenex out of her purse, sops it up. IRIS *helps her.
Both women are on the floor; they look at one another, then
they laugh.* HELEN *laughs even more than* IRIS*)*

IRIS

Hell, we'll regard it as a christening. An early christening.
(Pause. They look at each other. IRIS *gets a cigarette, lights
it)*

HELEN

You know, I'm a shy person.

IRIS

I know that.

HELEN

It's hard for me to express myself.

IRIS

I know that, Helen.

HELEN

Sometimes I would just like to lock my apartment, and double-lock
it and never go back. I mean, just take a suitcase and never go
back. I could go to—San Francisco, or Peoria, or Rio de Janeiro.
I have no obligations. I could go anywhere, and I could be anything. I could go back to school.

IRIS

(After a moment) So. Could you stay for supper?

HELEN

(With a little laugh) Yes. I'd like that. I'd like to stay.

IRIS

Listen. I've got the vitamin pills, and the calcium pills, all that
stuff . . . And I've got morning sickness. *(*HELEN *has not been
paying much attention)* Would you rather talk about something
else?

HELEN

Well—it's an area of experience I don't know anything about.

IRIS

For God's sake, nobody's a spinster any more!

HELEN

I have had a perfectly adequate sex life. And ı'm not in love with my brother. And I'm just not interested in pregnancy, all right? I mean— *(She tries to make a joke)* I mean, rabbits do it all the time. It's not such a big deal. *(Neither of them finds it funny)* You know, Iris, some people just—I really don't want anyone to be my whole life. I really don't.

IRIS

Oh, God, you don't know what you're missing, Helen. I wake up in the morning and I *want* to take his grapefruit and cut it in half and cut up all the little segments very neatly. You know what I mean?

HELEN

It's just not for me . . . I've never met someone I could love wholeheartedly. I used to think there was something wrong with me. People were planning to devote their lives to one another right and left.

IRIS

I have this feeling that if we go on talking like this, it's going to hurt my baby, so will you please shut up, Helen . . . I'm sorry, they say women get very emotional. Well, I'm very emotional, and I want to have nothing but happiness around my baby. For the next six months, I don't plan to have an argument. Or to listen to one.

(HELEN looks at her, holds out her arms, IRIS goes to her; HELEN hugs her, very maternally)

HELEN

You know, if it's a girl, I'd really like you to consider naming her after our mother.

SCENE 8
Iris in Rome

IRIS *has a piece of paper with her, a list on which the names of the donors and their addresses appear. She doesn't know how to find her way in this strange neighborhood. This is a slum, in the worst possible section of Rome. All around her is the sound of women shouting, children crying, cats yowling. A man,* ANTONIO, *is sitting on the steps of a tenement. He has a bottle of wine and is half drunk already. Iris walks hesitantly up to him.* ANTONIO *will only be able to speak in Italian. There could be subtitles to the scene.*

IRIS

Prego. Signore Antonio Vivaldi . . . Where do I find him?

ANTONIO

(In Italian) I'm Vivaldi, what do you want? (Sono Vivaldi. Cosa volete?)

IRIS

(Enunciating carefully) I'm looking for Antonio Vivaldi. *(She fishes in her purse for another piece of paper, looks at it, reads awkwardly from it in Italian)* I'm looking for Antonio Vivaldi.

ANTONIO

(In Italian) Damn it. I *am* Vivaldi. (Porca Madonna. Son' *io* Vivaldi.)

IRIS

Do you speak English?

ANTONIO

(Simultaneously, in Italian) Don't you speak Italian? (Non parlate Italiano, voi?)

IRIS

Antonio Vivaldi?

ANTONIO

(Pointing to himself) That's me. You want to hire me? I've gone honest. (Ecco mi. Ma che cazzo voleta? Son onestu orami. Cazzo.)

IRIS

Oh. You're Vivaldi . . . How do you do? Are you related to the composer?

(ANTONIO *stares at her.* IRIS *starts to find her Italian phrase book)*

ANTONIO

Get the hell out of here, will you? I want to drink privately. (Ma va mori' ammasato, va. Hai capito? Non vedi che sto bevando?)

IRIS

The composer. Musica . . . Maestro. Maestro.

ANTONIO

(He is afraid, ready to run away) Maestro? How'd you know they call me that? (Maestro? Maestro? Come sai che mi chiammaro così?)

IRIS

Don't be afraid. I just want to see—you had an operation. Hospital? . . . How do you say it? Hospitale? Dottore?

ANTONIO

You're sick? I was, too. Lousy doctors. (Sei malatta? Vatene! Disgraziati medici!)

IRIS

You had a transplant . . . An organ. Can I see it? *(She points to her eyes)*

ANTONIO

(He makes the evil eye at her) You're a witch! You want to curse me? What'd I ever do to you? (Ma sei una strega! Cosa vovi? Vuoi maledirmi?)

(He gets up, she pushes him down)

IRIS

I have to see it. You have to let me see it. I'll find it. I can tell by the scar. *(She starts examining his body, opening his shirt, looking for a clue to the organ. She is quite desperate and really hurting* ANTONIO*)* I have to see it. I need him.

ANTONIO

Help! Help! (Aiuto! Aiuto!) *(*ANTONIO *tries to beat her off, but* IRIS *is stronger. The fight turns serious.* IRIS *starts to choke him. He breaks away, makes an obscene gesture)* Crazy bitch! (Figlia d'una mignotta!)

IRIS

The hand! He got the hand! *(She makes a grab for it.* PHILIP *appears suddenly.* IRIS *is distracted from* ANTONIO*)* Phil?

PHILIP

(In Italian. He will have subtitles to translate his lines, too.) Leave me alone . . . Damn it. You've got to let me have some privacy. (Lasciarmi. Per l'amore di dio, ogni tanto devi lasciarme in pace.)

37

ANTONIO

Holy Jesus! There's a witch loose. (Porca miseria! Aiuto! Qui c'è una strega.) *(He runs off)*

IRIS

I don't understand you. I can't speak Italian. I'm lonely, Phil.

PHILIP

You've never known when to stop. It's time to stop now, Iris. (Non hai mai saputo smettere, Iris. Adesso smetti.)

IRIS

How do I get back to the hotel? *(PHILIP leaves her. She looks around, truly frightened)* Does anyone here speak English?

SCENE 9
KNOWING HOW IT IS GOING TO GO
BUT GOING ON ANYWAY

PHILIP *is in a hospital bed. There is a bouquet of flowers, candy, a couple of books.* IRIS *is sitting in a chair very close to the bed.* HELEN *is sitting in another chair, a little removed from the other two.*

HELEN

(To PHILIP*)* It's funny, isn't it? The last few days, I've never felt closer to you.

IRIS

Were you friends—when you were little?

HELEN

Sometimes. Sometimes we hated one another . . . When he was seven, he was all muscle. You know, one of those swaggering boys who play all day at getting dirty. He never read a book. I don't know when he changed. He always had a cut or a scab from falling, or a black eye. Oh, God, he was aggressive. It was hell growing up his sister.

PHILIP

Was it really?

HELEN

When's your next meal?

PHILIP

What difference does it make?

IRIS

It's five-thirty.

HELEN

I think I'll leave when they bring the tray in.

PHILIP

You can leave now. It's all right, Helen. You don't have to spend every day here.

HELEN

Oh. Well, I don't mind. Not at all. I have a vacation coming to me. And they won't take the rest of the time off without paying me. You'll see. I'm never out of the office with a cold or, you know, when my period comes, any of those things. I'm healthy as a horse, actually, so I never use up the sick leave anyway . . . I talk too much. *(She grinds to a slow halt)*

IRIS

Yes.

HELEN

I always did. Especially when there's a chance to say the wrong thing. Remember when I got in that freight elevator at work and whistled Dixie all the way up to my floor. *(She laughs uneasily)* And there was a black operator. Just when the—you know, the civil rights movement was starting up. And when I heard myself, I was so embarrassed. I didn't know what to do, so I kept on whistling Dixie. *(She laughs again)*

PHILIP

There's something about death that makes people stupid.

HELEN

Stop it, Phil.

PHILIP

I'm dying, Helen.

HELEN

I don't like to hear about it.

PHILIP

Really, you know, it's none of your business.

39

IRIS

Why don't you go have an early dinner. That way you can have a visit with him while I'm eating.

HELEN

He's spiteful. There's no reason to be spiteful. *(She leaves)*

IRIS

You are.

PHILIP

I've got a right to be.

IRIS

Maybe I'd better take a walk.

PHILIP

No. Please. I don't want to be alone. Not yet.

IRIS

(She holds his hand) Can I get you anything?

PHILIP

No.

IRIS

How about the pillow. Does it need any fluffing up.

PHILIP

I'm fine.

IRIS

It's hard to talk to you.

PHILIP

The doctor—that psychiatrist—she says in a while I'll want to be alone. Now—

IRIS

You're afraid.

PHILIP

God damn it! I'm thirsty. Get me something to drink, will you? Some ginger ale.

(He turns away from her. She moves off, encounters the DOCTOR*)*

DOCTOR

I'm sorry. It simply isn't operable.

IRIS

I don't believe that. My husband's a strong man. He's perfectly healthy. And he's young.

DOCTOR

We'd do much damage getting to it, Mrs. Uberman.

IRIS

I don't care. Even if he's an invalid. You've got to—

DOCTOR

The aneurism is leaking now . . . You understand? . . . It's a bubble, like a balloon in his artery. And it's growing bigger. When it bursts, suddenly, without any warning, well, that'll be it.

PHILIP

Where the hell are you? I'm thirsty. (IRIS *comes back to him*) Didn't they have any ice?

IRIS

Someone's bringing it.

PHILIP

I want to talk to him when he comes on rounds today. I want you to find out what the news is. About it.

IRIS

You know there isn't any, Phil. He told us. There's no way to know. You just have to keep still. The stiller you are, the better your chance is.

PHILIP

I moved just now. I tried to crank up the damned bed. Nothing happened.

IRIS

It could. You shouldn't do that. I'll ring for the nurse.

PHILIP

I didn't do any damage . . . You aren't even upset, are you.

IRIS

Of course I am. We've got to be calm. Both of us. Now try to relax.

PHILIP

I suppose the sooner I die the better off you'd be. It's expensive keeping me here.

IRIS

That sounds like Helen. *(She takes his hand again)*

PHILIP

Put your head down, on the bed. Like you did before. *(She does. He strokes it again)* How's the boy?

IRIS

Fine. He wants to come and visit . . . They still won't let me bring him in.

PHILIP

Maybe I'll make it till he's twelve. Only three more years.

IRIS

He's making you a steam engine. It's supposed to be finished next week.

PHILIP

That's fine.

IRIS

I've been trying to figure out a way that you could do some work.

PHILIP

On what?

IRIS

You've got so many unfinished things. I was going through the papers—do you mind? And I sorted them. There are three short articles that just need a little work. A book review. And the book.

PHILIP

The book's out. It's impossible. Too much. And all the research left.

IRIS

Couldn't I do some of that?

PHILIP

Don't sit up. Please.

IRIS

What's the matter?

PHILIP

Lock the door. There's a lock on it, isn't there?

IRIS

We can't. You know what the doctor said.

PHILIP

I want you.

IRIS

I know.

(They kiss)

PHILIP

Jesus.

IRIS

We have to settle for this.

PHILIP

I can't.

IRIS

Talk to me about it. Tell me about loving me.

PHILIP

I want you.

IRIS

You love me.

PHILIP

What'll you do? When—you know.

IRIS

I don't know.

PHILIP

You won't have to work.

IRIS

Maybe I will anyway.

PHILIP

You'll marry again.

IRIS

I don't know.

PHILIP

You will. You're too fucking sexy not to.

IRIS

Would you mind?

PHILIP

I'll be dead.

IRIS

I don't want to talk about it.

PHILIP

My golf clubs. I'd hate to see you give them away. Maybe the boy could use them when he's old enough.

IRIS

I wouldn't give them away.

PHILIP

Remember? I'm the only professor of the philosophy of literature to win the club's open. In its history.

IRIS

You're the only one who's entered.

PHILIP

It's still a distinction.

IRIS

I won't marry. If you don't want me to.

PHILIP

Don't make stupid promises.

IRIS

I keep thinking there must be something to say and I'm forgetting it. *(She kisses him again)*

PHILIP

Listen. Lock the door. It doesn't matter. An hour more or less. Please.

IRIS

You're sure?

PHILIP

Come to bed, honey.

IRIS

(She gets on the bed. They lie there for a moment) No. Be still.

PHILIP

Forget it.

IRIS

We can be careful . . . Come on. We do it my way.

PHILIP

Whoever would've thought it. That dying's an aphrodisiac.

SCENE 10
ASSORTED INFORMATION

IRIS *and* PHILIP *each at a lectern with scripts.*

IRIS

Part 1. The Meeting.

PHILIP

I was walking to work one morning.

IRIS

I was sitting in the library doing my research for a term paper.

PHILIP

And she came toward me, with an open umbrella. It wasn't raining.

IRIS

And he stumbled against the chair.

PHILIP

So I asked her why. I thought it was a joke. A sorority initiation or something.

IRIS

He apologized and asked me to have coffee. But I had a class to get to.

PHILIP

She invited me back to her apartment.

IRIS

We didn't see each other for a few weeks after that.

PHILIP

We went to bed that very night.

IRIS

I loved him then.

PHILIP

Part 2. The Ninth Anniversary.

IRIS

You'll be late for school.

PHILIP

I just decided to retire from teaching.

IRIS

And stay in bed all day?

PHILIP

Stay in bed with you all day.

IRIS

Come home early tonight.

PHILIP

Can't. There's a department meeting.

IRIS

Okay . . . Call the dean and give him your notice. Part 3. Getting Acquainted.

PHILIP

I was a champion marbles player when I was seven.

IRIS

Did you ever play hi-lo? You know, with the paddle and the rubber ball?

PHILIP

No. But I played ping-pong.

IRIS

Gnip gnop.

PHILIP

Did you win at it?

IRIS

Only once.

PHILIP

Well, then. You were all A's in graduate school.

IRIS

Almost. I got a B in library science.

PHILIP

Part 4. Domestic.

IRIS

You never wash out the bathtub.

PHILIP

I like handkerchiefs, not Kleenex.

IRIS

Please, no chicory in the coffee this week.

PHILIP

You'd better go on a diet.

IRIS

You'd better start jogging.

PHILIP

Where's my red tie?

IRIS

I threw it out. Wear the blue striped one.

PHILIP

We're out of toilet paper.

IRIS

Part 5. Phone calls . . . Philip?

PHILIP

Hurry up. I've got to get to my ten o'clock.

IRIS

I went to the doctor today.

PHILIP

What's wrong?

IRIS

He says I'm pregnant.

PHILIP

Are you sure?

IRIS

Well—the rabbit is.

PHILIP

Jesus.

IRIS

Are you glad?

PHILIP

How long?

IRIS

In June. That's six months.

PHILIP

I'll be on sabbatical.

IRIS

Are you glad?

PHILIP

Stunned. I think so. Listen . . .

IRIS

I can't. My dime's up.

PHILIP

I'll call you. What's the number?

IRIS

Just tell me.

PHILIP

Hello. Hello.
> *(He shrugs. Hangs up the phone. Then he picks it up again.*
> IRIS *picks hers up)*

IRIS

Hello?

PHILIP

I love you.

IRIS

I'm in labor.

PHILIP

My God. And I'm in London.

IRIS

They're coming every fifteen minutes. How did the paper go?

PHILIP

I'm going to write a book.

IRIS

What shall I call it?

PHILIP

If it's a boy, call him David.

IRIS

And if it's a girl?

PHILIP

You name it.

IRIS

Clara. After your mother.

PHILIP

Swell. Is it fifteen minutes yet?

48

IRIS

Not quite.

PHILIP

Is Helen there?

IRIS

I have to hang up now, dear.

PHILIP

I'm catching the next plane back.

IRIS

Get some rest . . . Are you there?

PHILIP

Do you need anything?

IRIS

I can't hear you.

PHILIP

I can't hear you. *(He can't hear, hangs up)*

IRIS

Oh, I want you here. I love you.

PHILIP

I love you.

IRIS

Hello. Operator. Operator, I've been disconnected.

PHILIP

Last section.

IRIS

Take an aspirin and come to bed.

PHILIP

You know, about swinging. I don't think I'd like it.

IRIS

Want to try it?

PHILIP

We could spend a few weeks with Masters and Johnson.

IRIS

There's no such thing as a vaginal orgasm.

PHILIP

Who cares?

49

IRIS

You're drunk.

PHILIP

I want—

IRIS

(At the same time) I love—

PHILIP

Why do you put the nightgown on if you're only going to have to take it off?

IRIS

It's sexy.

PHILIP

Did you take the pill?

IRIS

What about vasectomy?

PHILIP

No more kids.

IRIS

I think I'm starting change of life.

PHILIP

They have hormones now.

IRIS

Postscript. Honeymoon.

PHILIP

If anything happens to me, I want you to get married again, you understand?

IRIS

I'll be long gone and you'll be living with a twenty-year-old model.

PHILIP

It's a statistical fact. Men die first.

IRIS

I made a will.

PHILIP

There's a will in the safe deposit box.

IRIS

You won't die. You wouldn't. I insist on it. I'm going first.

PHILIP

I couldn't live without you.

IRIS

I couldn't live without you.

SCENE 11
IRIS ON TOP OF THE WORLD

IRIS *has a pack on her back, and in the manner of Chinese theatre, she performs a stylized, spiral motion that will indicate that she is climbing a mountain.* PHILIP *stands to one side, watching her. As the climb goes on,* IRIS *will grow more tired; there is less oxygen in the air.*

PHILIP

There's nothing left but my heart.

IRIS

Nothing.

PHILIP

Has the trip been successful.

IRIS

No. Not yet . . . I'm still hoping, though.

PHILIP

You should rest.

IRIS

The connections are wearing thin. I'm climbing to the top of the world, Phil . . . I thought it would be otherwise.

PHILIP

I expected more from dying, and it's so simple. And I've gone away too quickly. Iris?

IRIS

It's getting cold. I'd better move on.

> (IRIS *goes on in her endless spiral, the lights fading on her completely after a bit.* PHILIP *is alone, in his area. It is the moment of his death)*

SCENE 12
IRIS IN INDIA

IRIS *is sitting with a basket of food and wine; she has been eating.*
A MONK *comes in.*

IRIS
Good afternoon. I wondered when I'd see someone.

MONK
You found the food though.

IRIS
You speak English?

MONK
Whatever tongue may be necessary.

IRIS
Am I taking someone's meal?

MONK
May I sit with you?

IRIS
I was cold on the way up, but I'm quite comfortable, now. I expect
it's the sun through the clouds or something.

MONK
Do you plan to stay here?

IRIS
I was looking for something—someone.

MONK
We leave a meal out every day, for someone who may have come
without food.

IRIS
Oh. You get a lot of visitors, then?

MONK
No.

IRIS
Are there many people here? I don't see—you know, houses,
stores. I didn't even see any farms.

MONK
The soil is not good for growing things.

IRIS

Are you in charge?

MONK

We live in—openings of the mountain. You wouldn't notice them.

IRIS

You don't answer my questions.

MONK

I'm sorry. Ask one.

IRIS

I was trying to find someone. My husband died.

MONK

Yes.

IRIS

And I've been traveling, trying to find him.

MONK

His pieces.

IRIS

Yes. All over. And. They said. His heart. Could anyone do an operation like that up here?

MONK

Operation?

IRIS

A transplant.

MONK

That isn't what we did.

IRIS

I thought there was a mistake.

MONK

No mistake, the heart came here . . . Have you tried some of the wine? It's very good. It's made from spring flowers.

(*He reaches in the basket, takes out two glasses, pours the wine*)

IRIS

Thank you. But I don't like wine.

MONK

Cheers.

53

IRIS

Were you educated in England?

MONK

No. I've never been down this mountain.

IRIS

This is good . . . The wine. May I have some more? *(He pours some)* I'm sorry. I don't want to—intrude. Is this a religious community?

MONK

Yes.

IRIS

You're very handsome. *(Short pause)* I come from Indiana. Originally. I've lived most of my life in New York. In the United States . . . Should I worry about a sunburn? So high up. This is going to be the last stop on my trip. Then I'm going home . . . When I was little, my father gave me a book, about a boy and a girl who traveled all over the world. They had lived on a farm, but they left the farm and they went to Paris, France, and London. They even went to China. And when they came back, all the little girl wanted to do was to go out to the barn to see if her baby calf had grown any. I thought travel was something else. I expected to turn into a new person in each country. But what I've found is, I keep staying more and more the same. And I'm middle-aged . . . I think I'll do what Philip did. Then we'd have a chance, you know. The girl who gets my liver could marry the boy who got his bone marrow. If I die soon enough. Then we'd have more children. It bothers me not to have had more babies.

MONK

You could stay here with me.

IRIS

Do you find me pretty?

MONK

No. But I like you.

IRIS

Was that an eagle? Do they fly this high? I'll have to stay the night, I guess. I'd never get down the mountain by dark. And I stay with you?

MONK

No birds fly up here. It's going to rain.
>   *(He packs up the food that's left, the glasses, etc.)*

IRIS

What happened to Philip's heart? Who got it?

MONK

I did.

IRIS

You seem so healthy.

MONK

I am.

IRIS

You said there was no operation. Is it something new? Something
—Eastern?

MONK

I ate it.

LAST SCENE
MORE CONVERSATIONS BETWEEN TWO WOMEN

IRIS *and* HELEN *at* IRIS's *kitchen table. Iris is wearing paint-spotted blue jeans.*

HELEN

I thought you wouldn't want to be alone all day.

IRIS

I needed the coffee. And I needed a break from the painting. I'm
going to be stiff tomorrow.

HELEN

I noticed how healthy the plants were.

IRIS

David's coming home for a few days tonight. I wanted to get his
room all ready . . . But I can't put a wet bookcase in there.

HELEN

It's his birthday today, Phil's birthday.

IRIS

I know.

55

HELEN

I just meant—well, I was surprised to find you painting things today.

IRIS

I thought about painting this table purple. Like eating on an eggplant.

HELEN

Can I take you both out to supper? Pizza. He likes pizza . . . I got the nicest letter from him last week.

IRIS

David likes you.

HELEN

He's just like his father.

IRIS

No. Not really. Not at all.

HELEN

Whatever you say.

IRIS

Oh, come on, Helen.

HELEN

I've enrolled at the New School. Biology. And I'm going to take some math. Statistics . . . Something I can really get involved in . . . I've always felt very connected to science.

IRIS

All right, Helen. Phil's dead. I'm sorry . . . Now I have to go on working.

HELEN

You used to say he was your whole life.

IRIS

He was . . . I mean I thought he was. At that last place. While I was on my trip, Helen. I discovered that I had to make up my mind. To go on, or to stop. Whatever. So today, I decided to paint a bookcase. That's what I'm going to do. Even on my husband's birthday.

HELEN

I have to go to school.

(HELEN *leaves the kitchen. She goes to another area. She is in a tight light. She picks up a phone.* IRIS *picks up her phone)*

IRIS

I just can't go on talking about Phil every time we see one another, Helen.

HELEN

Why not?

IRIS

Because there's no point in it.

HELEN

Ever since you came back, you've been different. Are you in love with someone?

IRIS

Not on the phone, Helen.

HELEN

I'm sorry. It's been worrying me.

IRIS

How's school?

HELEN

I had to stop. All those fluorescent lights. They gave me headaches. And I can't go to school during the daytime. I mean, I don't want to give up my job.

IRIS

All right, Helen. No more about Phil, then.

HELEN

David's starting to look just like him. *(They hang up. Then* IRIS *picks hers up, followed by* HELEN*)* Hello?

IRIS

What's all this about your giving a cocktail party?

HELEN

For the victims of the Spanish Civil War.

IRIS

That was 1937.

HELEN

Well, some of them are still alive.

IRIS

All right. I'll come.

HELEN

I've been learning how to crochet.

IRIS

Isn't that hard on the eyes?

HELEN

Do you want me to make you an afghan?

IRIS

If you want to.

HELEN

How's David?

IRIS

He wants to be an engineer.

HELEN

I don't know how to go on, Iris. Really. I don't. *(HELEN comes back into the kitchen)* I don't know why. I—no, I wasn't even drunk. And I went home with him.

IRIS

Did you enjoy it?

HELEN

Yes.

IRIS

Well?

HELEN

What about you?

IRIS

I like being alone. For a while.

HELEN

You'll end up making someone else your whole life.

IRIS

Not ever again, Helen. No one.

HELEN

Sometimes I wonder if I'm capable of love.

IRIS

I love you, Helen.

HELEN

I love David. I'm sure of that . . . And you. I love you . . . Lately, for the last few years, I'm always afraid.

IRIS

About going on? *(*HELEN *nods)* I am too.

HELEN

I'm forty years old.

IRIS

When I was in India, I was on top of a mountain. And—it's not that I saw God—almost the reverse. I had this sure sensation, as firm and as real as a string of beads; mortality. I finally believed in mortality. I finally believed in mortality. Phil's dead. I'm going to die some time. Even my son will. I find that reassuring. *(She hands* HELEN *an envelope)* Here.

HELEN

What is it?

IRIS

The list. Of all the people who got his organs. I think you should take the trip. I think you should quit your job and pack one small suitcase and take the trip . . . I'll take care of your aquarium . . . You'll find out. It's good. Going crazy. I'm really glad I did it. Everything. Even being crazy. And then he'll be dead. For both of us. He'll be dead for the rest of our lives.

Window Dressing

by
JOANNA RUSS

"I remember being fascinated with store windows and going through a few years when I really tried to look like the mannequins —clothes, make-up, hair. I finally realized that no one ever managed it, that it's a device to make you spend money, a totally false idea. A couple of years after that, I wrote *Window Dressing.*"

Joanna Russ was born in 1937 and says she spent much of her childhood in the Bronx Botanical Gardens. Although she wrote her first play at eight, she was also busy turning out stories and comic books. She studied playwrighting at the Yale School of Drama but stopped writing plays three or four years after she got her MFA there. "I loved the theatre, but I felt, when I was working in it, that it was so barbarous and cruel to everyone that if I could work out an alternative, I'd be very happy." She continued writing science fiction (which she'd kept at all along) and has published many stories and three novels, *Picnic on Paradise* (1968), *And Chaos Died* (1970) and *The Female Man* (1975). She says about science fiction, "I feel that fantasy gives the writer more leeway than realism; you can show things more clearly."

Although long sections of her novels are written in dialogue with stage directions—"I had no place else to put it!"—Russ has not written plays in several years, but she would write them again —with large parts for women—if theatres were interested. *Window Dressing* was first produced in 1969 with other one-acts off-off-Broadway as an Actors Equity Showcase. In 1976, it was produced by the Boulder Feminist Theatre. Russ lives in Boulder and teaches writing and science fiction (as literature) at the University of Colorado.

CHARACTERS

MARCIA, a mannequin

IRVING

A WINDOW DESIGNER (no lines)

SCENE 1

A department-store window, looking out on the street. MARCIA, *a mannequin.*

MARCIA

I am more beautiful than you. Yes I am. I know I am. I can see myself in the glass. *(Gaily)* I went dancing at the Colony last night. Can't you tell? You can tell by my dress. It's a Colony dancing dress and no one else has ever worn it before. Oh, what a time we had! It was divine! It was madly gay! I danced and danced and danced and danced—*(Disappointed)* Nobody's paying the slightest attention. *(She calls softly to the invisible crowd passing in front of her window)* Hello . . . Hi there . . . Ta . . . Aa-oo . . . *(To herself)* Of course I don't mind. I don't mind at all. They'll turn the lights out soon, but if you think I mind—! . . . I won't be able to see myself. I won't know who I am. I won't have any memories, only the most awful nightmares, the most awful, awful—I don't mind. One has to be brave. When they turn the lights out in the evening, you can hear a little, sighing sound, like a hundred leaves all falling, all drifting and circling down. That's all of us. We die, each time the lights are turned out. Of course I don't mind. I just fix my eyes on a corner of the Park— I can see the Park, you know, right over there—and when the sun comes up, that's the first thing I see. I keep my eyes fixed on the fountain, on those trees. And that's the first thing I see every morning. *(Coaxing)* You can see me. Of course you can. Look at me. Look. No one's ever worn this dress before. Look how lovely my shoes are. I have eyelashes. Look! Look at me! Please, please look at me!

> *(Enter* IRVING, *who stops, stares at her, awestruck. He bites his nails. He scratches. Scruffy, grimy, badly dressed. Hunched over. She glows, poses, yearns, leans toward him. He is fascinated. He rubs his hands together. Then he*

65

jumps violently, as if stung, pulls his jacket closer around him and runs out. The lights fade. MARCIA *goes limp)*

MARCIA

We die . . . We die . . . in the dark.
(The lights go out)

SCENE 2

MARCIA *again in her window. A different pose. She wears a coat.*

MARCIA

Here I am. Isn't it lovely? I went riding in the Park last night. It was simply divine! Can't you tell? I'm wearing a riding coat. I went riding in an open carriage in the Park and the night—the night was simply enchanting! No one's ever worn this coat before. The window designer put it on me this morning. He's wonderful. He's like a god. He put on my shoes and he actually *talked* to me. He said: *(Naïvely)* "There you go, old girl, ruining another pair of shoes." That's what he said. He knows everything. Why, he once said—I had a desk in the window and a globe and a barrel of apples and a map and a chair and a basket and a window and a curtain and a—

(Enter IRVING. *She breaks off. He comes up to the window and leans against it. Very secretive. He looks about to see no one is watching, then gives himself up to adoring her)*

MARCIA

Hello. *(She is going through all sorts of small adjustments)* Aren't you handsome! Did you come to see me? Do you like me? I think you're wonderful. I'd like to see you again. I think you're awfully handsome. Come and see me. Come and talk to me. Talk to me. Say something. Tell me, tell me, talk to me, say something, say, say—

*(*IRVING *has not, of course, heard her; but he looks about, puts his mouth to the glass and—)*

IRVING

(Hoarsely) This is my lunch hour.
(And he bolts. The lights fade out)

SCENE 3

MARCIA, *in the window, revolving slowly, talking, putting on and taking off items of clothing, etc. Scarves, hats, shawls.* IRVING *is staring off in front of her. A montage.*

MARCIA

When you look at me, I feel as if someone were touching me.

IRVING

I work in a warehouse.

MARCIA

I feel something touching me and I can't bear it; it's so pleasant and so painful at once, I don't know what to do.

IRVING

You look rich.

MARCIA

I feel something like a fire, something going all through me, like a fire—

IRVING

You're a lady.

MARCIA

I don't know if I can stand it. I wonder if I want you to look at me at all.

IRVING

You're a real lady.

MARCIA

Look at me! I want you to look at me! *(He does)* Do you know what will happen to me? It happens to all of us. We get melted down or chopped up and we go back to being *things* and all the time we're *so* much more beautiful and *so* much more perfect than—than *real* women . . . *(With dignity)* Sometimes it occurs to me that I may end my days being used for land reclamation, but I don't cry—I never cry— *(Stifling a sob)* because—because I know—I just look—over there—

IRVING

You! You're better than all of them.

MARCIA

No. Not really.

IRVING

You understand.

MARCIA

No. Not really.

IRVING

You love me.

MARCIA

No. Not really. *(He kisses the window. She gasps)* I love you! *(He rushes off. The* WINDOW DESIGNER *comes in and begins to take off her clothes as the lights fade out)*

SCENE 4

The window. MARCIA *has both hands against the glass, tête-à-tête with* IRVING.

IRVING

You're so beautiful.

MARCIA

They're going to turn the lights out soon.

IRVING

You got pretty hair.

MARCIA

I'll have nightmares when they turn the lights out.

IRVING

You got pretty feet.

MARCIA

All of us have nightmares when they turn the lights out.

IRVING

You got long eyelashes.

MARCIA

I think we remember what it was like before we became so beautiful, when we were just lumps of wood or plaster. I think we remember factories and assembly lines and being ground and shaped and polished, being carried and sawed like things . . . I don't like to think about it.

IRVING

(Greatly daring) You got a great—*figure!*

MARCIA

(Gaily) The designer put a copy of a book in my window. There it is. It's by F. Scott Fitzgerald. I'm trying to read it, but it's not easy because I can't move my head very well and the book is turned upside down. But I can read the back cover. It's about a Daisy. Do you think I'm a Daisy?

IRVING

I think you're beautiful.

MARCIA

I think *you're* beautiful.

IRVING

You got lovely eyes.

MARCIA

Look . . . in my eyes.

> *(A long, long look. The lights in the window go out, showing* MARCIA *dimly. She is limp.* IRVING *looks about, surreptitiously takes out a glass-cutter, cuts the glass, breaks it,* * *and—throwing a sheet around* MARCIA—*prepares to carry her off. The lights go out)*

---

*A word to the nervous—not you who are reading this, of course. *You* know this is all in mime.

SCENE 5

IRVING's *room, a bleak room in a cheap boarding house—bed window, chair, bureau, bookcase with one shelf full of books and the rest bare. On one wall the only picture—a tiny snapshot* MARCIA, *wrapped in a sheet, stands in the center of the room* IRVING *unwraps her. She is perfectly still, in the pose of a window mannequin. She stares ahead. He adores her. Is beside himself Rushes to a little mirror on the bureau and frantically combs his hair. Rushes back. Touches her hand very carefully.* MARCIA *cries out, without altering her pose or her face. He seizes the head and kisses it. She cries out. He kisses her other hand, runs his hands tremulously over her face and hair, grabs her around the waist, then gets down on his knees and grabs her around the knees. At each touch,* MARCIA *is wrenched dreadfully, this way and that. A moment's silence. Her stiffness alters a little. She bends her head, to look at him.*

MARCIA

Hello.

IRVING

(On his knees) You're alive! You're alive!

MARCIA

(With dawning rapture) I can talk. *(*IRVING *springs up, hardly able to contain himself. He cannot talk from joy)* I can move. *(She moves her arms, a little stiffly)* I can walk. *(She does so, carefully)* I can walk! Look! I can walk! *(He watches, beaming)* I can smile! I can talk! I can dance! Dance! Dance! Dance!

> *(She begins to whirl about the room, slowly at first; then faster and faster, finishing up with a wild Charleston. Then she stops, rapturous)*

IRVING

My name is Irving.

> *(But* MARCIA *is too wrapped up in herself to listen. She's touching herself all over, feeling her new sensations, listening, flexing her fingers, touching herself with little, light, awed motions)*

IRVING

This is my room. Those are my books. I'm a reader. The imagina-tion—is just more—than the material things. I read, usually at night. *(Trying to interest her)* I thought somebody would catch me, in the street! . . . That's me. *(Indicating the snapshot)* A long time ago. Say, I thought somebody would catch me, I ran so fast—

MARCIA

(Who has not heard a word) Is this the Colony?

IRVING

No, this is my room.

MARCIA

Then I can't stay here. *(IRVING is horror-struck)* It wouldn't be right. *(Powdering her nose)* When a gentleman takes out a Daisy, he takes her to the Colony. I read that on the book jacket.

> *(IRVING runs and locks the door, putting the key out of sight on the molding above it)*

MARCIA

(Thoughtfully) Of course, perhaps you're going to take me to the Colony *later.*

IRVING

(Just making it back in time. Shouts desperately) Yes!

MARCIA

Well then, maybe it's all right. Are you a Princeton man?
> *(IRVING smiles sickly)*

MARCIA

Don't tell me you're a Yale man!

IRVING

Oh no, no!

MARCIA

(Suspicious) What college *did* you go to?

IRVING

(Mumbles) I—I didn't—

MARCIA

(Alarmed) I have to leave. *(She edges towards the door)* Really, I'm not dressed for it. I have to go to the Colony. I'm going to a dance. It's been delightful. Excuse me. I'm sure you're a gentleman—

(She discovers that the door is locked) Let me out! (IRVING *follows her, wringing his hands)* You let me out this instant!

(She wrenches at the door, he runs and grabs her, they struggle, all the time crying—)

IRVING

No, no, no! Don't! Don't!

MARCIA

(Determined) You're not a gentleman! Let go! Let go! Help! *Help!*
(And then she emits a real scream, for he—quite accidentally, for he is the timidest of mortals—tears the shoulder and half the bodice off her dress. She is wearing nothing underneath, of course, but she holds the rip numbly together with one hand. IRVING *is extremely frightened.* MARCIA *totters)*

MARCIA

(Numbed, a little dead) What am I doing here? Who am I? How did I get here? What am— Who— What did I— What I— do—I

*(*IRVING *has run and gotten his bathrobe, which he now throws around her. He ties it. Her dizziness disappears; she "stabilizes," as it were, looking no longer empty-headed, but simply fully human. Then she looks puzzled. She brings up her arm to look at the sleeve of the bathrobe. She feels it)*

MARCIA

(Sensibly) How very strange . . . I don't understand it . . . When I was a model in a store window, I got all the memories from the clothes I had on, and I only wore clothes that nobody had ever worn before, so the memories I got from them were very simple ones, the ones the designers had built into the clothes. And so my whole life was very simple, and very clear. Now I'm wearing your clothes and I should have all your thoughts and your memories. And I do. But I don't understand them. I don't understand them one little bit.

IRVING

That's my bathrobe.

MARCIA

I have them, but they don't make sense. They don't make any sense at all.

72

IRVING

I wear it every night.

MARCIA

Why do you stay here all the time? Why don't you go out? Why don't you ever talk to anybody?

IRVING

Uh—the imagination—is very superior—

MARCIA

Why didn't you go to school? Why don't you talk to the people at work? Why do you cross the street when you see anyone coming? Why do you count to yourself all the time? Why do you cross your fingers?

IRVING

So I come home and then I read—and—then—and then I—

MARCIA

Look here: you have to kiss me. *(IRVING is alarmed)* Yes, you do. I have it all figured out. I know all about kissing; I read about it on the book jacket. The reason I don't understand your memories is that I don't feel them. And I don't feel them because I'm not human. You have to kiss me.

IRVING

(Whispering) Why?

MARCIA

To make me human. To make me just like you.

IRVING

(He still can't believe it about the kissing) Do you *want* to?

MARCIA

Why, is it unhappy?

IRVING

Nah!

MARCIA

Then kiss me.

IRVING

You would *let* me?

> *(She holds out her arms. He grabs her violently and kisses her; then lets her go, breathing hard. She waits for her new humanity. Then it comes. She bends over, in great pain)*

MARCIA

(Agonized) Take me back! Take me back!

IRVING

Hey—

MARCIA

Why did you take me away! Why did you do it?

IRVING

W—well, what—

MARCIA

(Looking around the room) Oh, Jesus.

IRVING

Where are you going?

MARCIA

(With great loathing and misery, looking at the room and at him and seeing them both for the first time) Oh, Jesus, Jesus, Jesus, Jesus—

IRVING

No!

> *(She runs towards the window. And throws herself out.* IRVING, *who has made a last, desperate grab at her—in which he has practically fallen out of the window himself —retains only her head, which has come loose from her body and which he drops precipitously)*

IRVING

They'll get me!

> *(He takes a suitcase from under the bed, flings his books into it and a few pieces of clothing from the bureau and bolts out the door, throwing the key on the floor)*

MARCIA'S VOICE

(Slow, expressionless. She is dying) Back . . . bright light . . . blessed . . . beautiful . . . still . . . bright . . . lights . . . In the dark.

> *(And the lights go out)*
> *(Curtain)*

Breakfast
Past Noon

by
URSULE MOLINARO

"**B**reakfast Past Noon is prototypical rather than autobiographical. . . . I don't see myself as THE DAUGHTER, and still less as THE MOTHER—although I played THE MOTHER one night to show her exasperatingly well-meaning irrelevance as far as THE DAUGHTER'S life is concerned. . . . To my great satisfaction, most of the sons and daughters in my audience came to tell me afterwards that that was 'exactly like their mother.' "

Breakfast Past Noon was first produced at the East Village Theatre in 1971; there is a "vertical" companion play about the relationship between father and son.

Ursule Molinaro has written approximately fifteen one-act plays, which have been produced off- and off-off-Broadway. She has published three novels—Green Lights Are Blue (1967), Sounds of a Drunken Summer (1969) and The Borrower (1970) —and short stories in a wide range of magazines, most recently Superfiction and Triquarterly. Molinaro has also written "a paperback on sun-sign characteristics and affinities" called The Zodiac Lovers (1969) and a handbook on numerology, Life by the Numbers (1971). She received a Creative Artists Public Service (CAPS) fellowship in fiction from the New York State Council on the Arts (1973), and has just finished a new novel, The Autobiography of Cassandra, Princess and Prophetess of Troy, about the end of the era when "women were wise, men muscled, and all children legitimate." She lives in New York City.

CHARACTERS

THE MOTHER, sixty-eight, neat dress

THE DAUGHTER, forty-three, terry robe

THE SET

Two giant harp cases, side by side. MOTHER's harp case lid opens stage left, DAUGHTER's stage right.

All objects—telephone beside DAUGHTER's harp case, magazine, glasses and case, coffeepot, cup, saucer, ashtray, etc., which MOTHER or DAUGHTER take out of or put into harp cases—might be blatant outsized papier-mâché imitations of the real things.

Radio: Rock and roll (Good Guys or similar station) as background throughout. Turned up and down by DAUGHTER.

A beautiful day . . . any season.

MOTHER

(Sitting on rim of her wide-open harp case, reading a magazine, twisting her wedding ring—which she twists throughout the play— almost to the end. She looks up. Looks expectantly at DAUGH- TER*'s closed harp case. Reads some more)*

(Noon siren, long and loud)

(Puts both hands—one holding magazine, the other glasses case— to her ears to blot out siren. Looks expectantly at DAUGHTER*'s closed harp case. Pushes glasses far down on nose. Looks at* DAUGH- TER*'s harp case over top of glasses. Pushes glasses back up. Contin- ues to read magazine, twisting her wedding ring)*

DAUGHTER

(Lid of harp case slowly rises. A wedding-ringed hand appears, pushes lid all the way back. A tousled head yawns out)

MOTHER

(Watches DAUGHTER *over top of glasses)*

(Radio starts blaring inside DAUGHTER's harp case)

MOTHER

(Puts hands—holding objects—to her ears)

(Radio is adjusted inside DAUGHTER's harp case: first still louder, then somewhat toned down)

DAUGHTER

(Yawns. Swings legs out. Stands up. Stretches. Bends into harp case. Takes out cup and saucer. Sits down on rim of harp case, her back turned on MOTHER*)*

MOTHER

(Twists wedding ring; watches DAUGHTER *over top of glasses)*

DAUGHTER

(Reaches into harp case. Takes out coffeepot. Pours coffee into cup. Massages her forehead. Lifts cup to her lips)

MOTHER

(Closes magazine. Carefully places it inside her harp case. Looks at DAUGHTER*'s back over top of glasses. Removes glasses while looking at* DAUGHTER*'s back. Carefully fits glasses into case. Places*

case inside harp case. Looks at DAUGHTER*'s back. Gets up. Walks around own harp case, around top of* DAUGHTER*'s harp case. Stands in front of* DAUGHTER, *looking down at* DAUGHTER*)*

DAUGHTER

(Drinking coffee) Good morning: I said to her. As she had taught me to say to her when she made me get out of bed in the mornings when I was little.

Good morning: I said. Because she had come over to the table at which I had just sat down. She was standing in front of me ... Over me ... Her eyes watching. Watching me drink my coffee. *(She drinks)*

MOTHER

(Sitting down on rim of DAUGHTER*'s harp case, knee by knee with* DAUGHTER, *twisting wedding ring)* And I said: good afternoon. Because it *was after* noon. I had heard the noon siren scream a few minutes before she turned that radio on ... to that awful music ... That was no *music* ... Much too loud ... before she came out of her bedroom. And made coffee for herself. While I sat reading a magazine by the window. Waiting for her to get up.

I stopped reading and walked over to sit with her. To keep her company. As I used to do when she was still a little girl. When I used to sit with her and keep her company while she ate her breakfast before running off to school.

I said the siren sounded terribly loud. And asked if they had known it would be right on top of them when they rented their apartment. And remarked that landlords rarely mentioned those inconveniences to a prospective tenant. And that one ought to make sure for oneself before one rented an apartment.

I couldn't stand that screaming every noon, I said to her.

DAUGHTER

(Wriggles behind along harp-case rim to sit less close to MOTHER*)* I told her she didn't have to stand it every noon. *(She drinks)*

MOTHER

She'd had such sensitive ears as a little girl, I said. The smallest noise would bother her ... *(She twists wedding ring)* Like that radio, I said. Wouldn't she like me to turn it down a bit? *(She stands up to go and turn radio down)*

DAUGHTER

(Holding cup to her chin . . . with slightly shaking hand) I told her not to bother. That it was my wake-up music.

MOTHER

(Standing over DAUGHTER*)* I didn't ask her how she could call that noise music . . . I didn't want to irritate her. She was holding the cup to her chin. Her hand was shaking. And I told her so. *(She twists wedding ring)*

DAUGHTER

(Drinks) I nodded: yes. So it was.

MOTHER

(Sitting down again on rim of DAUGHTER*'s harp case, closer to* DAUGHTER*)* I asked her how that could be! She was only forty-two!

DAUGHTER

(Pulling herself away from MOTHER*)* I was forty-three. I said I was forty-three.

MOTHER

(Leaning toward DAUGHTER*)* But I was seventy! I said. And *my* hands didn't shake. *(She twists wedding ring)*

DAUGHTER

(Wriggling away from MOTHER*)* I said I thought she was sixty-eight.

MOTHER

(Leaning toward DAUGHTER*)* I was sure drinking coal-black coffee every morning . . . every afternoon . . . probably didn't help, I said. *(She twists wedding ring)*

DAUGHTER

(Wriggling away from MOTHER*)* I said it probably didn't. *(She drinks)*

MOTHER

(Wriggling after DAUGHTER*)* I asked her why she kept drinking it then? *(She twists wedding ring)*

> (Throughout the dialogue preceding DAUGHTER's bath, MOTHER continues to wriggle after DAUGHTER on harp-case rim; DAUGHTER continues to wriggle away . . . Until she finds herself sitting at foot of harp case on one buttock with no space left to withdraw to)

DAUGHTER

I said it helped me think.

MOTHER

I said she only *thought* it did. That it only made her nervous. How could she think when she was nervous.

DAUGHTER

I said: I seemed to manage somehow . . . *(She pours another cup)*

MOTHER

Another cup! I said. Why didn't she drink Sanka? *I* drank Sanka, I said. It tasted just as good.

DAUGHTER

It didn't to me, I said. *(She drinks)*

MOTHER

How did she know? I asked her. Had she tried it? It tasted just like *real* coffee . . . With a little milk and sugar, I said. I offered to fix her some—the way I fixed it for myself—the next morning . . . uhh . . . afternoon . . . She wouldn't be able to tell the difference, I told her.

DAUGHTER

I said I hated milk and sugar. That I'd rather drink hot water. *(She drinks)*

MOTHER

She used to *love* milk and sugar as a little girl, I reminded her. Why did she always have to be so *radical?* Did she think I was planning to poison her?

DAUGHTER

I said I hadn't been a little girl in years . . . *(She takes a pack of cigarettes from harp case; lights one . . . with slightly shaking hand)*

MOTHER

She would always be *my* little girl: I said. A boy was a son till he married a wife; a girl stayed a daughter for all of her life . . . I was looking at her shaking hand that was lighting a cigarette. Smoking probably didn't help. Either . . . I said.

DAUGHTER

I said it probably didn't. But that it helped other things. *(She inhales deeply)*

MOTHER

Like "thinking"? I asked. I was teasing her gently.

DAUGHTER

Yes: I said. And like leaving people alone.

MOTHER

I said that wasn't nice.

DAUGHTER

(Inhaling) Oh, I didn't know, I said. Leaving people alone could be *very* nice . . . . For *them* . . .

MOTHER

I repeated: that she was *not* nice. That I didn't see her that often

DAUGHTER

(Smokes; drinks coffee)

MOTHER

She didn't answer me. Or look at me. She sat drinking her coal-black coffee, puffing away at that cigarette. Visibly ruining the good health I had borne her with. Vice always found excuses, I said.

DAUGHTER

(Smokes; drinks coffee; strokes her forehead)

MOTHER

She didn't answer me. Or look at me. I couldn't help looking at her trembling hand which was holding the cigarette. I asked her to look at that poor hand.

DAUGHTER

(Smokes; drinks coffee; strokes her forehead)

MOTHER

She did *not* look at her hand. Or at me. She sat staring at some-thing . . . at nothing . . . behind/above my head. With narrowed eyes. Like a sphinx. As though I weren't there. I couldn't just sit by and watch her ruin the good health God had been kind enough to let me bear her with, I said. *(She fishes for ashtray in* DAUGH-TER*'s harp case)* I held the ashtray out to her. *(She does)* Here, I said. Put it out.

DAUGHTER

(Recoils)

MOTHER

She recoiled. From the ashtray. From her mother's hand. That was only trying to help her. That was *not* trembling at seventy . . . At sixty-eight . . . As though my hand were a poisonous snake . . . A wave of pity flooded my heart. I was only trying to *help* her, I said.

DAUGHTER

(Smokes; drinks coffee; strokes her forehead)

MOTHER

She didn't answer me. Or look at me. She just sat. Smoking. Drinking her wicked coffee. Staring beyond me. A narrow-eyed sphinx. I held out my hand across the breakfast table. *(She holds out hand)* Give *me* that cigarette, I said. *I'll* put it out.

DAUGHTER

(Gestures with cigarette as though to burn MOTHER*'s held-out hand. But doesn't)*

MOTHER

For a moment I thought she was going to burn my hand. I pulled it back. *(She does)* Perhaps I should *not* have pulled it back . . . I implored her: WHY—DON'T YOU—STOP—SMOK-ING!

DAUGHTER

I was trying not to see her concerned face. Not to hear her pleading tone. To "keep my cool," as Johnny would have said. *(She smiles a smile of reminiscence: Johnny)* But her persistence won . . . As it always had . . . Why don't *you* start! I said.

MOTHER

She was being deliberately unreasonable. I should not have answered. I should have changed the subject. To the weather. Which was beautiful. Perhaps I should have asked what she was planning to do with this beautiful day. Perhaps I should have suggested something she and I might have enjoyed doing together . . . In the sunshine. A leisurely walk. A bit of window-shopping. I refused to believe that she seriously wanted me to start smoking. She was only trying to distract me . . . by shocking me. Because she knew that I was right . . . It had already been one of her tricks, when she was still a little girl . . . When she had been a *bad* little girl. When she would try to distract me by shocking me . . . by trying to hurt me . . . from whatever reason I had for scolding her . . . Or for spanking her. Sometimes . . . Like the time she tried to stop me from hanging the cowbell around her little neck. When she was not quite five. When she couldn't be stopped from wandering off by herself . . . Out of earshot . . . Into the wheat field . . . That stood higher than she did. At not quite five . . . Where I might never have been able to find her again . . . Ever . . . Wandering through the wheat field all the way down to the creek . . . In which she might easily have drowned . . . When she upset me . . . succeeded in upsetting me . . . when she asked . . . at not quite five! . . . why I hadn't hung a cowbell around her daddy's neck? . . . Because her daddy had "wandered off" . . . She had succeeded in making me cry while I hung the cowbell around her little neck . . . Still, I didn't change the subject. I felt I couldn't afford to, if I wanted to help her stop smoking. I didn't see her that often. I pretended to take her seriously. I! Start smoking! I cried. At *my* age! What ever for! Did she want *my* hands to shake too!

DAUGHTER

I knew I should have "kept my cool" . . . as Johnny *(smile of reminiscence)* would have said. I should have changed the subject. To the weather. Which was harmless. Which was beautiful. I should have asked her if she didn't want to go for a walk for an hour or so . . . while I took my bath and got dressed . . . *(While Johnny called?)* But I was no longer used to words coming at me in the morning. Or afternoon . . . Whenever it was that I was getting up . . . I had grown used to approaching a new day quietly. On tiptoe. Over a slow cup of coffee. And a couple of cigarettes. To a rock'n'roll undertone . . . Before the world came in . . . Over the telephone . . . Her well-washed well-meaning face was blocking the sunshine beyond the window bars. The flowers I had planted. Our landlord's ivy. I tried not to see her neat sparing hair . . . *(She brushes hair out of forehead)* . . . Which I had inherited. Which was not neat. Still uncombed . . . Which was not yet quite so sparing. Not yet a greyish white. But would become just as sparing greyish white sooner or later . . . I wondered what Johnny *(smile of reminiscence)* thought about my hair. *If* he thought about it. I knew he thought about my painted toenails. He had told me he had thought about them . . . Did he see my hair for what it was: teased and color-rinsed and not very thick. An elaborate time-consuming cheat . . . Or was it just "white folks" hair to him? That could never be as *bad* as his own? I thought of Johnny's mother. Whom I had met. Once. At Johnny's insistence . . . With a permanent bandana around her head . . . Who refused to let him talk to me on the telephone after she'd met me . . . Told me he was out . . . Or asleep . . . when I called him at home . . . Mothers! I thought. I wished her hands *would* start to shake . . . Might shake some of her convictions as well, I said. Here! I said, holding out my pack of cigarettes. *(She holds out pack . . . with slightly shaking hand)* Have one! I said.

MOTHER

I said I didn't think she was glad to see me.

DAUGHTER

(Chain-lights another cigarette)

MOTHER

She didn't even protest. Her mouth looked like the rear end of a chicken, puckered around another cigarette she was pulling from the pack with her lips. Another one! I said. And on an empty stomach! Why didn't she *eat* something instead! I offered to fry her an egg or two. The way she'd used to like me to fry her eggs . . . turned over ever so lightly . . . before she'd run off to school in the mornings. When she was still a little girl . . . I thought the memory of the taste might give her an appetite. Distract her from her smoking.

DAUGHTER

I didn't remember having liked *my* eggs "turned over ever so lightly." I remembered only how *fat* her food had made me. At fourteen. Or at fifteen. A fat, undesirable teenager. Whose ego-image it had taken me years to outgrow . . . To shrink . . . I felt like throwing all those dieting, self-remodeling years in the well-meaning well-washed face across the table from me. But I didn't. I thought of Johnny *(smile of reminiscence).*

Keep your cool, man . . . Baby . . . Wondering when . . . *if*
. . . he would call . . . No, thank you, I said politely. It was
too early in the day for me to eat.

MOTHER

Too *early!* I said. It was *past noon!* Normal people were eating
lunch at this hour.

DAUGHTER

That was nice of the normal people, I said. *(She smokes intently)*

MOTHER

She was turning into a regular chimney. Hiding from me behind
a screen of smoke. I asked her to think of her poor lungs. That
were probably soot-black by now. The only deep breath I'd seen
her take since my arrival at six the previous evening had been at
the end of a cigarette.

DAUGHTER

(Smokes)

MOTHER

She didn't answer me. Or look at me. She was rejecting my help.
But I was her *mother!* And I didn't see her that often. Might not
see her again for a long time. Might *die* without *ever* seeing her
again. And *who* would have a mother's loving patience to help her
then? She'd have to go looking for *professional* help . . . I decided
to broach the subject from a different angle. Did she *always* get
up this late? I asked.

DAUGHTER

When I had worked late the night before: I said. Keeping my cool
. . . *(Smile of reminiscence)*

MOTHER

But she *hadn't* worked the night before, I said. They'd gone out
for dinner . . . Without me . . . Not quite two hours after my
arrival. I had broiled a lamb chop for myself. And read a bit before
going to bed. Since they had no television. She'd probably drunk
too much, too, I said.

DAUGHTER

Eating and drinking . . . with people you worked with . . . was part
of working sometimes, I said.

MOTHER

Vice always found excuses, I said. How could drinking be part of working! *I'd* never seen anybody do any work when he was drunk.

DAUGHTER

(Holds out pack of cigarettes . . . with slightly shaking hand) Have a cigarette! I said.

MOTHER

(Ignores offered pack) I said I wasn't as stupid as she thought. Even if *I* was not "creative."

DAUGHTER

(Smokes; drinks coffee; strokes forehead)

MOTHER

I had merely created *her*, I said.

DAUGHTER

Without any assistance from my departed father? I asked.

MOTHER

She was trying to shock me. Again. To distract me from trying to help her. But I remembered a lecture I had heard on the radio some time before . . . by that famous psychiatrist . . . whatever his name was . . . Haddad or something . . . Who helped mentally disturbed people . . . And drug addicts . . . And he'd said that in order to win your patient's permission to let you help him you had to pretend that everything he did . . . or said . . . was perfectly normal. That you couldn't afford to be shocked by anything. So I merely asked: Did she always have to reduce everything to the animal level? She didn't have to tell me . . . *me, a mother!* . . . how babies came into this world. I had done my share. And I knew that the man . . . uh . . . inspired life. Still . . . the woman . . .

DAUGHTER

. . . *per*spired? I laughed. Cutting her off. She looked hurt. I didn't want to be mean to her. I got up. *(She does)* Finished my coffee. *(She does)* Stubbed out my cigarette. *(She does)* I was going to take a bath, I said. *(She disappears into harp case, closing the lid)*

MOTHER

I said that was a good idea. But warned her not to let the water run so hot. That that didn't help either . . . I was warning a closed door. She had closed . . . and *locked!* . . . the bathroom door behind her. As though I were a stranger. As though I'd never seen her naked . . . She was opening it again . . . Realizing how absurd she'd been, I thought.

MOTHER

DAUGHTER

(Opens lid of harp case wide enough to stick head out) I asked her to call me . . . Please! . . . if anyone called. *(She withdraws head; closes lid of harp case)*

MOTHER

She was locking the door *again* . . . I knew who "anyone" was. He'd waked me up three times the night before. While they were out. Every time I'd try to doze off, the phone would start ringing. With that voice at the other end . . . It was ringing again . . .

(The telephone rings beside DAUGHTER's harp case)

I picked it up. Hello? I said. It *was* that voice again. No, I said. She still hadn't come home.

DAUGHTER

(Opens lid wide enough to stick head out) I'd heard the phone ring. I saw her hang up.

MOTHER

(Hangs up)

DAUGHTER

I asked her who had called.

MOTHER

I said whoever it was hadn't told me who he was.

DAUGHTER

Had she asked? I asked her.

MOTHER

I told her I hadn't had to. That it was the same voice that had waked me up three times the night before.

DAUGHTER

Johnny *had* called then. Several times. And she had not let him through to me. Self-righteously. The same way *his* mother refused to let *me* through to *him*. Why hadn't she told me someone— he—had called the night before? I asked her.

MOTHER

Because I'd finally fallen asleep by the time they'd come home, I said.

DAUGHTER

She might have told me in the morning . . . or afternoon . . . after I got up, I said. She'd had plenty of time to tell me then. And WHY!?! hadn't she called me a moment ago? When I had specifically asked her to call me if anyone—he—called . . .

MOTHER

Because *I* had more consideration for her bath than she had for her mother's sleep, apparently, I said. I hadn't wanted her to get out of the tub and catch cold just to talk to that kind of voice on the telephone. I would have called her if it had sounded important, I said.

DAUGHTER

I hadn't even climbed into the tub yet, I said. I'd been brushing my teeth. And didn't she think she might have left the decision of who was and who was not important up to me? I was, after all, forty-three. And it so happened that I'd been *waiting* for that particular call.

MOTHER

I said that she ought to be ashamed of herself. That I recognized a black man. Even over the telephone. And I wasn't going to be the go-between for that kind of business. She didn't expect me just to sit by and watch her wreck her marriage, did she? The same way she was wrecking her health. With alcohol. And coal-black coffee. And cigarettes!

DAUGHTER

What had she said to him? I asked.

MOTHER

I was her *mother!* I said. And I was determined to protect her. As long as God allowed me to live. Since her husband wasn't able to protect her, apparently. Or didn't care enough . . . Why hadn't she told me her husband had been unfaithful?

DAUGHTER

What had she said? On the telephone? I asked.

MOTHER

I wasn't going to sit by and watch while she disgraced herself, I said. That kind of business was bad enough with a white man. Did she want the entire neighborhood . . . all her friends . . . to point

a finger at her? That black man himself was probably laughing at
her . . . behind her back . . . Telling dirty jokes about her . . .

DAUGHTER

What had she said to him? I asked.

MOTHER

Perhaps I'd been *fortunate* to lose her father when I did. So young,
I said. Before it occurred to him to become unfaithful. Although
I doubted very much that that *would* have occurred to her father.
Ever. Her father's and my relationship had transcended the ani-
mal level . . .

Still, it was different for a man to do that sort of thing. A
woman's reputation was her most precious possession, I said. I
wasn't just going to sit by and watch her ruin the good reputation
I had started her out with. There had to be better ways to get even
with an unfaithful husband than ruining that reputation with a
black man, I said.

DAUGHTER

I asked her never to mind my husband. What he had or had not
done. To mind her own business . . . To have a cigarette . . . And
to tell me . . . PLEASE! . . . what she had said on the phone!
(The telephone rings)

MOTHER

(Reaching for receiver) The telephone was ringing again. I reached
to pick it up. I was standing right beside it. But she *was* my
business, I said. Whether she liked it or not. I was her *mother.* She
came charging over like a wild animal and wrestled the receiver
out of my hand.

DAUGHTER

(Has run over; tries to take phone from MOTHER. *They struggle)*

MOTHER

I told her she was hurting my hand.
(The ringing stops; the struggle breaks the connection)

DAUGHTER

*(Takes phone into arm, climbs back into harp case; forcefully
closing lid behind her)*

MOTHER

(Stands in front of DAUGHTER *'s closing harp case; shakes her head;*

looks at her hand; strokes it gently; flexing fingers) She was taking the telephone into the bathroom with her. I warned her: to be careful. Not to electrocute herself . . . Through the bathroom door. Which she was locking behind her as before . . . After slamming it in my face . . . My hand was hurting. I walked over to sit by the window again. *(She walks over to own harp case; sits down)* I felt too sad to read. I'd been looking forward to spending a little time with my daughter . . . I looked at the sunshine outside and asked God for help. For her. What could I do to help her? What should I say to her . . . that would not irritate her . . . After she'd come out of the bathroom . . . In which she seemed to be staying forever . . . It began to worry me. Perhaps she *had* electrocuted herself with the telephone . . . I wondered if it were better to go upstairs and ask the landlord for help? Or to find a street telephone booth and call a locksmith? Since she had locked herself in . . . I prayed to God to guard her against electrocuting herself. Even if He thought that she deserved it, maybe . . . Finally I hit on an idea: I would offer to cook dinner for them that night. I thanked God for the inspiration, and started composing a menu in my head to distract me from worrying . . . Until she came out of the bathroom . . .

DAUGHTER
(Lifts harp-case lid with wedding-ringed hand; climbs out, visibly bathed and elaborately combed; still in bathrobe. She sits down on rim of harp case. Starts filing her toenails)

MOTHER
(Gets up; walks around own harp case. Toward seated DAUGHTER*)* I didn't ask if she always spent so much time in the bathroom? Even when her mother was *not* visiting? . . . When she did all that work she told me she was doing? Nor did I mention how worried I'd been, since I couldn't have come to her rescue without breaking down the locked bathroom door . . . *(Standing in front of—over—seated daughter)* I forced my voice to sound casual. Light-hearted. When was her husband coming home? I asked.

DAUGHTER
(Continues to file toenails without looking up) What was she driving at now? I wondered. With the obstinacy I remembered

her for. Her mind running like an El, down the same old high-principled track . . . Johnny had *not* called back. What had she said to him? The night before? That morning . . . or afternoon? It was useless trying to call him at home. Even if he *was* at home . . . I didn't know when my husband was coming home, I said.

MOTHER

(Sitting down on rim of DAUGHTER's *harp case; twisting wedding ring)* She was rejecting my offer before I'd even made it. As though nothing good could come from me. For her. When she herself had come from me . . . As though there were nothing good about her life . . . But I didn't permit my voice to sound discouraged. That was strange, I said. After eighteen years of marriage she still didn't know when her husband came home from work?

DAUGHTER

(Filing toenails without looking up) Sixteen years. We had lived together for two years before we got legalized, I said. Hoping to shock her off the subject of my husband. Which was nothing but a detour. To get back onto the subject of Johnny, I thought. She was obviously trying to pry some kind of confession out of me. To find out if my husband *had* been unfaithful. And with whom? Which would lead into a good long heart-to-heart talk between mother and daughter. With a few hot tears spilled on mother's advice-dispensing shoulder. When she *had* no advice to give. At least not to me. At least not on that subject. Because she'd had little experience with marriage. Because my father had been away . . . traveling . . . most of the not quite six years during which he had been her husband. On paper, mostly. In letters. Before he died. When the El-car in which he was riding . . . in Chicago . . . jumped the track and plunged to the street . . . And she had not risked any new relationship after that. Out of commitment to me, supposedly . . . Like most people, she was offering what she did not have to give. No, I said. After sixteen years of marriage I still didn't know when my husband came home from work. Not any more than she had known when my father came back from his travels. My husband didn't know himself, most of the time. He didn't have a nine-to-five job, I said.

MOTHER

(Twisting wedding ring) I hadn't known about her living with her husband for two years before she got married. She had never told me before. It grieved me. For her sake. No wonder her husband was having affairs. If she herself had been an "affair" to him to begin with. But I didn't say anything. I merely asked: How she managed to cook dinner for him then? Wondering to myself— worrying a bit—how I'd manage to roast the duck I had planned on. For them. If I had no way of knowing what time to plan it for. I didn't want to serve it half-burned. Or half-raw. I was no French chef, after all . . .

DAUGHTER

(Starts painting toenails; bits of cotton between toes) Had I been too self-centered, thinking that she was thinking about me? I wondered. About my marriage. And Johnny . . . Not that I wanted her to think about it. Or me. In her proprietary way of thinking about me. As though I were an investment she had made. Worrying that it might not pay off . . . Perhaps her selfishness was more primitive—much more immediate—than I was giving her credit for. In my selfishness. Perhaps she was merely trying to pin me down about dinner. To pressure me into not letting her eat alone. Again. As she had the night before. To make me feel good and guilty, at least, if the pressure did not succeed. I said: we didn't eat at home every night. But when we did I either made a stew. Which kept stewing until my spouse entered the house. Or else I fried a steak. Which I dropped into the pan when I heard his key in the door.

MOTHER

Didn't alternating between stews and steaks get a bit tiresome? I asked. Wouldn't they both enjoy a change of menu . . . A roast duck, for instance?

DAUGHTER

(Intent on painting her toenails) She had lost me. I couldn't imagine what she was after now. Not cooking dinner for us? She'd never been particularly keen on cooking. Nor particularly good at it. The entire conversation proved only one thing: that we had

94

nothing to say to each other. I also made hamburger sometimes, I said. Or chops . . . and we often ate out . . .

MOTHER

Restaurant food wasn't the healthiest, I said.

DAUGHTER

(Fanning her toenails) Oh, I didn't know, I said. We went to pretty good places.

MOTHER

But didn't that cost a fortune? Nowadays? I asked. She'd spend two-thirds less cooking the same dishes at home.

DAUGHTER

(Fanning toenails) I said that was undoubtedly true. But then, in a restaurant, *I* didn't have to do the cooking . . . She forgot: I was a working woman, I said.

MOTHER

(Twisting wedding ring) Well, that evening she wouldn't have to do the cooking. *Or* go to an expensive restaurant, I said. In a gay voice. *I* was going to make dinner, I said. I'd roast them a duck, I'd thought . . .

DAUGHTER

(Fanning toenails) I could just picture my husband's gourmet face, biting into a soggy half-raw drumstick. Politely saying what an unusual cook she was. I said nothing. Hoping she would not insist.

MOTHER

(Twisting wedding ring) For a moment I thought she was going to accept my offer. And panicked a bit. At the thought of roasting a duck in a kitchen with which I was not familiar. And getting it just right in time for a time I didn't know. Seven? Seven-thirty? Eight o'clock? But I told myself that I'd manage. Somehow. With God's help. All she had to do was tell me where to shop for the duck, I said . . . Unless she preferred to come *with* me. It was such a beautiful day. Her lungs would enjoy a breath of fresh air.

DAUGHTER

(Pulls cigarette from pack with lips; lights it) I said fresh air wasn't one of New York's best features. And thanked her for her kind offer . . . And did not ask: why was she forever offering what she

95

didn't have to give . . . And told her not to bother. That it was not necessary.

MOTHER
(Twisting wedding ring) I asked myself if my reference to lungs and fresh air had prompted her to smoke another cigarette. And was sorry *if* it had. How careful one had to be with these addicts . . . I pretended not to notice. I was a better cook than she gave me credit for, I said gaily. Why didn't she let me prove it? . . Or did she think I was planning to poison her? and her husband?

DAUGHTER
(Smoking; blowing smoke on drying toenails) My husband and I were going out for dinner, I said.

MOTHER
(Twisting wedding ring) Again! I said. But they'd been out the night before! Were they going to let me eat alone? Again?

DAUGHTER
(Smokes; begins to file fingernails) Aha! I thought. Bracing myselr for a list of guilt-inspiring examples from the past. When *she* had turned down the most enticing invitations. To stay home with *me.* When I was "still a little girl" . . . I was afraid she'd have to eat alone again. Yes, I said.

MOTHER
(Twisting wedding ring) All their hard-earned money washed down their throats, I said. I was sure they could have bought a house with the money they had carried to restaurants in all those eighteen . . . sorry: sixteen . . . years. A big house. With a garden In the country, I said.

DAUGHTER
(Begins to paint fingernails) I said she was undoubtedly right. But that I wasn't interested in a big house in the country . . . That I couldn't afford to be interested. Because of my work. That I couldn't afford not to live in the city. That I had to be within ready reach. By telephone. *(She stubs out cigarette)*

MOTHER
(Twisting wedding ring) I did *not* ask: Had she to be within ready reach in the middle of the night? For black men to call her in the middle of the night? I merely said: that lots of people commuted.

96

And that, if *she* wasn't interested in a house . . . in the country . . . I was sure her husband was.

DAUGHTER

(Painting fingernails) I assured her that he was not.

MOTHER

(Twisting wedding ring) I said: and *I* was sure that her husband would have remained more interested in *her,* if she were interested in making a pleasant home for him. All husbands were interested in a pleasant home. And a pleasant dinner. I was sure her husband would become interested in her again, if she started making a pleasant home for him.

DAUGHTER

(Blowing on painted fingernails) She kept forgetting that I was a professional woman, I said. That I worked. Even if I did my work at home. And that, even if I *were* interested, I didn't have the time to take care of a house. Besides, what made her so sure my husband had lost interest in me? He was extremely interested. In my work, I said. We even collaborated on things, occasionally . . . *(She blows on painted fingernails)*

MOTHER

I said she knew very well that "interest in her work" was not what I'd had in mind. And that she didn't have to take from her working time to give a little more thought to making her husband a pleasant home . . . All she had to do was think a little less about black men . . . Who thought nothing of telephoning her in the middle of the night. Who shouldn't feel free to telephone her in the first place. Who only kept her from working . . . only interrupted her work . . . by telephoning morning noon and night . . . No husband could be expected to put up with that sort of thing forever, I said.

DAUGHTER

Oh, have a cigarette, I said. *(She holds pack out to* MOTHER, *careful not to spoil her still-wet nails)*

MOTHER

(Ignores offered pack) Maybe her husband didn't care . . . Enough . . . Any more . . . I said. But I cared. She couldn't expect me just

to sit by and watch her wreck her life! She was flesh of *my* flesh, I said. Blood of *my* blood . . .

MOTHER

DAUGHTER

I said: every time I heard the word *blood*, all I could think was *spill* . . . *(She pulls cigarette from pack with her lips; lights it; inhales deeply)*

MOTHER

Did she really *have* to smoke that cigarette? I asked. Just to spite me? Still? At her age? . . . She'd just put one out.

DAUGHTER

(Smoke-sigh) I said I'd be perfectly happy to let her smoke it in my stead. *(She holds cigarette to* MOTHER'*s face)*

MOTHER

(Averts her face) I said: Didn't she know I only meant well. That I only wanted to help her?

DAUGHTER

I couldn't help myself. *(She stuffs cigarette into* MOTHER'*s mouth)* My hands were stuffing the burning cigarette into her mouth. Deep down into her throat. My nail polish hadn't dried. It smeared on her cheek and chin. She bit my fingers . . .

MOTHER

(Speaks with increasing difficulty) I couldn't believe that she would really hurt me. Physically. That my own flesh would turn against me in bodily earnest. *(Her hands flail out; find* DAUGHTER'*s throat)* My hands found her throat . . . In self-defense . . . and tried to push her away from me . . . and pressed . . .

DAUGHTER

(Speaks with increasing difficulty) Her hands were around my throat. I could feel the hardness of her wedding ring. That used to hurt my cheek when she'd slap me when I was a little girl. When I had been "bad" . . . When she used to tell me that slapping me . . . with her hard wedding ring . . . hurt her more than it hurt my cheek . . . I couldn't believe that she was strangling me in earnest . . .

MOTHER and DAUGHTER

(Choke and strangle each other. Push each other. Fall into open harp cases)

Birth and After Birth

by
TINA HOWE

"I wrote *Birth and After Birth* out of my own experience, but also out of the experience of women I knew where I lived in the country. I was different because I always had my writing. I wrote this play for the suburban woman with no exit from her kitchen and a four-year-old seven feet tall." Tina Howe also speaks of the need to redress a balance: "As a mother, you experience moments of excruciating tenderness and love, but there is also great savagery —family life has been over-romanticized; the savagery has not been seen enough in the theatre and in movies . . ."

Tina Howe wrote her first play, a one-act, while a senior at Sarah Lawrence College. It was produced there, directed by her friend, the actress Jane Alexander. After that, Howe taught high school, first in Maine and then in Wisconsin. "I taught English, and they were always looking for someone to run the dramatics department —I would agree to do it on the condition that I could produce my own plays . . . That's how I learned what worked and what didn't work—if you can keep the attention of an audience of teenagers, then it's working . . ."

Her first full-length play is "still in a dark drawer somewhere"; the second, *The Nest*, was produced in 1970 off-Broadway by Ann McIntosh, Honor Moore and Thayer Burch; *Museum* was produced in 1976 at the Los Angeles Actors' Theatre and at the Public Theatre in New York. *Birth and After Birth* was first produced as a workshop at the Gotham Art Theatre in New York City in 1974 with the playwright directing. "My ambition," Tina Howe says, "is to get a thousand people in a dark room laughing themselves nearly to death, drenched in tears, rolling in the aisles, ambulances rushing to theatre doors." She lives in New York City with her husband and two small children.

CHARACTERS

SANDY APPLE   The mommy, in her early thirties

BILL APPLE   The daddy, in his middle thirties

NICKY   Their four-year-old son, played by a grownup

MIA FREED   An anthropologist without children, in her early thirties

JEFFREY FREED   An anthropologist without children, in his forties

Act One

The Apples' kitchen-playroom, the center of the house—a big, cheerful room with a few overstuffed chairs and all the usual kitchen appliances. A dining table and five chairs are in the center of the stage. There's also a closet in the room, and a large inherited mirror hanging on the wall.

The curtain rises. Today is NICKY*'s fourth birthday. It's very early in the morning, the stage is in near darkness.* SANDY *and* BILL *are in their bathrobes getting everything ready before* NICKY *gets up.* BILL *shakes a tambourine.*

SANDY
(Wrapping presents) Sssssssssssshhhhhhhhh!

BILL
God, I love tambourines!

SANDY
(Whispering) You'll wake him up.

BILL
What is it about tambourines?

SANDY
We'll never finish!

BILL
They kill me.

SANDY
Bill!

BILL
If I had my life to live over, I'd be a tambourine virtuoso.

SANDY
I haven't even started wrapping the masks yet.

BILL
Imagine being the . . . greatest tambourine virtuoso in the world . . .

SANDY

At least *you* got some sleep last night.

BILL

Concerts on every continent: Europe, Australia, South America
... *(Plays with enthusiasm, does a few flamenco steps)*

SANDY

There's still the puzzles and coloring books.

NICKY

(Bursts into the room in his pajamas) Where's my presents?
Where's my presents?

SANDY

(Drops everything) Oh, Nicky, you *scared* me!

BILL

(Snatches up a movie camera, starts filming NICKY*)* Don't do a
thing 'til Daddy gets his new camera!

NICKY

(Tears through the darkness looking for his presents) Where's my
presents? Where's my presents?

SANDY

Mommy and Daddy have been up all night getting everything
ready for Nicky's party. Does Nicky want to see what they've
done? One, two, three! *(She turns on the lights)*
> *(Crepe-paper streamers crisscross the ceiling, balloons hang
> in clusters, a huge* HAPPY BIRTHDAY *banner is stretched
> across the room. The table is set for five and seems to float
> under the weight of favors, candies, noisemakers and hats.
> Everything stops; even* NICKY *is stunned)*

BILL

(On top of it all with his camera) I'll bet you *never* expected
anything like this, old buddy, did you? Huh? You never dreamed
it would be like this!

SANDY

(Throws her arms around NICKY*)* Just look at you! Mommy's great
big four-year-old!

NICKY

Where's my presents? Where's my presents?

BILL

Daddy's present to Nicky is a whole movie of Nicky's party.

SANDY

Such a big boy . . . it seems like only yesterday I was bringing him home from the hospital.

BILL

Quik Foto has same-day service now, you know. Bring in the film at noon, pick up the printed reel at three.

NICKY

(Has found his presents, shrieks, dives into them head-first) Presents! Presents! Ooooooooooooh, look at all my presents!

BILL

Keep it up, Nick, you're doing great, just beautiful . . . beautiful .

SANDY

Nicky, you're not supposed to open presents now. Presents *after* cards, you know that's the way we do it! (Starts picking up the shredded wrapping)

> (NICKY *ignores her, tears open musical instruments, plays them)*

BILL

(Filming) Atta boy, Nick, show 'em how good you can play. Look at Daddy and play something. Over this way . . . look at Daddy!

SANDY

(As manic in her cleaning as NICKY *in his wrecking)* Nicky, I asked you to wait. We do cards first. That way we avoid all of this mess at the beginning.

BILL

Oh, Nicholas, are we making one hell of a movie!

NICKY

A red wagon! *(Pulls it around the room in rapture)*

BILL

Towards Daddy, honey, come towards Daddy. Oh, Christ, I don't believe this kid.

SANDY

(With a broom) Nicky, how is Mommy going to clean all this up? Do you want to have your party inside a great big mess?

BILL

Stop everything, Nick! Daddy just got an idea! Let's get some footage of Nicky pulling Mommy in his new red wagon! *(Rushes to* SANDY *and forces her into the wagon)* Come on, Mommy, Nicky's going to give you a ride.

SANDY

Hey, what are you doing? We have company coming tonight!

NICKY

(Jumping up and down) Nicky's going to pull his big Mommy present. *(Starts pulling)*

BILL

(Filming) Too much . . . Oh, Jesus . . . Jesus . . . Too much!

SANDY

(Drops her head in her hands) Please, Bill, I'm a mess. I haven't even brushed my teeth yet.

NICKY

(Pulling lickety-split) Look at Nicky go! Look at Nicky, Daddy. Nicky's pulling his big Mommy present! *(Laughs)*

SANDY

I've got to clean up.

BILL

Will you look at that kid go?! Don't tell *me* my son isn't football material!

> *(*NICKY *pulls* SANDY *all around the room making hairpin turns. He suddenly sees an unopened present and runs off to it)*

BILL

Hey, where are you going? You were doing great!

NICKY

More presents, more, more, *more!*

SANDY

(In the wagon, depressed) My breath smells.

BILL

Hey, Nick, what the hell? You were pulling Mommy and doing great. Now come back here and pick up that wagon handle!

SANDY

Nobody cares about anything around here. *(Starts combing her hair in the wagon)*

BILL

I've got an idea. Let's put in some of these presents *with* Mommy! *(Starts piling presents on top of* SANDY*)*

SANDY

I haven't even had a chance to pee.

NICKY

(Throws his last opened present across the room) Nicky's presents are all gone! (Starts to cry)

BILL

Daddy asked you to pick up the wagon handle and pull!

NICKY

I wanted a bunny! And I wanted a puppy . . . and a pony. *Where's my pony?* You said I could get a pony for my birthday!

SANDY

(Combing her hair) I stay up all night decorating the room, wrapping the presents, blowing up the balloons, making a really nice party, and what does he do? Just tears into everything. Rips it all up! Ruins everything. *(Gets out of the wagon and sits at the birthday table)*

BILL

All the presents are in the wagon. So get over here, Nicholas, and pull! *(Films)*

NICKY

(Kicks the wagon, cries) You promised me a pony. *You promised!*

SANDY

And not one thank you. I never heard one thank you for anything.

BILL

I'm waiting!

SANDY

Do you know what my mother would have done if I ruined all my birthday presents and never said thank you?

BILL

(Slams down his camera) Thanks a lot, Nicky. Thanks for ruining a great movie!

107

SANDY

She'd flush them down the toilet, that's what she'd do!
(NICKY *gets into the wagon, lies down, sucks his thumb.*
BILL *sits down with* SANDY *at the birthday table)*

BILL

Jesus Christ, Nicky.
(Silence)

SANDY

He shouldn't be up this early.

BILL

He got up too early.

SANDY

(To NICKY*)* I have a good mind to take you back up to your room!

BILL

If you ask me, he should be sent up to his room!

SANDY

Do you want Daddy to take you up to your room?

BILL

You'd better watch it, young man, or it's up to your room!

SANDY

How would you like to be sent up to your room on your birthday?
(Silence)

BILL

He got up too early.

SANDY

Come on, Bill, take him on up.
(Silence)

BILL

That kid gets away with murder. *(*SANDY *sighs)* Absolute murder
... *(*SANDY *sighs. There is a moment of silence.* BILL *imitates* NICKY
sucking. SANDY *sighs)* He sounds like some ... sea animal ... some
squid or something. *(Imitates the sound)*

SANDY

All children suck their thumb when they're upset.

BILL

You'll get warts on your tongue if you keep that up!

108

SANDY

I used to suck mine.

BILL

He'll push his teeth all out of shape.

SANDY

(Pops her thumb into her mouth) This one.

BILL

Do you know how much fixing that boy's teeth is going to cost?
About three thousand dollars, that's all!

SANDY

I sucked my thumb until I was twenty-two.

BILL

You'll have warts on your tongue and three-thousand-dollar braces
on your teeth!

SANDY

I used to suck it during lunch hour when I worked at the insurance
company. I'd go into the ladies' room, lock the door, sit on the
toilet, and just . . . suck my thumb. *(Laughs)* It sounds ridiculous,
a grown woman sucking her thumb on a toilet in the ladies' room.

BILL

Aside from the warts and the three-thousand-dollar braces, it's just
so goddamned disgusting! *(Imitates* NICKY *again)*

SANDY

Come to think of it, I didn't really stop sucking it until Nicky was
born.

BILL

. . . in the same category as nose-picking.

SANDY

(Scratching her head) It's funny how that sucking instinct gets
passed right on from the mother to her child.
   (Silence)

BILL

Four years old . . . Wow!

SANDY

(Scratching) Ever since I woke up this morning, I've had this
itching . . .

BILL

When a kid turns four, then it's time to buy a movie camera, right?

SANDY

It's strange, because I've never had dandruff . . .

BILL

Put away the Polaroid and bring out the Super 8.

SANDY

When I looked in the mirror this morning, I saw an old lady. Not *old* old, just used up. *(She scratches her head; a shower of sand falls out)* It's the weirdest thing, it doesn't look like dandruff or eczema, but more like . . . I don't know, like my head is drying up and leaking . . .

BILL

You see, if Daddy didn't take pictures on your birthday, then none of us would remember what you looked like when you were little.

SANDY

(Giggling) My head is leaking . . .

BILL

(Picks up his camera, starts shooting NICKY *at close range)* Time passes so fast, before you know it, you'll be an old man lying in a nursing home.

SANDY

(Shaking out more sand) My brains are drying up . . .

BILL

Not a lonely old man, Nick, but one with movies of his youth: birthday parties, Christmases, visits to the zoo.

SANDY

(Pulls out a fistful of hair) And now my hair, falling out by the roots.

BILL

Shit, you'll be the most popular guy in the nursing home. "Have you seen Mr. Apple's movies of his fourth birthday party?" the little old ladies will say.

SANDY

(Giggling) Poor Mommy's going bald.

110

BILL

From every floor the old people will crowd into your room, perch on the edge of your bed, block your door with their wheelchairs . . .

SANDY

(Scratching and leaking more sand) When she looked in the mirror this morning, she saw an old lady.

BILL

All for that one backwards glance at the radiance of youth.

SANDY

(Giggling) Poor old feeble leaking Mommy . . .

BILL

Someday you'll thank me for this.

SANDY

Bald as an egg.

BILL

Come on, give Daddy a big smile now.

NICKY

(Still in the wagon, sucking his thumb) I want to make my birthday wish.

BILL

(Holding out a mask for NICKY*)* Hey, Nick, how about putting this mask on? *(*SANDY *sighs)* Come on, give us a roar.

SANDY

Oh, put on the mask for Daddy!

NICKY

I want to blow out my candles and make my birthday wish.

SANDY

Oh, Nicky, *put it on!*

BILL

I tell you, when we show this movie to the Freeds tonight, eat their hearts out!

SANDY

(Puts the mask on NICKY*)* Look at Nicky! *(Laughs)*

BILL

Run around the room and pop out from behind the chairs.

NICKY

I don't have to if I don't want to.

BILL

Nicky, I said pop out from behind the chairs! Now, do it!

NICKY

I want raisins.

SANDY

Oooooh, my neck is stiff.

BILL

(Yanks NICKY *out of the wagon) Move!*

NICKY

(In his mask, lies on the floor) Raisins!

BILL

Will you *please* get him to run around the room and pop out from behind the chairs!

SANDY

Come on, Nicky.

NICKY

Raisins!

BILL

We're showing the movie to the Freeds tonight, so let's get going!

SANDY

That's right. Jeffrey and Mia are coming over to celebrate with us.

BILL

And if you'll just cooperate, Daddy will be able to give them one hell of a terrific show!

SANDY

You know how much Jeffrey and Mia love you, Nicky.

BILL

Jeff may take good slides, but I promise you he's never seen a movie like this!

SANDY

They're bringing you a special present and everything . . .

NICKY

Presents!

112

SANDY

And you know what great presents Jeffrey and Mia give!

BILL

Nobody gives presents like Jeffrey and Mia. So come on, Nick, pop out from behind the chairs.

SANDY

Remember the Imperial Chinese warrior doll they brought him last year?

NICKY

Presents, presents, presents . . .

SANDY

Jeffrey and Mia are first cousins, honey. Jeffrey and I have the same grandpa.

BILL

Will you move, goddammit!

SANDY

I've known Jeffrey ever since he was your age. We used to throw apples on sticks.

BILL

Nickyyyyyy!

SANDY

Mommy's planned such a wonderful party with our cousins.
  (Nothing happens)

BILL

(Lunges at NICKY*)* I said . . . move! *(*NICKY *runs around the room popping up from behind the chairs, but all so fast that* BILL *can't keep up with him)* Will you slow down, for Christsake?!
  *(*SANDY *laughs.* NICKY *stops and falls down flat inside his wagon)*

BILL

(Furious, slams down his camera) Thanks a lot, Nicholas. I'll remember that! *(He sits down)*
  (Long silence)

SANDY

My neck is so stiff I can hardly turn my head. *(Silence.* BILL *pulls a letter out of his pocket and reads it, depressed)* Four years ago

113

Nicky came out of my tummy and made me the happiest mommy in the world.

BILL

I wish you'd look at this letter sometime. *(SANDY sighs)* It came through the office mail last week. I told you about it the other day, remember?

SANDY

I'm a mommy!

BILL

It's from Continental Allied.

SANDY

Who ever thought that I'd be a mommy?

BILL

(Reading) "Dear Mr. Apple. It has come to the attention of the accounting department that certain papers in the Fiedler file are either missing or incomplete . . ."

SANDY

Hey, Nicky, I'm a mommy! *(NICKY puts on one of his masks. It's the face of a baby.* SANDY *is enchanted)* Oh, Nickyyyyyyyyyyy.

BILL

"You assured us last month that the Fiedler account had been settled."

SANDY

Does Nicky want to play Babies? *(Laughs)*

BILL

". . . or indeed, you never did close the account with Mr. Fiedler as you indicated . . ."

SANDY

Nicky, we can't play now, Mommy has to get the party ready.
(NICKY coos and gurgles inside his mask)

BILL

". . . Mr. Brill has brought to our attention the outstanding work you did on the Yaddler account . . ."

SANDY

Look at all the mess, honey. *(NICKY gurgles louder)* Don't you want to have a nice tidy birthday party with everything in its place? *(NICKY crawls over to SANDY, gets in her lap, hands her a mask of a pop-eyed Cinderella)* Ohhhhhh, Nicky, not now. . . .

BILL

". . . rest assured, everyone here at Continental Allied knows what a delicate procedure that was . . ."

SANDY

(Puts on her mask) Sweet baby.

> *(The game of Babies starts. NICKY is inspired: going limp, gurgling, cooing and laughing)*

SANDY

(Rocking NICKY) Do you know what baby Nicky looked like when he was born, hmmm? *(Kissing him) A shiny blue fish!* Mommy's little blue trout!

BILL

". . . We are full of admiration for the good judgment you showed on that particular account . . ."

NICKY

I was blue?

SANDY

Of course you were blue. All babies are blue when they're inside their mommies' tummies. It's because there's no air inside the little plastic bag they live in.

NICKY

I want to be blue again. I want to be blue again!

SANDY

Once the baby pops out of the plastic bag inside his mommy's tummy, he breathes air for the first time. And do you know what happens to him then?

BILL

". . . What puzzles us, Mr. Apple, is the professional inconsistency you exhibit in your work . . ."

SANDY

He turns bright pink! As pink as a seashell!

BILL

"Professional inconsistency."

SANDY

Actually, you were a little jaundiced at birth, so your skin was more golden than pink. Mommy's *gold fish!*

NICKY

I was gold?

SANDY

Fourteen-karat gold!

NICKY

Son of a bitch!

SANDY

Nicky!

BILL

What kind of a phrase is that, "professional inconsistency"?

SANDY

And your little arms were so skinny and waved every which way. Do you know what baby Nicky's arms looked like?

NICKY

Nicky was such a good baby, all blue and gold inside his plastic bag.

SANDY

French-fried potatoes, that's what your arms looked like!
  (SANDY and NICKY laugh)

BILL

Gibberish!

SANDY

And Nicky was such a hungry baby! Why, he drank fifteen bottles of sugar water only an hour after he was born!

NICKY

Oh, blue and gold Nicky was *soooooooo* thirsty! *(Slurps)*

SANDY

(Plugs an imaginary bottle in his mouth) The nurses on the floor had never seen anything like it! They stood around my bed and watched you drink one bottle after another: ten, eleven, twelve, thirteen . . . The head nurse lined up all the empty bottles in a row and took a picture with her camera!

116

BILL

There's talk around the office that Brill is going to ask for my resignation.

SANDY

Well, after drinking so much sugar water so fast, Nicky's tummy was all full of gas bubbles and Mommy had to burp him. *(Starts swatting his back and lying him in different positions)*

NICKY

Oh, Nicky's tummy full of gas bubbles!

SANDY

So she swatted him and slapped him until suddenly Nicky exploded with such a loud burp that he flew across the room and landed in the sink!

BILL

It's quite subtle, don't you think?

NICKY

Baby firsty, baby still firsty.

SANDY

Such a hungry baby!

BILL

And this was over a week ago. *(Pause) You're not even listening to me!* You don't give a good shit if I'm fired! All *you* care about is playing your moronic baby games with Nicky! *(He storms out of the room)*

        (Long silence. SANDY *takes off her mask)*

NICKY

Daddy's mad.

SANDY

Daddy's mad. *(*NICKY *sucks his thumb) Just look at this mess!*

NICKY

I don't like it when Daddy gets mad.

SANDY

God, Nicky, you have to destroy everything you touch, don't you?

NICKY

I want grape juice.

SANDY

I just don't understand you. One minute you're the sweet baby Mommy brought home from the hospital, and the next, you're a savage!

NICKY

(Tears off his mask) I said I want grape juice!

SANDY

We have company coming!

NICKY

(Stamping his feet and whirling through all the wrapping) I want grape juice. I want grape juice. I want grape juice!

SANDY

You don't care if Jeffrey and Mia walk into a shit house! *(Starts cleaning again)*

NICKY

(Wailing) I'm going to die if I don't have grape juice, and then you'll be sorry!

SANDY

Well, you can't have grape juice. You'll spoil your appetite for your birthday cake!

NICKY

I want grape juice. I want grape juice. *I want grape juice.*

SANDY

(Cleaning in a fury) Mommy said no grape juice.

NICKY

(Hurtling into the middle of her cleaning) Grape juice!

SANDY

(Slaps him hard with each word) Mommy!   Said!   No! *(Silence.* NICKY *makes a small strangled sound)* Oh, God. *(*NICKY *faints flat out on the floor.* SANDY *stands over him, helpless)* Oh, God. *(Nothing happens)* Billlllllllll! Nicky's fainted!

BILL

(Flies into the room, props NICKY *up in his arms and starts walking him)* What happened?

SANDY

Oh, Bill, help him. *(Starts to cry)*

(SANDY's and BILL's reactions to NICKY's fit are completely outrageous, a parody of parental panic)

BILL

Quick, the ice!

SANDY

(Dashes to the refrigerator, takes out the ice, wraps it in a dish towel and presses it to NICKY's temples) It's all right, Nicky, Mommy's got some ice, Mommy will make you all better.

BILL

Come on, Nicker, move those legs of yours! Let's see some action! *(To SANDY) Will you get more ice!*

SANDY

(Tries to force the ice down NICKY's mouth as BILL drags him around the room) Open wide, darling, Mommy wants to get some of this nice cold ice against your tongue and cool Nicky off. Open wide . . . poor Nicky, did Mommy get mad and hit her boy?

BILL

(Swings NICKY upside down and shakes him by the feet, then swings him in wide circles) Keep that circulation going! Keep those veins and arteries open! Come on, Sandy, for Christsake, will you get the tourniquet?

SANDY

(Runs about, panicked) Oh, Bill, help him, *help him! The tourniquet! I forgot the tourniquet! (She wraps a dish towel around his head)*

BILL

Will you hurry up before he forms a blood clot!

SANDY

Nicky . . . Nicky . . .

BILL

Come on, we'd better get him over to the sink! *(Drags NICKY to the sink, turns on the water full blast, shoves his head under)* That's the boy, let the water splash in your face. Now try and open your mouth and take a deep breath.

119

SANDY

He isn't moving, Bill, he's still all limp . . . *Get him to open his eyes at least! I want to see his eyes!*

BILL

Will you please get me the goddamned flashlight?!

SANDY

Oh, the flashlight . . . how could I have forgotten the flashlight? *(Gets it, shines it in* NICKY*'s eyes)* Oh, Nicky, open your eyes for Mommy. Come on, honey, let Mommy peek into your pretty eyes . . .

BILL

(Abruptly swings NICKY *to the floor, throws him down, spreads him out and sits on his stomach, giving him artificial respiration, pumping his arms back and forth. To* SANDY*)* Get on his legs, hurry up. *(Chanting)* Up and back, up and back, up and back.

SANDY

(Pumping his legs) Maybe he needs more ice. I don't think he got any in his mouth.

BILL and SANDY

(Faster and faster) Breathe. In and out. In and out. In and out.
(Their chanting reaches a crescendo. Time passes, NICKY *twitches.* SANDY *and* BILL *stop, sigh, wait. Silence)*

NICKY

(Weakly) Sing to me.

SANDY

(Cradling him in her arms)
  Hush, little baby, don't say a word,
  Momma's gonna buy you a mockingbird,
  And if that mockingbird don't sing,
  Momma's gonna buy you a diamond ring.
  (Silence)

BILL

We got it in time. *(*SANDY *keeps humming)* Jesus.

SANDY

What would I do if this ever happened when you weren't here?

BILL

Well, luckily, it only seems to happen when I *am* here.

120

SANDY

I don't know what I'd do without you.

BILL

Nick Apple is four years old today!

NICKY

It hurts being born.

SANDY

I know, honey. I know.

NICKY

It hurts Nicky's head and stomach.

BILL

Tell me, Nick, how does it feel being four? Do you feel any different?

SANDY

"Four" sounds so old.

NICKY

I feel . . . sweeter.

SANDY

(Laughing, hugs him) Oh, Nicky.

BILL

And what else?

NICKY

Softer.

BILL

You nut.

NICKY

. . . and cuter.

SANDY

Oh, Nickyyyyy.

NICKY

. . . and furrier!

BILL

Furrier?

NICKY

(Sticks out his hands) When I woke up this morning, I saw fur on my hands, white fur.

121

BILL

(Looks at NICKY*'s hands) The kid's got white fur growing on his hands!*

SANDY

(Mock-stricken) My baby!

BILL

(Grabbing NICKY*'s arm, inspecting it) The kid's got fur growing up his arm!*

NICKY

Nicky's turning into a furry rabbit.

SANDY

Oh, Nicky!

NICKY

I like being a furry rabbit!

SANDY

My baby! What will we do?

NICKY

Look, there's fur on my tongue, too!

BILL

Well, son of a gun!

NICKY

And on my teeth . . .

BILL

We'll have to get carrots and lettuce . . .

SANDY

What will the neighbors say?

BILL

(Whispering) They'll never know . . . We'll keep it a secret.

SANDY

Bill, I'm scared.

NICKY

(Whispering) I'll only leave the house at night . . .

BILL

During the day he'll stay in his room . . .

NICKY

I'll hide under my bed.

BILL

We'll build vast underground tunnels . . . no one will suspect a thing . . .

NICKY

By day I'll hide under my bed eating carrots, and at night I'll roam the countryside.

SANDY

Ooooooh, Nicky!

BILL

For long periods of time he'll disappear altogether.

NICKY

I'll be known as . . . Rabbit Boy.

BILL

He'll become a champion of rabbits in distress.

NICKY

I'll learn rabbit magic.

BILL

He'll cast spells. He'll turn buildings into giant carrots!

NICKY

Let's play Rabbit Says.

SANDY

Oh, Nicky, not now.

NICKY

(Standing on a chair) Rabbit says, "Raise your hands!"

BILL

Later, Nick.

SANDY

Please, honey.

NICKY

Rabbit says, "Raise your hands!"

BILL

We have the whole rest of the day.

NICKY

Rabbit says, "Raise your hands!" *(SANDY and BILL raise their hands)* Rabbit says, "Scratch your nose." *(SANDY and BILL scratch their noses)* Rabbit says, "Lift your right leg." *(SANDY and BILL do everything he says)* Rabbit says, "Lift your left leg." Rabbit says,

"Stick out your tongue."*Reach for the sky! (*SANDY *and* BILL *do all these things;* NICKY *laughs, claps his hands)* I tricked you, I tricked you! Rabbit says, "Rub your belly." Rabbit says, "Hop on two feet." *Hop on one foot! (*SANDY *and* BILL *do)* You did it! You did it! *(The game gets faster)* Rabbit says, "Lie on the floor." Rabbit says, "Get up." Rabbit says, "Fart."

> *(*BILL *makes a farting noise in his armpit)*

SANDY

Not this again!

NICKY

Rabbit says, "Fart again."
> *(*BILL *does)*

SANDY

I'm not playing, it's disgusting.

NICKY

Rabbit says, "Fart three times in a row."
> *(*BILL *does)*

SANDY

It isn't funny, Nicholas!

NICKY

Rabbit says, "Run after Nicky and play Fart Tag."
> *(*BILL *chases* NICKY, *making a farting sound every time he tags him)*

SANDY

If this is the only way you can celebrate Nicky's birthday, it's just pathetic! *(Sits down and stares into space)*
(Bill and Nicky pantomime their game)
My front teeth feel loose . . . *(Leans over, shakes a shower of sand from her hair)* It's the strangest thing—ever since I got up this morning I've been smelling the sea. We're hundreds of miles away from it, but that bitter salty smell of low tide is unmistakable. I noticed it the moment I woke up . . . *(Inhales, shakes out more sand)* Nicky, I'd like you to come back to the table now and open your cards.

BILL

(Sits NICKY *in his lap, rumples his hair)* Nicky's four!

124

NICKY

I love you, Daddy.

SANDY

He got more cards than he did last year.
(BILL *starts tickling* NICKY)

NICKY

(Laughing) Don't!

SANDY

(Opening a card, reads)
  "This little pony comes galloping by,
    With a smile on his face and a gleam in his eye.
    Seems it's somebody's birthday, 'neigh, neigh, neigh,'
    Somebody special who's four today!"
From Walt and Sally, and look, they sent five dollars.

BILL

(Still tickling NICKY*)* Is Nicky ticklish?

NICKY

(Screams with pleasure) Stop . . . Stop!

SANDY

(Reading another card)
  "May God in his glory look down from the sky,
    With a birthday blessing for a wonderful guy."
The Blys. How thoughtful.

BILL

I tell you, Nick, we're going to have a great party tonight!

SANDY

Will you look at this! Nicky got a card from Mrs. Tanner, his
nursery school teacher, and they have a policy of not sending out
individual cards on the children's birthdays. *(In a singsong)* I guess
someone is Mrs. Tanner's favorite! *(Long pause)* It's important for
a child to form attachments outside the home.

BILL

(With NICKY *quietly on his lap)* Children need guidelines!

SANDY

You can't stress self-discovery enough!

125

BILL

If a child isn't given love at home, he'll be emotionally crippled for the rest of his life!

SANDY

I believe in discipline!

BILL

You can't tell me that children don't learn from observation!

SANDY

Tolerance through acceptance!

BILL

Self-respect is built on sharing!

SANDY

Reading readiness precedes cognition!
    (Silence)

BILL

If I ever caught Nicky with matches, right out! I'd toss him right out of the house!
    (Another silence)

SANDY

You know, Bill, I feel sorry for Jeffrey and Mia. I wish there was something we could do.

BILL

It's not our business!

SANDY

But not to have children . . .

BILL

You can't run other people's lives.

SANDY

Neither of them wants children!

BILL

Their careers are very important to them

NICKY

I love birthdays!

SANDY

But they're missing so much.

NICKY

What I love the most is blowing out the candles and making my wish.

SANDY

What if tonight . . .

NICKY

Sally told me all birthday wishes come true.

SANDY

. . . they changed their minds and decided to have a baby?

BILL

Jeffrey and Mia have been married for twelve years. I don't think they're going to change their minds about having children at Nicky's birthday party.

SANDY

But what if they did?

NICKY

I know just the wish I'm going to make!

BILL

It won't happen.

SANDY

But what if they just . . . did . . . because of us and Nicky and how happy we all are.

NICKY

And it's going to come true because Sally told me it would!

SANDY

Oh, Bill, I bet they change their minds tonight, you wait and see!

BILL

What's going to happen tonight is that we're going to have one hell of a party for Nicky, and I'm going to show one hell of a movie!

SANDY

I have a feeling . . .

NICKY

When can I blow out the candles and make my wish?

SANDY

Imagine being a woman and not wanting to experience childbirth.

BILL

People are different.

SANDY

But never to have your own baby . . .

NICKY

When can I blow out the candles and make my wish?

SANDY

It would be so good for both of them.

BILL

As anthropologists studying children of primitive cultures, they
see a lot of suffering.

NICKY

I want to make my birthday wish.

BILL

Once you've seen babies dying of starvation, I'm sure you think
twice about bringing more people into the world.

SANDY

But their baby wouldn't starve!

NICKY

I want to make my birthday wish!

SANDY

They'd have such a beautiful baby.

BILL

They're not interested in having a beautiful baby, they're interested in primitive children!

NICKY

Mommy, can I make my birthday wish now?

SANDY

*No, you cannot make your wish now, Mommy's talking to Daddy
and it's very important.* How can they understand primitive children if they don't have children of their own?

BILL

Just because I understand their reasons for not wanting children
doesn't mean I agree with them!

NICKY

Daddy, can I make my birthday wish now?

SANDY

Well, you don't have to be so pompous about it. People do change!

BILL

It's very unlikely.

SANDY

But it could happen . . .

BILL

Well, anything *could* happen, but that doesn't mean . . .

NICKY

Please, Daddy, can I make my . . .

SANDY

Shit, Nicky, can't you let Mommy and Daddy have a conversation?!

BILL

Mommy and Daddy are talking now.

NICKY

(Starts to cry) It's not fair . . . it's not fair . . .

SANDY

(To BILL*)* He's impossible!

BILL

Can't you just wait . . .
        *(*NICKY *cries louder)*

SANDY

Keep this up, Nicky, and there won't *be* any birthday party!

NICKY

(Puts on a mask to hide his crying) Go on, yell at me and be mean, I don't care because I still haven't made my birthday wish and when I make it it will come true because Sally said so!
        (He exits. Long silence)

SANDY

(Glances at herself in the mirror) When I looked in the mirror this morning, I saw an old lady. Not *old* old, just used up. *(Takes off her slipper and dumps out a stream of sand)*

BILL

Kids!

SANDY

(Sighs) I don't know.
        (Silence)

BILL

(Holding a party favor) Remember those surprise balls we used to get at parties when we were kids? Those endless ribbons of paper all rolled up with little metal toys inside?

SANDY

He has such a temper.

BILL

It's funny, you never see them around any more. *(Pause)* We had some birthday parties in those days! One birthday I'll never forget, and that was my eleventh! *Shit, what a party!*

SANDY

My eighth was the best. I invited the entire class. It was on a Saturday afternoon and we strung white streamers from one end of the dining room to the other.

BILL

My mother let me invite the whole class. Thirty-three kids came!

SANDY

All the girls got Story Book dolls for favors, and the boys got yo-yos that glowed in the dark. And instead of having cake and ice cream, my mother made this incredible baked Alaska.

BILL

We decorated the whole place in red: red streamers, red balloons, red tablecloth . . .

SANDY

When she brought it to the table, everyone gasped. It was three feet high and covered with peaks of egg white.

BILL

Shit, everything was red! My mother even put red food coloring into the cake.

SANDY

I can still remember how that first bite of baked Alaska tasted . . .

BILL

That was the birthday I got my red bike. And when we'd finished eating the red cake and red raspberry ice cream, we played games.

SANDY

I don't know where we got the room, but we actually set up twenty-seven chairs for musical chairs.

BILL

Darts, ducking for apples . . .

SANDY

We played it once, then twice.

BILL

Then we set up the chairs and played musical chairs.

SANDY

By the fifth round we decided to alter the rules a little . . .

BILL

. . . but after a while we changed the rules.

SANDY

When you sat down in a chair, you grabbed someone of the opposite sex and they sat in your lap.

BILL

It was getting boring with the same old rules.

SANDY

. . . and then you had to . . . had to . . .

BILL

So you grabbed a girl and both sat on the chair together.

SANDY

. . . you had to . . . had to . . .

BILL

And you kissed the girl for as long as you could without coming up for air, and whoever got in a chair and kissed for the longest time played in the next round.

SANDY

We played musical chairs.

BILL

After the kissing part, we began unbuttoning the girls' blouses and putting our hands inside. *(He pulls* SANDY *onto his lap)*

SANDY

We played it once, twice, then three times.

BILL

(Nuzzles her) . . . and feeling what there was to feel. Oh, it was nice, it was very nice.

SANDY

By the fifth round we decided to alter the rules a little.

131

BILL

(His hands in her robe) And each time the music stopped, you grabbed another girl and reached down into another blouse . . .

SANDY

When you sat down in a chair *(Giggles)*, you grabbed someone of the opposite sex and he sat in your lap.

BILL

After a while we forgot all about the musical part of the game and everyone was just lying all over the chairs, kissing and feeling up.

SANDY

I don't know why the grownups didn't . . .

BILL

(Caressing SANDY*)* Some of us even got our pants off.

SANDY

(Laughing) Bill!

BILL

(More and more amorous) . . . and we pulled down the shades . . .

SANDY

Someone might come in . . .

BILL

Tommy Hartland and I got five girls under the table.

SANDY

(Resisting) Oh, Bill.

BILL

But by the time we got our jockies off, the girls panicked and were back in the game with someone else, and there were Tommy Hartland and I, horny as hell, surrounded by all these goddamned red streamers and strawberry gumdrops.

SANDY

I remember, my mother made this baked Alaska. It was covered with egg whites . . .

BILL

Come on, give us a kiss.

SANDY

Don't, Nicky might come in . . .

BILL

Nicky's not coming in, just relax.

SANDY

Please, Bill, not now, I just can't . . . Nicky . . .

(They struggle. NICKY *bursts into the room, dressed up in* SANDY*'s underwear. A slip trails off his shoulders, a bra is draped around his waist, a stocking hangs from his neck. He's stricken with hurt and jealousy at what he sees)*

(All together)

NICKY

Mommy!

SANDY

(Flying off BILL*'s lap) Nicky!*

BILL

You little prick!

NICKY

I want grape juice!

BILL

What in hell are you doing in your mother's underwear?

SANDY

That's a twelve-fifty bra you've got wrapped around your waist.

BILL

Boy, I never even *dreamed* of going through my mother's underwear!

NICKY

I want grape juice! I want grape juice!

SANDY

I just don't . . .

BILL

That child should be punished.

NICKY

(Louder still) And I . . . want . . . ice . . . in . . . my . . . grape . . . juice!

BILL

Well, you can't have ice in your grape juice, you little—

SANDY

(Shoving a glass of grape juice at NICKY*)* Here's your damned grape juice, without ice . . . nice and *warm!*

133

NICKY

(Hurls the glass to the floor) Then I won't drink it!

SANDY

(Rushing to her brooms) Look out, broken glass!

BILL

Did you see what he just did? He deliberately threw his glass on the floor!

NICKY

(Lunges headlong into the glass) I want to make my birthday wish! I want to make my birthday wish!

BILL

(Pulling him back) Mommy said look out!

NICKY

(Starts to cry) Daddy hurt me, Daddy hurt me.

SANDY

(Sweeping) It's all over the floor. Don't anybody go near there until I get it cleaned up!

BILL

I didn't hurt him, for Chrissake, I was just trying to get him away from the glass before he cut himself.

NICKY

You did so hurt me, you stupid idiot! (Kicks BILL *in the shins)*

BILL

(Slugging NICKY *with each word) Don't . . . you . . . ever . . . hit . . . your . . . father! (*NICKY *wails)* Did you see that? Your son just kicked me in the shin. *(Examines the wound)*

SANDY

(Sweeping) If you ever deliberately break a glass like that again . . .

BILL

He broke the skin . . .

SANDY

I've had enough. Take him up to his room and let's just forget about the party!

BILL

My own son drew blood.

SANDY

I'll phone Jeffrey and Mia and tell them to forget the whole thing.

BILL

You'd better get the peroxide to sterilize it with.

SANDY

(NICKY *lies down in his wagon and makes his strangled sound*)
Come on, Bill, take him up to his room. We're calling the party
off.

NICKY

But what about my cake?

SANDY

No birthday party for Nicky this year.

NICKY

. . . and the candles?

BILL

You can spend the rest of the day up in your room.

NICKY

What about my wish? *(Starts to cry)*

SANDY

The child must be punished.

BILL

It's your own fault, Nicky, we gave you every chance.

NICKY

You mean I won't have any party at all?

SANDY

We warned you.

BILL

It hurts us more than it does you.

SANDY

You've got to learn some time, Nicholas!

BILL

Maybe next year you'll be a better boy.

SANDY

I asked you to wait and open your presents after the cards!

NICKY

No party? No wish?

BILL

We certainly don't enjoy doing this, Nicky.

SANDY

No party, and that's that. *(Crying,* NICKY *runs out of the room)* I'm sorry, Nicky.

BILL

We gave you every chance.

SANDY

We gave him every chance.

(Curtain)

Act Two

It is early in the evening of the same day.

The curtain rises: SANDY, BILL and NICKY sit around the birthday table all dressed up in party clothes. They wear little paper hats, and are blowing noisemakers and making barnyard sounds.

> (SANDY *clucks like a chicken;* BILL *howls like a coyote;* NICKY *grunts and oinks)*

BILL

One, two, three—change!

> (SANDY *meows;* BILL *grunts like a gorilla;* NICKY *barks)*

BILL

One, two, three—change!

> (SANDY *whinnies;* BILL *whistles like a thrush;* NICKY *bleats like a goat)*

BILL

One, two, three—change!

> (SANDY *clucks like a chicken;* NICKY *hoots like an owl)*

BILL

Stop! Mommy's out of the game! She already clucked before!

> (BILL *roars like a lion;* NICKY *makes fish noises and faces)*

BILL

(Faster) One, two three—change!

> (BILL *hisses like a snake;* NICKY *gobbles like a turkey)*

BILL

One, two, three—change!

> (BILL *grunts like a gorilla;* NICKY *sqeaks like a mouse)*

BILL

Stop the game! Daddy already made gorilla grunts before, Nicky wins!

BILL and SANDY
(Applaud and whistle) Yea, Nicky, yea, Nicky!

NICKY
Let's play again.

SANDY
(Laughing) You're too good for us.

NICKY
Let's play again!

SANDY
They should be here any minute now.

BILL
Is everybody ready for one hell of a party?

SANDY
The movie's all developed?

BILL
The movie's developed and ready to roll!

SANDY
Oh, Nicky, I can hardly wait!

BILL
They will eat their hearts out when they see this film!

SANDY
The whole day would be perfect if only Jeffrey and Mia changed their minds about not having children. Tonight, with us.

BILL
I've always admired Jeffrey as a photographer, but frankly I think he overrates himself.
(NICKY runs around the room making animal sounds)

SANDY
They have exciting careers now, but what about when they're sixty and retired and all alone in the world.

BILL
Just because he does a lot of traveling he fancies himself a professional photographer!

NICKY
(Braying in their ears) Let's play again.

SANDY
If she waits too long, it will be too late. Remember Diane Oak?

Diane Oak waited until she was forty-five before she had Jonathan, and by then her cervix had shriveled up and wouldn't even open for the birth.

NICKY

What's a cervix?

SANDY

She passed her ninth month, tenth, eleventh, twelfth . . . nothing happened. Finally they had to induce her in her fifteenth.

NICKY

What's a cervix?

SANDY

When that poor baby was finally pulled out by Caesarean section, he weighed thirty-six pounds and had a full set of teeth.

NICKY

What's a cervix?

BILL

It's a part of a lady.

NICKY

What part?

SANDY

The part the baby comes out of, sweetheart.

BILL

(Whispering) The hole.

NICKY

The poopie hole?

BILL

Not the poopie hole! The baby hole!

NICKY

Where's the baby hole?

(BILL indicates on himself where it is)

SANDY

I certainly wouldn't want Mia to go through what Diane Oak did. All her female plumbing was ripped to shreds by that child.

BILL

Babies come out of the baby hole, and poopie comes out of the poopie hole.

139

SANDY

Of course they could always adopt, but it just isn't the same.

NICKY

Where's the poopie hole?

(BILL *indicates on himself where it is*)

SANDY

How she and Jeffrey can call themselves authorities on children when they've never had one of their own . . .

NICKY

Does Mia have a baby hole?

SANDY

She's never felt life moving inside her. It's sad.

BILL

Of course Mia has a baby hole. All women have baby holes.

NICKY

Then why doesn't a baby come out of it?

SANDY

We have so much compared to them.

BILL

Why doesn't a baby come out of Mia's baby hole?

SANDY

Of course we don't get to travel like they do, we don't have their kind of freedom . . .

NICKY

Why doesn't a baby come out of Mia's baby hole?

SANDY

. . . and we don't speak all the languages they do.

BILL

Maybe there is one in there, but he's stuck.

NICKY

(Laughs) Stuck in with the poopie.

SANDY

They get out more than we do.

NICKY

(Laughing) How does a lady tell whether she's going to have a baby or a poopie?

SANDY

Of course Mia looks younger than me . . .

BILL

Because if it's a baby inside her, her tummy swells up, and if it's a poopie inside her . . .

(NICKY *starts laughing again*)

SANDY

She's missing the most basic experience a woman can have, and when you come right down to it, all she's left with are memories of *other* people's children.

NICKY

Why doesn't a baby come out of Mia's baby hole?

SANDY

Tape recordings and photographs of strangers . .

BILL

Because she doesn't want to.

SANDY

Slides of foreign urchins eating raw elephant meat. I feel sorry for her.

BILL

We all have different needs.

SANDY

(Getting louder) It's just pathetic. Trying to have her own family through other people's children, and not even American children, but poor starving—

(The doorbell rings)

BILL and SANDY

They're here.

SANDY

(Whispering) Oh, God, they heard us!

BILL

(Whispering) Don't be silly, they couldn't possibly have heard us.

SANDY

(Head in hands) They heard us.

BILL

(Going to the door) They didn't hear us.

141

SANDY

They heard us.

NICKY

Heard what?

SANDY

Sssssssshhhhhhhh!

(BILL *opens the door;* MIA *and* JEFFREY *enter, out of breath.*
JEFFREY *is professorial,* MIA *is a fragile beauty)*
(All together)

JEFFREY

(Shaking hands with BILL*)* I'm sorry we're so late. Mia was delivering a paper at an anthropology convention and she got tied up
with a lot of questions at the end. *(Kisses* SANDY*)* Sandy, I'm sorry.
(Sets down a slide projector and several boxes of slides)

MIA

(Kissing BILL*)* Bill, forgive us. I was giving a paper at a convention
and some visiting professors from Manila had all these questions
. . . *(Kisses* SANDY*)* Sandy, we finally made it!

SANDY

(Kisses both JEFFREY *and* MIA*)* Jeffrey! Mia! It's so good to see
you. Come in, please!

BILL

(Slapping JEFFREY *on the back)* We were beginning to worry
about you. Come in . . .

(Slight pause)

(All together again)

BILL

(Kisses MIA*)* Mia, you look beautiful, as always. Come in!

MIA

(Kisses NICKY*)* Nicky, four years old!

JEFFREY

(Shakes hands with NICKY*)* Happy birthday, Nicky.

NICKY

I'm four today. Four!

(Silence)

(All together)

142

BILL

(Leading them into the room) Come on in.

SANDY

We were beginning to worry . . .
        (Pause)

MIA

Oh, Sandy, look at what you've done!
                        (All together)

BILL

Well, folks, everybody ready for a great party?

SANDY

Nicky's been so excited . . .

MIA

Jeffrey, look what they've done!
        (Embarrassed laughter, a pause)
                        (All together)

BILL

There's nothing like a kid's fourth birthday!

MIA

We'll give Nicky his present at the table with the cake and ice
cream.
        (They laugh, embarrassed)
                        (All together)

SANDY

It just wouldn't have been a real celebration without you!

NICKY

I got a wagon and masks.

BILL

. . . and wait till you see the movie we made . . .
        (They laugh, embarrassed; a pause)

JEFFREY

When the Tunisian hill child turns four, he's blindfolded and led
into a swamp to bring back the body of a mud turtle for a tribal
feast.

SANDY

How fascinating.
        (Silence)

MIA

If he fails, he's expelled from the tribe.

JEFFREY

. . . and left on the plains to be picked apart by giant caw-caws.

SANDY

How horrifying!
(Silence)

MIA

In the Tabu culture, four is believed to be a magical age. I once saw a four-year-old Tabu girl skin a six-hundred-pound zebra and then eat the pelt!

BILL

Son of a bitch!

NICKY

I can write my name.

MIA

How wonderful.

JEFFREY

I saw the same child nurse a dead goat back to life.

BILL

Jesus!

JEFFREY

With her own milk!

NICKY

I pulled Mommy in my wagon.

MIA

How wonderful.

SANDY

Come, let's sit down around the table.

MIA

(Sitting) Sandy, everything is just . . . beautiful!

JEFFREY

(Sitting) It's really amazing what you can do to a room with a little imagination and some crepe paper.

NICKY

(To MIA*)* Do you have a baby hole?

SANDY

Nicky!

(All are seated around the table)

BILL

Nicky and I made a great movie this morning, didn't we, Nick?

NICKY

Daddy and I made a movie.

MIA

How wonderful.

SANDY

Bill and Nicky are very close.

(Silence)

SANDY

They've always been close. Ever since Nicky was born they were close.

NICKY

(To MIA*)* Do you have a baby hole?

SANDY

(Fast) It's really quite unusual to find a father and son that are as close as Bill and Nicky.

(Awkward silence)

BILL

I wasn't at all close to my father.

SANDY

I was very close to my father.

MIA

I was close to my mother.

SANDY

I hated my mother.

BILL

I don't remember my mother.

JEFFREY

My mother and father were very close.

BILL

That's interesting, because my mother and father weren't close at all.

(Silence)

MIA

Sandy, this room is a work of art! I've never seen anything like it.

SANDY

Well, how often does your favorite son turn four?

NICKY

I got a lot of presents.

MIA

You must have been up all night.

NICKY

I got a wagon.

MIA

I'll bet you did!

SANDY

. . . *and* birthday cards. Nicky got twenty-seven birthday cards this year, including one from Mrs. Tanner, his nursery school teacher. And they have a strict policy of not sending out individual cards on the children's birthdays. You know, they might forget somebody. So naturally Nicky was thrilled . . . I mean, to be singled out like that . . . *(Hands* MIA *the card)*

MIA

(Reading) "Happy birthday, Nicky. Sincerely, Mrs. Tanner."

SANDY

(To NICKY*)* Mrs. Tanner sent that especially to you, breaking all the school rules!

MIA

(Examining the card) That's funny, this looks like your handwriting.

SANDY

So, cousins, how long will you be with us before you disappear over the horizon again on the back of some camel?

MIA

Her Y's and N's are exactly like yours.

SANDY

(Snatching the card away) People will start thinking you don't like American children, the way you're always running off to interview toddlers in Iceland and Nigeria. *(Laughs nervously)*

NICKY

I pulled Mommy in my wagon.

BILL

He's very strong for his age.

JEFFREY

One of the interesting things about the Berbers is that parents regard spiritual strength much more highly than physical strength.

NICKY

I pulled Mommy and all my presents too!

MIA

Almost any Berber child can converse with desert vegetation.

SANDY

Really?

JEFFREY

To my mind, there are no children the equal of Berber children!

NICKY

I got instruments for my birthday.

MIA

That's wonderful, Nicky.

SANDY

I know we spoil him, but we just can't help it.

BILL

We spoil the living crap out of that kid and we love every minute of it, right, Nick?

NICKY

Daddy made a movie of me.

SANDY

Bill and Nicky are very close.

NICKY

(Putting on a mask) I got masks for my birthday.

SANDY

Nicky and his masks . . .

BILL

Give that kid a mask, any kind of mask, and he's in seventh heaven!

MIA

We've always been fascinated by masks and the whole phenomenon of taking on the identity of someone else.

(NICKY *runs around the room, grunting*)

JEFFREY

Remember those animal-head masks we were given in New Guinea?

SANDY

He gets so excited on his birthday.

BILL

He's been up since six this morning.

JEFFREY

Mia and I were given animal-head masks in New Guinea that were made out of a paste of dried insects.

MIA

You had the feeling that if you left one on too long, your face would slowly blend right into the mask and lose all human features.

SANDY

Uuuuuugh.

BILL

Nicky has an unusually vivid imagination.

SANDY

You should hear his dreams . . .

BILL

All about man-eating chairs and flying dogs.

SANDY

Really wild!

(NICKY *makes more and more noise running around the room grunting*)

SANDY

All right, Nicky, that's enough!

BILL

Come on, Nick, quiet down.

SANDY

He's been up since five-thirty this morning.

BILL

(*Chasing* NICKY) Okay, Nicky, let's take off the mask and calm down.

NICKY

(Running) I don't want to take my mask off!

BILL

(Wrests it away after finally catching him) You're being too wild!

NICKY

(Wails) I want my mask, I want my mask!

SANDY

Let him keep his mask on. Poor thing, he's exhausted. He was up at four-thirty this morning.

BILL

Okay, okay, you can have your mask back, but no more being wild . . . *understand?*

> *(*NICKY *puts the mask back on, sits in his chair, sucks his thumb through the mask. Silence)*

BILL

(Whispering) Take your thumb out of your mask.

> *(*NICKY *doesn't)*

SANDY

It's the strangest thing, but ever since I got up this morning I've been smelling the sea. *(Runs her hands through her hair; a shower of sand falls out)*
> *(Silence)*

BILL

Tell us again, just how many languages can the two of you speak?

JEFFREY

Seventeen.

MIA

Thirteen.

SANDY

Jeffrey and Mia can speak fifteen languages, Nicky.

BILL

My maternal grandmother was Canadian and always spoke French around the house.

SANDY

My maternal grandmother was Dutch.

BILL

But us kids never learned it.

JEFFREY

Canadian French isn't considered a pure language, it's a dilution . . .

SANDY

I'm part Dutch on one side and Swedish on the other.

BILL

I'm pure Canadian and a little Irish.

NICKY

What am I?

BILL

No, wait, I forgot, I have some Greek blood in me too.

SANDY

Oh, Mia, say a few words in something for Nicky!

NICKY

What am I?

SANDY

Mia's going to say something in a funny language, honey.

NICKY

What am *I?*

BILL

(Angry) Canadian, Dutch, Swedish, and a little Greek!
(Silence)

MIA

Talla zoo zoo feeple zip.

NICKY

(Laughing) What did you say?

SANDY

(Laughing) Isn't it a riot?

BILL

(Laughing) Jesus Christ!

What did she say?

MIA

Happy birthday!

NICKY

Say something else.

SANDY

Oh, say more!

MIA

Dun herp zala zala cree droop soy nitch.

SANDY

(Roaring with laughter) Stop, stop!

NICKY

Say it again, say it again!

BILL

Oh, God!

MIA

Dun herp zala zala cree droop soy nitch.

BILL

(Laughing) What . . . what was it?

MIA

Merry Christmas!
 *(*SANDY, BILL *and* NICKY *all roar with laughter)*

SANDY

That was Merry Christmas?

NICKY

Say, "Nicky is four years old today."

MIA

(Also laughing) Ooola oola zim dam zilco reet treet comp *graaaaa,
Nicky!*
 (All laugh)

SANDY and NICKY

Again, again!

MIA and JEFFREY

(Chanting and clowning) Ooola oola zim dam zilco reet treet
comp *graaaaa, Nicky!*
 (All laugh)

BILL

(To NICKY*)* How would you like to be able to speak like that?

NICKY

(Gravely) Lim biddle ree yok slow iffle snee buddle twee rat ith
twank.

BILL and SANDY

(Laughing) Oh, Nicky, Nicky.

SANDY

We always have such a good time when you two come over!

MIA

We wouldn't miss Nicky's birthday for the world.

SANDY

Who else has cousins that speak fifteen languages?

BILL

Hey, I haven't told Jeff and Mia about Charley E.Z. yet, this crazy guy that works in our office.

SANDY

Oh, Bill . . .

BILL

Did I tell you about Charley E.Z.?

SANDY

He made the whole thing up.

BILL

There's a shakedown going on at the office, and quite a few of the top-level guys are being let go. And the things they do to try and hang on. Unbelievable. I guess something comes over a guy when he feels his job threatened . . .

SANDY

Bill, really, I . . .

BILL

There's this guy Charles E. Zinn—Charley E.Z., we call him. He's a junior officer who recently lost an important account, so word came down that Charley E.Z. was going to be axed.

JEFFREY

I don't think I've ever heard you mention a Charley E.Z. before.

SANDY

He made it all up.

BILL

He'd been getting these letters accusing him of "professional inconsistency." Have you ever heard such a phrase—"professional inconsistency"?

MIA

(Laughing) I have a feeling this is going to be another of Bill's wild stories.

BILL

So the word came down that Charley E.Z. was going to lose his job.

JEFFREY

Oh, no!

MIA

How awful!

JEFFREY

Poor guy.

BILL

So Charley E.Z. took action. And where did he take action? In the elevator! *(Lowers his voice)* For the past few months between three and four in the afternoon Charley has been getting into the elevator and taking his clothes off, starting with his jacket and shirt, then pants, socks, shoes, underwear. But the first time he did it, it was cold turkey. *(NICKY pantomimes the action as BILL tells the story. He takes off all his clothes except his underwear and stands in the closet facing the audience. At the appropriate moment, he opens the door like an elevator door)* He changed in the executive men's room, stuffed all his clothes into a duffel bag, glided into the hall when no one was looking, rang for the elevator, stepped in . . . and began his long, lonely, naked journey.

SANDY

(Laughing) Oh, Bill!

BILL

You see, there's a special control panel in the elevator that lets the operator open and shut the door whenever he wants. So if Charley E.Z. is cruising around between the fourth and fifth floors, say, and someone rings on Main and the door starts to open, just a crack, and Charley sees someone he doesn't know, he just zaps the CLOSE DOOR button, the door slams shut and Charley zooms back up, safe with his secret.

SANDY

(Laughing, to MIA) Isn't he crazy?

MIA

(Laughing) Completely . . .

BILL

Charley's first day in the elevator: He's in there, cold turkey, nothing on, not even a cuff link. The bell rings on five. Charley braces himself, the elevator rises, stops, the door opens and in steps this account executive. He doesn't notice anything. Charley's cool, but by the time they're between two and Main, he looks at Charley. No one says a word, Charley lets him off at Main. One minute later, he gets another call. Guess who?

ALL

The account executive!

BILL

The account executive!
    (All laugh)

BILL

Well, for the rest of the afternoon the two of them just kept riding up and down, down and up. One of the secretaries on two said that when the elevator stopped at her floor she caught a fleeting glimpse of two naked men rolling around on the floor, laughing.

MIA

I can't imagine anyone actually doing that.

BILL

Lately he's taken to props: disguises, musical instruments, special effects. *(NICKY opens and shuts the closet door, wearing a variety of masks and playing on his different instruments)* Last week he was in there with a viola and the entire accounting department.

SANDY

And they all take their clothes off?

BILL

Take them off and throw them down the elevator shaft.

SANDY

Imagine businessmen doing that!

MIA

I never realized there was such an allure for the forbidden in business.

BILL

(Whispering) I've heard that next week he's hired a string trio to play Schubert in the service elevator.

SANDY

Bill took a wonderful movie of Nicky opening his presents this morning.

BILL

The point is that everybody at Continental Allied loves Charley E.Z. now. The letters about "professional inconsistency" have stopped coming . . . and he's doing just great . . .

(Silence)

MIA

Don't you think it's time we gave Nicky his present, Jeffrey?

NICKY

(Opening the door) Up, please. Elevator going up. Please move to the rear of the car to make room for the people getting on. *(Slams the door)*

SANDY

(Knocks on the door) Jeffrey and Mia want to give you your present now, honey.

JEFFREY

(Puttering by his slides and projector) Nicholas, you've never gotten a present like this!

SANDY

Presents!

MIA

(Helping JEFFREY*)* I just hope he likes it, you never know with children. But we put a great deal of thought into it.

SANDY

Nicky . . .

NICKY

(Opens the door) Main floor, everybody off. *(Quickly slams the door)*

SANDY

(Lowering her voice) Please, Nicky, you're embarrassing us.

JEFFREY

You've got a movie screen somewhere, don't you?

155

BILL

(Turns on a light to reveal a whole area that's all set up with a screen, movie projector, tables, ashtrays) Say no more.

JEFFREY

Great! *(Pulls the screen out to the center of the stage, sets it up)*

SANDY

It's the strangest thing, but one of my front teeth is loose. People don't lose their front teeth, do they?

MIA

The Qua tribe starts out with all their permanent adult teeth and then at the age of sixteen every one falls out to be replaced at the age of thirty-five with an entire new set of baby teeth. It's a complete mystery to dental science.

SANDY

How disgusting.

MIA

We were taping interviews with Qua mothers a few months ago. Wonderful people: highly resourceful. They used to prepare these aromatic banquets for us out of tree bark.

SANDY

Uuuuugh! I could never eat that native food. It always looks made out of human excrement.

MIA

Qua *women* have no teeth at all.

JEFFREY

They eat by grinding their food into a paste between large stones and then lapping it up.

SANDY

(Hand over her mouth) Uuuuuuugh!

JEFFREY

Okay, folks, we're ready to go. Get Nicky, his present is all set.

SANDY

(Hugging MIA) He's always so thrilled to see you!

BILL

Come out, come out, wherever you are!

SANDY

Family means so much to him.

156

JEFFREY

(Switches off the lights) The show is about to begin.

SANDY

Oooooh, Nicky, I wonder what it is!

BILL

(Angrily opens the door) Nicholas, will you get the hell out of there!

SANDY

You're being very rude, Nicky. Mommy isn't going to forget this.

BILL

(Drags NICKY *out of the closet. He's dressed again) Now come over here and sit down!*

> *(*BILL *sits* NICKY *down. All the birthday chairs have been rearranged to face the movie screen. The grownups all sit down. A silence)*

JEFFREY

(Rises, waves his hand over the slide projector and box of slides) Happy birthday, Nicky.

MIA

Happy birthday.
(Silence)

NICKY

What is it?

JEFFREY

Your own projector with slides of children from all over the world.
> *(He starts showing slides of children in native dress doing all kinds of remarkable things. Every few seconds a new picture is flashed on the screen)*

SANDY

Ooooooooh, Nicky!

BILL

What a present!

SANDY

(Groaning) Ooooooooooh, Nicky, look!

MIA

We took them all.

SANDY

They're just beautiful.

157

BILL

Son of a bitch!

JEFFREY

We figured this would be something he could work himself . . .

MIA

And learn from.

BILL

I've never seen such clarity of color. What kind of film were you using?

SANDY

And Jeffrey and Mia said you could keep them!

NICKY

Isn't there anything else?

BILL

Shit! That's color!

NICKY

. . . something to unwrap?

JEFFREY

All you do is load the projector and then push this button every time you want to see a different slide. Your mommy and daddy can help you with it.

NICKY

This is it?

MIA

These are some of the children we worked with last year.

SANDY

Jeffrey and Mia lead very special lives, honey. They travel all over the world studying poor children.

JEFFREY

Oh, look! The Io children. They decorate their faces with an iridescent paint made out of powdered giraffe hooves.

MIA

It's very bad for their skin, actually.

SANDY

I can imagine.

MIA

They're wonderful children. Highly motivated. Jeffrey and I got very close to them.

NICKY

I wish I could meet them.

MIA

Well, maybe someday, Nicky.

NICKY

I wish I could play with them. I don't have anybody to play with.

SANDY

Nicky, that isn't true. You have Daddy and me to play with, and you go to nursery school three mornings a week.

JEFFREY

Actually, these slides don't represent the most amazing part of our trip last year . . .

NICKY

I don't have anybody to play with.

JEFFREY

. . . our penetration into the Bush.

SANDY

I didn't know anybody was allowed.

NICKY

I wish those children could come to my house.

JEFFREY

We penetrated the Bush and saw things no human being has ever seen.

NICKY

Nobody plays with me.

SANDY

Oh, tell us everything!

JEFFREY

(Turns off the projector) We encountered a civilization untouched by the Industrial Revolution. People living in the Stone Age.
    (The lights go dim and eerie)

SANDY

Ooooooooh, cave men.

159

JEFFREY

There are a Bush people called the Whan See who are still arboreal.

(SANDY *gasps*)

BILL

Jeeeez.

NICKY

I'm lonely.

BILL

Ssssssh!

JEFFREY

They live in trees and never come down to the ground.

MIA

What was so remarkable about them was they were obviously Homo sapiens and not simian, yet they had this one extraordinary feature . . .

(SANDY *screams*)

BILL

Christ, I hope you had your camera with you.

MIA

. . . a freakish biological throwback.

JEFFREY

Each and every one of them had a tail!

(SANDY, BILL *and* NICKY *gasp*)

MIA

We couldn't believe our eyes the first time we saw them swinging through the trees. We'd been cutting our way through deep brush when we suddenly heard this chattering above us. It sounded like children giggling. We looked up. And there were these . . . people . . . swinging through the branches by their tails.

JEFFREY

About the size of Orientals, clean-shaven, Mongoloid bone structure, delicate features, fair . . .

MIA

. . . and covered with the most incredible silvery down that glittered so brightly we had to shade our eyes.

(SANDY, BILL *and* NICKY *gasp*)

BILL

Did you get any pictures?

MIA

And they had the most musical way of speaking . . . a kind of sighing almost.

> (NICKY *picks up a cello and begins playing the Bach unaccompanied cello suites*)

JEFFREY

At first we were afraid they'd run away when they saw us, but they didn't. They just became very still and stared down at us.

MIA

I had no idea Nicky could play the cello so well.

SANDY

Oh, yes, Nicky's always been musical.

JEFFREY

Because they exuded such docility, I reached up my hand to one and said, "We're American anthropologists, we come in peace."

SANDY

What a perfect thing to say!

BILL

Beautiful . . . beautiful.

JEFFREY

They became very excited and all started talking at once.

BILL

At least you had a tape recorder on you.

MIA

I've never seen such eyes . . . a kind of creamy pink . . . like looking into some strawberry parfait.

SANDY

Weren't you scared?

JEFFREY

You see, we, without tails and wearing clothes, were just as strange to their eyes.

MIA

After Jeffrey spoke, I said a few words, and then our guide gave them chewing gum.

MIA

Then as a body, they furled and unfurled their long silvery tails and chanted, "Whan See." So we chanted it back.

JEFFREY and MIA

(Chanting) Whan See, Whan See, Whan See . . .

JEFFREY

Then one of them motioned that we should climb up a tree and join them. So we climbed up into some low branches, and they gingerly approached us, touching our hair and skin.

SANDY

I would have died!

MIA

They were an exceedingly gentle people who had no words in their simple vocabulary for hate, war or anger.

JEFFREY

We spent an entire week with them.

MIA

It's amazing how fast you can adjust to living in a tree.

SANDY

I would have died . . .

JEFFREY

And not once in all that time did we ever see one of them drop down to the ground, even though they could stand erect, run, and even dance on their hind legs.

MIA

You should have seen them dance! They'd wrap their tails around a branch and then start rocking back and forth, swaying higher and higher until suddenly they'd let go . . . and spin off through the trees like meteors . . .

JEFFREY

While the older members of the tribe banged on drums made out of hollow tree stumps.

MIA

Our last day there they asked us to join them, and the leader gripped me around the waist with his tail and started whirling me through the air. Everything was spinning and pulsating. There was this strong smell about him . . . cinnamon . . . cinnamon dust sprinkled through his fur . . . he spun me higher and higher and then suddenly . . . let go. We both went flying through the air . . . his arms holding me close . . . oh . . . it was . . . just . . . everything rushing by . . . the sun on my face . . . that fragrance of cinnamon . . .

BILL

Jesus . . .

SANDY

Oh, Mia . . .

JEFFREY

Other tribes in the Bush have repeatedly tried to capture the Whan See because of their great beauty and grace, but once a Whan See touches ground, he dies. Something happens to their centers of gravity. Their balance goes haywire.

SANDY

(Covering her ears) I can't listen . . .

BILL

Think of the shots you could have gotten with a Leica!

JEFFREY

In spite of their utter ignorance of science and technology, they displayed incredible artistic sophistication. They did these bark carvings with their teeth that were absolutely stunning!

MIA

It was a form of relaxation for them to sit on a branch in the shade and then bite into the tree trunks, tearing out delicate designs.

JEFFREY

Their virtuosity was astonishing. On the one hand, they could do representational carvings depicting familiar Bush objects, but then they also did these highly abstract designs that resembled some ancient calligraphy.

MIA

And of course that constant gnawing on tree bark provided them with excellent dental hygiene.

SANDY

I've never heard anything like this.

JEFFREY

They also did exquisite lacework, tearing into large pawpaw leaves.

SANDY

You should write a book.

BILL

Christ, I hope you got some pictures out of it!

MIA

The whole thing was like a dream . . . except . . .

JEFFREY

Except . . .

SANDY

Oh, no, they do something awful you haven't told us.

MIA

We didn't find out about it until our last night, otherwise we'd still be there.

JEFFREY

Neither of us wanted to leave. We'd have given up everything to stay with them.

MIA

Our careers, our fieldwork, our publications . . .

JEFFREY

Sometimes at night we'd watch them make love, their silvery bodies radiating a kind of shimmering electricity. And everybody would watch: all the children, grandparents, everyone.

MIA

But that last evening we saw the flaw . . .

JEFFREY

. . . the style . . .

MIA

. . . the moral defect.

SANDY

No!

BILL

They eat their young!
(SANDY screams)

BILL

I knew it.

SANDY

(Covering her ears) Don't . .

MIA

Our last evening there a young girl went into childbirth.

SANDY

Oh, no.

MIA

As usual, everyone gathered around to watch, since they had no awareness of modesty or privacy.

JEFFREY

No one doctor or midwife was in charge—the delivery was the responsibility of all the women of the tribe.

MIA

As the girl was in the final throws of labor, the older women reached out their hands to help her . . .

SANDY

I can't bear it, it will be awful!

MIA

Finally her moment came, the head was being born. She gave a shrill yelp of pain and joy.

(SANDY *gasps*)

MIA

. . . and the baby was born . . .

SANDY

Oooooooh.

MIA

But the very instant it emerged, they lifted up the tiny creature and . . . and . . .

SANDY

(Hands flying to her heart) No!

MIA

It's too awful.

BILL

One of the elders popped it into his mouth!
(SANDY *screams*)

MIA

They lifted up the tiny creature and reinserted it back into its mother's womb.

SANDY and BILL

But that's impossible.

MIA

(Upset) And they did it again and again and again and again . . .

SANDY

It couldn't . . .

BILL

Son of a . . .

MIA

And the mother kept urging them on. As soon as the baby would be born another time, she'd motion them to . . . stuff him back in. It was obviously some ritual, there was some minimal number of reinsertions a mother had to withstand. *(Low voice)* After the baby was born for the last time, the girl sat up and kissed the hands of all the women who'd helped her.

SANDY

I just can't believe . . .

BILL

Now, that's one thing I'd have to see with my own eyes . . .

SANDY

It's barbaric . . . unnatural.

BILL

Did   you   get   any   shots?

MIA

Do you have any idea how many times that baby was born?

JEFFREY

Only the strongest survive.

BILL

If you got any pictures at all, you could sell them to one of the national magazines and make a bundle.

MIA

Seventeen times that baby came out of the womb and sixteen times he was pushed back in. The pain that girl bore was beyond description.

BILL

Of course, you would have needed some kind of powerful flash attachment, floodlights even.

MIA

She kept making this little sound way in the back of her throat, a rending like she was being torn apart.

SANDY

But why? Why did she allow it?

JEFFREY

You have to remember, these were a highly primitive people who took things literally. When a civilized woman has a baby, she too is possessive, only in more subtle ways. She's possessive of her birth experience and delights in retelling it. She's possessive of her baby and tries to keep him helpless for as long as possible. Well, these Stone Age women were just acting out that same possessiveness by reinserting the baby into its mother's womb. Through fetal insertion, you see, the primitive mother could experience her moment of motherhood over and over and over again.

(Silence)

MIA

After the fourth reinsertion, her uterus went into profound shock. And how that baby squealed. It wasn't human after a while, but mangled . . . and drenched . . . like some rodent . . . some little . . . hamster.

SANDY

I'm going to be sick.

JEFFREY

(Putters with the slides, taking them out and holding them up to the light) I've got to go through these and make sure I leave Nicky the right ones. Let's see—oh, yes, Caracas! What's this one of Nepal doing in here? *(He mutters on, improvising)*

MIA

After a while they motioned me to join them, they pulled me over to where she lay.

SANDY

I wish you'd stop this.

MIA

It was such a beautiful night, the air was so warm . . .

(SANDY screams)

MIA

I didn't understand what they wanted me to do at first, so I just stood there.

SANDY

I haven't been feeling well today. When I looked in the mirror this morning, I saw an old woman.

MIA

Then someone gripped my hand, guiding it towards the girl, towards her birth canal. I felt something warm and moist. I looked down, I was holding the baby's head. Such a tiny head, about the size of a softball and covered with that same silvery down, except it was all wet and matted down. It was so slippery I was afraid I'd drop it, and then this hand closed over mine and brought the baby hard up against his mother's birth canal, which opened again, received him, held him.

SANDY

I've been smelling the sea ever since I got up . . .

MIA

Her body convulsed, the baby came out again: five, six, seven times . . .

SANDY

My front teeth feel loose . . .

MIA

After a while I noticed that I was doing it by myself, no one was holding my hands, *I* was inserting the baby.

SANDY

I feel so tired all the time.

MIA

You know what it felt like? Stuffing a turkey. Stuffing a fifty-pound turkey with some little . . . hamster.

SANDY

Nicky . . . oh, my Nicky . . .

MIA

And there was this overpowering cinnamon smell. I started laughing.

SANDY

Nicky is four today. My son is four years old.

MIA

. . . and then they all started laughing, with those light sighing voices. All the women wrapped their long arms around each other, threw back their heads and laughed.

SANDY

Oh, Mia! *You* should have a baby. It's so wonderful!

MIA

This great swell of musical sound rose up as the young mother stiffened, screamed, experienced birth again and again and . . .

SANDY

It couldn't have happened.

MIA

The baby died.

SANDY

Not even a Stone Age woman can withstand the abnormal.

MIA

The baby died.

SANDY

(Whispering) You're afraid.

MIA

It died in my hands.

SANDY

You're afraid to have a baby.

MIA

It just stopped moving and went all stiff.

SANDY

You're afraid something will be wrong.

MIA

The mother didn't realize.

SANDY

We're all afraid . . . but . . . it . . . isn't . . . like . . . that . . .

MIA

I was responsible and it died. *(She starts to cry)*
        *(*NICKY *stops playing, puts his cello away)*

SANDY

Of course there *are* sacrifices . . .

169

MIA

(Rocking back and forth) The mother didn't realize. She'd fainted, and when she came to, she reached for him and bared her breast to him and cupped his tiny head in her hand . . . but he didn't move . . .

SANDY

There are sacrifices.

BILL

There are sacrifices.

SANDY

For the first few years you'd have to stay home. You certainly wouldn't want to bring a newborn into the Sahara Desert or anything.

MIA

His tiny body fit into hers so perfectly.

SANDY

There are sacrifices, but you gladly make them!

BILL

You couldn't take an infant into some mud village with no sanitary or medical facilities.

MIA

She kept drawing his little head closer and closer . . .

SANDY

Your child's welfare always comes first.

BILL

It's difficult to imagine the sacrifices you have to make as a parent until you've actually had your own child.

MIA

Suddenly she sensed something was wrong. She looked up into the semicircle of women and searched their faces.

SANDY

You'd have to forget about your career for six or seven years, maybe even longer.

BILL

There'd be great resentment on your child's part if you left him to visit other children.

SANDY

Strangers, people you don't even know.

BILL

It's perfectly understandable.

SANDY

I wouldn't trade motherhood for anything in the world!

BILL

Sandy and Nicky are very close.

SANDY

Of course you can always adopt, but it just isn't the same as having your own.

MIA

She lifted the baby off her breast and held him tightly in her hands.

SANDY

(Leads MIA *to the center of the room, eases her down to the floor)* It isn't like that.

BILL

Sandy and Nicky are very close.

MIA

Nothing happened. He didn't move. She breathed into his mouth. She slapped his face. She pulled at the down on his arms. She dug at his closed eyes with sticks, but . . . *nothing happened . . .*

SANDY

(Easing MIA *on her back)* It isn't like that . . .

MIA

No life in his body anywhere . . . She understood at last and opened her mouth . . . and this scream . . . tore from her throat . . .

SANDY

(On the floor next to MIA*)* I knew it would happen tonight. I told Bill you'd change your mind, you'd have your own, you'd want your own . . .

MIA

Then in one awful moment she hugged her baby close, stood up on one of the branches and hurled herself to the ground, plunging two hundred feet straight down.

BILL

(Crouching next to SANDY *and* MIA*)* You can't really know about kids until you've had your own.

MIA

They rushed through the air and were lost in the night.

SANDY

It isn't like that. It just isn't like that. You'll see, Mia . . .

BILL

Sandy and Nicky are very close.

SANDY

Just relax and breathe. In . . . and out . . . In and out . . . In and out . . .

BILL

(Attends MIA *as a doctor, checks her vital signs)* Her pulse is racing.

SANDY

Breathe with the contraction. Hold your breath when the contraction's over, slowly let it out. In and out . . . In and out . . .

MIA

. . . lost in the night.

BILL

(Breathes with SANDY*)* In . . . and out . . . In . . and out . . .

SANDY

Nicky, we need you too.

> *(*NICKY *joins the charade with great concentration and flair. He takes blood pressure, administers shots, writes on charts. Their voices are disembodied, as if heard through a haze of painkillers)*

JEFFREY

(Engrossed with his slides throughout) I'd completely forgotten about the Sook! They don't bury their dead, but prop them up against trees, sort of like decorations. *(Looks at more slides, improvises)*

SANDY

We'll help you. We won't leave you.

BILL

(Keeps breathing) In and out . . . In and out . . . In and out . . .

NICKY

Blood pressure: 150 over 277. Heart racing, irregular cardiovascular pattern.

MIA

They were lost in the night.

SANDY

Don't stiffen up . . . relax and breathe . . . relax and breathe . . . *(Breathes with* BILL*)*

JEFFREY

(Holding up a slide) Lahore! Remember that afternoon we took a walk in the foothills!

SANDY

It's the most beautiful thing that can happen to a woman. Breathe in . . . and out . . . In and out . . .

> *(In spite of herself,* MIA *starts breathing in tempo with* SANDY. SANDY, BILL, *and* NICKY *keep up a steady breathing pattern, breaking it only to speak)*

SANDY

Good girl . . . That's right . . . Hold it . . . Let it out slowly . . .

MIA

Oh! Something's happening . . .

NICKY

Pulse: 60 over 80. Blood pressure: 230 over 98. She should be dilated about seven centimeters by now.

> *(Their breathing gets faster)*

MIA

(Screams in pain) Oh! . . . Oh! What's happening to me? I don't want this . . . please . . . I . . . *Oh!*

JEFFREY

The Brazilian nomad has a life span of a hundred and twenty years, give or take a few.

MIA

(Breathing) In and . . . Oh . . . Oh! . . . God! Help me!

SANDY

(Holding her hand) You're going just beautifully. The first is always the hardest.

173

BILL

The first is always the hardest.

NICKY

The first is always the hardest.

SANDY

. . . but the most rewarding.

BILL

Certainly the most rewarding.

NICKY

Rewarding . . .

MIA

I . . . don't . . . want . . . this!

SANDY

Concentrate on your breathing.

MIA

Can't you do something? *Can't you stop it? God! . . . Oh! Stop it!*

JEFFREY

Here's that skeleton of a goat we came across in Mexico.

BILL

(Struggling to hold her down) You'd better give me a hand. She's fighting.

SANDY

(Helps BILL *pin her down)* When you feel the contraction this time, push against it. Push . . . Breathe . . . Push, hold . . . Breathe! *Push, hold, breathe.* It's no good, she's fighting. Nicky.

NICKY

(Sits on her legs) She's going to pass out if she keeps up like this.

SANDY

She'll have to be put to sleep.

MIA

(Screaming) Let me up . . . Please stop this . . . I want to get . . . Please . . . Oh . . . Oh!

JEFFREY

(Looking at the slide) Lars Kronniger!

NICKY

If you don't cooperate with us, you'll have to be put to sleep and miss everything.

174

SANDY

That's right, you'll miss everything.

BILL

You don't want to miss everything, do you?

NICKY

Her pulse is 450 over 6 and her blood pressure is 6 over 450. That can't be right!

SANDY

You've got to relax.

BILL

We'll have to put her to sleep.

SANDY

Push, hold, breathe . . . Push, hold, breathe . . .

MIA

I . . . don't . . . please . . . I . . . Oh! . . . You can't do this . . . I . . . Please . . . Leave me alone . . . Oh! You can't . . . Oh . . . Ohhhh! (She passes out)

(All together)

SANDY

They'd have such a beautiful child.

BILL

It's no good when you fight it.

NICKY

What a shame. What a shame.
(Silence)

SANDY

Well, I guess some people just . . . can't have children.

BILL

You can't pass a camel through the eye of a needle.

NICKY

One man's meat is another man's poison.
(Long silence)

SANDY

Well! What do you say we bring out Nicky's cake?!

BILL

Let's bring out Nicky's cake!

NICKY

(Dances up and down, races to the table) My cake, my cake, my cake!

BILL

(Prods JEFFREY *away from his slides, escorts him to his seat)* We're bringing out the cake.

JEFFREY

(Holding a slide up to the light as he sits down) You know, it's funny about these slides of the Whan See. Not one of them came out. There must have been something about that down on their bodies that set up a toxic reaction to the film I was using.

BILL

Wait 'til you see this cake!

SANDY

(Lights the candles on the table) I just love candlelight.

NICKY

I get to make my wish now.

BILL

Sandy makes one hell of a birthday cake!

NICKY

I can't wait to make my wish.

SANDY

I wish Mia would get up and join us. It just isn't a party without her.

NICKY

I want Mia at the table.

SANDY

Why won't she get up?

BILL

I don't like this.

SANDY

(More and more upset) Oh, Bill . . .

NICKY

(Rises) What's wrong with Mia?

> *(Silence.* JEFFREY *lifts* MIA *from the floor, drags her to the table and sits her in a chair.* MIA *sits upright for several seconds and then slumps over on the table. Never for a*

*moment does she seem dead or seriously ill. Rather, there's
something vaguely comical about her collapse as with
Nicky's fit early in the morning)*

JEFFREY

It happens all the time.
  (Silence)

SANDY

What have I done?

NICKY

Why won't Mia sit up?

BILL

(Patting MIA *on the face)* Come on, Mia . . . wake up . . .

SANDY

Oh, God.

JEFFREY

It won't do any good slapping her. When she's out, she's out.

SANDY

Oh, Bill . . .

BILL

(Rougher with her) Wake up, Mia!

NICKY

Is she dead?
  *(*SANDY *screams)*

BILL

(To SANDY*)* Maybe you should get some cold water.

SANDY

(Leaps up, gets some cold water, sprinkles it on MIA*'s face)* Mia?
Mia?

BILL

(Lifting MIA *up, holding her under the arms)* Come on, let's walk
her.

NICKY

She's dead. *She's dead!*

SANDY

She is not dead, she just passed out, that's all!

JEFFREY

It's pointless to do anything. She'll wake up when she's ready.

177

SANDY

She's not moving, Bill.

BILL

I know she's not moving. What do you think I am, blind?

SANDY

You don't have to yell!

NICKY

Mia's dead. Mia's dead!

SANDY

Will you shut up, Nicky!

BILL

Maybe I should lie her down on the floor again. *(He does)*

SANDY

Oh, Mia, I'm sorry.

NICKY

You killed her!

BILL

We did not kill her, she just fainted.

NICKY

You killed her, I saw you kill her!

JEFFREY

She'll pull out of it.

SANDY

I didn't mean to hurt you.

BILL

Isn't there any kind of medication that she carries with her?

JEFFREY

(Angry) I *told* you. There's *nothing* you can do about it. You never should have started all this in the first place!

SANDY

(To BILL*)* Prop her up again, she's so scary this way.

BILL

(Leans MIA *up against a chair leg)* There!

NICKY

You killed her.

BILL

Stop it, Nicky, or it's back to your room!

NICKY

How could you kill somebody on my birthday? *I* wasn't even that bad.

JEFFREY

Leave her alone!
    (Silence)

SANDY

I never should have said all that about having her own baby.

NICKY

I'd never . . . kill anybody!

BILL

(Raising his hand to him) Nickyyyyyy!

SANDY

I shouldn't have forced her.

BILL

You'd think she'd carry some kind of medication.
    *(*MIA *slides down to the floor again with a thud.* SANDY *and* NICKY *scream)*

BILL

(Peels back MIA*'s eyelids)* We must have some smelling salts or something . . .

JEFFREY

I said take your hands off her!

NICKY

(Starts to cry) I'm scared.

BILL

Now what do we do?

JEFFREY

We finish the party so we can go home and forget the whole thing.

BILL

(Trying to cheer up) Sure, let's bring out the cake!

NICKY

I don't want any cake.

BILL

Of course you want cake, it's your birthday, isn't it? Sandy, get the cake.

SANDY

How can we eat birthday cake when she's . . .

BILL

Get the cake!

NICKY

(Cries) I don't like this party any more.

> *(SANDY exits to get the cake)*

BILL

(Starts to pick up MIA *again)* Maybe it would be nicer if we could bring her over to the table again.

JEFFREY

(Out of his seat, pushes BILL *aside)* Don't touch her! You've done enough.

> *(He lifts* MIA *back to her seat, where she slumps over the table.* SANDY *enters carrying the cake, its candles blazing)*

BILL

Isn't that some cake? Come on . . . let's sing!

BILL and SANDY

(A bit mournful)
> Happy birthday to you,
> Happy birthday to you,
> Happy birthday, dear Nicky,
> Happy birthday to you!
> *(SANDY sets the cake down in front of* NICKY*)*

BILL

Huhhhhh, is that *some cake?* Come on, Nick, let's hear your wish.

NICKY

I . . . can't.

BILL

Nicky can't make his fourth-birthday wish? I don't believe it!

SANDY

Oh, Nicky!

BILL

(Whispering) Come on, try.
> *(Pause)*

NICKY

(Concentrates, takes a deep breath) I wish . . . I had a brother.
(Blows out the candles)

BILL

Good old Nick, you never know what he's going to say.

SANDY

My Nicky . . .

JEFFREY

That's quite a wish.

NICKY

I wish I had . . . three brothers!

SANDY

(Laughing) What about poor Mommy?

NICKY

I want three brothers to play with.

JEFFREY

All children need siblings.

BILL

Boy, that's all we need, three more kids.

JEFFREY

It would do Nicky good to have siblings.

NICKY

I'm lonely.

JEFFREY

The only child is more prone towards psychosis in later years . . .

NICKY

(Stamping his feet) I want three brothers for my birthday!

SANDY

He's overtired. We never should have let him come down from
his room this afternoon.

BILL

Next time you'll stay in your room!
        (MIA *slides to the floor with a thud. Grim silence)*

NICKY

I want five brothers! No, I want eleven brothers . . . thirty-seven brothers . . . a hundred brothers . . . six hundred brothers! I want nine hundred brothers!

SANDY

Oh, Nicky . . .

NICKY

Nine hundred brothers!

SANDY

But don't we have fun together? We play Babies with the masks. Daddy makes movies of us. We play Rabbit Says.

NICKY

(Wailing) I want nine hundred brothers!

SANDY

I'd like to give birth to nine hundred more babies . . . but I can't.

NICKY

Why not?

SANDY

I've been trying.

BILL

We've been trying a long time.

SANDY

Ever since you were born.

NICKY

I'm lonesome.

SANDY

There's nothing Mommy loves more than having babies, you know that, Nicky.

BILL

We've been to special doctors.

NICKY

I want someone to play with!

SANDY

No one can seem to find any medical reason why we can't conceive again, it's just one of those . . .

NICKY

I want to share my room with nine hundred brothers!

SANDY

(Upset) The doctor said if you try too hard the mommy's eggs won't come down right.

BILL

Don't . . .

SANDY

(Teary) You see, every mommy has all these unborn eggs inside her and . . .

NICKY

I want a sister!

BILL

(His arm around SANDY*)* Stop . . .

SANDY

The timing has to be just right or else the egg won't turn into a baby.

BILL

He's too young to understand.

JEFFREY

The barren woman of the Gabon Tua tribe is considered a witch.

SANDY

It's such a wonderful feeling . . . life . . . fluttering . . . inside you . . .

NICKY

Maybe you could even have twins!

JEFFREY

The barren Tot woman is taken out and drowned!

NICKY

Or triplets!

SANDY

(In tears again) Sometimes I imagine I can still feel you . . . turning inside me . . .

BILL

We haven't given up, Nicky. We're still trying!

JEFFREY

In Arabic cultures, however, the barren woman is . . .

BILL

Will you shut up?!
(Pause)

SANDY

When I looked in the mirror this morning I saw an old lady who could only conceive once.

JEFFREY

(Rises, hauls MIA *up under the arms)* Well, we have a plane to catch tomorrow.

BILL

Don't leave yet, we haven't shown you our movie of Nicky!

SANDY

My hair is falling out by the roots and I could only conceive once.

JEFFREY

I'm afraid we have to go. We're flying to Lisbon.
        *(*MIA *starts coming to, making little meowing, stretching sounds)*

BILL

(Barring JEFFREY*'s way)* Now just one minute, you said you'd see our movie!

NICKY

I want to see the movie! I want to see the movie!

MIA

What happened?

SANDY

Please stay.

BILL

I went to a lot of extra trouble having this film developed today.

SANDY

We saw your slides.

BILL.

Fair is fair!

MIA

(Stretching) Uuuuuuuuuh!

NICKY

I want to see the movie!

184

MIA

(Rises, staggers) Oooooooooh.

JEFFREY

We have two stopovers, one in Los Angeles and one in Mexico
City.

SANDY

Nicky was looking forward to your watching it with us.

MIA

I feel as if I've been run over by a train. *(Still staggering, she laughs
at herself)*

JEFFREY

You ready, darling?

MIA

(Tottery, laughing) I guess so.
        *(*SANDY *laughs with her)*

JEFFREY

(Shaking Nicky's hand) Well, Nicky, it was a great party. We'll
send you a postcard from Lisbon. *(*MIA *does a lurching little dance
around the room.* SANDY *giggles helplessly)* You can peel off the
stamp for your collection.

BILL

Nicky's stamp collection is already worth over three hundred dollars!
        *(*MIA *veers over to* NICKY *and steadies herself holding his
        face in her hands)*

MIA

Nicky . . .

BILL

(Pointing to NICKY *and mouthing the letters)* He's very B–R–I–G–
H–T.

MIA

. . . you're a love.

SANDY

Stay!

MIA

. . . so helpless . . . *(She kisses him)*

JEFFREY

Mia, we have a plane to catch tomorrow!

MIA

We do have a plane to catch tomorrow . . . and a very intriguing urban culture to study!

SANDY

. . . just a minute more!

JEFFREY

(At the door) The post office will forward our mail!

MIA

We'll send stamps . . . lots of stamps!
(They're gone. Silence)

BILL

That son of a bitch.

SANDY

(By the door) They left.

BILL

We sat through his lousy slides, but do you think he'd have the courtesy to watch our movie??! "The post office will forward our mail!" *Jesus!*

SANDY

They left.

NICKY

I want to see the movie!
(SANDY yelps, her hand flying to her mouth)

BILL

Well, shit on him, we'll see the movie without them!

SANDY

My front tooth just fell out!

NICKY

I want to see my movie!

SANDY

(Shows it to BILL) My front tooth just fell out.

BILL

(Sets up the projector and screen) You'll see your movie, Nick, don't worry.

SANDY

I'll have to call the dentist tomorrow. I can't walk around like this.
(Flashes a smile with a blacked-out front tooth)

BILL

(Dims the lights) All right, folks, is everybody ready for one hell
of a movie?

NICKY

Faster! Faster!

SANDY

(Showing NICKY*)* Look at Mommy's tooth, Nicky. What do you
think? *(*BILL *sings a fanfare)* It looks so . . . small . . . lying in my
hand.

NICKY

Will the whole movie be just of me?

SANDY

The other one is loose too.

(Blurred images start up on the screen)

BILL

(Starts clapping in anticipation) Hey, Nicky!

NICKY

(Imitating BILL*)* Hey, Daddy!

BILL

(Clapping) Hey, Sandy!

NICKY

(Imitating) Hey, Mommy!

SANDY

(Dreamy) Nicky on his fourth birthday . . . my Nicky . . .

BILL

(Clapping joyously) Four years old!

NICKY

(Throws his arms around SANDY *and* BILL*)* Look! Look! Look! Look!
(They freeze in an endless embrace)

SANDY

Four years ago today, Nicky, you made us the happiest family in
the world!

(The curtain slowly falls)

Mourning Pictures

by
HONOR MOORE

*The mourning picture, which usually showed a grave-
stone with the survivors grieving beside it, was an art
form popular in the early nineteenth century, especially
in New England. Young women stitched or painted
them for bereaved friends.*

"**I** remember being on the Eastern Shuttle going to visit my mother in Washington, D.C., while she was dying of cancer. There were all these very strong feelings inside me that seemed to have an almost independent life. I was just sitting there, and none of the other passengers knew, or, I thought, would have wanted to know, what I was feeling. So I opened my journal and wrote, 'Ladies and gentlemen, my mother is dying . . .' because I couldn't say it—that was the first part of *Mourning Pictures*."

At the age of ten, Honor Moore collaborated with her sixth-grade class on a play about Ancient Egypt. That was the beginning of an obsession which kept her in the theatre, in nearly every capacity, for many years. In 1970, after co-producing *The Nest* by Tina Howe off-Broadway, she began to write full time. "Because I always performed my poems and because of my theatre background, it seemed natural to say yes when Mary Silverman and Lyn Austin asked me to write a play about my mother's dying, instead of the book of poems I'd planned." *Mourning Pictures*, Moore's first play, was produced by Austin and Silverman at the Lenox Arts Center with Leora Dana and Kathryn Walker in the leading roles; Kay Carney directed, and Susan Ain composed the music. In November 1974, the same production moved to the Lyceum Theatre on Broadway.

Moore has traveled extensively around the country, giving readings of her poems (including excerpts from *Mourning Pictures*). She has taught women's writing workshops at the Manhattan Theatre Club and the Henry Street Settlement House, and contributes reviews and articles to *Ms.* Her poems have been published in *Chrysalis, The Nation, Amazon Quarterly, American Review* and other magazines and in *The New Woman's Survival Sourcebook* and *We Become New: Poems by Contemporary American Women*. She won a CAPS Fellowship in playwrighting in 1976 from the New York Council on the Arts, is at work completing her first collection of poems, and has begun a second play. She lives in New York City.

CHARACTERS

MARGARET, twenty-seven   A poet. Lives in New York City, but spends time at an old house in Kent, a small town in Connecticut.

ABIGAIL, nineteen   A student. Shares an apartment with David, her boyfriend.

DAVID, twenty   A student. His twentieth birthday occurs during the play.

MAGGIE, fifty   A mother of nine (including Margaret and Abigail) who has finished bringing up her children and is on the threshold of a new, independent life.

PHILIP, fifty-two   Maggie's husband. His life work has been helping people. That he is a clergyman is almost incidental.

DR. RUMBACH, about fifty   The surgeon. There are traces of his German background in his speech.

DR. THOMAS BERRYMAN, early forties   The vitamin therapist. Psychiatrist who has been converted to organic medicine.

DR. POTTER, about eighty   A chiropractor-nutritionist. Has been healing people for fifty years. Folksy.

DR. CASSIDY   A young surgeon.

SINGER

The doctors should be played by one actor. The songs, sung by a woman singer on stage but far to one side, are a counterpoint to the action.

The action takes place during a recent year, in Washington, D.C., with certain incidents in New York City and Connecticut. Places should be suggested with lighting and with minimal scenery and props in specific areas of a unit set.

Part One

MARCH THROUGH MAY

March 29. Afternoon.
Kent, Connecticut.

MARGARET
The telephone rings. I answer.
Hello? I hear nothing.
It frightens me.

MAGGIE
Margaret.

MARGARET
It's my mother. It doesn't sound
like her. A week ago I wrote
her, I love you.

MAGGIE
Margaret.

MARGARET
Not the perfunctory "I
love you." A new one. The real one.

MAGGIE
I went to the gynecologist.
She examined me.
Tomorrow I go to
the hospital for tests. She found—

MARGARET
Alone in a red coat she walks
down a long white hall—

MAGGIE
                                    She
found a lump in my right
side. Margaret—

MARGARET
In bed in a room. They
hold her wrist.

MAGGIE
I'm scared!

MARGARET
I love you.

MAGGIE
Why is this happening?

MARGARET
I'm here, Mom. I love you.

I refuse to share her terror.
My new ability to say
"I love you" right out to
my own mother is an
act of courage great enough to
save the whole world.

March 31. Two A.M.
Kent, Connecticut.

MARGARET
I am sleeping. The phone rings. It is dark.
The clock says two. It is my father.

PHILIP
I just
want to tell you—Maggie's
in the hospital.

MARGARET
I was sleeping. Wasn't
it just for tests?

PHILIP
We don't know for sure—

MARGARET
I don't want to wake up.

PHILIP
                    —the surgeon
says it's probably cancer.
The question is how far the tumor's spread.

MARGARET
I can't comfort him. I want to go back
to sleep.

PHILIP
        I'm sorry.

MARGARET
        I'll call—

PHILIP
                    I'll call after
we know more.

MARGARET
        I know this call
at two A.M. means he wants more than to
tell me—

PHILIP
        Good night, Margaret.

MARGARET
                    —but I am cold.
I run to bed. It is easy to sleep.

April 3. Eight A.M.
New York. Airport.

MARGARET
The next phone call: she has cancer.
They must remove a tumor
    from her colon or
she will die immediately.
While they operate
    they will biopsy
her liver to learn if the lump
under her breast is malignant.

195

Eight A.M. in the Air Shuttle
Terminal. I am going
    to see her. I buy
Newsweek and the *New York Times.* I
stand in line for Washington.
    I see an old friend
pass. He doesn't see me. I don't
give up my place to say hello.

April 3. Afternoon.
Washington, D.C. Hospital.

MAGGIE *is in a hospital bed. There is a basket of spring flowers*
in the room.

MARGARET

I want to see her before the surgery.
    (After seeing her)
She looks different than she did
just two weeks ago at her fiftieth
birthday party.
She is a sick woman.

*(*MARGARET *kisses her mother,*
    then sits down beside the bed)
MAGGIE

(Warm) Hi. When did you get in?
MARGARET

I came straight from the airport.
MAGGIE

Did someone meet you?
MARGARET

I rented a car. I wanted to be independent.
MAGGIE

Good idea.
MARGARET

When will they operate?

MAGGIE

Seven-thirty A.M. Tomorrow.

MARGARET

I thought Thursday!

MAGGIE

They moved it up.

MARGARET

(About the flowers) Who sent those divine things?

MAGGIE

I haven't even looked.

MARGARET

(Taking card from basket) I love opening things! *(Looks at card)*
It's from the Lawrences.

MAGGIE

She had it.

MARGARET

I didn't know that—

MAGGIE

Years ago. Then she had something in her stomach last month.
They were terrified, but it was just a cyst. Nothing. Nothing like
mine. *(After a silence)* Everything was just starting! Do you have
a Kleenex? *(MARGARET gives her one)* I want you to know I've
made a new will. It's harder this way, but your father and I
promised we wouldn't have secrets. We've asked Dr. Rumbach to
tell us both everything at the same time. And we planned my
funeral, just in case tomorrow isn't successful.

> *(MAGGIE and MARGARET are quiet during the song, as if
> each is alone)*

SONG

> A ring or two.
> The turquoise beads.
> The green-striped chair.
> What will she leave me
> Except alone by myself?
> No one to have the final word!

What will she leave me—
A will,
A legal sheaf of papers
Sealed with blood-red wax—
They put it in a vault until you die—
Not forever—
Just until you die!

A ring or two.
The painting on the stairs
Her mother did
Of her asleep at three
That looks a lot like me—
Will she leave me that?

The turquoise beads
The green-striped chair
The old French silverware
The antique quilt
I bought for her—
Will I get it back?

April 5.
Washington, D.C. Hospital.
Ultramodern intensive-care unit.

DR. RUMBACH

Our surgery to remove the tumor has been successful.
We were able to sew her colon back together.
It will mend.
Now we wait for the results of the liver biopsy. If
the tests are positive, there is only time: Liver
cancer is inoperable.

PHILIP

Margaret and I go to see her in the new intensive-care
unit. She has two I.V.'s stuck in her arm.

MAGGIE

(Waking)   Doesn't
this look like a spaceship?

198

MARGARET
Yes.

PHILIP

How do you feel?

(DR. RUMBACH comes into the room)

MAGGIE
Hello, Doctor.

(He leans over, takes MAGGIE*'s hand and whispers that her tests are positive, that the cancer has spread to her liver. The audience doesn't hear him.* MAGGIE *moans)*

There's no hope, no hope at all!

MARGARET

(Walks out of the room)

Do you know when something terrible is happening
to you—or you think it is, you're not sure—
the relief you feel
when you find out it's really true?
When you finally
know your mother has cancer and might die,
how you feel, at last, legitimate?

April 6.
Washington, D.C. Hospital
Intensive-care unit.

MAGGIE *sits up abruptly, as if healthy.*

MAGGIE
I was in this hospital three years ago
in an identical room after
the impact of a STOP-running car hitting
broadside socked a Volkswagen gearshift
stick straight into my abdomen. Right after,
I felt fine. Hours after, I complained
my stomach hurt. On the table they found my
body cavity filled with blood. It
took nine hours. They cut away seven-tenths of
my liver. Luckily the surgeon

199

on duty was a liver man. Within five
   months my liver grew back (it is the
only human organ that can), I got well
   and we all thought I was good as new,
better, and I was, probably, for a while.

April 6.
Washington, D.C. Hospital.

MARGARET *waits at home alone for news.* ABIGAIL *and* DAVID *wait in a consulting room.* DR. RUMBACH *comes in.*

DR. RUMBACH

I wish I had never met your mother. I am so sorry. I regret I made her well after the accident. You know the liver tests were positive. What can I tell you?

ABIGAIL

Is it all through her?

DR. RUMBACH

The cancer has spread through all five lobes . . .

MARGARET

   Off-white against the wine color the liver is,
   like a web, irregular like the patterns fat makes
   in raw beef—

DR. RUMBACH

. . . to the stomach and the top of the lungs.

ABIGAIL

Is her liver still working?

DAVID

Some of it has to be.

DR. RUMBACH

Twenty percent is still working. The liver is a vital organ. Without a liver, we don't survive.

ABIGAIL

One tumor?

DR. RUMBACH

You know we took the tumor out of the colon. This gives her more

time—but we cannot operate and the tumor next to the liver is
the size of a grapefruit.

MARGARET

A large soft ball, the size of a softball
women use to play.

ABIGAIL

How long—

MARGARET

Floating.
Attached delicately with strands.

ABIGAIL

How long do people with this kind of cancer usually live?

DR. RUMBACH

Six months. At the most.

MARGARET

He tried to tell us more.
He said we have to prepare ourselves.
I didn't want to hear any more.
The walls in that room started to move.
I didn't want to hear.

April 10. Night.
Kent, Connecticut.

ABIGAIL

(In Washington, answering the telephone) Hello.

MARGARET

Hi. I wanted to know how things are.

ABIGAIL

Aunt Julia got here last night. She looks so sad.

MARGARET

I'll be down Friday. Will she still be there?

ABIGAIL

Until Saturday, when Pop gets back.

MARGARET

Oh.

ABIGAIL

He went up to New York to see that liver cancer specialist.

MARGARET

How's Mom?

ABIGAIL

Out of intensive care, in one of those big rooms for a few days.

MARGARET

Like after the accident—

ABIGAIL

Yes.

MARGARET

Is she feeling any better?

ABIGAIL

I think so. David and I took some clothes over this morning and she was all smiley. Then she fell asleep. I woke up this morning crying. I guess my dreams couldn't handle all my grief—

MARGARET

I'm dreaming a lot—

ABIGAIL

Margaret—

MARGARET

Yes.

ABIGAIL

I was sleeping.

MARGARET

Oooh, I'm sorry. You go back.

ABIGAIL

I'm sorry. I mean, I love you. I just can't talk any more.

April 13. Afternoon.
Washington, D.C. Hospital.

Flowers and get-well presents surround MAGGIE's *bed.*

MARGARET
At the hospital with Julia, my mother's

sister, it's like a party—she wears a
pretty nightgown and sits up. I forget
she is sick. I forget where I am.
In the middle of a conversation
about the weather, the children and flowers:

MAGGIE

Julia, I'm leaving Mark Mumma's engagement
ring to give his bride someday. I want you
to wear it until then, it's so pretty.
You wouldn't mind giving it up for Mark?

MARGARET

Julia says "No, Maggie, I wouldn't mind."
I feel like an intruder, a child, six,
overhearing parents' plans for Christmas.
All of a sudden she is quite yellow.

MAGGIE

I'd like to take a nap now. I loved seeing
you girls. Why don't you come back tomorrow?

(MARGARET *moves away from the room*)

MARGARET

Outside the room in a vestibule with
one aqua wall, Julia's face goes red. I
hold her as she cries. "Why do these terrible
things happen to the people you love!"

April 15. Morning.
Washington, D.C. Hospital.

MARGARET

She is sleeping, I watch her. I calm my breathing.
I shut my eyes and concentrate on what I feel
inside my body.

I open my eyes. The room is full of sun. She's still
there, on her right side, on the blue sheets, breathing.

In some primitive birth rituals, the father mimes
labor contractions nearby as the woman gives birth.

203

With my mind I try to feel what she feels and send
her some of my health.

MAGGIE

(Opens her eyes) Hi, sweetie.

(DR. CASSIDY walks in jauntily, wearing a white lab coat)
Good morning! Have you met my oldest daughter?

DR. CASSIDY

No, I don't believe I have. *(He shakes* MARGARET's *hand)*

MARGARET

How do you do?

MAGGIE

Will you get some golf in later?

DR. CASSIDY

I sure hope to.

MAGGIE

You're lucky. It's such a beautiful day!

DR. CASSIDY

(To MARGARET*)* You have quite a mom.

MARGARET

Yes.

DR. CASSIDY

Will you excuse us a moment?

MARGARET

Sure. *(She goes out into the corridor)*

DR. CASSIDY

Well, how are we feeling today?

MAGGIE

Uncomfortable still.

DR. CASSIDY

That will continue a few days.

*(DR. CASSIDY shuffles through his bag, finds his stethoscope
and begins the examination, which continues as* MARGARET
paces outside)

MARGARET

I go out to wait. This is the penthouse wing.
Huge rooms. Carpets. To make you forget.
Flowers—white, pink—through a half-open door.

Drawn faces watch a presence on a bed
the door blocks. I see lumps,
feet under a sheet. Do they still walk? Will
she take more than six months to die? Will I
have an invalid mother? I'm tired of waiting.

DR. CASSIDY

Margaret—

MARGARET

I make my walk casual—

DR. CASSIDY

Your mother wants you.

(DR. CASSIDY exits. MARGARET goes back into the room)

MAGGIE

Will you help me walk?

(MAGGIE awkwardly sits up. MARGARET awkwardly helps her. She gets MAGGIE's slippers from under the bed and helps her put them on)

MAGGIE

Maybe I should wear something warmer.

(MARGARET gets MAGGIE's bathrobe from a hook near the bed and helps her put it on. MAGGIE extends her arms. She is ready to stand up. MARGARET, not knowing what to expect, but finding MAGGIE lighter than she thought, helps her mother to her feet. They walk slowly up the long corridor once and back again. MARGARET holds MAGGIE around the waist to help her balance)

This helps me heal, but God it hurts!

MARGARET

We pass a white-haired man. A bent woman with glasses helps him.

MAGGIE

(As if the old man is where audience is) Good morning. How are you today? *(They get back to MAGGIE's room. MARGARET carefully helps her off with the slippers and bathrobe and back into bed, then stands waiting, holding the bathrobe)* That's all right. I don't need anything. *(About the bathrobe)* Just hang it up.

205

(DR. CASSIDY pokes his head in)

DR. CASSIDY

Just wanted to say goodbye—

MAGGIE

My daughter took me on a walk all the way up the hall and back.
Pretty good, don't you think?

DR. CASSIDY

Terrific! *(He exits)*

MAGGIE

I'm so pleased about our walk! Yesterday I went only half as far.

MARGARET

It must really hurt.

MAGGIE

Not as much today.

MARGARET

How much longer do you think you'll be here?

MAGGIE

It depends what I do next.

MARGARET

What do you think you will do?

MAGGIE

Not chemotherapy. I remember Mrs. Falk. She had it. I'm not
going to do it. It's just a holding action, never a cure. I want
my last days, if they are my last days, to be as happy as they
can be.

MARGARET

I agree.

MAGGIE

I want the little ones to remember me as me—not as some
charred, alienated vegetable they can't know.

> *(MARGARET kisses her mother goodbye and moves out of the
> hospital area)*

MARGARET

> I drive to the airport, return
> the rented car, fly back to
> New York, to my life.
> That night, I go out with close friends—

I say little, I hear voices, I can't
    distinguish words. I hate
the way they look at me. I want
to be in Washington, the room with
    the flowers. With her.

May 5. Afternoon.
Washington, D.C.

ABIGAIL

Today Poppy and David and I went to the hospital to bring Mom
back. Not back home, but to the Simons', our neighbors, who live
down the street. They both work during the day, so Mom thought
she would have more peace and quiet there than she would at
home with all the kids running in and out. People will come
to stay with her for a few days at a time—Margaret comes
early tomorrow morning. Ann, my other older sister who's married and twenty-four, will have the next shift. And I'll be there
a lot.

May 6. Morning.
Washington, D.C. The Simons' house.

PHILIP *sits studying.* MAGGIE *is asleep upstairs.* MARGARET *comes*
in carrying an overnight bag.

MARGARET

Hi.

PHILIP

(Gives her a big hug and kiss) So glad you're here.

MARGARET

Phew. God, I hate to fly. It exhausts me for a week.

PHILIP

(Apologetic) Would you like some freeze-dried coffee?

MARGARET

No, I don't think so, thanks.

MARGARET

He looks so out of place.

PHILIP

Maggie's sleeping. I was just finishing up for Sunday.

MARGARET

A sermon?

PHILIP

Someone else is taking the morning service. This is just a little talk for some students in the afternoon.

MARGARET

You're going to keep working?

PHILIP

I want time with her. After I pull together some last things, I'm going to take a short leave.

MARGARET

Why didn't she go straight home?

PHILIP

It would have been a lot easier—

MARGARET

Things have been—

PHILIP

Heavy. The surgery made her very weak.

MARGARET

What's going to happen?

PHILIP

She's decided against chemotherapy.

MARGARET

She told me. But what else—

PHILIP

There's a whole cancer-cure underground.

MARGARET

I thought it was too far along for us to have any hope—

MAGGIE

(Shouts from her bedroom upstairs) Philip! Philip!

PHILIP

Yes.

MAGGIE

What are you saying about me?

MARGARET
We should go upstairs.
(They go to MAGGIE*'s bedroom)*

SONG
*(*MARGARET*'s point of view)*
"What are you saying about
   me now?"
Can't you see my father and I
   are trying to speak?

MARGARET
Hi, Mom.
*(*MAGGIE *says nothing)*

You say our sounds come
   from the mouth of a
   prison warden!
You say our sounds come
   from the mouth of a
   reform school matron!

PHILIP
Can I get something for you,
sweetie?
*(*MARGARET *goes toward her)*

What are you saying about
   me now?
That we are two against one?
That we are the living who
   conspire against the dying?

MAGGIE
How can you talk behind my
back? You don't understand!
What were you saying about
me? I'm not a child. *(Like a
child)* You don't understand.
I'm lost. Everything's gone.
Lost.

In blue, she sees wisteria,
   bright lavender she planted
With her own hands, before
   any of this began—

PHILIP
Do you want to sit up for a
while?

MARGARET

I'll sit with you.

MAGGIE

I want to go downstairs. Why don't you go? Margaret can help me.

MARGARET

We'll manage. You go on.

PHILIP

I'll be back.

*(*PHILIP *exits)*

MARGARET

She is like a cat gone mad, hissing from fear. I am afraid to touch her. I don't know where the wound is.

The sounds we make surround her—

"Please understand how far I'm lost!"

She is like a cat gone mad, hissing from fear—

I am afraid to touch her.

I don't know where the wound is.

*(*MARGARET *helps* MAGGIE *into her slippers, supports her as she stands. They begin the walk to the living room. They had both imagined* MAGGIE *was more recovered than she is)*

MAGGIE

(A yelp) Jesus!

MARGARET

Are we going too fast?

MAGGIE

No. No. I'm fine. *(After a few steps)* It hurts like hell!

MARGARET

(Adjusts her grip) We're almost there. *(They reach the sofa.* MARGARET *carefully sits* MAGGIE *down)*

MAGGIE

I didn't think it would be this hard. I'm sorry.

MARGARET

It's all right. It hurts. Just . . . just . . . Why don't you . . . Can you sleep?

MAGGIE

I'll shut my eyes a little while.

PHILIP

(From another area) In the beginning I thought she should have

210

chemotherapy. I thought refusing was her way, after all our truth, of denying what was happening to her. Then Dr. Rumbach said he agreed—that chemotherapy has side effects which change the emotions. He suggested we take a bottle of Johnny Walker Black and a Caribbean cruise—*carpe diem*—but Maggie's never been the kind to sit around doing nothing.

> *(ABIGAIL and DAVID come in. ABIGAIL is carrying a bag of groceries. When they see MAGGIE is asleep, they quiet down, but they are still full of giggles)*

MAGGIE

(Wakes up) Where's Abigail?

DAVID

In the kitchen. We brought some ginger ale.

MAGGIE

Oh! Can I have some?

> *(MARGARET leaves the room)*

DAVID

Would you like me to rub your feet?

> *(MAGGIE offers a foot. MARGARET and ABIGAIL come in. ABIGAIL carries a glass of ginger ale. She gives it to MAGGIE. DAVID is still rubbing MAGGIE's feet)*

MAGGIE

I feel so much better! It's the mornings. I wake up at five and feel I'm no one no where. I can't do anything for myself. Ooooooh, David! That feels divine!

ABIGAIL

It's great to rub your feet. In China there are doctors who treat each organ by rubbing a different part of your foot.

MAGGIE

MMMmmmmmmmm.

> *(DAVID continues to rub MAGGIE's feet with ABIGAIL looking on as PHILIP speaks again)*

PHILIP

When I first heard about the O'Briens, I was suspicious. Probably because I'm an old square at heart. But I wanted to give Maggie

211

as many options as I could, so David and I went to see them. Eighteen months ago, doctors told Mrs. O'Brien she had six months—she's only twenty-five!—but she and her husband were enough into the counterculture bit not to despair. They began to read everything they could and eventually were put in touch with some people in the Southwest, a psychic and a nutritionist, to whom they sent a blood sample and a photograph. The psychic analyzed the blood sample and the photograph—not chemically, but with something, a small weight on the end of a string which apparently went bloop-de-doop, doop, every which way. Then the nutritionist prescribed certain herbs and diet supplements. It sounded nuts to me, but Mrs. O'Brien really seems to have recovered. More important, though, is the kind of people they are— really open and genuine—and in my life, the Church, I've met a lot of quack healers.

MAGGIE

(DAVID *is telling her a story*) Then what happened?

DAVID

Well, he said, "Rewrite it!"

MAGGIE

God.

MARGARET

(*Comes in*) Ready, Abbie?

ABIGAIL

Mom, we're going to take a walk.

MAGGIE

See you soon.

(MARGARET *and* ABIGAIL *go out*)

MAGGIE

(*To* DAVID) So you like it there still.

DAVID

Yes. I'm really learning. When I quit school, I never thought I'd go to college, but here I am—

MAGGIE

I know what you mean. When I started taking the courses last fall, I thought, how extraordinary to be able to do this, after nearly thirty years and nine children, back in school and learning so much! *(She stops talking, puts her hand across her face, shakes her head)* I'm sorry. *(*DAVID *helps* MAGGIE *on with her bathrobe and back to her bedroom, careful to support her)* That's what I said to Margaret this morning, "I'm sorry." It bores me so! I'm tired of asking.

DAVID

Yes—

MAGGIE

Margaret's strong, but I didn't know how bad I'd be when I asked her to be here. *(Takes herself in hand)* Well, I won't say any more about that! *(*DAVID *helps her into bed)* You take care of Abigail so well! *(He just looks at her)* Will you refill my ginger ale? *(*DAVID *goes out, and returns after a while with a new glass of ginger ale. Simultaneously,* MARGARET *and* ABIGAIL *walk, stopping occasionally)*

ABIGAIL

. . . all my time with her. Even before this
I wanted that. We could have gone away
to school—

MARGARET

—you and David—

ABIGAIL

—but we came here. We finally got our own
apartment, but we'd come home twice a week!

MARGARET

Strange—

ABIGAIL

Then I took the same
prose-writing class she did. I used to stare
as if I had to memorize her. Now
I want to touch her: I
brush her hair, rub her feet, wrists, back—to help
her energy; read to her when she's tired.
At school Thursdays is

213

when I miss her most: I have my Coke alone
our free half-hour, try hard to picture her
on the next counter stool
and, sometimes, when a funny thing from school
flashes through my mind, I hear her laugh!

MARGARET
I'm so glad you exist.

May 8. Evening.
Washington, D.C. The Simons' porch.

MARGARET
You must understand I came home wanting
the good talks we always had, but she's too weak.
Three days I cook, carry her up, down stairs,
    watch visitors come, go.
But because she is weak, she is no one.
I am alone in a house I cannot
make familiar and I am tired. Each
    morning at six, five: My
name. My name. I climb out of a dream, stumble
to her, she yelping with fear—I suppress
mine, soothe hers. I'm locked up in her—why
    am I so selfish? Last
night she wanted a bath. Abigail
asked to do it. I was relieved. This morning
she said "Abigail has such a gift for
    healing. She gave me the
most gentle bath, made me feel my body
was mine again." What do I have a gift for?
Later Mrs. Simon said "Come with me."
    She took me, showed me trees—
Spring is early here—she told me her dreams,
plans, and asked nothing, just that I walk slow
with her through the night, past houses, dark, dogs . . .

214

The air is cool. I breathe.
I will go home and rest, come back next week.

May 10. Afternoon.
Kent, Connecticut.

MARGARET

My father called today. He sounded better than he has in weeks.
He's found a doctor he feels comfortable with. Mom will meet
him today. His name is Dr. Berryman. He's a Harvard-educated
former psychiatrist who's been converted to homeopathy.

May 10.
Washington, D.C.

DR. BERRYMAN

Mononucleosis at forty. Fever
a hundred and four—I could not lift myself
from bed for months.
You feel you have no blood. My body was
burning, burning. They couldn't heal me. Heal
myself or burn away—

I began to feed myself to make me
live: minerals, wheat sprouts, kelp, alfalfa,
lemon, lime, anything
real. I gave up force, chemicals, the knife.
I accepted magic "Heal like with like"
learned what stories a dark

speck in your eye's iris can tell. I waited
to think with my body, let the sun come
freely through my skin—
I didn't burn. Meditating day after
day, listening to my breathing, my blood,
I found my way back.

215

May 20. Noon.
Washington, D.C. Outdoors.

(DR. BERRYMAN *shows* MAGGIE *meditating postures, and how to*
breathe, as they speak. The others watch)

DR. BERRYMAN

At noon each day without rain, stand fifteen
minutes—no less, full abdomen exposed—
in the sun. Shut your eyes.
In your mind, see dark poisons leave you,
leave your body free to heal itself—

MAGGIE

Leave my body, leave me.

At the same time I try to feel them leave,
then I lie down flat, under the sun, half
an hour, middle bare
again—a kind of trance—and, eyes shut, form
a message—my insides make the words—sweet
clear sun, come into me.

I'm sure the neighbors think I'm crazy: Why
doesn't she just relax and die? But I
will not. I feel something
being wrenched down there. It hurts, then I feel
the sun-heat baking me, and like magic,
some diamond-sweet relief.

May 20. Afternoon.
New York City. Dr. Potter's office.

MARGARET

I go to an eighty-year-old chiropractor and
nutritionist. I want to be massaged, healed with someone's hands.
I need care. I sit in a wing chair, ache for his hands—
First he talks to me about my structure, points out disasters

216

on a lit-up, full-length X-ray of my spine.
He starts the interview gently.

DR. POTTER

How's your energy?

MARGARET

I can't work in the afternoon.

DR. POTTER

What kind of work do you do?

MARGARET

I'm a poet.

DR. POTTER

How often are the headaches?

MARGARET

Most days.

DR. POTTER

Do you sit up straight when you type?

MARGARET

I try.

DR. POTTER

How much mental
work do you do each day?

MARGARET

About four hours.

DR. POTTER

Did you know that mental work uses fifteen times the
energy of physical work?

MARGARET

No.

DR. POTTER

Do you exercise?

MARGARET

Some.

DR. POTTER

Can you nourish yourself?

MARGARET

What?

DR. POTTER

               Do you know how to feed
your children the right foods?

MARGARET

          I'm single. I eat balanced meals.

DR. POTTER

Do you cook properly?

MARGARET

    I try to.

DR. POTTER

      Often
cooking drains all the nutritious properties—

MARGARET

                I know.

DR. POTTER

—from our foods, and we don't know it. We've eaten fodder,
cotton batting! The blood has gotten nothing. Then your
body must eliminate all the waste, which sometimes it just
can't do entirely.

MARGARET

      Yes.

DR. POTTER

      We're not perfect!
Congestion, constipation result. You don't feel well;
toxins collect and irritate, finally poison your tissues.
This is why we recommend the vegetable juices.
Purification. Begin with a quart of carrot each day,
fourteen days, then switch to half-beet–half-carrot—

MARGARET

Yes.

DR. POTTER

—ten more days. Then the last week you add the green juice.

MARGARET

What kind?

DR. POTTER

    Any of your greens: celery, cucumber, lettuce—

then we'll have your blood free of toxicity, back to
zero! Of course, you can't get back more than you started out with!

DR. POTTER

MARGARET

I get a juicer.

DR. POTTER

Not just any juicer.
Most machines we see are centrifugal. They don't grind
sufficient to release the minerals which digestion can't.
Only the Walker machine. Expensive, very rare—

MARGARET

Where do I get one?

DR. POTTER

You see, the secret's elimination:
Draining out all the wastes. And prevention. Pre-
ven-tion! Why, I had a lady with cancer in here
just a few months ago and we cleared it up with vegetable
juices. So you hear what I'm telling you, my dear! We've
got to free your circulation, get a fresh clean blood supply
to your nerves—

MARGARET

STOP! Stop, I can't hear these things now.
You see, my mother has cancer. Her liver,
and all through her . . .

DR. POTTER

(Genuine) I'm sorry. I didn't know.

May 20.
New York

MARGARET

Ladies and gentlemen, my mother is
dying. You say "Everyone's mother dies."
I bow to you, smile. Ladies, gentlemen,
my mother is dying. She has cancer.
You say "Many people die of cancer."
I scratch my head. Gentle ladies, gentle

219

men, my mother has cancer, and, short of
some miracle, will die. You say "This has
happened many times before." You say "Death
is something which repeats itself." I bow.
Ladies and gentlemen, my mother has cancer
all through her. She will die unless there's
a miracle. You shrug. You gave up religion
years ago. Marxism too. You don't believe
in anything. I step forward. My mother
is dying. I don't believe in miracles.
Ladies and gentlemen, one last time: My
mother's dying. I haven't got another.

Part Two

JUNE THROUGH SEPTEMBER

June 1. Early afternoon.
Washington, D.C. The house.

MAGGIE *is up and around. She has recovered from her surgery.*
Everyone is enthusiastic about the new cure.

DAVID
Maggie's been on Dr. Berryman's treatments
fourteen days, and she's looking much better—

PHILIP
Someone gave us those restaurant food racks
on wheels. They're out back, tall with lots of shelves,
layers of aluminum trays. Each tray
can be a planter for some of the wheat.

DAVID
Wheat is loaded with vitamin A and
minerals, but it tastes terrible, like
watercress when you're not in the mood—that
green taste: you think a leaf is edible—
but you're wrong!

MAGGIE
No one else would go near it, but *he* didn't
think I should have to drink alone.

PHILIP
When you've used up a tray of sprouts, empty
it on the compost out back, refill it
with earth and a little fertilizer
and put it in a warm oven for two
hours. This sterilizes it, then you're
ready to plant. Let each batch germinate
in the cellar in the dark. After three—

ABIGAIL

No, four—

PHILIP

Too many cooks. After four days, move them
outdoors onto one of the racks. And then—

ABIGAIL

—when the grasses are six inches tall—

DAVID

—cut off a bunch with kitchen shears and put
it through that huge grinder on the kitchen
counter. It's specially made, from Vermont,
but, unfortunately, *you* have to crank it!

MAGGIE

I take a cup a day, quick like this, then
someone gives me a sprout poultice at four—

PHILIP

I'm going. I'll be back for supper.

MAGGIE

Have a good game!

DAVID

Bye, Philip.

ABIGAIL

See you later!

You cut cheesecloth into squares and put them
in a bowl of wheat sprout juice to soak. When
you're ready to start the poultice, you wring
each piece slightly (so it doesn't get all
over), then build a gloppy green cloth mound
on her belly.

DAVID

The quickest route
to the liver is right through the skin.

MAGGIE

Then

I'm supposed to nap. I'm always sure I
can't sleep, but Berryman always says "Just
close your eyes." So I do, and the poultice starts

to vibrate! My mind is very clear—then
I feel calm all over and—poof!—dreamland!
DAVID
Wheat is just the weird part. She has to take
a hundred—more—vitamin and mineral
pills a day, all at different times, to build
up her strength. We put them all in bottles
on top of the bookshelf in her room: Breakfast
Pills, After Breakfast Pills, Lunch Pills, Before
Nap Pills, Supper Pills, Bedtime Pills. Six rows,
all coded so anyone can do them.
ABIGAIL
Next to the pills on the shelf is a blue
spiral notebook we keep for Berryman.
We check off the pills there and write down how
she's feeling and what she says about it
so when the doctor comes in the evening,
we'll remember to ask him everything.

July 10.
Kent, Connecticut.

MARGARET
We spent the first summer here clearing—
we cut down saplings and planted grass seed
to extend the lawn to the brook—
And we have roses! My mother gave me
seven my twenty-seventh birthday. They
arrived in April brown and dry. We dug
holes two feet deep, built mounds in the bottoms
to support the pyramids of sleeping
roots, and flooded the plants with water,
centering each in a gelatinous pack
of mud and humus. In May the red spuds
became new canes. We've had roses three weeks.
MARGARET
(Answering the telephone) Hello.

223

MAGGIE

Hello, dear.

MARGARET

Is that you, Mom?

MAGGIE

I feel wonderful.

MARGARET

Your voice sounds so much stronger.

MAGGIE

Yes.

MARGARET

Dr. Berryman.

MAGGIE

I can't tell you what a difference he makes. I feel myself getting stronger, and I have no pain. I'm taking *nothing* for pain.

MARGARET

I hear you take a lot of vitamins.

MAGGIE

It's disgusting. I thought I'd taken a lot of pills in my time, but forty at once is over the line.

MARGARET

Have you been going out?

MAGGIE

Well, I'm not quite ready for tennis, but Mrs. Claremont lent us the pool, and I've been once. It's just heaven. And I've been rocketing along with my writing.

MARGARET

You have?

MAGGIE

Dictating two hours a day. I'm never going back to the other. Never. Dictation's a breeze. Edith sits with her back to me, takes it all down, and comes back the next day with typed pages!

MARGARET

I'm so jealous!

MAGGIE

We're determined to get me into print.

July 12. Afternoon.
Washington, D.C. The house.

MAGGIE *is sitting in the living room editing transcripts of her writing.* DR. BERRYMAN *comes in.*

MAGGIE

Hello, Dr. Berryman. Take a load off your feet.

DR. BERRYMAN

(Sitting down) How is it today?

MAGGIE

(Pats her stomach) Much less pain.

DR. BERRYMAN

Good. *(Puts a thermometer in her mouth)* I want to start you on more citrus juices.

MAGGIE

(In spite of the thermometer in her mouth) Orange?

DR. BERRYMAN

All of them. Mixed. Lemon, lime, grapefruit.

MAGGIE

I can still have ginger ale—

DR. BERRYMAN

You decide. Whenever you can, I want you to take citrus for your liquid. We want as much C in natural form as we can get. *(He takes the thermometer out of her mouth)* You've been normal since last night?

MAGGIE

Yes.

DR. BERRYMAN

Good.

MAGGIE

When do we start phase two?

(The examination continues as PHILIP *speaks)*

PHILIP

(From another area) When Tom Berryman took Maggie's case, he said he'd start by building her up physically. Surgery under any circumstance is exhausting and she's had so much, we have to be

225

very careful. When she's strong, we start a second phase: actually destroying the cancer cells. Sometimes this treatment turns the body around: The process of the disease reverses, tumors shrink, disappear. These remissions do happen, but usually in cases less advanced than Maggie's.

DR. BERRYMAN

We'll start Monday, but you have to be prepared for more discomfort.

MAGGIE

I know.

DR. BERRYMAN

Pain.

MAGGIE

I'm ready.

DR. BERRYMAN

I don't want to start before you can take it.

MAGGIE

I want to be healed. Otherwise, what's the point of all this? We could go on forever having pleasant interesting conversations.

DR. BERRYMAN

Monday.

MAGGIE

Doctor. Tom. You will be honest with me. Please tell me. Is there hope?

DR. BERRYMAN

There is some hope, some chance. You are one of the most determined patients I have ever had. I believe there is some hope.

July 20. Afternoon.
Washington, D.C. The house.

MAGGIE *is sitting in the living room.*

MAGGIE

No change of plans allowed. I said "Get out."
Polly to Cape Cod with her friend Laura;
Sarah to camp, Laughing

Lakes a third time, and James to survive with
adult sanction in Wyoming for six weeks.
Outward Bound—they spend five

days at the end in small groups with no food,
just knives and canned heat. Mark's in Mexico.
Susan called from Duluth
en route West: "Hello, the Volvo broke down!"
It's quieter. Philip leaves tomorrow—
he needs to get away.

My trip? Here. Full air-conditioning.
Friends. Sprouts. Older children: Abbie, David,
Ann with husband Ted;
Margaret, consort Tim; Paul from Oregon.
My sister Julia. One at a time for
easy company and help.

PHILIP

(From another area) I don't really want to leave. I want to be with
her now. She wants me to go away. She says I need a rest. I need
a rest? Will I rest when I think of her every second? Yes, I will
go. It's her life.

*(*DR. RUMBACH *comes in.* PHILIP *watches from his area)*

DR. RUMBACH

How are you—long time.

MAGGIE

Dr. Rumbach. *(Stands slowly)* I'm feeling really well.

DR. RUMBACH

I see! You got the tan without taking the cruise!

MAGGIE

I like to get my vitamins from natural sources.

DR. RUMBACH

What is he giving you for the pain?

MAGGIE

I have no pain.

DR. RUMBACH

None?

MAGGIE

(Touches her stomach) I feel this from time to time, but nothing I'd call pain.

DR. RUMBACH

I'm delighted you didn't do chemotherapy.

MAGGIE

Thanks for your advice.

DR. RUMBACH

You really seem yourself.

(Takes MAGGIE's *pulse.* PHILIP *comes in)*

PHILIP

How is she?

DR. RUMBACH

I tell you, it's really fantastic. She's so much better than I would have expected.

PHILIP

She's been very much herself the last two weeks.

DR. RUMBACH

It's extraordinary.

PHILIP

What do you think of my going away?

DR. RUMBACH

She wants you to—you could use the mountain air—Go ahead.

PHILIP

So you think there's hope.

DR. RUMBACH

We always proceed as if there is hope. But what do I think? I can't really say. I don't know this treatment. What I will say is that she is doing very well, much better than I had hoped.

July 25. Afternoon.
Washington, D.C. The house.

MARGARET
I brought these all the way from Kent
wrapped in newspaper. I wanted her to

see some of the roses she gave me. It's
almost a month since I've been here.
(She comes into the living room)

MAGGIE

Hi, sweetie!

MARGARET

(Holding out the flowers) I brought you these!

MAGGIE

They're so huge. What have you been feeding them?

MARGARET

Just ordinary food.

MAGGIE

You look beautiful.

MARGARET

You look so healthy! How do you feel?

MAGGIE

I had a bad day yesterday, but today—

MARGARET

Emotionally?

MAGGIE

No. Pain. He's increased the lemon drops.

MARGARET

Lemon drops?

MAGGIE

Phase two. The mysterious illegal vitamin from Europe.

MARGARET

Oh.

MAGGIE

We swore to Berryman we'd never utter its true name.

MARGARET

They hurt?

MAGGIE

They're supposed to hurt. The more they hurt, the more cells are
being destroyed, the better I'm getting.

*(*ABIGAIL *comes in.* MARGARET *rushes to her. They hug)*

MARGARET

Hi!

229

ABIGAIL

(To MAGGIE*)* It's time for your Lunch Pills.

MAGGIE

Ugh. Will you get them for me?

MARGARET

I'll do it. *(She leaves)*

MAGGIE

I always seem to be worse when Margaret comes.

ABIGAIL

You're feeling much better than yesterday. He said it would be this way at first.

MAGGIE

You'll call when you get to your apartment?

ABIGAIL

Yes. Goodbye.

> (MARGARET *comes in carrying a clear plastic glass brimming with pills)*

MARGARET

You're going?

ABIGAIL

To class. See you later. *(She leaves.)*

MAGGIE

(Pouring pills, all different shapes, sizes, colors, into her hand) Have you ever?

MARGARET

No.

MAGGIE

(Takes pills, lots, five or six at a time during the conversation) I can't wait for you to meet Berryman.

MARGARET

He's here every day?

MAGGIE

We never know!

MARGARET

His clock is organic too—

MAGGIE

Every other day, in the evening.

MARGARET

Why at night?

MAGGIE

He starts his rounds in the afternoon, and he takes a lot of time
with each patient, getting your vibes.

MARGARET

You talk . . .

MAGGIE

Yes, and he examines you: stethoscope, blood pressure, so on.
Sometimes he sits and holds my hand very hard and looks into my
eyes, deeply. Fascinating.

MARGARET

You get a sense of what's going on in there.

MAGGIE

He makes me feel I have some control over my life.

MARGARET

You haven't finished all your pills.

MAGGIE

(Puts the remaining pills in her pocket) Some control over my life.
(As they walk toward the bedroom) Listen. I'm going to take my
nap, then I thought we'd have early dinner, just the two of us. I
don't feel like lots of people tonight.

MARGARET

I'll see Abbie later.

MAGGIE

Tomorrow.

MARGARET

After dinner—

MAGGIE

(Insists) Tomorrow.

MARGARET

But you're going to bed.

MAGGIE

(Sudden anger) You can see her any time!

MARGARET

(Stunned.) Okay.

MAGGIE

I'm a little fragile.

MARGARET

I'm sorry, Mom.

MAGGIE

Let's talk about it after my nap. *(She lies down and goes to sleep)*

MARGARET

(Leaves the bedroom) I've been trying not to notice. Her stomach's swollen. The liver. The tumor. *(She walks to another area)* I walk around the block, go talk to Mrs. Simon. I feel better.

(MAGGIE has finished her nap. MARGARET comes in)

MAGGIE

While you were out, Abigail called and I asked them for dinner. I thought, what the heck! I've got you here three days.

ABIGAIL

(From another area) I was eight when Margaret went away to college, so I always think of her as a visitor. But I think that's changed. I even think she's changed—I guess since she started living with Tim three years ago. Loving a person makes you more open, more feeling. She always used to be running.

(It is after supper and MAGGIE is in bed)

MARGARET

It was great to see you out on the porch! I loved you sitting there, feet up like Cleopatra, waving to everyone!

MAGGIE

I really have been very well. How's Tim?

MARGARET

He'll be down here with me next time.

MAGGIE

I envy you. You've been so wise about yourself. Both of you. Your choices—

MARGARET

I don't think of them as choices. I just think I bumbled fortuitously. I wonder about children, for instance.

MAGGIE

You'd be crazy to have children.

MARGARET

Why?

MAGGIE

You love your independence too much. Not that you wouldn't be a good mother—

MARGARET

You had enough for both of us.

July 26. Morning.
Washington, D.C.

MARGARET

By the time I wake up at ten, Berryman has called. They've decided to stop the lemon drops for a day so her body can consolidate, so she can get some rest. *(A flash)* And I had a dream! Mom in a wheelchair in a green field with light around her. The tumor has died, but she hasn't. She's getting better.

July 26. Afternoon.
Washington, D.C.

DAVID *is at the house.* PHILIP *calls from the mountains, where he is on vacation with the younger children.*

DAVID

(Answering the telephone) Hello.

PHILIP

Hi. What's the report.

DAVID

She's not having lemon drops today and she feels better.

PHILIP

Margaret's there?

DAVID

She and Abigail went shopping. I'm holding the fort.

PHILIP

Well, Sarah and her little friend from camp got here last night and Polly gets in on a bus this afternoon.

233

DAVID
What's it like there? It's so hot here, I can't believe it.

PHILIP
Bright. Sunny. About seventy degrees.

DAVID
Mmmmmmm.

PHILIP
Jamie and his group are rocketing around. He's insisted we climb
a mountain this afternoon.

DAVID
Silver?

PHILIP
No, Long Tom. The only one with no trail.

DAVID
Have fun!

July 26. Late night.
Washington, D.C. The house.

MARGARET
She says she will have dinner.
She says she wants one of the lamb chops
I bought exactly enough: two apiece.
I didn't count her.
She didn't want meat last night.
I make her a plate:
the chop cut into tiny pieces,
corn on the cob, salad.
She doesn't feel well enough to come down
I ask David to take the food to her
because I am too hungry.
Later she calls me:

MAGGIE
Margaret.

MARGARET
I go to her room. She has not touched
the lamb. One long hand is wrapped around her

eyes. Crying. We've been
laughing downstairs.
I know she wants me
to take her plate away. I say "Do
you want me to take your
plate away?" She nods, her face still covered.
I take the plate noisily. "Do you want
something to drink?" Her hands still
hide her face. "I'll get you some
ginger ale." I take the dirty glass,
dirty plastic straw. I leave the room, close
the door behind me,
prevent myself from slamming
it. Halfway down the
stairs, I stop and put the dishes down,
sit there and remember
as hard as I can where I am, hard as
I can: I am myself, a woman,
nursing a woman who may be dying.
My mother can't feed me any more.

July 28. Late night.
New York. Airport.

MARGARET
I see Manhattan, a map
in lights. The island shape
disappears. We are landing.
Tim meets me.
Summer's half over.

August 10. Night.

PHILIP *calls from the mountains.* MARGARET *is in Kent, Connecticut.* ABIGAIL *is at the house in Washington.*

235

PHILIP

(On the telephone) It's me.

MARGARET

How are you?

PHILIP

I'm flying to Washington. Maggie's in the hospital tonight. Berryman thought she'd have less pain if they could drain her excess fluids.

MARGARET

Pop?

PHILIP

Yes?

MARGARET

Do you think she'll ever get out?

ABIGAIL

(From another area) We brought her back from the hospital. She feels lighter, she says, like after having a baby.

MARGARET

(Answering the telephone) Hello?
      (It is the next day. PHILIP *is in Washington. He has moved to the bedroom area)*

PHILIP

She's even stronger today. Amazing!

MARGARET

What are your plans?

MAGGIE

(Insistent. From her bed) I'm fine. I want the little girls to finish their vacation with a parent!

PHILIP

Maggie, they know!

MAGGIE

Please, darling, I want some time.

PHILIP

(To MARGARET *on the telephone)* I'll go back on Friday.

MARGARET

If you change your plans for her, she has to give up.

MOURNING PICTURES

Labor Day weekend. Afternoon.
Washington, D.C. The house.

MAGGIE *is taking more naps and feels great discomfort and pain,*
both exacerbated by the heat.

MARGARET

If she could only sleep.
Her body is an ochre barrel made
of shiny skin.
She rolls from right to left, from left
to right on the white sheets.
If she could only sleep. Her mouth is a line.
Her eyes flicker open, no energy to see, close.
She rolls back the other way.
    (MARGARET goes to MAGGIE's bedside)

MARGARET

The new-painted cabinets are bright white. The
beige rugs I bought last month have settled on
the children's floors upstairs. I tell her so.

MAGGIE

    (Drowsy)
I want the little ones to have nice things.

MARGARET

The light woodwork is wonderful!

MAGGIE

    (Suddenly clear)
I think Susan's room lacks something.

MARGARET

We decide that six-foot Susan's specially
ordered seven-foot bed needs a dust ruffle,
then she falls asleep.
    (Stage-whisper)
Mom! Mom! I'm going to Woodward and
Lothrop to get the dust ruffle! Because
I have known her voice for twenty-seven
years, I know she answers

MAGGIE

(Barely audible)

Yes, darling.

MARGARET

(Echo)

Yes, darling.

I am afraid to touch the shiny skin,
but I do, my arms spread wide
enough for a barrel.

I have thought the cancer was in my control.
If I decide she will recover, it will go away.

September 10. Early evening.
Washington, D.C. The house.

MAGGIE *is in bed.* DR. BERRYMAN *is at her side.*

MAGGIE

Oh, Doctor! I'm in such pain. *(Grabs his arm)* Doctor! I'm so damn scared. I can't do it. *(A spasm of pain)* Doctor!

DR. BERRYMAN

Maggie. Maggie. *(He takes her hand off his arm and takes both her hands)* I want you to let the fear give you some rest.

MAGGIE

(Shouts) Ahghh!

DR. BERRYMAN

You're in a dark place. Wild darkness. Something down there pulls—

MAGGIE

(Jerks her hand from his, rage) I'm the one that's here. You're— why, you're standing up!

DR. BERRYMAN

I'm going to give you something for the pain.

MAGGIE

I didn't want to give up, Tom, but I couldn't!

(BERRYMAN *makes one more calming gesture and leaves.*
ABIGAIL *is waiting*)

ABIGAIL

(To BERRYMAN*)* Way down since last night?

DR. BERRYMAN

These things go in cycles.

ABIGAIL

She'll come up?

DR. BERRYMAN

Should, a little. Give her the pain medicine any time she asks for
it. Pull back on the pills, she doesn't have the strength.

ABIGAIL

The protein?

DR. BERRYMAN

Her body knows things we can't. Don't force anything.

MARGARET

(From another area)
There are practical nurses around the clock
now. They sit outside her room, hands clasped,
waiting. My mother's usual caring is gone—
all she has for these night strangers is
a forced smile. I would like to sit here all night,
but I would have to do it from love,
and love is an insufficient nursing school.
(DAVID *goes to* MAGGIE*'s bedside and begins to rub her
feet, very carefully*)

DAVID

Hi.
(MARGARET *comes to the bedside and sits*)

ABIGAIL

(From another area)
I wonder how it makes her feel, all
these visitors. I sit here juggling
them on the telephone: The visitor
from Indianapolis, her stepmother—who
will come when.

239

Are they coming because they think
they'll never see her again?

*(MAGGIE comes out of her haze long enough to see
MARGARET)*

MAGGIE

Oh darling, someday when I feel better, we'll go to
Oregon, to the delphinium farms, to the place where
roses come from, and some winter we'll take our trip
to Milan, to the opera. And I will come visit you again.

*(MARGARET nods yes. MAGGIE dozes. MARGARET stays
by her bedside. ABIGAIL brings juice, sits for a while,
leaves, as the song is sung)*

SONG

There's so much I want to tell you
   about the garden:
The lettuce and the carrots, how they
   tasted all summer, and
The roses you gave me are still blooming,
   but it's late September
How pretty you look,
How much I love you,
   but it's late September
And everything I say says, I want—

It's my turn to feed you, but your lips
   are dry and cracked
Your face so thin your mouth can't
   even open.
I'd like to feed you the things you fed me:
Chicken in fancy sauces and crème brûlée,
Spinach made your special way—
I'd like to tell you all my new recipes:
   Spaghetti you would love
   And salad made with mint!

> But your lips are dry and cracked,
> Your face so thin your mouth can't
>   even open—
> I want to come here giving, not
>   wanting
> But everything I say says "I want."
> I want to come to you giving, not
>   wanting
> But everything I say says "I want."

(During the end of the song, PHILIP *comes into the bedroom.* MARGARET *and* DAVID *leave)*

MAGGIE

(Coming up, sees PHILIP, *tries to smile)* I'd like to sit up. *(*PHILIP *helps her sit by adjusting her bed)*

PHILIP

Hard.

MAGGIE

It was worse this morning. *(A spasm of pain. She winces.* PHILIP *wants to help)* No. No! *(Apologetic)* I didn't want to put you through this.

PHILIP

(Takes her hand) I love you.

MAGGIE

I'm glad you're back. Very glad.
    *(*PHILIP *hugs her. She falls asleep)*

PHILIP

I remember her on the beach, dark against the white sand. Her body was so beautiful—smooth, smiling. Oh, God! I can't believe this is happening!
    *(*MAGGIE*'s face shows pain again.* PHILIP *lowers the bed to a flatter position)*

MAGGIE

(Out of her haze) I think Margaret better take some pictures of her house. I won't be well enough to travel for quite a while.

241

SONG

It's dark, almost noon—
It's been that way
So many days I've tried to take
    the pictures you asked for:
the house, painted new white,
the wicker chairs you gave me,
How they look on the porch—

(PHILIP leaves. DAVID comes in for his shift)

MARGARET

(From another area) Labor Day is over. I am back at my desk, paying bills. I can't write until I pay my bills. *(The telephone rings, twice)* Abbie!

If I called the weather man,
He'd say the sun's been out
Five days out of seven,
    but I don't remember,
I've only seen the dark.
I've only seen the almost noon.

ABIGAIL

Have you sent the pictures of Mom for the faith healer?

MARGARET

I'll send them today.

MAGGIE

Right now.

MARGARET

Yes. Yes.

So I'll wait until the sun
    comes out, throws
The shadow of the apple tree
    all over the lawn,
Brightens the living room,
Shows me the world again,
    the fields across the road.

MARGARET

We make love. I shut my eyes. I am her
with her eyes shut. I can't see myself. How
do I know I'm me and not her? My lips
dry. I run my tongue through the slot between
my teeth and upper lip to clear out stale
saliva. I have seen her do that. I
touch my belly, imagine it a barrel.

242

I am her. My eyes are closed. How do I
know I am not her? I have always been her,
and it's never mattered before who was
who. I open my eyes, feel them flicker
open like hers, open my arms. I am
not moving. How do I know I won't have
pain, as much as she does, when I move?

I see you. I love you. I don't want to die.

September 17.

MARGARET *is in Connecticut. The others are in Washington
sitting around* MAGGIE*'s bed.*

MARGARET
This morning on its door the A&P thanked us
concisely for our "faithful patronage"
and stopped selling for good.
Noon: the phone, Abigail,
ABIGAIL
This is the end.
Her fluids came back. She's saying strange things—
last night,
MAGGIE
I feel like twins!
MARGARET
"Mind/body split," I hear my voice attempt.
ABIGAIL
I guess—
MARGARET
Abbie says—
ABIGAIL
—she's only half here,
and later Tom came—

(DR. BERRYMAN goes to the bedside)
She said right to him—

MAGGIE

Oh, Doctor, I'm gone!

MARGARET

I hang up. Lock the house. Drive the eighty
miles, not fast. Will I
be in time to talk to her again, see her?
New York. I fill two bags, a week's clothes, my
long black dress—

ABIGAIL

I have never been here before.

DAVID

My friend has.
His two fathers died within three years, his
natural father, then his stepfather.
I ask him what he remembers. He says
"Only the black ambulance that came before
my second father died. It was terrible
in those days when ambulances
and police cars were painted black."

MARGARET

—call to say
which shuttle. Hear this:

PHILIP

She went—ambulance
the hospital—half-hour ago—too much pain—
her fluids tapped again.

*(DAVID and ABIGAIL remove a coverlet, leaving only the
sheets. When MARGARET arrives at the bedside, it has
become a hospital bedside)*

MARGARET

The hospital straight from the airport. She
has oxygen feeds in each nostril, their
gurgling source is hitched to
the flowered wall above her. Is it like fresh

air, cool on her brain? There's an I.V. just
below the shoulder: Food

straight into the blood. Her hands look like birds'
claws on the sheets. They say she nearly died
this afternoon; that's why
she's all hooked up. I thought we were against
keeping her going. The afternoon nurse
comes in, gives her a shot.

"It's for pain. Are you her daughter, dear? You
look just like her. She's a lovely woman."
Mom. I don't say it out loud,
but I want her awake, her eyes open.
Hello, Mom. I love you so much. I'm here.
I hold her hand. She sleeps.

September 20. Afternoon.
Washington, D.C. Hospital.

MARGARET
Today she wants to go. I'm sure of it.
MAGGIE
(Staccato bursts)
I am on a bridge alone.
MARGARET
What?
DAVID
On a bridge?
MAGGIE
(Loud and fast)
I can see all the people—
Doctor.
DAVID
People.
MAGGIE
—on the other side. Oh, God!

245

(ABIGAIL *comes in*)
Where's the doctor?

MAGGIE

(Singsong)
Goodbye. Goodbye.
I really must go now.
I love you, darlings.
I must go to sleep.
Such a long journey.
Abbie, you go upstairs and get
my red coat. David, you
get the car keys, top left
drawer . . .

(MAGGIE *starts vigorously
to get out of bed. They
restrain her, replace sheets*)

MAGGIE

A man in orange. Bright.
A man in black.

(Her body jerks, one long scream of terror)
AAAAaaaaaahhhhhhh.

(They hold her down)

MARGARET

I press the call. The nurse comes,
gives her a hypo, straightens the bed.
This calms her, maybe deprives her.

(PHILIP *enters the room, beckons to* ABBIE *and*
DAVID)

PHILIP

Paul's here.

ABIGAIL

My brother Paul!

SONG

Paul arrives from Oregon.
Twenty-five, wearing maroon platform shoes,
And a great big white cowboy hat.
He is very tall and very thin—

246

His shirts are flowered—
He is from another place.
In his white cuffed pants,
He looks gorgeous and seedy.
My father says,
Did he ride on a plane
in those clothes?

September 21. Night.
Washington, D.C. Hospital.

MAGGIE *is alone. She sits up as if totally well.*

MAGGIE

What has happened to all the cures?
The miracle wheat sprout juice.
The hundreds of vitamins.
The predigested protein they gave me hourly
which tasted like melted muscles.
Where are the cruel hard chemicals they said
could never cure? but I wonder—
atom bombs do end wars.

And the faith healer who didn't know
how sick I was, who told the doctor
to get me through October fifteenth, then I'd survive.
The childhood friends who waited on me,
my daughters, sons, my neighbors.
Helen, who brought a yellow cup to sweeten
the vile nutritious teas.

Where are they?

I am swollen, drugged senseless and alone
on a white bed in a small hospital room.
You have all betrayed me.

247

September 28. Afternoon.
Washington, D.C. Hospital.

Since BERRYMAN *is not officially a medical doctor, he has not been treating* MAGGIE *in the hospital;* RUMBACH *has. This is* BERRYMAN's *first hospital visit. They speak slowly because she is very weak.*

MAGGIE

Oh, Doctor—Thank God you've come! *(He takes her hand)*

DR. BERRYMAN

Yes.

MAGGIE

It wasn't my fault—

DR. BERRYMAN

We did our best.

MAGGIE

So long.

DR. BERRYMAN

Goodbye.

October 1. Afternoon.
Washington, D.C. Hospital.

As PHILIP *speaks,* ABIGAIL, DAVID *and* MARGARET *enter and sit around* MAGGIE's *bed to give a sense of the larger group.*

PHILIP

All the children packed in this small room: I
hold Sarah, the youngest, on my lap—she
fingers one blond braid, can't look. Jamie is
solemn. Polly holds her mother's hand, and
watches—she's seen dying creatures before.
My oldest son, Paul. Mark, his dark hair wild
like Maggie's. Ann, hair pulled back, holds her blond
husband. Very blue eyes. Tall Susan, blue-

248

jeaned, at the foot. Tim's arms hold Margaret,
Abigail holds David. We're all touching—a wreath.
Maggie opens her million-kilowatt eyes, turns
her head from side to side. Is she counting?
She sees me. I know it.

MAGGIE

I love you, Philip. *(She looks around)* I love everybody!

ABIGAIL

(Stands)
Everyone has been here two weeks.
We have begun to plan the funeral.
The men have bought dark suits, but
last night she seemed stronger.
Aunt Julia has decided to stay. She asked
me and I said I thought we all needed her.

October 2. Afternoon.
Washington, D.C. The hospital room.

MARGARET *is at* MAGGIE's *bedside. As she speaks, she moves out
of the room, into the corridor.*

MARGARET

The mouth is closed, determined. The eyeballs
move under shut lids. The hands shake, grasp
the metal bed bars, then jiggle loose, lost
until they find something else to touch: bed
surface, swollen stomach, white gown. She tugs
her gown, kicks the sheets off, pulls
the gown up. Naked, shaved: That's where I came
from. I turn away. Something heaves through me,
leaves me used up. I go out. It is hot,
tropical. Black men in green suits pull beds-
on-wheels rapidly from room to room, ward
to operating theatre, X-ray lab—
the steady metallic rattle does not

249

disturb. Priest in black, doctor in white, stand,
confer. Three nurses finish the P.M.
shift. I am still here. I am counting squares.
One foot's almost bigger than a square. I'm
alone. My sandaled white feet
are bigger than anyone else's, my
health is an excess. I'm twenty-seven
and I still feel the same. I am sixteen:
Look at my pale feet, my sandals. Watch them
swell—another tropical climate just as hot.
Red-brown men in diapers whack water
buffalo home at dusk. Our speeding car
stops for this even on The Mall, bordered
with skinny sleepers suspended on hand-
woven webbing from hand-lashed frames; the poor
in this country carry their beds on their
backs. Here, Lahore. The sky sick-
white. Palm trees bend above us, moisten the
air. We wait. An old man, white hair to his
muslin-covered genitals, sleeps, curled up
on the ground. A woman, black face bubbled
with scars, carries a wide-eyed, smooth-skinned child
who begs with a handless wrist. A tonga
shoots by. The driver strikes his broken mare;
his fare, a woman in purdah. Her hands bounce
on her linen lap—they are round, and young.
We sit chewing pahn. Juice the color of
blood dribbles from our mouths. We pick betel
leaf from between our teeth.
The hospital basement, steam table.
Food. For waiting. I have no appetite.
"Iced tea, please." I suck it through the punctured
plastic top. The elevator stops.
A young black man in a green suit pushes
his cargo off. I turn from her
old eyes: a brick row house crumbling, a front
porch. September. Red climbing roses blousy

without her pruning. Where is her daughter?
"The food's dirty here. No wonder everyone dies all the time!" The sixteen-year-old,
afraid to suck raw sugar
cane that last day in Anarkali Bazaar,
named for the girl dancer beheaded because
some emperor of the Punjab loved her.
Sixteen years old: "Will that old man simply
die one day as he sleeps? How do you know
he's dead?" By the smell. "In America, my
country, this could never happen. They care
for you old and sick. No one dies here. My
mother says she will live to be—well,
old enough to have white hair down her back,
sit on a porch rocking, sipping something,
without children, remembering
her life." I count the squares of asphalt tile—
brown, off-white: eleven across some places,
eight near the nurse's station. One hundred
and twenty-eight long. I just hold this
in my head, then multiply. I have no
paper, no pencil. I'll count again tonight.

The music begins for DAVID's *birthday party.* MARGARET
*moves downstage as the others enter and begin to sing the
birthday song. The music is boisterous; they sing enthusiastically and dance)*

SONG

There is a birthday in this house. David is twenty.
He lives with Abbie—they have been here every day
    since June.
Sometimes when they are needed, they spend the night
Sometimes they stay because they want to.
And when she wakes up, remembering each terrible
    thing about her life,
David comes across the hall and talks to her about
    philosophy, about Samuel Beckett,

251

And brings her something she'd like to eat: corn on the
  cob or a Sara Lee.
And in the morning, when she is feeling well,
She sits up and eyes like diamonds with excitement
She says, "David came in at four A.M. and made me milk
  and a piece of corn!
And we had a great talk and we solved all the problems
Of the world's great religions! He is such a lovely boy!"
  (They speak over the music)

SINGER

He is such a lovely boy.

PHILIP

He is such a lovely boy.

MARGARET

He is such a lovely boy.

ABIGAIL

He is such a lovely boy.

ALL

Tonight he's twenty. Abbie arranged a party and we
  ordered a cake from University Pastry.
And no one said anything at all about the greatest
  birthday party-giver of them all,
Who couldn't be here tonight.

SINGER

Who couldn't be here tonight.

ABIGAIL

Who couldn't be here tonight.

DAVID

Who couldn't be here tonight.

PHILIP

Who couldn't be here tonight.

October 3. Evening.
Washington, D.C. Margaret's bedroom.

MARGARET

I was just going to bed.

DAVID

We're going to the hospital. We thought you might like to come.

MARGARET

I've been up every night! I have to get some sleep.

DAVID

The night nurse says tonight—

MARGARET

She said that yesterday!

ABIGAIL

We're only going to stay a little. You go to sleep.

(ABIGAIL, DAVID *and* PHILIP *go to the hospital room, sit next to bed where* MAGGIE *is lying peacefully.* DR. BERRYMAN *stands upstage in the shadows. In a moment, it is clear that* MAGGIE *has died.* PHILIP *leaves the room to call* MARGARET.)

MARGARET

(Answering the telephone) Hello.

PHILIP

Maggie died a few minutes ago. Maybe you want to come over to the hospital.

(MARGARET *comes into the hospital room)*

MARGARET

Her dark hair is combed back,
spread on the white pillow.
Her cheek flesh falls thin
from the bones. The hollows
are gentle. I kiss her on the
forehead. She is not cold.

The lights dim to darkness.

Wedding Band

A Love/Hate Story
in Black and White

by ALICE CHILDRESS

"The woman on whom I based Julia was often mentioned by my mother and grandmother when I was growing up. . . . When plots and people won't go away, I find I must write them." *Wedding Band* was presented during the 1972–73 season at the Public Theatre, directed by Childress and Joseph Papp, with Ruby Dee and James Broderick in the leading roles. The following year Childress adapted the play for television, and it was broadcast nationally on ABC with Dee and J. D. Cannon playing Julia and Herman.

Childress was born in Charleston, North Carolina, and grew up in Harlem. She was a member of the American Negro Theatre for ten years as an actress, writer and director. In 1952 her *Gold Through the Trees* became the first play by a black woman to be produced professionally on the American stage, and in 1955, her *Trouble in Mind* earned her an Obie, the first won by a woman playwright. *Wine in the Wilderness*, her third play, was presented on National Educational Television; others include *Mojo, String, Martin Luther King at Montgomery*. Childress has also published two plays for young people to read, *When the Rattlesnake Sounds* about Harriet Tubman and *Let's Hear It for the Queen* (both 1976). From 1966 to 1968 she was a fellow of the Radcliffe Institute in Cambridge, Massachusetts, and in 1971, edited *Black Scenes*, the first collection of scenes chosen for the training of young black actors. Her first novel, *A Hero Ain't Nothin' but a Sandwich*, was published in 1973 and has been made into a movie from her screenplay. Childress lives in Harlem and is at work on a new novel.

CHARACTERS
(In order of appearance)

JULIA AUGUSTINE

TEETA

MATTIE

LULA GREEN

FANNY JOHNSON

NELSON GREEN

THE BELL MAN

PRINCESS

HERMAN

ANNABELLE

HERMAN'S MOTHER

Act One

SCENE 1

TIME: *Summer 1918 . . . Saturday morning. A city by the sea . . . South Carolina, U.S.A.*

SCENE: *Three houses in a backyard. The center house is newly painted and cheery-looking in contrast to the other two, which are weather-beaten and shabby. Center house is gingerbready, with odds and ends of "picked-up" shutters, picket railing, wrought-iron railing, newel posts, a Grecian pillar, odd window boxes of flowers. Everything clashes with a beautiful, subdued splendor; the old and new mingle in defiance of style and period. The playing areas of the houses are raised platforms furnished according to the taste of each tenant. Only one room of each house is visible.* JULIA AUGUSTINE *(tenant of the center house) has recently moved in, and there is still unpacking to be done. Paths are worn from the houses to the front yard entry. The landlady's house and an outhouse are offstage. An outdoor hydrant supplies water.*

JULIA *is sleeping on the bed in the center house.* TEETA, *a girl about eight years old, enters the yard from the house on stage right. She tries to control her weeping as she examines a clump of grass. The muffled weeping disturbs* JULIA's *sleep. She starts up, half rises from her pillow, then falls back into a troubled sleep.* MATTIE, TEETA's *mother, enters carrying a switch and fastening her clothing. She joins the little girl in the search for a lost quarter. The search is subdued, intense.*

MATTIE
You better get out there and get it! Did you find it? Gawd, what've I done to be treated this way! You gon' get a whippin' too.

FANNY
(Enters from the front entry. She is landlady and the self-appointed fifty-year-old representative of her race) Listen, Mattie . . . I want some quiet out here this mornin'.

259

MATTIE

Dammit, this gal done lost the only quarter I got to my name. *(LULA enters from the direction of the outhouse carrying a covered slop jar. She is forty-five and motherly)* "Teeta," I say, "go to the store, buy three cent grits, five cent salt pork, ten cent sugar; and keep your hand closed 'roun' my money." How I'm gonna sell any candy if I got no sugar to make it? You little heifer! *(Goes after* TEETA, *who hides behind* LULA*)*

LULA

Gawd, help us to find it.

MATTIE

Your daddy is off sailin' the ocean and you got nothin' to do but lose money! *I'm gon' put you out in the damn street, that's what!* *(TEETA cries out. JULIA sits up in the bed and cries out)*

JULIA

No . . . no . . .

FANNY

You disturbin' the only tenant who's paid in advance.

LULA

Teeta, retrace your steps. Show Lula what you did.

TEETA

I hop-hop-hop . . . *(Hops near a post-railing of* JULIA*'s porch)*

MATTIE

What the hell you do that for?

LULA

There 'tis! That's a quarter . . . down in the hole . . . Can't reach it . . .

> *(JULIA is now fully awake. Putting on her housedress over her camisole and petticoat.* MATTIE *takes an axe from the side of the house to knock the post out of the way)*

MATTIE

Aw, *move*, move! That's all the money I got. I'll tear this damn house down and you with it!

FANNY

And I'll blow this police whistle.

> *(JULIA steps out on the porch. She is an attractive brown woman, about thirty-five years old)*

MATTIE

Blow it . . . blow it . . . blow it . . . hot damn— *(Near tears. She decides to tell* JULIA *off also)* I'll tear it down—that's right. If you don't like it—come on down here and whip me.

JULIA

(Nervous but determined to present a firm stand) Oh, my . . . Good mornin', ladies. My name is Julia Augustine. I'm not gonna move.

LULA

My name is Lula. Why you think we wantcha to move?

FANNY

Miss Julia, I'm sorry your first day starts like this. Some people are ice cream and others just cow-dung. I try to be ice cream.

MATTIE

Dammit, I'm ice cream too. Strawberry. *(Breaks down and cries)*

FANNY

That's Mattie. She lost her last quarter, gon' break down my house to get it.

JULIA

(Gets a quarter from her dresser) Oh my, dear heart, don't cry. Take this twenty-five cents, Miss Mattie.

MATTIE

No, thank you, ma'm.

JULIA

And I have yours under my house for good luck.

FANNY

Show your manners.

TEETA

Thank you. You the kin'est person in the worl'.

> *(*LULA *enters her house.* TEETA *starts for home, then turns to see if her mother is coming)*

MATTIE

(To JULIA*)* I didn't mean no harm. But my husband October's in the Merchant Marine and I needs my little money. Well, thank you. *(To* TEETA*)* Come on, honey bunch.

> *(She enters her house stage right.* TEETA *proudly follows.* LULA *is putting* NELSON*'s breakfast on the table at stage left)*

261

FANNY

(Testing strength of post) My poor father's turnin' in his grave. He built these rent houses just 'fore he died . . . And he wasn't a carpenter. Shows what the race can do when we wanta. *(Feels the porch railing and tests its strength)* That loud-mouth Mattie used to work in a white cat-house.

JULIA

A what?

FANNY

Sportin' house, house of . . . A whore house. Know what she used to do?

JULIA

(Embarrassed) Not but so many things *to* do, I guess.
　　　*(*FANNY *wants to follow her in the house, but* JULIA *fends her off)*

FANNY

Used to wash their joy-towels. Washin' joy-towels for one cent apiece. I wouldn't work in that kinda place—would you?

JULIA

Indeed not.

FANNY

Vulgarity.

JULIA

(Trying to get away) I have my sewing to do now, Miss Fanny.

FANNY

I got a lovely piece-a blue serge. Six yards.
　　　(She attempts to get into the house, but JULIA *deftly blocks the door)*

JULIA

I don't sew for people. *(*FANNY *wonders why not)* I do homework for a store . . . hand-finishin' on ladies' shirtwaists.

FANNY

You 'bout my age . . . I'm thirty-five.

JULIA

(After a pause) I thought you were younger.

FANNY

(Genuinely moved by the compliment) Thank you. But I'm not

262

married 'cause nobody's come up to my high standard. Where you get them expensive-lookin', high-class shoes?

JULIA

In a store. I'm busy now, Miss Fanny.

FANNY

Doin' what?

JULIA

First one thing then another. Good day.

(JULIA *thinks she has dismissed her. Goes in the house.* FANNY *quickly follows into the room . . . picks up a teacup from the table)*

FANNY

There's a devil in your teacup . . . also prosperity. Tell me 'bout yourself, don't be so distant.

JULIA

It's all there in the tea-leaves.

FANNY

Oh, go on! I'll tell you somethin' . . . that sweet-face Lula killed her only child.

JULIA

No, she didn't.

FANNY

In a way-a speakin'. And then Gawd snatched up her triflin' husband. One nothin' piece-a man. Biggest thing he ever done for her was to lay down and die. Poor woman. Yes indeed, then she went and adopted this fella from the colored orphan home. Boy grew too big for a lone woman to keep in the house. He's a big, strappin', over-grown man now. I wouldn't feel safe livin' with a man that's not blood kin, 'doption or no 'doption. It's 'gainst nature. Oughta see the muscles on him.

JULIA

(Wearily) Oh, my . . . I think I hear somebody callin' you.

FANNY

Yesterday the white folks threw a pail-a dirty water on him. A black man on leave got no right to wear his uniform in public. The crackers don't like it. That's flauntin' yourself.

263

JULIA

Miss Fanny, I don't talk about people.

FANNY

Me neither. *(Giving her serious advice)* We high-class, quality people oughta stick together.

JULIA

I really do stay busy.

FANNY

Doin' what? Seein' your beau? You have a beau, haven'tcha?

JULIA

(Realizing she must tell her something in order to get rid of her) Miss Johnson . . .

FANNY

Fanny.

JULIA

(Managing to block her toward the door) My mother and father have long gone on to Glory.

FANNY

Gawd rest the dead and bless the orphan.

JULIA

Yes, I do have a beau . . . But I'm not much of a mixer. *(She now has* FANNY *out on the porch)*

FANNY

Get time, come up front and see my parlor. I got a horsehair settee and a four-piece, silver-plated tea service.

JULIA

Think of that.

FANNY

The first and only one to be owned by a colored woman in the United States of America. Salesman told me.

JULIA

Oh, just imagine.

> *(*MATTIE *enters, wearing a blue calico dress and striped apron)*

FANNY

My mother was a genuine, full-blooded, qualified, Seminole Indian.

264

TEETA

(Calls to her mother from the doorway) Please . . . Mama . . . Mama
. . . Buy me a hair ribbon.

MATTIE

All right! I'm gon' buy my daughter a hair ribbon.

FANNY

Her hair is so short you'll have to nail it on. *(*FANNY *exits to her
house)*

MATTIE

That's all right about that, Fanny. Your father worked in a stinkin'
phosphate mill . . . yeah, and didn't have a tooth in his head. Then
he went and married some half Portuguese woman. I don't call
that bein' in no damn society. I works for my livin'. I makes candy
and I takes care of a little white girl. Hold this nickel 'til I get back.
Case of emergency I don't like Teeta to be broke.

JULIA

I'll be busy today, lady.

MATTIE

(As she exits, carrying a tray of candy) Thank you, darlin'.

TEETA

Hey, lady, my daddy helps cook food on a big war boat. He peels
potatoes. You got any children?

JULIA

No . . . Grace-a Gawd. *(Starts to go in house)*

TEETA

Hey, lady! Didja ever hear of Philadelphia? After the war that's
where we're goin' to live. Philadelphia!

JULIA

Sounds like heaven.

TEETA

Jesus is the President of Philadelphia.

*(*TEETA *sweeps in front of* JULIA*'s house. Lights come up in*
LULA*'s house.* NELSON *is eating breakfast. He is a rather
rough-looking muscly fellow with a soft voice and a bitter-
sweet sense of humor. He is dressed in civilian finery and
his striped silk shirt seems out of place in the drab little
room.* LULA *makes paper flowers, and the colorful bits of*

265

paper are seen everywhere as finished and partially finished flowers and stems, also a finished funeral piece. A picture of Abraham Lincoln hangs on the upstage wall. LULA *is brushing* NELSON*'s uniform jacket)*

LULA

Last week the Bell Man came to collect the credit payment he says . . . "Auntie, whatcha doin' with Abraham Lincoln's pitcher on the wall? He was such a poor president."

NELSON

Tell the cracker to mind his damn business.

LULA

It don't pay to get mad. Remember yesterday.

NELSON

(Studying her face for answers) Mama, you supposed to get mad when somebody throw a pail-a water on you.

LULA

It's their country and their uniform, so just stay out the way.

NELSON

Right. I'm not goin' back to work in that coal-yard when I get out the army.

LULA

They want you back. A bird in the hand, y'know.

NELSON

A bird in the hand ain't always worth two in the bush.

LULA

This is Saturday, tomorrow Sunday . . . thank Gawd for Monday; back to the army. That's one thing . . . Army keeps you off the street.

(We hear the sound of THE SHRIMP MAN *passing in the street)*

THE SHRIMP MAN

(Offstage) Shrimp-dee-raw . . . I got raw shrimp.

*(*NELSON *leaves the house just as* JULIA *steps out on her porch to hang a rug over the rail.* TEETA *enters* GREEN *house)*

NELSON

Er . . . howdy-do, er . . . beg pardon. My name is Nelson. Lula Green's son, if you don't mind. Miss . . . er . . . Mrs.?

266

JULIA

(After a brief hesitation) Miss . . . Julia Augustine.

NELSON

Miss Julia, you the best-lookin' woman I ever seen in my life.
I declare you look jus' like a violin sounds. And I'm not talkin'
'bout pretty. You look like you got all the right feelin's, you
know?

JULIA

Well, thank you, Mr. Nelson.

NELSON

See, you got me talkin' all outta my head. *(LULA enters, TEETA
follows eating a biscuit and carrying a milk pail . . . she exits toward
street)* Let's go for a walk this evenin', get us a lemon phosphate.

JULIA

Oh, I don't care for any, Mr. Nelson.

LULA

That's right. She say stay home.

JULIA

(To NELSON) I'm sorry.

NELSON

Don't send me back to the army feelin' bad 'cause you turn me
down. Orange-ade tonight on your porch. I'll buy the oranges, you
be the sugar.

JULIA

No, thank you.

NELSON

Let's make it—say—six o'clock.

JULIA

No, I said no!

LULA

Nelson, go see your friends. *(He waves goodbye to JULIA and exits
through the back entry)* He's got a lady friend, her name is Merrilee Jones. And he was just tryin' to be neighborly. That's how
me and Nelson do. But you go on and stay to yourself. *(Starts
toward her house)*

JULIA

Miss Lula! I'm sorry I hurt your feelin's. Miss Lula! I have a
gentleman friend, that's why I said no.

LULA

I didn't think-a that. When yall plan to cut the cake?

JULIA

Not right now. You see . . . when you offend Gawd you hate for it to be known. Gawd might forgive but people never will. I mean . . . when a man and a woman are not truly married . . .

LULA

Oh, I see.

JULIA

I live by myself . . . but he visits . . . I declare I don't know how to say . . .

LULA

Everybody's got some sin, but if it troubles your heart you're a gentle sinner, just a good soul gone wrong.

JULIA

That's a kind thought.

LULA

My husband, Gawd rest the dead, used to run 'round with other women; it made me kind-a careless with my life. One day, many long years ago, I was sittin' in a neighbor's house tellin' my troubles; my only child, my little boy, wandered out on the railroad track and got killed.

JULIA

That must-a left a fifty-pound weight on your soul.

LULA

It did. But if we grow stronger . . . and rise higher than what's pullin' us down . . .

JULIA

Just like Climbin' Jacob's Ladder . . . *(Sings)* Every round goes higher and higher . . .

LULA

Yes, rise higher than the dirt . . . that fifty-pound weight will lift and you'll be free, free without anybody's by-your-leave. Do something to wash out the sin. That's why I got Nelson from the orphanage.

JULIA

And now you feel free?

LULA

No, not yet. But I believe Gawd wants me to start a new faith; one that'll make our days clear and easy to live. That's what I'm workin' on now. Oh, Miss Julia, I'm glad you my neighbor.

JULIA

Oh, thank you, Miss Lula! Sinners or saints, didn't Gawd give us a beautiful day this mornin'!

(The sound of cowbells clanking and the thin piping of a tin and paper flute. TEETA *backs into the yard, carefully carrying the can of milk.* THE BELL MAN *follows humming "Over There" on the flute. He is a poor white about thirty years old, but time has dealt him some hard blows. He carries a large suitcase, the American flag painted on both sides; cowbells are attached.* THE BELL MAN *rests his case on the ground. Fans with a very tired-looking handkerchief. He cuts the fool by dancing and singing a bit of a popular song as he turns corners around the yard)*

THE BELL MAN

(As LULA *starts to go in the house)* Stay where you at, Aunty! *(To* JULIA*)* You used to live on Thompson Street. How's old Thompson Street?

JULIA

(A slightly painful memory) I moved 'bout a year ago, moved to Queen Street.

THE BELL MAN

Move a lot, don'tcha? *(Opens suitcase)* All right, everybody stay where you at! *(Goes into a fast sales spiel)* Lace-trim ladies' drawers! Stockin's, ladies' stockin's . . . gottem for the knock-knees and the bow-legs too . . . white, black and navy blue! All right, no fools no fun! The joke's on me! Here we go! *(As he places some merchandise in front of the* WOMEN, *does a regular minstrel walk-around)* Anything in the world . . . fifty cent a week and one long, sweet year to pay . . . Come on, little sister!

TEETA

(Doing the walk-around with THE BELL MAN*)*
　　And a-ring-ting-tang
　　And-a-shimmy-she-bang

While the sun am a-shinin' and the sky am blue . . .
And a-ring-ting-tang.
And-a-shimmy-she-bang
While the sun am a-shinin' and the sky am blue . . .

LULA

(Annoyed with TEETA*'s dancing with* THE BELL MAN*)* Stop all that shimmy she-bang and get in the house! *(Swats at* TEETA *as she passes)*

THE BELL MAN

(Coldly) Whatcha owe me, Aunty?

LULA

Three dollars and ten cent. I don't have any money today.

THE BELL MAN

When you gon' pay?

LULA

Monday, or better say Wednesday.

JULIA

(To divert his attention from LULA*)* How much for sheets?

THE BELL MAN

For you they on'y a dollar. *(*JULIA *goes to her house to get the money.* THE BELL MAN *moves toward her house as he talks to* LULA*)* Goin' to the servicemen's parade Monday?

LULA

Yes, sir. My boy's marchin'. *(She exits)*

THE BELL MAN

Uh-huh, I'll getcha later. Lord, Lord, Lord, how'dja like to trot 'round in the sun beggin' the poorest people in the world to buy somethin' from you. This is nice. Real nice. *(To* JULIA*)* A good friend-a mine was a nigra boy. Me 'n' him was jus' like that. Fine fella, he couldn't read and he couldn't write.

JULIA

(More to herself than to him) When he learns you're gon' lose a friend.

THE BELL MAN

But talkin' serious, what is race and color? Put a paper bag over your head and who'd know the difference. Tryin' to remember me,

270

ain'tcha. I seen you one time coming out that bakery shop on Thompson Street, didn' see me.

THE BELL MAN

JULIA

Is that so?

THE BELL MAN

(Sits on the bed and bounces up and down) Awwww, Great Gawd-a-mighty! I haven't been on a high-built bed since I left the back woods.

JULIA

Please don't sit on my bed!

THE BELL MAN

Old country boy, that's me! Strong and healthy country boy . . . *(Not noticing any rejection)* Sister, Um in need for it like I never been before. Will you 'commodate me? Straighten me, fix me up, will you? Wouldn't take but five minutes. Um quick like a jack rabbit. Wouldn't nobody know but you and me. *(She backs away from him as he pants and wheezes out his admiration)* Um clean, too. Clean as the . . . Board-a Health. Don't believe in dippin' inta everything. I got no money now, but ladies always need stockin's.

JULIA

(Trying to keep her voice down, throws money at his feet) Get out of my house! Beneath contempt, that's what you are.

THE BELL MAN

Don't be lookın' down your nose at me . . . actin' like you Mrs. Martha Washington . . . Throwin' one chicken-shit dollar at me and goin' on . . .

JULIA

(Picking up wooden clothes hanger) Get out! Out, before I take a stick to you.

THE BELL MAN

(Bewildered, gathering his things to leave) Hell, what I care who you sleep with! It's your nooky! Give it way how you want to. I don't own no run-down bakery shop, but I'm good as those who do. A baker ain' nobody . . .

JULIA

I wish you was dead, you just oughta be dead, stepped on and dead.

THE BELL MAN

Bet that's what my mama said first time she saw me. I was a fourteenth child. Damn women! . . . that's all right . . . Gawd bless you, Gawd be with you and let his light shine on you. I give you good for evil . . . God bless you! *(As he walks down the porch steps)* She must be goin' crazy. Unfriendly, sick-minded bitch! *(TEETA enters from LULA's house. THE BELL MAN takes a strainer from his pocket and gives it to TEETA with a great show of generosity)* Here, little honey. You take this sample. You got nice manners.

TEETA

Thank you, you the kin'est person in the world.

(THE BELL MAN exits to the tune of clanking bells, and LULA enters)

JULIA

I hate those kind-a people.

LULA

You mustn't hate white folks. Don'tcha believe in Jesus? He's white.

JULIA

I wonder if he believes in me.

LULA

Gawd says we must love everybody.

JULIA

Just lovin' and lovin', no matter what? There are days when I love, days when I hate.

FANNY

Mattie, Mattie, mail!

JULIA

Your love is worthless if nobody wants it.

(FANNY enters carrying a letter. She rushes over to MATTIE's house)

FANNY

I had to pay the postman two cent. No stamp.

TEETA

(Calls to JULIA) Letter from Papa! Gimme my mama's five cents!

FANNY

(To TEETA*)* You gon' end your days in the Colored Women's Jailhouse.

> (PRINCESS, *a little girl, enters, skipping and jumping. She hops, runs and leaps across the yard.* PRINCESS *is six years old.* TEETA *takes money from* JULIA*'s outstretched hand and gives it to* FANNY*)*

TEETA

(To MATTIE*)* Letter from Papa! Gotta pay two cent!

FANNY

Now I owe you three cent . . . or do you want me to read the letter?

> (PRINCESS *gets wilder and wilder, makes Indian war whoops.* TEETA *joins the noise-making. They climb porches and play follow-the-leader.* PRINCESS *finally lands on* JU-LIA*'s porch after peeping and prying into everything along the way)*

PRINCESS

(Laughing merrily) Hello . . . hello . . . hello.

JULIA

(Overwhelmed by the confusion) Well— Hello.

FANNY

Get away from my new tenant's porch!

PRINCESS

(Is delighted with FANNY*'s scolding and decides to mock her)* My new tennis porch!

> (MATTIE *opens the letter and removes a ten-dollar bill. Lost in thought, she clutches the letter to her bosom)*

FANNY

(To MATTIE*)* Oughta mind w-h-i-t-e children on w-h-i-t-e property!

PRINCESS

(Now swinging on JULIA*'s gate)* . . . my new tennis porch!

FANNY

(Chases PRINCESS *around the yard)* You, Princess! Stop that!

> (JULIA *laughs, but she is very near tears)*

MATTIE

A letter from October.

FANNY

Who's gon' read it for you?

MATTIE

Lula!

PRINCESS

My new tennis porch!

FANNY

Princess! Mattie!

MATTIE

Teeta! In the house with that drat noise!

FANNY

It'll take Lula half-a day. *(Snatches letter)* I won't charge but ten cent. *(Reads)* "Dear, Sweet Molasses, My Darlin' Wife . . ."

MATTIE

No, I don't like how you make words sound. You read too rough.
(We hear sudden offstage yells and screams from TEETA *and* PRINCESS *as they struggle for possession of some toy)*

PRINCESS

(Offstage) Give it to me!

TEETA

No! It's mine!

MATTIE

(Screams) Teeta!
(The children are quiet)

FANNY

Dear, Sweet Molasses—how 'bout that?

JULIA

(To FANNY*)* Stop that! Don't read her mail.

FANNY

She can't read it.

JULIA

She doesn't want to. She's gonna go on holdin' it in her hand and never know what's in it . . . just 'cause it's hers!

FANNY

Forgive 'em, Father, they know not.

JULIA

Another thing, you told me it's quiet here! You call this quiet? I can't stand it!

FANNY

When you need me come and humbly knock on my *back* door. *(She exits)*

MATTIE

(Shouts to FANNY*)* I ain't gonna knock on no damn back door! Miss Julia, can you read? *(Offers the letter to* JULIA*)* I'll give you some candy when I make it.

JULIA

(Takes the letter) All right. *(*LULA *takes a seat to enjoy a rare social event. She winds stems for the paper flowers as* JULIA *reads)* Dear, sweet molasses, my darlin' wife.

MATTIE

Yes, honey. *(To* JULIA*)* Thank you.

JULIA

(Reads) Somewhere, at sometime, on the high sea, I take my pen in hand . . . well, anyway, this undelible pencil.

LULA

Hope he didn't put it in his mouth.

JULIA

(Reads) I be missin' you all the time.

MATTIE

And we miss you.

JULIA

(Reads) Sorry we did not have our picture taken.

MATTIE

Didn't have the money.

JULIA

(Reads) Would like to show one to the men and say this is my wife and child . . . They always be showin' pictures.

MATTIE

(Waves the ten-dollar bill) I'm gon' send you one, darlin'.

JULIA

(Reads) I recall how we used to take a long walk on Sunday

afternoon . . . *(Thinks about this for a moment)* . . . then come home and be lovin' each other.

MATTIE

I recall.

JULIA

(Reads) The Government people held up your allotment.

MATTIE

Oh, do Jesus.

JULIA

(Reads) They have many papers to be sign, pink, blue and white, also green. Money can't be had 'til all papers match. Mine don't match.

LULA

Takes a-while.

JULIA

(Reads) Here is ten cash dollars I hope will not be stole.

MATTIE

(Holds up the money) I got it.

JULIA

(Reads) Go to Merchant Marine office and push things from your end.

MATTIE

Monday. Lula, le's go Monday.

LULA

I gotta see Nelson march in the parade.

JULIA

(Reads) They say people now droppin' in the street, dyin' from this wartime influenza. Don't get sick—buy tonic if you do. I love you.

MATTIE

Gotta buy a bottle-a tonic.

JULIA

(Reads) Sometimes people say hurtful things 'bout what I am, like color and race . . .

MATTIE

Tell 'em you my brown-skin Carolina daddy, that's who the hell you are. Wish I was there.

276

JULIA

(Reads) I try not to hear 'cause I do want to get back to your side. Two things a man can give the woman he loves . . . his name and his protection . . . The first you have, the last is yet to someday come. The war is here, the road is rocky. I am *ever* your lovin' husband, October.

MATTIE

So-long, darlin' . . . I wish I had your education.

JULIA

I only went through eighth grade. Name and protection. I know you love him.

MATTIE

Yes'm, I do. If I was to see October in bed with another woman, I'd never doubt him 'cause I trust him more than I do my own eyesight. Bet yall don't believe me.

JULIA

I know how much a woman can love. *(Glances at the letter again)* Two things a man can give . . .

MATTIE

Name and protection. That's right, too. I wouldn't live with no man. Man got to marry me. Man that won't marry you thinks nothin' of you. Just usin' you.

JULIA

I've never allowed anybody to *use* me!

LULA

(Trying to move her away stage right) Mattie, look like rain.

MATTIE

A man can't use a woman less she let him.

LULA

(To MATTIE*)* You never know when to stop.

JULIA

Well, I read your letter. Good day.

MATTIE

Did I hurtcha feelin's? Tell me, what'd I say.

JULIA

I—I've been keepin' company with someone for a long time and . . . we're not married.

277

MATTIE

For how long?

LULA

(Half-heartedly tries to hush MATTIE, *but she would also like to know)* Ohhh, Mattie.

JULIA

(Without shame) Ten years today, ten full, faithful years.

MATTIE

He got a wife?

JULIA

(Very tense and uncomfortable) No.

MATTIE

Oh, a man don't wanta get married, work on him. Cut off piece-a his shirttail and sew it to your petticoat. It works. Get Fanny to read the tea leaves and tell you how to move. She's a old bitch but what she sees in a teacup is true.

JULIA

Thank you, Mattie.

LULA

Let's pray on it, Miss Julia. Gawd bring them together, in holy matrimony.

JULIA

Miss Lula, please don't . . . You know it's against the law for black and white to get married, so Gawd nor the tea leaves can help us. My friend is white and that's why I try to stay to myself.

(After a few seconds of silence)

LULA

Guess we shouldn't-a disturbed you.

JULIA

But I'm so glad you did. Oh, the things I can tell you 'bout bein' lonesome and shut out. Always movin', one place to another, lookin' for some peace of mind. I moved out in the country . . . Pretty but quiet as the graveyard; so lonesome. One year I was in such a *lovely* colored neighborhood but they couldn't be bothered with me, you know? I've lived near sportin' people . . . they were very kindly but I'm not a sporty type person. Then I found this place hid way in the backyard so quiet, didn't see another soul . . . And that's why I thought yall wanted to tear my house down this mornin' . . . 'cause you might-a heard 'bout me and Herman . . . and some people are . . . well, they judge, they can't help judgin' you.

MATTIE

(Eager to absolve her of wrongdoing) Oh, darlin', we all do things we don't want sometimes. You grit your teeth and take all he's got; if you don't, somebody else will.

LULA

No, no, you got no use for 'em so don't take nothin' from 'em.

MATTIE

He's takin' somethin' from her.

LULA

Have faith, you won't starve.

MATTIE

Rob him blind. Take it all. Let him froth at the mouth. Let him die in the poorhouse—bitter, bitter to the bone!

LULA

A white man is somethin' else. Everybody knows how that low-down slave-master sent for a different black woman every night . . . for his pleasure. That's why none of us is the same color.

MATTIE

And right now today they're mean, honey. They can't help it; their nose is pinched together so close they can't get enough air. It makes 'em mean. And their mouth is set back in their face so hard and flat . . . no roundness, no sweetness, they can't even carry a tune.

LULA

I couldn't stand one of 'em to touch me intimate no matter what he'd give me.

JULIA

Miss Lula, you don't understand. Mattie, the way you and your husband feel, that's the way it is with me 'n' Herman. He loves me . . . We love each other, that's all, we just love each other. *(After a split second of silence)* And someday, as soon as we're able, we have to leave here and go where it's right . . . Where it's

279

legal for everybody to marry. That's what we both want . . . to be
man and wife—like you and October.

LULA

Well, I have to cut out six dozen paper roses today. *(Starts for her
house)*

MATTIE

And I gotta make a batch-a candy and look after Princess so I can
feed me and Teeta 'til October comes back. Thanks for readin'
the letter. *(She enters her house)*

JULIA

But Mattie, Lula—I wanted to tell you why it's been ten years—
and why we haven't—

LULA

Good day, Miss Julia. *(Enters her house)*

JULIA

Well, that's always the way. What am I doin' standin' in a backyard explainin' my life? Stay to yourself, Julia Augustine. Stay to
yourself. *(Sweeps her front porch)*

　　I got to climb my way to glory
　　Got to climb it by myself
　　Ain't nobody here can climb it for me
　　I got to climb it for myself.
　　　　　　(Curtain)

SCENE 2

TIME: *That evening. The curtain is still closed;* MATTIE, LULA
and KIDS *can be heard singing and laughing.*

　　As curtain opens, JULIA *has almost finished the unpacking. The
room now looks quite cozy. Once in a while she watches the clock
and looks out the window.* TEETA *follows* PRINCESS *out of* MATTIE's
house and ties her sash. PRINCESS *is holding a jump-rope.*

MATTIE

(Offstage. Sings)
> My best man left me, it sure do grieve my mind
> When I'm laughin', I'm laughin' to keep from cryin' . . .

PRINCESS

(Twirling the rope to one side) Ching, ching, China-man eat dead rat . . .

TEETA

(As PRINCESS *jumps rope)* Knock him in the head with a baseball bat . . .

PRINCESS

You wanta jump?

TEETA

Yes.

PRINCESS

Say "Yes, ma'm."

TEETA

No.

PRINCESS

Why?

TEETA

You too little.

PRINCESS

(Takes bean-bag from her pocket) You can't play with my bean-bag.

TEETA

I 'on care, play it by yourself.

PRINCESS

(Drops rope, tosses the bag to TEETA*)* Catch. *(*TEETA *throws it back.* HERMAN *appears at the back-entry. He is a strong, forty-year-old workingman. His light-brown hair is sprinkled with gray. At the present moment he is tired.* PRINCESS *notices him because she is facing the back fence. He looks for a gate or opening but can find none)* Hello.

TEETA

Mama! Mama!

HERMAN

Hello, children. Where's the gate?

(HERMAN passes several packages through a hole in the fence; he thinks of climbing the fence, but it is very rickety. He disappears from view. MATTIE dashes out of her house, notices the packages, runs into LULA's house, then back into the yard. LULA enters in a flurry of excitement; gathers a couple of pieces from the clothesline. MATTIE goes to inspect the packages)

LULA

Don't touch 'em, Mattie. Might be dynamite.

MATTIE

Well, I'm gon' get my head blowed off, 'cause I wanta see.

(NELSON steps out wearing his best civilian clothes: neat-fitting suit, striped silk shirt and bulldog shoes in oxblood leather. He claps his hands to frighten MATTIE)

MATTIE

Oh, look at him. Where's the party?

NELSON

Everywhere! The ladies have heard Nelson's home. They waitin' for me!

LULA

Don't get in trouble. Don't answer anybody that bothers you.

NELSON

How come it is that when I carry a sack-a coal on my back you don't worry, but when I'm goin' out to enjoy myself you almost go crazy.

LULA

Go on! Deliver the piece to the funeral.

(She hands him a funeral piece. MATTIE proceeds to examine the contents of a paper bag)

NELSON

Fact is, I was gon' stay home and have me some orange drink, but Massa beat me to it. None-a my business no-how, dammit.

(MATTIE opens another bag. HERMAN enters through the front entry. FANNY follows at a respectable distance)

282

MATTIE

Look, rolls and biscuits!

LULA

Why'd he leave the food in the yard?

HERMAN

Because I couldn't find the gate. Good evening. Pleasant weather. Howdy-do. Cool this evenin'. *(Silence)* Err—I see where the Allies suffered another set-back yesterday. Well, that's the war, as they say.

> *(The* WOMEN *answer with nods and vague throat clearings.* JULIA *opens her door, he enters)*

MATTIE

That's the lady's husband. He's a light colored man.

PRINCESS

What is a light colored man?

> *(The children exit with* MATTIE *and* NELSON. FANNY *exits by front entry,* LULA *to her house)*

JULIA

Why'd you pick a conversation? I tell you 'bout that.

HERMAN

Man gotta say somethin' stumblin' round in a strange backyard.

JULIA

Why didn't you wear your good suit? You know how people like to look you over and sum you up.

HERMAN

Mama and Annabelle made me so damn mad tonight. When I got home Annabelle had this in the window. *(Removes a cardboard sign from the bag . . . printed with red, white, and blue crayon:* WE ARE AMERICAN CITIZENS*)*

JULIA

"We are American citizens." Why'd she put it in the window?

HERMAN

Somebody wrote cross the side of our house in purple paint . . . "Krauts . . . Germans live here"! I'd-a broke his arm if I caught him.

JULIA

It's the war. Makes people mean. But didn't she print it pretty.

HERMAN

Comes from Mama boastin' 'bout her German grandfather, now it's no longer fashionable. I snatched that coward sign outta the window . . . Goddammit, I says . . . Annabelle cryin', Mama hollerin' at her. Gawd save us from the ignorance, I say . . . Why should I see a sign in the window when I get home? That Annabelle got flags flyin' in the front yard, the backyard . . . and red, white and blue flowers in the grass . . . confound nonsense . . . Mama is an ignorant woman . . .

JULIA

Don't say that . . .

HERMAN

A poor ignorant woman who is mad because she was born a sharecropper . . . outta her mind 'cause she ain't high-class society. We're redneck crackers, I told her, that's what.

JULIA

Oh, Herman . . . no, you didn't . . .

HERMAN

I did.

JULIA

(Standing) But she raised you . . . loaned you all-a her three thousand dollars to pour into that bakery shop. You know you care about her.

HERMAN

Of course I do. But sometimes she makes me so mad . . . Close the door, lock out the world . . . all of 'em that ain't crazy are coward. *(Looks at sign)* Poor Annabelle—Miss Wartime Volunteer . . .

JULIA

She's what you'd call a very Patriotic Person, wouldn't you say?

HERMAN

Well, guess it is hard for her to have a brother who only makes pies in time of war.

JULIA

A brother who makes pies and loves a nigger!

HERMAN

Sweet Kerist, there it is again!

284

JULIA

Your mama's own words . . . according to you—I'll never forget them as long as I live. Annabelle, you've got a brother who makes pies and loves a nigger.

HERMAN

How can you remember seven or eight years ago, for Gawd's sake? Sorry I told it.

JULIA

I'm not angry, honeybunch, dear heart. I just remember.

HERMAN

When you say honeybunch, you're angry. Where do you want your Aunt Cora?

JULIA

On my dresser!

HERMAN

An awful mean woman.

JULIA

Don't get me started on your mama and Annabelle. *(Pause)*

HERMAN

Julia, why did you move into a backyard?

JULIA

(Goes to him) Another move, another mess. Sometimes I feel like fightin' . . . and there's nobody to fight but you . . .

HERMAN

Open the box. Go on. Open it.

JULIA

(Opens the box and reveals a small but ornate wedding cake with a bride and groom on top and ten pink candles) Ohhh, it's the best one ever. Tassels, bells, roses . . .

HERMAN

. . . daffodils and silver sprinkles . . .

JULIA

You're the best baker in the world.

HERMAN

(As he lights the candles) Because you put up with me . . .

JULIA

Gawd knows that.

HERMAN

. . . because the palms of your hands and the soles of your feet are pink and brown . . .

JULIA

Jus' listen to him. Well, go on.

HERMAN

Because you're a good woman, a kind, good woman.

JULIA

Thank you very much, Herman.

HERMAN

Because you care about me.

JULIA

Well, I do.

HERMAN

Happy ten years . . . Happy tenth year.

JULIA

And the same to you.

HERMAN

(Tries a bit of soft barbershop harmony)
    I love you as I never loved before *(JULIA joins him)*
    When first I met you on the village green
    Come to me e'er my dream of love is o'er
    I love you as I loved you
    When you were sweet— Take the end up higher—
    When you were su-weet six-ateen.
Now blow!
    (They blow out the candles and kiss through a cloud of smoke)

JULIA

(Almost forgetting something) Got something for you. Because you were my only friend when Aunt Cora sent me on a sleep-in job in the white folks' kitchen. And wasn't that Miss Bessie one mean white woman? *(Gives present to HERMAN)*

HERMAN

Oh, Julia, just say she was mean.

JULIA

Well, yes, but she was white too.

HERMAN

A new peel, thank you. A new pastry bag. Thank you.

JULIA

(She gives him a sweater) I did everything right but one arm came out shorter.

HERMAN

That's how I feel. Since three o'clock this morning, I turned out twenty ginger breads, thirty sponge cakes, lady fingers, charlotte russe . . . loaf bread, round bread, twist bread and water rolls . . . and—

JULIA

Tell me about pies. Do pies!

HERMAN

Fifty pies. Open apple, closed apple, apple crumb, sweet potato and pecan. And I got a order for a large wedding cake. They want it in the shape of a battleship. *(HERMAN gives JULIA ring box. JULIA takes out a wide, gold wedding band—it is strung on a chain)* It's a wedding band . . . on a chain . . . To have until such time as . . . It's what you wanted, Julia. A damn fool present.

JULIA

Sorry I lost your graduation ring. If you'd-a gone to college what do you think you'd-a been?

HERMAN

A baker with a degree.

JULIA

(Reads) Herman and Julia 1908 . . . and now it's . . . 1918. Time runs away. A wedding band . . . on a chain. *(She fastens the chain around her neck)*

HERMAN

A damn fool present.

(JULIA drops the ring inside of her dress)

JULIA

It comforts me. It's your promise. You hungry?

HERMAN

No.

JULIA

After the war, the people across the way are goin' to Philadelphia.

HERMAN

I hear it's cold up there. People freeze to death waitin' for a trolley car.

JULIA

(Leans back beside him, rubs his head) In the middle of the night a big bird flew cryin' over this house— Then he was gone, the way time goes flyin' . . .

HERMAN

Julia, why did you move in a backyard? Out in the country the air was so sweet and clean. Makes me feel shame . . .

JULIA

(Rubbing his back) Crickets singin' that lonesome evenin' song. Any kind-a people better than none a-tall.

HERMAN

Mama's beggin' me to hire Greenlee again, to help in the shop. "Herman, sit back like a half-way gentleman and just take in money."

JULIA

Greenlee! When white folks decide . . .

HERMAN

People, Julia, people.

JULIA

When people decide to give other people a job, they come up with the biggest Uncle Tom they can find. The *people* I know call him a "white-folks nigger." It's a terrible expression so don't you ever use it.

HERMAN

He seems dignified, Julia.

JULIA

Jus' 'cause you're clean and stand straight, that's not dignity. Even speakin' nice might not be dignity.

HERMAN

What's dignity? Tell me. Do it.

JULIA

Well, it . . . it . . . It's a feeling— It's a spirit that rises higher than the dirt around it, without any by-your-leave. It's not proud and

it's not 'shamed . . . Dignity "Is" . . . and it's never Greenlee
. . . I don't know if it's us either, honey.

HERMAN

(Standing) It still bothers my mother that I'm a baker. "When you
gonna rise in the world!" A baker who rises . . . *(Laughs and coughs
a little)* Now she's worried 'bout Annabelle marryin' a sailor. After
all, Annabelle is a concert pianist. She's had only one concert
. . . in a church . . . and not many people there.

JULIA

A sailor might just persevere and become an admiral. Yes, an
admiral and a concert pianist.

HERMAN

Ten years. If I'd-a known what I know now, I wouldn't-a let Mama
borrow on the house or give me the bakery.

JULIA

Give what? Three broken stoves and all-a your papa's unpaid bills.

HERMAN

I *got* to pay her back. And I can't go to Philadelphia or wherever
the hell you're saying to go. I can hear you thinkin', Philadelphia,
Philadelphia, Phil—

JULIA

(Jumping up. Pours wine) Oh damnation! The hell with that!

HERMAN

All right, not so much hell and damn. When we first met you were
so shy.

JULIA

Sure was, wouldn't say "dog" 'cause it had a tail. In the beginnin'
nothin' but lovin' and kissin' . . . and thinkin' 'bout you. Now I
worry 'bout gettin' old. I do. Maybe you'll meet somebody
younger. People do get old, y'know. *(Sits on bed)*

HERMAN

There's an old couple 'cross from the bakery . . . "Mabel," he yells,
"where's my keys!" . . . Mabel has a big behind on her. She wears
his carpet slippers. "All right, Robbie, m'boy," she says . . . Robbie
walks kinda one-sided. But they're havin' a pretty good time. We'll
grow old together both of us havin' the same name. *(Takes her in*

his arms) Julia, I love you . . . you know it . . . I love you . . . *(After a pause)* Did you have my watch fixed?

JULIA

(Sleepily) Uh-huh, it's in my purse. *(Getting up)* Last night when the bird flew over the house—I dreamed 'bout the devil's face in the fire . . . He said "I'm comin' to drag you to hell."

HERMAN

(Sitting up) There's no other hell, honey. Celestine was sayin' the other day—

JULIA

How do you know what Celestine says?

HERMAN

Annabelle invited her to dinner.

JULIA

They still trying to throw that white widow-woman at you? Oh, Herman, I'm gettin' mean . . . jumpin' at noises . . . and bad dreams.

HERMAN

(Brandishing bottle) Dammit, this is the big bird that flew over the house!

JULIA

I don't go anywhere, I don't know anybody, I gotta do somethin'. Sometimes I need to have company—to say . . . "Howdy-do, pleasant evenin', do drop in." Sometimes I need other people. How you ever gonna pay back three thousand dollars? Your side hurt?

HERMAN

Schumann came in to see me this mornin'. Says he'll buy me out, ten cents on the dollar, and give me a job bakin' for him . . . it's an offer—can get seventeen hundred cash.

JULIA

Don't do it, Herman. That sure wouldn't be dignity.

HERMAN

He makes an American flag out of gingerbread. But they sell. Bad taste sells. Julia, where do you want to go? New York, Philadelphia, where? Let's try their dignity. Say where you want to go.

JULIA

Well, darlin', if folks are freezin' in Philadelphia, we'll go to New York.

HERMAN

Right! You go and size up the place. Meanwhile I'll stay here and do like everybody else, make war money . . . battleship cakes, cannonball cookies . . . chocolate bullets . . . they'll sell. Pay my debts. Less than a year, I'll be up there with money in my pockets.

JULIA

Northerners talk funny— "We're from New Yorrrk."

HERMAN

I'll getcha train ticket next week.

JULIA

No train. I wanta stand on the deck of a Clyde Line boat, wavin' to the people on the shore. The whistle blowin', flags flyin' . . . wavin' my handkerchief . . . So long, so long, look here—South Carolina . . . so long, hometown . . . goin' away by myself— *(Tearfully blows her nose)*

HERMAN

You gonna like it. Stay with your cousin and don't talk to strangers.

(JULIA gets dress from her hope chest)

JULIA

Then when we do get married we can have a quiet reception. My cut-glass punch bowl . . . little sandwiches, a few friends . . . Herman? Hope my weddin' dress isn't too small. It's been waitin' a good while. *(Holds dress in front of her)* I'll use all of my hope-chest things. Quilts, Irish linens, the silver cups . . . Oh, honey, how are you gonna manage with me gone?

HERMAN

Buy warm underwear and a woolen coat with a fur collar . . . to turn against the northern wind. What size socks do I wear?

JULIA

Eleven, eleven and a half if they run small.

HERMAN

. . . what's the store? Write it down.

JULIA

Coleridge. And go to King Street for your shirts.

HERMAN

Coleridge. Write it down.

JULIA

Keep payin' Ruckheiser, the tailor, so he can start your new suit.

HERMAN

Ruckheiser. Write it down.

JULIA

Now that I know I'm goin' we can take our time.

HERMAN

No, rush, hurry, make haste, do it. Look at you . . . like your old self.

JULIA

No, no, not yet—I'll go soon as we get around to it. *(Kisses him)*

HERMAN

That's right. Take your time . . .

JULIA

Oh, Herman.

> (MATTIE *enters through the back gate with* TEETA. *She pats and arranges* TEETA's *hair.* FANNY *enters from the front entry and goes to* JULIA's *window)*

MATTIE

You goin' to Lula's service?

FANNY

A new faith. Rather be a Catholic than somethin' you gotta make up. Girl, my new tenant and her—

MATTIE

(Giving FANNY *the high-sign to watch what she says in front of* TEETA*)* . . . and her husband.

FANNY

I gotcha. She and her husband was in there havin' a orgy. Singin', laughin', screamin', cryin' . . . I'd like to be a fly on that wall.

> (LULA *enters the yard wearing a shawl over her head and a red band on her arm. She carries two chairs and places them beside two kegs)*

LULA

Service time!
> (MATTIE, TEETA *and* FANNY *enter the yard and sit down.*
> LULA *places a small table and a cross)*

FANNY

(Goes to JULIA's *door and knocks)* Let's spread the word to those
who need it. *(Shouts)* Miss Julia, don't stop if you in the middle-a
somethin'. We who love Gawd are gatherin' for prayer. Got any
time for Jesus?

ALL

(Sing) When the roll is called up yonder.

JULIA

Thank you, Miss Fanny.
> (FANNY *flounces back to her seat in triumph.* JULIA *sits on
> the bed near* HERMAN)

HERMAN

Dammit, she's makin' fun of you.

JULIA

(Smooths her dress and hair) Nobody's invited me anywhere in
a long time . . . so I'm goin'.

HERMAN

(Standing) I'm gonna buy you a Clyde Line ticket for New York
City on Monday . . . this Monday.

JULIA

Monday?

HERMAN

As Gawd is my judge. That's dignity. Monday.

JULIA

(Joyfully kissing him) Yes, Herman! *(She enters yard)*

LULA

My form-a service opens with praise. Let us speak to Gawd.

MATTIE

Well, I thang Gawd that—that I'm livin' and I pray my husband
comes home safe.

TEETA

I love Jesus and Jesus loves me.

ALL

Amen.

FANNY

I thang Gawd that I'm able to rise spite-a those who try to hold me down, spite-a those who are two-faceted, spite-a those in my own race who jealous 'cause I'm doin' so much better than the rest of 'em. He preparest a table for me in the presence of my enemies.

MATTIE

That's enough, Fanny.

FANNY

Double-deal Fanny Johnson all you want but me 'n' Gawd's gonna come out on top.

(ALL *look to* JULIA)

JULIA

I'm sorry for past sin—but from Monday on through eternity—I'm gonna live in dignity accordin' to the laws of God and man. Oh, Glory!

LULA

Glory Hallelujah!

(NELSON *enters a bit unsteadily . . . struts and preens while singing*)

NELSON

Come here, black woman . . . whoooo . . . eee . . . on Daddy's knee . . . (etc.)

LULA

(Trying to interrupt him) We're testifyin' . . .

NELSON

(Throwing hat on porch) Right! Testify! Tonight I asked the prettiest girl in Carolina to be my wife, and Merrilee Jones told me . . . I'm sorry, but you got nothin' to offer. She's right! I got nothin' to offer but a hard way to go. Merrilee Jones . . . workin' for the rich white folks and better off washin' their dirty drawers than marryin' me.

LULA

Respect the church! *(Slaps him)*

NELSON

(Sings) Come here, black woman (etc.) . . .

JULIA

Oh, Nelson, respect your mother!

NELSON

Respect your damn self, Julia Augustine! *(Continues singing)*

LULA

How we gonna find a new faith?

NELSON

(Softly) By tellin' the truth, Mama. Merrilee ain't no liar. I got nothin' to offer, just like October.

MATTIE

You keep my husband's name outta your mouth.

NELSON

(Sings) Come here, black woman . . .

FANNY and CONGREGATION

(Sing)

   Ain't gon' let nobody turn me round, turn me round,
     turn me round
   Ain't gon' let nobody turn me round . . .

HERMAN

(Staggers out to porch) Julia, I'm going now, I'm sorry . . . I don't feel well . . . I don't know . . . *(Slides forward and falls)*

JULIA

Mr. Nelson . . . won'tcha please help me . . .

FANNY

Get him out of my yard.

     (NELSON and JULIA help HERMAN in to bed. Others freeze in yard)

     (Curtain)

Act Two

SCENE 1

TIME: *Sunday morning.*

SCENE: *The same as Act One except the yard and houses are neater. The clothesline is down. Off in the distance someone is humming a snatch of a hymn. Church bells are ringing.* HERMAN *is in a heavy, restless sleep. The bedcovers indicate he has spent a troubled night. On the table are medicine bottles, cups and spoons.* JULIA *is standing beside the bed, swinging a steam kettle; she stops and puts it on a trivet on top of her hope chest.*

FANNY

(Seeing her) Keep usin' the steam kettle.
> *(*HERMAN *groans lightly)*

MATTIE

(Picks up scissors) Put the scissors under the bed, open. It'll cut the pain.

FANNY

(Takes scissors from MATTIE*)* That's for childbirth.

JULIA

He's had too much paregoric. Sleepin' his life away. I want a doctor.

FANNY

Over my dead body. It's gainst the damn law for him to be layin' up in a black woman's bed.

MATTIE

A doctor will call the police.

FANNY

They'll say I run a bad house.

JULIA

I'll tell 'em the truth.

MATTIE

We don't tell things to police.

296

FANNY

When Lula gets back with his sister, his damn sister will take charge.

MATTIE

That's his family.

FANNY

Family is family.

JULIA

I'll hire a hack and take him to a doctor.

FANNY

He might die on you. That's police. That's the workhouse.

JULIA

I'll say I found him on the street!

FANNY

Walk into the jaws of the law—they'll chew you up.

JULIA

Suppose his sister won't come?

FANNY

She'll be here. (FANNY *picks up a teacup and turns it upside down on the saucer and twirls it*) I see a ship, a ship sailin' on the water.

MATTIE

Water clear or muddy?

FANNY

Crystal clear.

MATTIE

(*Realizing she's late*) Oh, I gotta get Princess so her folks can open their ice cream parlor. Take care-a Teeta.

FANNY

I see you on your way to Miami, Florida, goin' on a trip.

JULIA

(*Sitting on window seat*) I know you want me to move. I will, Fanny.

FANNY

Julia, it's hard to live under these mean white folks . . . but I've done it. I'm the first and only colored they let buy land 'round here.

297

JULIA

They all like you, Fanny. Only one of 'em cares for me . . . just one.

FANNY

Yes, I'm thought highly of. When I pass by they can say . . . "There she go, Fanny Johnson, representin' her race in-a approved manner" . . . 'cause they don't have to worry 'bout my next move. I can't afford to mess that up on account-a you or any-a the rest-a these hard-luck, better-off-dead, triflin' niggers.

JULIA

(Crossing up right) I'll move. But I'm gonna call a doctor.

FANNY

Do it, we'll have a yellow quarantine sign on the front door . . . "Influenza." Doctor'll fill out papers for the law . . . address . . . race . . .

JULIA

I . . . I guess I'll wait until his sister gets here.

FANNY

No, you call a doctor, Nelson won't march in the parade tomorrow or go back to the army, Mattie'll be outta work, Lula can't deliver flowers . . .

JULIA

I'm sorry, so very sorry. I'm the one breakin' laws, doin' wrong.

FANNY

I'm not judgin' you. High or low, nobody's against this if it's kept quiet. But when you pickin' white . . . pick a wealthy white. It makes things easier.

JULIA

No, Herman's not rich and I've never tried to beat him out of anything.

FANNY

(Crossing to JULIA*)* Well, he just oughta be and you just shoulda. A colored woman needs money more than anybody else in this world.

JULIA

You sell yours.

FANNY

All I don't sell I'm going to keep.

HERMAN

Julia?

FANNY

(Very genial) Well, well, sir, how you feelin', Mr. Herman? This is Aunt Fanny . . . Miss Julia's landlady. You lookin' better, Mr. Herman. We've been praying for you. *(*FANNY *exits to* TEETA's *house)*

JULIA

Miss Lula—went to get your sister.

HERMAN

Why?

JULIA

Fanny made me. We couldn't wake you up.
(He tries to sit up in bed to prepare for leaving. She tries to help him. He falls back on the pillow)

HERMAN

Get my wallet . . . see how much money is there. What's that smell?
(She takes the wallet from his coat pocket. She completes counting the money)

JULIA

Eucalyptus oil, to help you breathe; I smell it, you smell it and Annabelle will have to smell it too! Seventeen dollars.

HERMAN

A boat ticket to New York is fourteen dollars— Ohhhh, Kerist! Pain . . . pain . . . Count to ten . . . one, two . . . *(*JULIA *gives paregoric water to him. He drinks. She puts down glass and picks up damp cloth from bowl on tray and wipes his brow)* My mother is made out of too many . . . little things . . . the price of carrots, how much fat is on the meat . . . little things make people small. Make ignorance—y'know?

JULIA

Don't fret about your people, I promise I won't be surprised at anything and I won't have unpleasant words no matter what.

HERMAN

(The pain eases. He is exhausted) Ahhh, there . . . All men are born which is—utterly untrue.

> *(*NELSON *steps out of the house. He is brushing his army jacket.* HERMAN *moans slightly.* JULIA *gets her dress-making scissors and opens them, places the scissors under the bed)*

FANNY

(To NELSON *as she nods towards* JULIA*'s house)* I like men of African descent, myself.

NELSON

Pitiful people. They pitiful.

FANNY

They common. Only reason I'm sleepin' in a double bed by myself is 'cause I got to bear the standard for the race. I oughta run her outta here for the sake-a the race too.

NELSON

It's your property. Run us all off it, Fanny.

FANNY

Plenty-a these hungry, jobless, bad-luck colored men, just a-itchin' to move in on my gravy-train. I don't want 'em.

NELSON

(With good nature) Right, Fanny! We empty-handed, got nothin' to offer.

FANNY

But I'm damn tired-a ramblin' 'round in five rooms by myself. House full-a new furniture, the icebox forever full-a goodies. I'm a fine cook and I know how to pleasure a man . . . he wouldn't have to step outside for a thing . . . food, fun and finance . . . all under one roof. Nelson, how'd you like to be my business adviser? Fix you up a little office in my front parlor. You wouldn't have to work for white folks . . . and Lula wouldn't have to pay rent. The war won't last forever . . . then what you gonna do? They got nothin' for you but haulin' wood and cleanin' toilets. Let's you and me pitch in together.

NELSON

I know you just teasin', but I wouldn't do a-tall. Somebody like me ain't good enough for you noway, but you a fine-lookin' woman,

300

though. After the war I might hit out for Chicago or Detroit
. . . a rollin' stone gathers no moss.

FANNY

Roll on. Just tryin' to help the race.

(LULA *enters by front entry, followed by* ANNABELLE, *a
woman in her thirties. She assumes a slightly mincing air
of fashionable delicacy. She might be graceful if she were
not ashamed of her size. She is nervous and fearful in this
strange atmosphere. The others fall silent as they see her.*
ANNABELLE *wonders if* PRINCESS *is her brother's child. Or
could it be* TEETA, *or both?)*

ANNABELLE

Hello there . . . er . . . children.

PRINCESS

(Can't resist mocking her) Hello there . . . er . . . children. *(Giggles)*

ANNABELLE

(To TEETA*)* Is she your sister?

(ANNABELLE *looks at* NELSON *and draws her shawl a little
closer)*

TEETA

You have to ask my mama.

NELSON

(Annoyed with ANNABELLE*'s discomfort)* Mom, where's the flat-
iron?

(He turns and enters his house. LULA *follows.* MATTIE *and*
CHILDREN *exit)*

FANNY

I'm the landlady. Mr. Herman had every care and kindness 'cept
a doctor. Miss Juliaaaa! That's the family's concern. *(*FANNY *opens
door, then exits)*

ANNABELLE

Sister's here. It's Annabelle.

JULIA

(Shows her to a chair) One minute he's with you, the next he's
gone. Paregoric makes you sleep.

ANNABELLE

(Dabs at her eyes with a handkerchief) Cryin' doesn't make sense

301

a-tall. I'm a volunteer worker at the naval hospital . . . I've nursed
my mother . . . *(Chokes with tears)*

JULIA

(Pours a glass of water for her) Well, this is more than sickness.
It's not knowin' 'bout other things.

ANNABELLE

We've known for years. He is away all the time and when old
Uncle Greenlee . . . He's a colored gentlemen who works in our
neighborhood . . . and he said . . . he told . . . er, well, people do
talk. *(*ANNABELLE *spills water,* JULIA *attempts to wipe the water
from her dress)* Don't do that . . . It's all right.

HERMAN

Julia?

ANNABELLE

Sister's here. Mama and Uncle Greenlee have a hack down
the street. Gets a little darker we'll take you home, call a physician . . .

JULIA

Can't you do it right away?

ANNABELLE

'Course you could put him out. Please let us wait 'til dark.

JULIA

Get a doctor.

ANNABELLE

Our plans are made, thank you.

HERMAN

Annabelle, this is Julia.

ANNABELLE

Hush.

HERMAN

This is my sister.

ANNABELLE

Now be still.

JULIA

I'll call Greenlee to help him dress.

ANNABELLE

No. Dress first. The colored folk in *our* neighborhood have great respect for us.

HERMAN

Because I give away cinnamon buns, for Kerist sake.

ANNABELLE

(To JULIA*)* I promised my mother I'd try and talk to you. Now— you look like one-a the nice coloreds . . .

HERMAN

Remember you are a concert pianist, that is a very dignified calling.

ANNABELLE

Put these on. We'll turn our backs.

JULIA

He can't.

ANNABELLE

(Holds the covers in a way to keep his midsection under wraps) Hold up. *(They manage to get the trousers up as high as his waist but they are twisted and crooked)* Up we go! There . . . *(They are breathless from the effort of lifting him)* Now fasten your clothing. *(*JULIA *fastens his clothes)* I declare, even a dead man oughta have enough pride to fasten himself.

JULIA

You're a volunteer at the naval hospital?

HERMAN

(As another pain hits him) Julia, my little brown girl . . . Keep singing . . .

JULIA

> We are climbin' Jacob's ladder,
> We are climbin' Jacob's ladder,
> We are climbin' Jacob's ladder, Soldier of the Cross . . .

HERMAN

The palms of your hands . . .

JULIA

(Singing) Every round goes higher and higher . . .

HERMAN

. . . the soles of your feet are pink and brown.

ANNABELLE

Dammit, hush. Hush this noise. Sick or not sick, hush! It's ugliness. *(To* JULIA*)* Let me take care of him, please, leave us alone.

JULIA

I'll get Greenlee.

ANNABELLE

No! You hear me? No.

JULIA

I'll be outside.

ANNABELLE

(Sitting on bed) If she hadn't-a gone I'd-a screamed. *(*JULIA *stands on the porch.* ANNABELLE *cries)* I thought so highly of you . . . and here you are in somethin' that's been festerin' for years. *(In disbelief)* One of the finest women in the world is pinin' her heart out for you, a woman who's pure gold. Everything Celestine does for Mama she's really doin' for you . . . to get next to you . . . But even a saint wants some reward.

HERMAN

I don't want Saint Celestine.

ANNABELLE

(Standing) Get up! *(Tries to move* HERMAN*)* At the naval hospital I've seen influenza cases tied down to keep 'em from walkin'. What're we doin' here? How do you meet a black woman?

HERMAN

She came in the bakery on a rainy Saturday evening.

ANNABELLE

(Giving in to curiosity) Yes?

MATTIE

(Offstage. Scolding TEETA *and* PRINCESS*)* Sit down and drink that lemonade. Don't bother me!

HERMAN

"I smell rye bread baking." Those were the first words . . . Every day . . . Each time the bell sounds over the shop door I'm hopin' it's the brown girl . . . pretty shirtwaist and navy-blue skirt. One

day I took her hand . . . "Little lady, don't be afraid of me"
. . . She wasn't . . . I've never been lonesome since.

ANNABELLE

(Holding out his shirt) Here, your arm goes in the sleeve. *(They're
managing to get the shirt on)*

HERMAN

(Beginning to ramble) Julia? Your body is velvet . . . the sweet
blackberry kisses . . . you are the night-time, the warm, Carolina
night-time in my arms . . .

ANNABELLE

(Bitterly) Most excitement I've ever had was takin' piano lessons.

JULIA

(Calls from porch) Ready?

ANNABELLE

No. Rushin' us out. A little longer, please. *(Takes a comb from her
purse and nervously combs his hair)* You nor Mama put yourselves
out to understand my Walter when I had him home to dinner.
Yes, he's a common sailor . . . I wish he was an officer. I never
liked a sailor's uniform, tight pants and middy blouses . . . but they
are in the service of their country . . . He's taller than I am. You
didn't even stay home that one Sunday like you promised. Must-a
been chasin' after some-a them blackberry kisses you love so well.
Mama made a jackass outta Walter. You know how she can do.
He left lookin' like a whipped dog. Small wonder he won't live
down here. I'm crazy-wild 'bout Walter even if he is a sailor.
Marry Celestine. She'll take care-a Mama and I can go right on
up to the Brooklyn Navy Yard. I been prayin' so hard . . . You
marry Celestine and set me free. And Gawd knows I don't want
another concert.

HERMAN

(Sighs) Pain, keep singing.

ANNABELLE

Dum-dum-blue Danube. *(He falls back on the pillow. She bathes
his head with a damp cloth)*

JULIA

(As NELSON enters the yard) Tell your mother I'm grateful for her
kindness. I appreciate . . .

NELSON

Don't have so much to say to me. *(Quietly, in a straightforward manner)* They set us on fire 'bout their women. String us up, pour on kerosene and light a match. Wouldn't I make a bright flame in my new uniform?

JULIA

Don't be thinkin' that way.

NELSON

I'm thinkin' 'bout black boys hangin' from trees in Little Mountain, Elloree, Winnsboro.

JULIA

Herman never killed anybody. I couldn't care 'bout that kind-a man.

NELSON

(Stopping, turning to her) How can you account for carin' 'bout him a-tall?

JULIA

In that place where I worked, he was the only one who cared . . . who really cared. So gentle, such a gentle man . . . "Yes, ma'am" . . . "No, ma'am," "Thank you, ma'am . . ." In the best years of my youth, my Aunt Cora sent me out to work on a sleep-in job. His shop was near that place where I worked. . . . Most folks don't have to *account* for why they love.

NELSON

You ain't most folks. You're down on the bottom with us, under his foot. A black man got nothin' to offer you . . .

JULIA

I wasn't lookin' for anybody to do for me.

NELSON

. . . and *he's* got nothin' to offer. The one layin' on your mattress, not even if he's kind as you say. He got nothin' for you . . . but some meat and gravy or a new petticoat . . . or maybe he can give you meriny-lookin' little bastard chirrun for us to take in and raise up. We're the ones who feed and raise 'em when it's like this . . . They don't want 'em. They only too glad to let us have their kin-folk. As it is, we supportin' half-a the slave-master's offspring right now.

JULIA

Go fight those who fight you. He never threw a pail-a water on you. Why didn't you fight them that did? Takin' it out on me 'n Herman 'cause you scared of 'em . . .

NELSON

Scared? What scared! If I gotta die, I'm carryin' one 'long with me.

JULIA

No you not. You gon' keep on fightin' me.

NELSON

. . . Scared-a what? I look down on 'em, I spit on 'em.

JULIA

No, you don't. They throw dirty water on your uniform . . . and you spit on me!

NELSON

Scared, what scared!

JULIA

You fightin' me, me, me, not them . . . never them.

NELSON

Yeah, I was scared and I'm tougher, stronger, a better man than any of 'em . . . but they won't letcha fight one or four or ten. I was scared to fight a hundred or a thousand. A losin' fight.

JULIA

I'd-a been afraid too.

NELSON

And you scared right now, you let the woman run you out your house.

JULIA

I didn't want to make trouble.

NELSON

But that's what a fight is . . . trouble.

LULA

(In her doorway) Your mouth will kill you. (To JULIA) Don't tell Mr. Herman anything he said . . . or I'll hurt you.

307

JULIA

Oh, Miss Lula.

LULA

Anyway, he didn't say nothin'.

(HERMAN'S MOTHER *enters the yard. She is a "poor white" about fifty-seven years old. She has risen above her poor farm background and tries to assume the airs of "quality." Her clothes are well-kept–shabby. She wears white shoes, a shirtwaist and skirt, drop earrings, a cameo brooch, a faded blue straw hat with a limp bit of veiling. She carries a heavy black oilcloth bag. All in the yard give a step backward as she enters. She assumes an air of calm well-being. Almost as though visiting friends, but anxiety shows around the edges and underneath.* JULIA *approaches and* HERMAN'S MOTHER *abruptly turns to* MATTIE)*

HERMAN'S MOTHER

How do.

(MATTIE, TEETA *and* PRINCESS *look at* HERMAN'S MOTHER. HERMAN'S MOTHER *is also curious about them*)

MATTIE

(In answer to a penetrating stare from the old woman) She's mine. I take care-a her. *(Speaking her defiance by ordering the children)* Stay inside 'fore y'all catch the flu!

HERMAN'S MOTHER

(To LULA*)* You were very kind to bring word . . . er . . .

LULA

Lula, ma'am.

HERMAN'S MOTHER

The woman who nursed my second cousin's children . . . she had a name like that . . . Lulu we called her.

LULA

My son, Nelson.

HERMAN'S MOTHER

Can see that.

(MATTIE *and the children exit.* FANNY *hurries in from the front entry. Is most eager to establish herself on the good side of* HERMAN'S MOTHER. *With a slight bow. She is carrying the silver tea service)*

FANNY

Beg pardon, if I may be so bold, I'm Fanny, the owner of all this property.

HERMAN'S MOTHER

(Definitely approving of FANNY*)* I'm . . . er . . . Miss Annabelle's mother.

FANNY

My humble pleasure . . . er . . . Miss . . . er . . .

HERMAN'S MOTHER

(After a brief, thoughtful pause) Miss Thelma.
(They move aside, but FANNY *makes sure others hear)*

FANNY

Miss Thelma, this is not Squeeze-gut Alley. We're just poor, humble, colored people . . . and everybody knows how to keep their mouth shut.

HERMAN'S MOTHER

I thank you.

FANNY

She wanted to get a doctor. I put my foot down.

HERMAN'S MOTHER

You did right. *(Shaking her head, confiding her troubles)* Ohhhh, you don't know.

FANNY

(With deep understanding) Ohhhh, yes, I do. She moved in on me yesterday.

HERMAN'S MOTHER

Friend Fanny, help me to get through this.

FANNY

I will. Now this is Julia, she's the one . . .
*(*HERMAN'S MOTHER *starts toward the house without looking at* JULIA. FANNY *decides to let the matter drop)*

HERMAN'S MOTHER

(To LULA*)* Tell Uncle Greenlee not to worry. He's holdin' the horse and buggy.

309

NELSON

(Bars LULA*'s way)* Mama. I'll do it.

(LULA *exits into her house.* FANNY *leads* HERMAN'S
MOTHER *to the chair near* HERMAN*'s bed)*

ANNABELLE

Mama, if we don't call a doctor Herman's gonna die.

HERMAN'S MOTHER

Everybody's gon' die. Just a matter of when, where and how. A
pretty silver service.

FANNY

English china. Belgian linen. Have a cup-a tea?

HERMAN'S MOTHER

(As a studied pronouncement) My son comes to deliver baked
goods and the influenza strikes him down. Sickness, it's the war.

FANNY

(Admiring her cleverness) Yes, ma'am, I'm a witness. I saw him
with the packages.

JULIA

Now please call the doctor.

ANNABELLE

Yes, please, Mama. No way for him to move 'less we pick him up
bodily.

HERMAN'S MOTHER

Then we'll pick him up.

HERMAN

About Walter . . . your Walter . . . I'm sorry . . . *(*JULIA *tries to
give* HERMAN *some water)*

HERMAN'S MOTHER

Annabelle, help your brother. *(*ANNABELLE *gingerly takes glass
from* JULIA*)* Get that boy to help us. I'll give him a dollar. Now
gather his things.

ANNABELLE

What things?

HERMAN'S MOTHER

His possessions, anything he owns, whatever is his. What you been
doin' in here all this time?

*(*FANNY *notices* JULIA *is about to speak, so she hurries her*

through the motions of going through dresser drawers and throwing articles into a pillowcase)

FANNY

Come on, sugar, make haste.

JULIA

Don't go through my belongings.
(She tears through the drawers, flinging things around as she tries to find his articles. FANNY *neatly piles them together)*

FANNY

(Taking inventory) Three shirts . . . one is kinda soiled.

HERMAN'S MOTHER

That's all right, I'll burn 'em.

FANNY

Some new undershirts.

HERMAN'S MOTHER

I'll burn them too.

JULIA

(To FANNY*)* Put 'em down. I bought 'em and they're not for burnin'.

HERMAN'S MOTHER

(Struggling to hold her anger in check) Fanny, go get that boy. I'll give him fifty cents.

FANNY

You said a dollar.

HERMAN'S MOTHER

All right, dollar it is. *(*FANNY *exits toward the front entry. In tense, hushed, excited tones, they argue back and forth)* Now where's the billfold . . . there's papers . . . identity . . . *(Looks in* HERMAN*'s coat pockets)*

ANNABELLE

Don't make such a to-do.

HERMAN'S MOTHER

You got any money of your own? Yes, I wanta know where's his money.

JULIA

I'm gettin' it.

HERMAN'S MOTHER

In her pocketbook. This is why the bakery can't make it.

HERMAN

I gave her the Gawd-damned money!

JULIA

And I know what Herman wants me to do . . .

HERMAN'S MOTHER

(With a wry smile) I'm sure you know what he wants.

JULIA

I'm not gonna match words with you. Furthermore, I'm too much of a lady.

HERMAN'S MOTHER

A lady oughta learn how to keep her dress down.

ANNABELLE

Mama, you makin' a spectacle outta yourself.

HERMAN'S MOTHER

You a big simpleton. Men have nasty natures, they can't help it. A man would go with a snake if he only knew how. They cleaned out your wallet.

HERMAN

(Shivering with a chill) I gave her the damn money.

(JULIA takes it from her purse)

HERMAN'S MOTHER

Where's your pocket-watch, or did you give that too? Annabelle, get another lock put on that bakery door.

HERMAN

I gave her the money to go—to go to New York.

(JULIA drops the money in HERMAN'S MOTHER's lap. She is silent for a moment)

HERMAN'S MOTHER

All right. Take it and go. It's never too late to undo a mistake. I'll add more to it. (She puts the money on the dresser)

JULIA

I'm not goin' anywhere.

HERMAN'S MOTHER

Look here, girl, you leave him 'lone.

ANNABELLE

Oh, Mama, all he has to do is stay away.

HERMAN'S MOTHER

But he can't do it. Been years and he can't do it.

JULIA

I got him hoo-dooed, I sprinkle red pepper on his shirttail.

HERMAN'S MOTHER

I believe you.

HERMAN

I have a black woman . . . and I'm gon' marry her. I'm gon' marry her . . . got that? Pride needs a paper, for . . . for the sake of herself . . . that's dignity—tell me, what is dignity—Higher than the dirt it is . . . dignity is . . .

ANNABELLE

Let's take him to the doctor, Mama.

HERMAN'S MOTHER

When it's dark.

JULIA

Please!

HERMAN'S MOTHER

Nightfall. *(JULIA steps out on the porch but hears every word said in the room)* I had such high hopes for him. *(As if HERMAN is dead)* All my high hopes. When he wasn't but five years old I had to whip him so he'd study his John C. Calhoun speech. Oh, Calhoun knew 'bout niggers. He said, *"Men are not born . . . equal, or any other kinda way . . . MEN are made"* . . . Yes, indeed, for recitin' that John C. Calhoun speech . . . Herman won first mention and a twenty-dollar gold piece . . . at the Knights of The Gold Carnation picnic.

ANNABELLE

Papa changed his mind about the Klan. I'm glad.

HERMAN'S MOTHER

Yes, he was always changin' his mind about somethin'. But I was proud-a my menfolk that day. He spoke that speech . . . The officers shook my hand. They honored me . . . "That boy a-yours gonna be somebody." A poor baker-son layin' up with a nigger woman, a overgrown daughter in heat over a common sailor. I

313

must be payin' for somethin' I did. Yesiree, do a wrong, God'll whip you.

ANNABELLE

I wish it was dark.

HERMAN'S MOTHER

I put up with a man breathin' stale whiskey in my face every night . . . pullin' and pawin' at me . . . always tired, inside and out . . . *(Deepest confidence she has ever shared)* Gave birth to seven . . . five-a them babies couldn't draw breath.

ANNABELLE

(Suddenly wanting to know more about her) Did you love Papa, Mama? Did you ever love him? . . .

HERMAN'S MOTHER

Don't ask me 'bout love . . . I don't know nothin' about it. Never mind love. This is my harvest . . .

HERMAN

Go home. I'm better.

> *(*HERMAN'S MOTHER'*s strategy is to enlighten* HERMAN *and also wear him down. Out on the porch,* JULIA *can hear what is being said in the house)*

HERMAN'S MOTHER

There's something wrong 'bout mismatched things, be they shoes, socks, or people.

HERMAN

Go away, don't look at us.

HERMAN'S MOTHER

People don't like it. They're not gonna letcha do it in peace.

HERMAN

We'll go North.

HERMAN'S MOTHER

Not a thing will change except her last name.

HERMAN

She's not like others . . . she's not like that . . .

HERMAN'S MOTHER

All right, sell out to Schumann. I want my cash-money . . . You got no feelin' for me, I got none for you.

314

HERMAN

I feel . . . I feel what I feel . . . I don't know what I feel . . .

HERMAN'S MOTHER

Don't need to feel. Live by the law. Follow the law—law, law of the land. Obey the law!

ANNABELLE

We're not obeyin' the law. He should be quarantined right here. The city's tryin' to stop an epidemic.

HERMAN'S MOTHER

Let the city drop dead and you 'long with it. *Rather* be dead than disgraced. Your papa gimme the house and little money . . . I want my money back. *(She tries to drag* HERMAN *up in the bed)* I ain't payin' for this. *(Shoves* ANNABELLE *aside)* Let Schumann take over. A man who knows what he's doin'. Go with her . . . Take the last step against your own! Kill us all. Jesus, Gawd, save us or take us—

HERMAN

(Screams) No! No! No! No!

HERMAN'S MOTHER

Thank Gawd, the truth is the light. Oh, Blessed Savior . . . *(*HERMAN *screams out, starting low and ever going higher. She tries to cover his mouth.* ANNABELLE *pulls her hand away)* Thank you, Gawd, let the fire go out . . . this awful fire.

*(*LULA *and* NELSON *enter the yard)*

ANNABELLE

You chokin' him. Mama . . .

JULIA

(From the porch) It's dark! It's dark. Now it's very dark.

HERMAN

One ticket on the Clyde Line . . . Julia . . . where are you? Keep singing . . . count . . . one, two . . . three. Over there, over there . . . send the word, send the word . . .

HERMAN'S MOTHER

Soon be home, son.

*(*HERMAN *breaks away from the men, staggers to* MATTIE's *porch and holds on.* MATTIE *smothers a scream and gets the children out of the way.* FANNY *enters)*

315

HERMAN

Shut the door . . . don't go out . . . the enemy . . . the enemy . . . *(Recites the Calhoun speech)* Men are not born infants are born! They grow to all the freedom of which the condition in which they were born permits. It is a great and dangerous error to suppose that all people are equally entitled to liberty.

JULIA

Go home—Please be still.

HERMAN

It is a reward to be earned, a reward reserved for the intelligent, the patriotic, the virtuous and deserving; and not a boon to be bestowed on a people too ignorant, degraded and vicious . . .

JULIA

You be still now, shut up.

HERMAN

. . . to be capable either of appreciating or of enjoying it.

JULIA

(Covers her ears) Take him . . .

HERMAN

A black woman . . . not like the others . . .

JULIA

. . . outta my sight . . .

HERMAN

Julia, the ship is sinking . . .

*(*HERMAN'S MOTHER *and* NELSON *help* HERMAN *up and out)*

ANNABELLE

(To JULIA *on the porch)* I'm sorry . . . so sorry it had to be this way. I can't leave with you thinkin' I uphold Herman, and blame you.

HERMAN'S MOTHER

(Returning) You the biggest fool.

ANNABELLE

I say a man is responsible for his own behavior.

HERMAN'S MOTHER

And you, you oughta be locked up . . . workhouse . . . jail! Who you think you are!?

316

JULIA

I'm your damn daughter-in-law, you old bitch! The Battleship
Bitch! The bitch who destroys with her filthy mouth. They could
win the war with your killin' mouth. The son-killer, man-killer-
bitch . . . She's killin' him 'cause he loved me more than anybody
in the world.

(FANNY returns)

HERMAN'S MOTHER

Better off . . . He's better off dead in his coffin than live with the
likes-a you . . . black thing! *(She is almost backing into JULIA's
house)*

JULIA

The black thing who bought a hot-water bottle to put on your sick,
white self when rheumatism threw you flat on your back . . . who
bought flannel gowns to warm your pale, mean body. He never ran
up and down King Street shoppin' for you . . . I bought what he
took home to you . . .

HERMAN'S MOTHER

Lies . . . tear outcha lyin' tongue.

JULIA

. . . the lace curtains in your parlor . . . the shirtwaist you wearin'
—I made them.

FANNY

Go *on* . . . I got her. *(Holds JULIA)*

HERMAN'S MOTHER

Leave 'er go! The undertaker will have-ta unlock my hands off her
black throat!

FANNY

Go on, Miss Thelma.

JULIA

Miss Thelma my ass! Her first name is Frieda. The Germans are
here . . . in purple paint!

HERMAN'S MOTHER

Black, sassy nigger!

JULIA

Kraut, knuckle-eater, redneck . . .

HERMAN'S MOTHER

Nigger whore . . . he used you for a garbage pail . . .

JULIA

White trash! Sharecropper! Let him die . . . let 'em all die . . . Kill him with your murderin' mouth—sharecropper bitch!

HERMAN'S MOTHER

Dirty black nigger . . .

JULIA

. . . If I wasn't black with all-a Carolina 'gainst me I'd be mistress of your house! *(To* ANNABELLE*)* Annabelle, you'd be married livin' in Brooklyn, New York . . . *(To* HERMAN'S MOTHER*)* . . . and I'd be waitin' on Frieda . . . cookin' your meals . . . waterin' that damn red, white and blue garden!

HERMAN'S MOTHER

Dirty black bitch.

JULIA

Daughter of a bitch!

ANNABELLE

Leave my mother alone! She's old . . . and sick.

JULIA

But never sick enough to die . . . dirty ever-lasting woman.

HERMAN'S MOTHER

(Clinging to ANNABELLE, *she moves toward the front entry)* I'm as high over you as Mount Everest over the sea. White reigns supreme . . . I'm white, you can't change that.

(They exit. FANNY *goes with them)*

JULIA

Out! Out! Out! And take the last ten years-a my life with you and . . . when he gets better . . . keep him home. Killers, murderers . . . Kinsmen! Klansmen! Keep him home. *(To* MATTIE*)* Name and protection . . . he can't gimme either one. *(To* LULA*)* I'm gon' get down on my knees and scrub where they walked . . . what they touched . . . *(To* MATTIE*)* . . . with brown soap . . . hot lye-water . . . scaldin' hot . . . *(She dashes into the house and collects an armful of bedding)* Clean! . . . Clean the whiteness outta my house . . . clean everything . . . even the memory . . . no more love

. . . Free . . . free to hate-cha for the rest-a my life. *(Back to the porch with her arms full)* When I die I'm gonna keep on hatin' . . . I don't want any whiteness in my house. Stay out . . . out . . . *(Dumps the things in the yard)* . . . out . . . out . . . out . . . and leave me to my black self!

(Blackout)

SCENE 2

TIME: *Early afternoon the following day.*

PLACE: *The same.*

In JULIA's *room, some of the hope-chest things are spilled out on the floor, bedspread, linens, silver cups. The half-emptied wine decanter is in a prominent spot. A table is set up in the yard. We hear the distant sound of a marching band. The excitement of a special day is in the air.* NELSON's *army jacket hangs on his porch.* LULA *brings a pitcher of punch to table.* MATTIE *enters with* TEETA *and* PRINCESS; *she is annoyed and upset in contrast to* LULA's *singing and gala mood. She scolds the children, smacks* TEETA's *behind.*

MATTIE

They was teasin' the Chinaman down the street 'cause his hair is braided. *(To* CHILDREN*)* If he ketches you, he'll cook you with onions and gravy.

LULA

(Inspecting NELSON's *jacket)* Sure will.

TEETA

Can we go play?

MATTIE

A mad dog might bite-cha.

PRINCESS

Can we go play?

319

MATTIE

No, you might step on a nail and get lockjaw.

TEETA

Can we go play?`

MATTIE

Oh, go on and play! I wish a gypsy would steal both of 'em!
(JULIA *enters her room*)

LULA

What's the matter, Mattie?

MATTIE

Them damn fool people at the Merchant Marine don't wanta give
me my 'lotment money.

JULIA

*(Steps out on her porch with deliberate, defiant energy. She is
wearing her wedding dress . . . carrying a wine glass. She is over-
demonstrating a show of carefree abandon and joy)* I'm so happy!
I never been this happy in all my life! I'm happy to be alive, alive
and living for my people.

LULA

You better stop drinkin' so much wine. *(She enters her house)*

JULIA

But if you got no feelin's they can't be hurt!

MATTIE

Hey, Julia, the people at the Merchant Marine say I'm not married to October.

JULIA

Getcha license, honey, show your papers. Some of us, thang
Gawd, got papers!

MATTIE

I don't have none.

JULIA

Why? Was October married before?

MATTIE

No, but I was. A good-for-nothin' named Delroy . . . I hate to call
his name. Was years 'fore I met October. Delroy used to beat the

hell outta me . . . tried to stomp me, grind me into the ground
. . . callin' me such dirty names . . . Got so 'til I was shame to look
at myself in a mirror. I was glad when he run off.

JULIA

Where'd he go?

MATTIE

I don't know. Man at the office kept sayin' . . . "You're not married
to October" . . . and wavin' me 'way like that.

JULIA

Mattie, this state won't allow divorce.

MATTIE

Well, I never got one.

JULIA

You shoulda so you could marry October. You have to be married
to get his benefits.

MATTIE

We was married. On Edisto Island. I had a white dress and flowers
. . . everything but papers. We couldn't get papers. Elder Burns
knew we was doin' best we could.

JULIA

You can't marry without papers.

MATTIE

What if your husband run off? And you got no money? Readin'
from the Bible makes people married, not no piece-a paper. We're
together eleven years, that oughta be legal.

JULIA

(Puts down glass) No, it doesn't go that way.

MATTIE

October's out on the icy water, in the wartime, worryin' 'bout me
'n Teeta. I say he's my husband. Gotta pay Fanny, buy food. Julia,
what must I do?

JULIA

I don't know.

MATTIE

What's the use-a so much-a education if you don't know what to
do?

JULIA

You may's well just lived with October. Your marriage meant nothin'.

MATTIE

(Standing, angry) It meant somethin' to me if not to anybody else. It means I'm ice cream, too, strawberry. *(She heads for her house)*

JULIA

Get mad with me if it'll make you feel better.

MATTIE

Julia, could you lend me two dollars?

JULIA

Yes, that's somethin' I can do besides drink this wine.

> *(*JULIA *goes into her room, to get the two dollars. Enter* FANNY, TEETA *and* PRINCESS*)*

FANNY

Colored men don't know how to do nothin' right. I paid that big black boy 'cross the street . . . thirty cents to paint my sign . . . *(Sign reads . . .* GOODBYE COLORED BOYS . . . *on one side; the other reads . . .* FOR GOD AND CONTRY*)* But he can't spell. I'm gon' call him a dumb darky and get my money back. Come on, children!

> *(*CHILDREN *follow laughing)*

LULA

Why call him names!?

FANNY

'Cause it makes him mad, that's why.

> *(*FANNY *exits with* TEETA *and* PRINCESS. JULIA *goes into her room.* THE BELL MAN *enters carrying a display board filled with badges and flags . . . buttons, red and blue ribbons attached to the buttons . . . slogans . . .* THE WAR TO END ALL WARS. *He also carries a string of overseas caps [paper] and wears one. Blows a war tune on his tin flute.* LULA *exits)*

THE BELL MAN

"War to end all wars . . ." Flags and badges! Getcha emblems! Hup-two-three . . . Flags and badges . . . hup-two-three! Hey, Aunty! Come back here! Where you at?

(He starts to follow LULA *into her house.* NELSON *steps out on the porch and blocks his way)*

NELSON

My mother is in her house. You ain't to come walkin' in. You knock.

THE BELL MAN

Don't letcha uniform go to your head, boy, or you'll end your days swingin' from a tree.

LULA

(Squeezing past NELSON *dressed in skirt and open shirtwaist)* Please, mister, he ain't got good sense.

MATTIE

He crazy, mister.

NELSON

Fact is, you stay out of here. Don't ever come back here no more.

THE BELL MAN

(Backing up in surprise) He got no respect. One them crazies. I ain't never harmed a bare-assed soul but, hot damn, I can got madder and badder than you. Let your uniform go to your head.

LULA

Yessir, he goin' back in the army today.

THE BELL MAN

Might not get there way he's actin.'

MATTIE

(As LULA *takes two one-dollar bills from her bosom)* He sorry right now, mister, his head ain' right.

THE BELL MAN.

(Speaks to LULA *but keeps an eye on* NELSON*)* Why me? I try to give you a laugh but they say, "Play with a puppy and he'll lick your mouth." Familiarity makes for contempt.

LULA

(Taking flags and badges) Yessir. Here's somethin' on my account . . . and I'm buyin' flags and badges for the children. Everybody know you a good man and do right.

THE BELL MAN

(To LULA*)* You pay up by Monday. *(To* NELSON*)* Boy, you done cut off your mama's credit.

LULA

I don't blame you, mister. *(BELL MAN exits)*

NELSON

Mama, your new faith don't seem to do much for you.

LULA

(Turning to him) Nelson, go on off to the war 'fore somebody kills you. I ain't goin' to let nobody spoil my day.

> *(LULA puts flags and badges on punchbowl table. JULIA comes out of her room with the two dollars for MATTIE— hands it to her. Sound of Jenkins Colored Orphan Band is heard [Record: "Ramblin' " by Bunk Johnson])*

JULIA

Listen, Lula . . . Listen, Mattie . . . it's Jenkin's Colored Orphan Band . . . Play! Play, you Orphan boys! Rise up higher than the dirt around you! Play! That's struttin' music, Lula!

LULA

It sure is!

> *(LULA struts, arms akimbo, head held high. JULIA joins her; they haughtily strut toward each other, then retreat with mock arrogance . . . exchange cold, hostile looks . . . A Carolina folk dance passed on from some dimly remembered African beginning. Dance ends strutting)*

JULIA

(Concedes defeat in the dance) All right, Lula, strut me down! Strut me right on down!

> *(They end dance with breathless laughter and cross to LULA's porch)*

LULA

Julia! Fasten me! Pin my hair.

JULIA

I'm not goin' to that silly parade, with the colored soldiers marchin' at the end of it. *(LULA sits on the stool. JULIA combs and arranges her hair)*

LULA

Come on, we'll march behind the white folks whether they want us or not. Mister Herman's people got a nice house . . . lemon trees in the yard, lace curtains at the window.

JULIA

And red, white and blue flowers all around.

LULA

That Uncle Greenlee seems to be well-fixed.

JULIA

He works for the livery stable . . . cleans up behind horses . . . in
a uniform.

LULA

That's nice.

JULIA

Weeds their gardens . . . clips white people's pet dogs . . .

LULA

Ain't that lovely? I wish Nelson was safe and nicely settled.

JULIA

Uncle Greenlee is a well-fed, tale-carryin' son-of-a-bitch . . . and
that's the only kinda love they want from us.

LULA

It's wrong to hate.

JULIA

They say it's wrong to love too.

LULA

We got to show 'em we're good, got to be three times as good,
just to make it.

JULIA

Why? When they mistreat us, who cares? We mistreat each other,
who cares? Why we gotta be so good jus' for them?

LULA

Dern you, Julia Augustine, you hard-headed thing, 'cause they'll
kill us if we not.

JULIA

They doin' it anyway. Last night I dreamed of the dead slaves—
all the murdered black and bloody men silently gathered at the
foot-a my bed. Oh, that awful silence. I wish the dead could
scream and fight back. What they do to us . . . and all they
want is to be loved in return. Nelson's not Greenlee. Nelson is a
fighter.

LULA

(Standing) I know. But I'm tryin' to keep him from findin' it out.
*(*NELSON, *unseen by* LULA, *listens)*

JULIA

Your hair looks pretty.

LULA

Thank you. A few years back I got down on my knees in the
courthouse to keep him off-a the chain gang. I crawled and cried,
"Please, white folks, yall's everything, I'se nothin', yall's everything." The court laughed—I meant for 'em to laugh . . . then
they let Nelson go.

JULIA

(Pitying her) Oh, Miss Lula, a lady's not supposed to crawl and
cry.

LULA

I was savin' his life. Is my skirt fastened? Today might be the last
time I ever see Nelson. *(*NELSON *goes back in house)* Tell him how
life's gon' be better when he gets back. Make up what *should* be
true. A man can't fight a war on nothin' . . . would you send a man
off—to die on nothin'?

JULIA

That's sin, Miss Lula, leavin' on a lie.

LULA

That's all right—some truth has no nourishment in it. Let him feel
good.

JULIA

I'll do my best.

*(*MATTIE *enters carrying a colorful, expensive parasol. It is
far beyond the price range of her outfit)*

MATTIE

October bought it for my birthday 'cause he know I always wanted
a fine-quality parasol.

*(*FANNY *enters through the back entry,* CHILDREN *with her.
The mistake on the sign has been corrected by pasting* OU
over the error)

FANNY

(Admiring MATTIE's *appearance)* Just shows how the race can look

326

when we wanta. I called Rusty Bennet a dumb darky and he wouldn't even get mad. Wouldn't gimme my money back either. A black Jew.

(NELSON enters wearing his private's uniform with quarter-master insignia. He salutes them)

NELSON

Ladies. Was nice seein' you these few days. If I couldn't help, 'least I didn't do you no harm, so nothin' from nothin' leaves nothin'.

FANNY

(Holds up her punch cup; LULA *gives* JULIA *high sign)* Get one-a them Germans for me.

JULIA

(Stands on her porch) Soon, Nelson, in a little while . . . we'll have whatsoever our hearts desire. You're comin' back in glory . . . with honors and shining medals . . . And those medals and that uniform is gonna open doors for you . . . and for October . . . for all, all of the servicemen. Nelson, on account-a you we're gonna be able to go in the park. They're gonna take down the no-colored signs . . . and Rusty Bennet's gonna print new ones . . . Everybody welcome . . . Everybody welcome . . .

MATTIE

(To TEETA*)* Hear that? We gon' go in the park.

FANNY

Some of us ain't ready for that.

PRINCESS

Me too?

MATTIE

You can go now . . . and me too if I got you by the hand.

PRINCESS

(Feeling left out) Ohhhhh.

JULIA

We'll go to the band concerts, the museums . . . we'll go in the library and draw out books.

MATTIE

And we'll draw books.

327

FANNY

Who'll read 'em to you?

MATTIE

My Teeta!

JULIA

Your life'll be safe, you and October'll be heroes.

FANNY

(Very moved) Colored heroes.

JULIA

And at last we'll come into our own.

> (ALL *cheer and applaud.* JULIA *steps down from porch)*

NELSON

Julia, can you look me dead in the eye and say you believe all-a that?

JULIA

If you just gotta believe somethin', it may's well be that.

> *(Applause)*

NELSON

(Steps up on JULIA's *porch to make his speech)* Friends, relatives and all other well-wishers. All-a my fine ladies and little ladies— all you good-lookin', tantalizin', pretty-eyed ladies—yeah, with your *kind* ways and your *mean* ways. I find myself a thorn among six lovely roses. Sweet little Teeta . . . the merry little Princess. Mattie, she so pretty 'til October better hurry up and come on back here. Fanny—uh—tryin' to help the race . . . a race woman. And Julia—my good friend. Mama—the only mama I got, I wanta thank you for savin' my life from time to time. What's hard ain't the goin', it's the comin' back. From the bottom-a my heart, I'd truly like to see y'all, each and every one-a you . . . able to go in the park and all that. I really would. So, with a full heart and a loaded mind, I bid you, as the French say, Adieu.

LULA

(Bowing graciously, she takes NELSON's *arm and they exit)* Our humble thanks . . . my humble pleasure . . . gratitude . . . thank you . . .

> (CHILDREN *wave their flags)*

FANNY

(To the CHILDREN*)* Let's mind our manners in front-a the down-town white people. Remember we're bein' judged.

PRINCESS

Me too?

MATTIE

(Opening umbrella) Yes, you too.

FANNY

(Leads the way and counts time) Step, step, one, two, step, step.
(MATTIE, FANNY *and the* CHILDREN *exit.* HERMAN *enters yard by far gate, takes two long steamer tickets from his pocket.* JULIA *senses him, turns. He is carelessly dressed and sweating)*

HERMAN

I bought our tickets. Boat tickets to New York.

JULIA

(Looks at tickets) Colored tickets. You can't use yours. *(She lets tickets flutter to the ground)*

HERMAN

They'll change and give one white ticket. You'll ride one deck, I'll ride the other . . .

JULIA

John C. Calhoun really said a mouthful—men are not born—men are made. Ten years ago—that's when you shoulda bought tickets. You chained me to your mother for ten years.

HERMAN

(Kneeling, picking up tickets) Could I walk out on 'em? . . . Ker-ist sake. I'm that kinda man like my father was . . . a debt-payer, a plain, workin' man—

JULIA

He was a member in good standin' of The Gold Carnation. What kinda robes and hoods did those plain men wear? For downin' me and mine you won twenty dollars in gold.

HERMAN

I love you . . . I love work, to come home in the evenin' . . . to enjoy the breeze for Gawd's sake . . . But no, I never wanted to

go to New York. The hell with goddamn bread factories . . . I'm
a stony-broke, half-dead, half-way gentleman . . . But I'm what I
wanta be. A baker.

JULIA

You waited 'til you was half dead to buy those tickets. I don't want
to go either . . . Get off the boat, the same faces'll be there at the
dock. It's that shop. It's that shop!

HERMAN

It's mine. I did want to keep it.

JULIA

Right . . . people pick what they want most.

HERMAN

(Indicating the tickets) I did . . . you threw it in my face.

JULIA

Get out. Get your things and get out of my life. (The remarks
become counterpoint. Each rides through the other's speech. HER-
MAN goes in house) Must be fine to own somethin'—even if it's
only four walls and a sack-a flour.

HERMAN

(JULIA has followed him into the house) My father labored in the
street . . . liftin' and layin' down cobblestone . . . liftin' and layin'
down stone 'til there was enough money to open a shop . . .

JULIA

My people . . . relatives, friends and strangers . . . they worked and
slaved free for nothin' for some-a the biggest name families down
here . . . Elliots, Lawrences, Ravenals . . . (HERMAN is wearily
gathering his belongings)

HERMAN

Great honor, working for the biggest name families. That's who
you slaved for. Not me. The big names.

JULIA

. . . the rich and the poor . . . we know you . . . all of you . . . Who
you are . . . where you came from . . . where you goin' . . .

HERMAN

What's my privilege . . . Good mornin', good afternoon . . . pies
are ten cents today . . . and you can get 'em from Schumann for
eight . . .

JULIA

"She's different" . . . I'm no different . . .

HERMAN

I'm white . . . did it give me favors and friends?

JULIA

. . . "Not like the others" . . . We raised up all-a these Carolina children . . . white and the black . . . I'm just like all the rest of the colored women . . . like Lula, Mattie . . . Yes, like Fanny!

HERMAN

Go here, go there . . . Philadelphia . . . New York . . . Schumann wants me to go North too . . .

JULIA

We nursed you, fed you, buried your dead . . . grinned in your face —cried 'bout your troubles—and laughed 'bout ours.

HERMAN

Schumann . . . Alien robber . . . waitin' to buy me out . . . My father . . .

JULIA

Pickin' up cobblestones . . . left him plenty-a time to wear bed-sheets in that Gold Carnation Society . . .

HERMAN

He never hurt anybody.

JULIA

He hurts me. There's no room for you to love him and me too . . . *(Sits)* it can't be done—

HERMAN

The ignorance . . . he didn't know . . . the ignorance . . . Mama . . . they don't know.

JULIA

But *you* know. My father was somebody. He helped put up Roper Hospital and Webster Rice Mills after the earthquake wiped the face-a this Gawd-forsaken city clean . . . a fine brick-mason he was . . . paid him one-third-a what they paid the white ones . . .

HERMAN

We were poor . . . No big name, no quality.

331

JULIA

Poor! My gramma was a slave wash-woman bustin' suds for free!
Can't get poorer than that.

HERMAN

(Trying to shut out the sound of her voice) Not for me, she didn't!

JULIA

We the ones built the pretty white mansions . . . for free . . . the
fishin' boats . . . for free . . . made your clothes, raised your food
. . . for free . . . and I loved you—for free.

HERMAN

A Gawd-damn lie . . . nobody did for me . . . you know it . . . you
know how hard I worked—

JULIA

If it's anybody's home down here it's mine . . . everything in the
city is mine—why should I go anywhere . . . ground I'm standin'
on—it's mine.

HERMAN

(Sitting on foot of the bed) It's the ignorance . . . Lemme be,
lemme rest . . . Ker-ist sake . . . It's the ignorance . . .

JULIA

After ten years you still won't look. All-a my people that's been
killed . . . It's your people that killed 'em . . . all that's been in
bondage—your people put 'em there—all that didn't go to school
—your people kept 'em out.

HERMAN

But I didn't do it. Did I do it?

JULIA

They killed 'em . . . all the dead slaves . . . buried under a blanket-a
this Carolina earth, even the cotton crop is nourished with hearts'
blood . . . roots-a that cotton tangled and wrapped 'round my
bones.

HERMAN

And you blamin' me for it . . .

JULIA

Yes! . . . For the one thing we never talk about . . . white folks
killin' me and mine. You wouldn't let me speak.

HERMAN

I never stopped you . . .

JULIA

Every time I open my mouth 'bout what they do . . . you say
. . . "Ker-ist, there it is again . . ." Whenever somebody was
lynched . . . you 'n me would eat a very silent supper. It hurt me
not to talk . . . what you don't say you swallow down . . . *(Pours
wine)*

HERMAN

I was just glad to close the door 'gainst what's out there. You did
all the givin' . . . I failed you in every way.

JULIA

You nursed me when I was sick . . . paid my debts . . .

HERMAN

I didn't give my name.

JULIA

You couldn't . . . was the law . . .

HERMAN

I shoulda walked 'til we came to where it'd be all right.

JULIA

You never put any other woman before me.

HERMAN

Only, Mama, Annabelle, the customers, the law . . . the ignorance
. . . I honored them while you waited and waited—

JULIA

You clothed me . . . you fed me . . . you were kind, loving . . .

HERMAN

I never did a damn thing for you. After ten years look at it—I
never did a damn thing for you.

JULIA

Don't low-rate yourself . . . leave me something.

HERMAN

When my mother and sister came . . . I was ashamed. What am
I doin' bein' ashamed of us?

JULIA

When you first came in this yard I almost died-a shame . . . so
many times you was nothin' to me but white . . . times we were

angry . . . damn white man . . . times I was tired . . . damn white man . . . but most times you were my husband, my friend, my lover . . .

HERMAN

Whatever is wrong, Julia . . . not the law . . . *me;* what I didn't do, with all-a my faults, spite-a all that . . . You gotta believe I love you . . . 'cause I do . . . That's the one thing I know . . . I love you . . . I love you.

JULIA

Ain't too many people in this world that get to be loved . . . really loved.

HERMAN

We gon' take that boat trip . . . You'll see, you'll never be sorry.

JULIA

To hell with sorry. Let's be glad!

HERMAN

Sweetheart, leave the ignorance outside . . . *(Stretches out across the bed)* Don't let that doctor in here . . . to stand over me shakin' his head.

JULIA

(Pours water in a silver cup) Bet you never drank from a silver cup. Carolina water is sweet water . . . Wherever you go you gotta come back for a drink-a this water. Sweet water, like the breeze that blows 'cross the battery.

HERMAN

(Happily weary) I'm gettin' old, that ain' no joke.

JULIA

No, you're not, Herman. My real weddin' cake . . . I wanta big one . . .

HERMAN

Gonna bake it in a washtub . . .

JULIA

We'll put pieces of it in little boxes for folks to take home and dream on.

HERMAN

. . . But let's don't give none to your landlady . . . Gon' get old and funny-lookin' like Robbie m'boy and . . . and . . .

JULIA

And Mable . . .

HERMAN

(Breathing heavier) Robbie says, "Mable, where's my keys" . . .
Mable— Robbie— Mable—

> *(Lights change, shadows grow longer.* MATTIE *enters the yard)*

MATTIE

Hey, Julia! *(Sound of carriage wheels in front of the main house.*
MATTIE *enters* JULIA's *house. As she sees* HERMAN*)* They 'round
there, they come to get him, Julia.

> *(*JULIA *takes the wedding band and chain from around her neck, gives it to* MATTIE *with tickets)*

JULIA

Surprise. Present.

MATTIE

For me?

JULIA

Northern tickets . . . and a wedding band.

MATTIE

I can't take that for nothing.

JULIA

You and Teeta are my people.

MATTIE

Yes.

JULIA

You and Teeta are my family. Be my family.

MATTIE

We your people whether we blood kin or not. *(She exits to her own
porch)*

FANNY

(Offstage) No . . . No, ma'am. *(Enters with* LULA. LULA *is carrying the wilted bouquet)* Julia! They think Mr. Herman's come
back.

> *(*HERMAN'S MOTHER *enters with* ANNABELLE. *The old lady
> is weary and subdued.* ANNABELLE *is almost without feeling.*
> JULIA *is on her porch waiting)*

JULIA

Yes, Fanny, he's here. *(*LULA *retires to her doorway.* JULIA *silently stares at them, studying each woman, seeing them with new eyes. She is going through that rising process wherein she must reject them as the molders and dictators of her life)* Nobody comes in my house.

FANNY

What kinda way is that?

JULIA

Nobody comes in my house.

ANNABELLE

We'll quietly take him home.

JULIA

You can't come in.

HERMAN'S MOTHER

(Low-keyed, polite; humble simplicity) You see my condition. Gawd's punishin' me . . . Whippin' me for somethin' I did or didn't do. I can't understand this . . . I prayed, but ain't no understandin' Herman's dyin'. He's almost gone. It's right and proper that he should die at home in his own bed. I'm askin' humbly . . . or else I'm forced to get help from the police.

ANNABELLE

Give her a chance . . . She'll do right . . . won'tcha?

> *(*HERMAN *stirs. His breathing becomes harsh and deepens into the sound known as the "death rattle."* MATTIE *leads the* CHILDREN *away)*

JULIA

(Not unkindly) Do whatever you have to do. Win the war. Represent the race. Call the police. *(She enters her house, closes the door and bolts it.* HERMAN'S MOTHER *leaves through the front entry.* FANNY *slowly follows her)* I'm here, do you hear me? *(He tries to answer but can't)* We're standin' on the deck-a that Clyde Line Boat . . . wavin' to the people on the shore . . . Your mama, Annabelle, my Aunt Cora . . . all of our friends . . . the children . . . all wavin' . . . "Don't stay 'way too long . . . Be sure and come back . . . We gon' miss you . . . Come back, we need you" . . . But we're goin' . . . The whistle's blowin', flags wavin' . . .

We're takin' off, ridin' the waves so smooth and easy . . . There now . . . (ANNABELLE *moves closer to the house as she listens to* JULIA) . . . the bakery's fine . . . all the orders are ready . . . out to sea . . . on our way . . . *(The weight has lifted, she is radiantly happy. She helps him gasp out each remaining breath. With each gasp he seems to draw a step nearer to a wonderful goal)* Yes . . . Yes . . . Yes . . . Yes . . . Yes . . . Yes . . .

Curtain

The Abdication

by
RUTH WOLFF

"**I** was never sure Cleopatra or Joan of Arc would have acted the way Shakespeare or Shaw said. . . . These were men of great vision and insight, but I often feel their heroines are boys in disguise. . . . Only when women can see themselves through other women's eyes will we know who we are."

Ruth Wolff has written five historical plays about great women: *Eleanor of Aquitaine* (about the twelfth-century queen who married two kings), *The Fall of Athens* (a reinterpretation of the story of Antigone), *George and Frederic* (about George Sand and her affair with Chopin), *Empress of China* (about Tsu Hsi, "a concubine who became a ruler because she was the cleverest person around") and *The Abdication.* "I want to create major roles for actresses—I see that as my function."

"Christina is the most disturbed of the women I've written about—the most in conflict about being a woman. . . ." In researching *The Abdication,* Wolff read Christina's actual letters to Cardinal Azzolino. "It was true that she had a great love for this man. . . . She made him her executor, and when she died, the first thing he did was to destroy all his letters to her—he was about to destroy hers to him when he died." The play was first produced in Bath, England, by the Bristol Old Vic, and was later made into a movie, from Wolff's screenplay, starring Liv Ullmann and Peter Finch.

Wolff is currently writing a screenplay for Ellen Burstyn about Loreta Velasquez, who fought for the Confederacy during the Civil War. Two of Wolff's plays, *Folly Cove* and *Still Life with Apples,* were presented at the O'Neill Theatre Center, and *Arabic Two* was performed in New York. Wolff was awarded a Rockefeller playwrighting fellowship to Wesleyan University and had a play, *Eden Again,* commissioned by The Kennedy Center for the Bicentennial. She lives in New York City with her architect husband and teen-age son.

CHARACTERS
(In order of appearance)

BIRGITO

DOMINIC

CHRISTINA

AZZOLINO

TINA

OXENSTIERNA

CHRIS

CHARLES

EBBA

MAGNUS

TIME: The main action of the play takes place in Rome, 1655.

PLACE: An antechamber in the Vatican.

SETTING: A raked platform surrounded by vertical panels which can rise, fall and pivot to create a space in which scenes flow easily from present action to other places, other times.

The setting should be abstract, less concerned with physical reality than with evocation of character, mood and state of mind.

342

Act One

The curtain is up as the audience enters.

The antechamber is deserted except for an empty ceremonial chair which dominates the space. Music. The lights come up slowly on the empty chair.

After a moment, BIRGITO, *a dwarf, enters warily from outside, down left. He explores the room, then approaches the chair, moving around it, running his fingers over it.*

DOMINIC, *a young priest, enters busily from the interior of the Vatican, carrying documents. The dwarf sees him and attempts to hide under the chair.*

DOMINIC

Who is there? *(No answer)* I said *who is there? (He goes toward the chair)* Come out! Come out of there!

> *(He reaches under and pulls* BIRGITO *out by the nape of the neck.* BIRGITO *struggles in his grip.* CHRISTINA *enters from the outside, wearing a traveling cape)*

CHRISTINA

Let him go!

> *(In spite of himself,* DOMINIC *obeys instantly)*

DOMINIC

Who—? *(*BIRGITO *bites* DOMINIC *on the hand.* DOMINIC *cries out and drops all his papers)* He bit me!

CHRISTINA

(To BIRGITO*)* How does he taste? *(*BIRGITO *makes a wry face)* In that case, don't make a habit of it.

> *(She takes off her cape, revealing herself to be wearing men's clothes and carrying a riding crop)*

DOMINIC

Just a minute! Who are you?

CHRISTINA

Tell the Pope I'm here.

DOMINIC

You can't just break in—!

CHRISTINA

(Examining the room) I am Christina.

DOMINIC

You—?

CHRISTINA

Yes.

DOMINIC

Christina of Sweden?

CHRISTINA

Why not?

DOMINIC

Because . . . because . . . *(He looks at her clothing, her unqueenly disarray, her dwarf, then comes up with)* . . . she is not expected for three days!

CHRISTINA

Nevertheless, she is here.

DOMINIC

But, Madame—

CHRISTINA

Tell the Pope I have arrived to throw myself at his feet and to become his newest and most ardent Catholic! Tell him I was so eager to see him that I galloped on ahead of all my retinue. Tell him I have sworn not to take my first communion till I receive it from his hand. Tell him I— *(She breaks off. She looks suddenly lost, vulnerable, deeply troubled.* BIRGITO *approaches her, recalling her to herself. She turns to* DOMINIC *impatiently)* Well? . . . Go! *(She cracks her whip.* DOMINIC *jumps. She laughs)* We won't steal anything. *(He hesitates for a moment, then scoops up his scattered papers and leaves)* Caught them off guard, didn't I? *(*BIRGITO *smiles with satisfaction.* CHRISTINA *strides about the room)* Well, Birgito, what do you think? Will the Vatican suit us? *(*BIRGITO *performs some mocking stunts, parodies of piety and reverence)* Are you glad we gave up Sweden for Rome? *(He shivers with cold, then pantomimes languishing under the sun)* Yes, yes, how glorious! To be out of the cold and under the Italian sun at last! Sometimes I thought we'd never make it. But here we are, safe, sound and

344

about to be greeted by the Pope! How I've longed to meet him
. . . *(In pantomime* BIRGITO *questions how he should greet His
Holiness. Should he shake hands? Bow? Salute?)* You kiss his ring!
And then—you leave me alone with him. *(Again the look of
troubled longing comes over her)* I have only just arrived, but
I have a feeling the Pope and I are going to be the best of
friends . . .

> *(She sits on the chair, throwing one leg over the arm.* DOM-
> INIC *reenters and stops abruptly)*

DOMINIC

Madame!

CHRISTINA

Yes?

DOMINIC

In the Pope's antechamber, the only one who sits on that chair
is the Pope!

CHRISTINA

Well, I wouldn't want to offend him in my first five minutes
. . . *(She rises)* Is he coming?

DOMINIC

He is in his apartments.

CHRISTINA

Oh, then I'm to be taken to him. Good. Is this the way?

> *(She starts to exit toward the papal quarters stage right.*
> DOMINIC *hurries to block her path)*

DOMINIC

Madame, please! Not yet—

CHRISTINA

Oh?

DOMINIC

There are formalities—

CHRISTINA

Oh, let's dispense with those! Tell the Pope I permit him not to
stand on ceremony.

DOMINIC

This ceremony, I'm afraid, is necessary.

345

CHRISTINA

Ceremony is *never* necessary. I thought when I gave up the crown I'd be through with all that nonsense.

DOMINIC

This ceremony is hardly nonsense.

CHRISTINA

Well, what is it?

DOMINIC

Before you can see the Pope, you must confess.

CHRISTINA

Confess!

DOMINIC

A ritual cleansing.

CHRISTINA

I could better use a bath!

DOMINIC

For the good of your soul—

CHRISTINA

My soul has survived abdication, conversion and a thousand miles of jogging in square-wheeled carriages. I shall not make the rest of the journey on my knees!

DOMINIC

But, Madame—

CHRISTINA

Besides, I've already poured out my soul in letters to His Holiness. Why does he want me to whisper it all over again into his ear?

DOMINIC

Oh, you won't be confessed by *him!*

CHRISTINA

Who, then?

DOMINIC

Another.

CHRISTINA

Some ancient cleric hiding behind his curtains muttering "Yes, my daughter." "No, my daughter"?

DOMINIC

Please, Madame—

346

CHRISTINA

I shall not expose my soul to some faceless creature!

(CARDINAL AZZOLINO *enters. He is a handsome, forceful man in his middle forties*)

AZZOLINO

Do it eye to eye, then.

DOMINIC

Father—

AZZOLINO

She's quite right. The curtains are put on the confessional to make things easier for the penitent. But I can see that Christina, the former Queen of Sweden, is not one for the easiest way.

CHRISTINA

I expected the Pope to take me in his arms and bless me. I did not expect to be held in his antechamber—

AZZOLINO

I quite understand.

CHRISTINA

I am a Queen!

AZZOLINO

An *ex*-Queen—if you will forgive the distinction.

CHRISTINA

I have rank—

AZZOLINO

Great rank—as do we all in the eyes of God.

CHRISTINA

And what have I in the eyes of the Pope?

AZZOLINO

He has not seen you.

CHRISTINA

Then I insist you give him the opportunity immediately!

AZZOLINO

(Coolly) Dominic, tell the Pope he may retire for the evening. It is obvious that his daughter will not be ready to be received by him tonight. *(Furious,* CHRISTINA *slaps her riding crop against the throne)* And, Dominic . . .

347

DOMINIC

Yes, Father?

AZZOLINO

Kindly remove the chair. I've been noticing for some time—it needs reupholstering. *(DOMINIC starts to remove the chair. BIRGITO, who has been hidden under it, jumps out to block his path)* What have we here?

CHRISTINA

My companion of the road, Birgito.
(She gestures for him to let DOMINIC pass. DOMINIC goes out with the chair)

AZZOLINO

Where are your maidservants?

CHRISTINA

I prefer the company of men. Birgito serves me well. I've named him after the only Swedish saint. She was a lady, of course, and as beautiful as virtue, while he is a man, and as ugly as sin. Outside of that, they are identical! *(BIRGITO pantomimes)* He's asking you if you see the resemblance.

AZZOLINO

"Asking" me?

CHRISTINA

He cannot speak—except in gestures . . . Oh, don't try to "overhear" him, only I can understand.
(BIRGITO makes signs to her)

AZZOLINO

What does he say?

CHRISTINA

He says we should go back to Sweden!
(AZZOLINO laughs)

AZZOLINO

(To BIRGITO) After such a long journey, at least you will consent to spend the night. *(BIRGITO looks to CHRISTINA for advice. She nods. He indicates he will accept the invitation. DOMINIC reenters)* Dominic, show Birgito to the Queen's apartments.

DOMINIC

Yes, Father.

*(*DOMINIC *and* BIRGITO *start out)*

AZZOLINO

And, Dominic—

DOMINIC

Yes, Father?

AZZOLINO

Please be on your best behavior. Remember, you are escorting a saint . . . *(Posing as a holy relic,* BIRGITO, *escorted by* DOMINIC, *marches out)* I apologize for Brother Dominic. His request for you to confess apparently surprised you.

CHRISTINA

It did.

AZZOLINO

When he's been at it longer, he'll be more diplomatic.

CHRISTINA

I hope so.

AZZOLINO

It's a mere formality. If you prefer, we can wait till you are less tired—

CHRISTINA

I am never tired.

AZZOLINO

I only thought you might like to—

CHRISTINA

I always look like this. Rest does not improve me . . . Tell me, Cardinal . . . You *are* a Cardinal? I don't misread the costume?

AZZOLINO

I am a Cardinal.

CHRISTINA

This . . . formality . . . before I can see the Pope—is it usual Vatican procedure?

AZZOLINO

Frequently.

CHRISTINA

Do you never make exceptions?

AZZOLINO

Sometimes.

CHRISTINA

Then surely I can be one—

AZZOLINO

I am afraid not.

CHRISTINA

Why?

AZZOLINO

There are doubts.

CHRISTINA

About what?

AZZOLINO

The sincerity of your conversion.

CHRISTINA

I gave up a *crown* to become a convert!

AZZOLINO

So it seems . . .

CHRISTINA

No one in the history of the world has ever made such a sacrifice!

AZZOLINO

So anxious were you to become a Catholic.

CHRISTINA

So anxious.

AZZOLINO

Then why did it take you a year to make the journey from Stockholm to Rome?

CHRISTINA

The roads were muddy.

AZZOLINO

And the ballrooms of Hamburg, Antwerp and Brussels? Were they muddy, too?

CHRISTINA

They were divine!

AZZOLINO

The *Church* is divine.

CHRISTINA

Ah, but in quite a different way—

AZZOLINO

In your letters to the Pope you said you would travel as a pilgrim, incognito!

CHRISTINA

I tried to.

AZZOLINO

With an entourage of two hundred and fifty-five!

CHRISTINA

Can Catholics not have footmen?

AZZOLINO

Within reason. They dress within reason, too. The women do not go about dressed as men.

CHRISTINA

I wear what I please! Will you measure my faith by my clothes and my servants?

AZZOLINO

I will measure your faith—by your faith.

CHRISTINA

Which you obviously find wanting.

AZZOLINO

Since your abdication, you've been cavorting over the face of Europe—

CHRISTINA

I was enjoying myself for the first time in my life!

AZZOLINO

And what made you suddenly decide to cut short the merrymaking and descend on the Vatican?

(CHRISTINA *looks at him. She will not answer the question*)

CHRISTINA

I insist on seeing the Pope. At once!

AZZOLINO

That is impossible.

CHRISTINA

But he led me to believe he would greet me as a daughter the moment I arrived!

AZZOLINO

And so he hoped to.

CHRISTINA

Then why am I still standing here?

(AZZOLINO *takes a small book from his pocket and shows it to her*)

AZZOLINO

Because of this.

(CHRISTINA *looks at it—she doesn't have to see inside*)

CHRISTINA

So . . . it has reached you . . .

AZZOLINO

Yes. It has reached us. *(He reads the cover)* "The Pleasures and Depravities of Christina, Queen of Sweden."

CHRISTINA

A promising title.

AZZOLINO

I understand copies are being sold in seven languages.

CHRISTINA

The anonymous author must be getting rich.

AZZOLINO

Have you read it?

CHRISTINA

I haven't time to waste on scandal. Don't tell me you have?

AZZOLINO

I've read it, yes.

CHRISTINA

So you share the public's appetite for royal meat!

AZZOLINO

Not exactly. Do you refute the book?

CHRISTINA

No. I laugh at it! And so should you! Or can't the Church be expected to appreciate a dirty joke?

AZZOLINO

We can enjoy a dirty joke—if that's what it is, Christina. There's only one reason we don't find it amusing.

CHRISTINA

And what is that?

AZZOLINO

(Taking out a packet of letters) These seem to prove that a great deal of what the book says . . . is true.

CHRISTINA

And what are those?

AZZOLINO

Letters—from priests and bishops all along your route.

CHRISTINA

You had me spied upon!

AZZOLINO

There was no need. Your actions were all too open . . . You associated with people of the basest character. You roamed the streets, carousing every night. You commanded for your pleasure entertainments of the most disreputable nature. Some say you took part in them—

CHRISTINA

Anything else?

AZZOLINO

What more would you like? *(Thumbing through the letters)* Sacrilege? Debauchery? Perversion?

CHRISTINA

Go on, it's getting better . . .

AZZOLINO

Tales are told of you in every dining hall and tavern in Europe. With your escapades you are single-handedly keeping a continent of gossips alive!

CHRISTINA

Then why didn't you stop me coming?

AZZOLINO

To judge for ourselves.

CHRISTINA

And now that you see me? *(AZZOLINO looks at her silently, unable to hide his disapproval)* So even here in the Temple of the Spirit, you believe in the ones who comb their hair!

AZZOLINO

There are those in the College of Cardinals who refuse to believe a word against you. They think your conversion is a wonderful coup for Catholicism. They are eager to welcome you into the faith.

CHRISTINA

Thank them.

AZZOLINO

There are others, however, who *do* believe the stories—or at least believe the *people* believe them. They feel your presence here will bring discredit to the Holy City. They are determined to keep you out.

CHRISTINA

Why not have a battle of Cardinals in St. Peter's Square?

AZZOLINO

I am the battlefield. I have been assigned to question you.

CHRISTINA

Which side are you on?

AZZOLINO

I am neutral.

CHRISTINA

There is no such thing!

AZZOLINO

Then, let us say . . . I will be fair.

CHRISTINA

(Bitterly) Thank you very much . . . Will you be the one to pass final judgment?

AZZOLINO

I shall make recommendations to the Pope.

CHRISTINA

And will he act on them?

AZZOLINO

I think so.

354

CHRISTINA

Then my fate is in your hands.

AZZOLINO

In your own, I would say.

CHRISTINA

I refuse to submit to this!

AZZOLINO

Then you will stay in the vestibule forever.

CHRISTINA

Then I will stay in the vestibule forever. But I *will* see the Pope!

AZZOLINO

Madame, the Pope cannot be *used!*

CHRISTINA

"Used"!

AZZOLINO

You cannot escape your life by hiding in the Vatican!

CHRISTINA

I came here for a haven and a refuge!

AZZOLINO

You came here after God-knows-what political intrigues, debaucheries and perversions and expect the Pope to welcome you, showing he approves?

CHRISTINA

You insult me to suggest I came all this way to rebel against the Holy Father!

AZZOLINO

I want some evidence that if you are to be the Vatican's eternal guest, you will abide by its rules and not be a constant embarrassment!

CHRISTINA

What do you think I would do? Break your china? Ride my horse through your crypts?

AZZOLINO

You cannot become a Catholic for your own convenience!.

CHRISTINA

For whose, then?

AZZOLINO

If you have done these things and are repentant, you will be accepted.

CHRISTINA

If I have done these things and am *not* repentant?

AZZOLINO

You will not.

CHRISTINA

And what if I have *not* done these things?

AZZOLINO

That's why I want to hear your story.

CHRISTINA

And what if I don't choose to tell?

AZZOLINO

Then you are free to go.

CHRISTINA

Go? . . . Where?

AZZOLINO

Back to Sweden, perhaps.

CHRISTINA

You know that is impossible.

AZZOLINO

You seemed to enjoy Antwerp.

CHRISTINA

There is nothing for me there.

AZZOLINO

Spain, then? Or France? *(She doesn't reply)* Well, where can a lady go when she has given up a Protestant throne to become a Catholic? When she arrives to spend the rest of her life in Rome, but the Pope refuses to let her in? Who would care to entertain a woman without God *or* country? What place would she have in the world, such a woman, who has been used to so much, and who expected in Rome—what?—some kind of spiritual crown?

CHRISTINA

You forget. I was received into the Church three weeks ago, at Innsbruck. I am already a convert!

356

AZZOLINO

Then go where other converts go.

CHRISTINA

Where do they go?

AZZOLINO

Why—anywhere.

CHRISTINA

Anywhere . . . *(Lost and confused, she looks at him)*

AZZOLINO

(After a moment) There is no "anywhere" for the former Queen of Sweden, is there?

CHRISTINA

No.

AZZOLINO

Then she must be accepted by the Pope.
(Silence. She understands)

CHRISTINA

What is your name?

AZZOLINO

Azzolino.

CHRISTINA

How long have you been a Cardinal, Azzolino?

AZZOLINO

Long enough.

CHRISTINA

Have you ever confessed a Queen?

AZZOLINO

No.

CHRISTINA

Does the prospect disconcert you?

AZZOLINO

I assume you're mortal.

CHRISTINA

Come, Azzolino! Let's get ourselves some good French wine, and when I've drunk enough, I'll tell you the story of my life!

AZZOLINO

I wish to hear the story of your life without wine!

CHRISTINA

(Laughing) Not even a little sacramental sip?

AZZOLINO

Your eternal soul is at stake and you laugh!

CHRISTINA

And what do you want?

AZZOLINO

Seriousness. Obedience.

CHRISTINA

Seriousness and obedience!

(The lights change. TINA *appears. She is* CHRISTINA *as* CHRISTINA *remembers herself at an earlier age, meek and docile, dressed in a gown the color of ivory, a pale and waxen image. With* TINA *is* AXEL OXENSTIERNA, *her very just, very correct Prime Minister. They are rehearsing for the coronation.* TINA *carries the orb and scepter and wears the ceremonial cape.* AXEL *carries the crown)*

TINA

(Dimly in the background, unseen by AZZOLINO*)* Yes, Oxenstierna. Yes, Oxenstierna.

CHRISTINA

Have I come all this way once more to play the Doll Queen?

AZZOLINO

I beg your pardon?

OXENSTIERNA

Good girl, Your Majesty. Chin up high—

TINA

Yes, Oxenstierna. Yes, Oxenstierna.

CHRISTINA

(Imitating the voice of TINA*)* "Yes, Azzolino. Yes, Azzolino." Is this what you want?

AZZOLINO

I don't understand you.

OXENSTIERNA

Smile once to your left, once to your right—

CHRISTINA

I became Queen at six, you know. All I could do was smile and obey my Prime Minister.

OXENSTIERNA

Pause by the throne and curtsy to the left.

(CHRISTINA *mockingly imitates what* TINA *is doing*)

AZZOLINO

I am not asking you to become a puppet.

CHRISTINA

Aren't you?

AZZOLINO

But there are certain standards of conduct—

OXENSTIERNA

Good girl, Your Majesty, now to the right—

CHRISTINA

What will you give me if I do as you wish?

OXENSTIERNA

How would you like to stay up until midnight?

AZZOLINO

All I can offer is absolution—

TINA

Thank you, Oxenstierna.

CHRISTINA

Why should I need absolution?

OXENSTIERNA

Now bend your left knee and lower your head—

TINA

Yes, Oxenstierna. Yes, Oxenstierna.

(OXENSTIERNA *places the crown on her head*)

CHRISTINA

I was the best-behaved child you could ever wish to know!

AZZOLINO

(Holding the book) That isn't what they say about you here.

(CHRIS *dashes in. The more jaunty side of* CHRISTINA, *she,
too, is dressed in ivory—but as a dashing young man. She
snatches the crown from* TINA*'s head, and puts it on her
own*)

CHRIS

I'm going to fall flat on my face! *That* will entertain the
multitudes!

359

OXENSTIERNA

(To CHRIS*)* Christina!

AZZOLINO

They say you grew up like a boy—rebellious and rude—

CHRIS

(Snatching the orb and scepter) What do I do with these—
a juggling act?

OXENSTIERNA

Christina, you must rehearse your coronation.

CHRIS

(Holding the orb) You know, Oxy, this reminds me of your
head! Here, catch! *(She throws it at him)*

AZZOLINO

They say you had the language of a guttersnipe—

CHRIS

I warn you, I'm going to have to piss in the middle of the
ceremony!

*(She pantomimes vulgarly with the scepter, then twirls the
crown around it.* TINA *runs after her, trying to recapture the
sacred symbols)*

TINA

Stop it! Stop it!

*(*CHRIS *laughs)*

OXENSTIERNA

You must behave yourself!

(A fight develops between CHRIS *and* TINA. OXENSTIERNA
throws up his hands and exits)

AZZOLINO

Well, which of these creatures are you?

CHRISTINA

None of them! Both of them! Neither!

*(*CHRIS *and* TINA *disappear)*

AZZOLINO

This chapter says you're the harlot of the northern hemisphere.

CHRISTINA

How picturesque!

AZZOLINO

This chapter says you are a man in disguise.

CHRISTINA

And a harlot, too! Some trick!

AZZOLINO

Why did you never marry?

CHRISTINA

(Sarcastically) I was far too busy.

AZZOLINO

Why did you give up the crown?

CHRISTINA

(With heavy irony) To devote myself to lust.

AZZOLINO

Answer my questions!

CHRISTINA

So you can report my answers to the Pope? Is he somewhere in the darkness now, listening?

AZZOLINO

Like God, he does not have to listen in order to hear.

CHRISTINA

(Shouting) Listen, God! Pope! Cardinals! Bishops! Washerwomen!

AZZOLINO

Christina—

CHRISTINA

Today's confession is tomorrow's gossip! I'm saving them the trouble of whispering behind their hands!

AZZOLINO

The confessional is sacrosanct. One does not shout in it.

CHRISTINA

What does one do in it?

AZZOLINO

One tells what troubles one most deeply.

CHRISTINA

(Her tone belying her words) Nothing troubles me.

AZZOLINO

(Deeply) Why did you give up the crown?

CHRISTINA

It was too heavy.

AZZOLINO

Why did you never marry?

CHRISTINA

I am allergic to gold rings.

AZZOLINO

Why did you become a Catholic?

CHRISTINA

To come to a better climate!

AZZOLINO

Is it true that—

CHRISTINA

Oh, yes! Everything is true! What do they accuse me of? Murder? Rape? The seven deadly sins? Anything you like! I caused the storm that wrecked the Spanish fleet! I personally infected Holland with the plague! Next week Vesuvius and I have a surprise in store for the citizens of Pompeii! Oh, yes. I'm guilty! Guilty!

AZZOLINO

I've had enough of this! The Pope will have to give the assignment to somebody else. I am tired of dealing with refugees from the courts of Europe who flock here for the wrong reasons. The Vatican is not some kind of holy wayside inn! I do not take the Church and what it has to offer lightly.

CHRISTINA

Nor do I, Azzolino.
    (Pause)

AZZOLINO

Then, I give you one more chance.

CHRISTINA

(Echoing him) To open my heart to you?

AZZOLINO

To tell me the truth!
    (Pause)

CHRISTINA

I have nothing to tell.

AZZOLINO

In that case, I am wasting my time. *(He holds up the documents)*
These will stand. ·

> *(He starts to stride out.* TINA *enters)*

TINA

Let's play the truth game!

CHRISTINA

I don't want to play the truth game!

TINA

Charles!

> *(*AZZOLINO *turns back to* CHRISTINA*)*

AZZOLINO

Your entire future is at stake and you call it a game?

CHRISTINA

(Laughing) Azzolino! Azzolino!

TINA

Ebba!

AZZOLINO

I don't understand you!

CHRISTINA

How touchy you are!

TINA

Magnus!

CHRISTINA

I was thinking of something I used to play when I was young.

TINA

We each have to tell the absolute truth!

CHRISTINA

A truth game. I was rather good at it.

AZZOLINO

Now, *that* astounds me.

CHRISTINA

I used to play it with my cousin Charles, *(*CHARLES *appears)* my
dear friend, Ebba, *(*EBBA *appears)* and that most handsome of all
young gentlemen, Magnus Gabriel de la Gardie! *(*MAGNUS *appears)*

363

MAGNUS

Anyone who lies has to pay a forfeit! Anyone who lies has to forfeit a kiss!

(He runs after the girls. They squeal with laughter)

CHRISTINA

(In the spirit of the game) What would you like to know the truth about?

AZZOLINO

(Lightly) Everything!

(CHRISTINA *laughs*)

MAGNUS

What's the biggest lie you've ever told?

EBBA

About my age. I always say I'm two years older.

MAGNUS

I lied about where I was last Christmas Eve.

CHARLES

Where were you?

MAGNUS

Behind the stables.

CHARLES

What were you doing?

MAGNUS

I'll tell you this much: it had nothing to do with horses!

(CHARLES *reacts puritanically, then continues*)

CHARLES

My biggest lie . . . was about mathematics. Once . . . I cheated.

TINA

Charles!

MAGNUS

What about you, Christina?

TINA

I never lie.

AZZOLINO

Was that the truth?

CHRISTINA

Was and is. Absolutely!

AZZOLINO

Didn't you ask each other any harder questions?

CHRISTINA

Of course—

TINA

Now we each have to tell . . . our greatest virtue.

MAGNUS

My courage.

EBBA

My looks.

TINA

Charles . . . ?

CHARLES

I can't think of anything—

MAGNUS

Forfeit! Forfeit!

TINA

No. It's true. There's nothing to say. Charles is Charles. That's all there is to it!

CHRISTINA

Charlie has no character at all! Charlie is absent! Charlie is invisible!

AZZOLINO

Who is this fellow who's invisible?

CHRISTINA

The present King of Sweden, Charles the Tenth!

EBBA

Now it's your turn, Christina.

AZZOLINO

You abdicated to *him?*

CHRISTINA

Does that surprise you? It seems to be an advantage for a King— to have no character.

MAGNUS

What's your greatest virtue, Christina?

365

TINA

I am always in command of myself. I never let my emotions
get out of control.

CHRISTINA

(Under her breath) Good girl, good girl . . .

TINA

Now each of us has to tell . . . our greatest fault!

EBBA

My greatest fault is: at a ball, I can never decide which
partner to choose—I have so many!

CHARLES

My greatest fault is . . . my greatest fault is . . . I really don't
know!

CHRISTINA

He never did.

MAGNUS

My greatest fault is my eagerness to throw myself into the
thick of the battle, thus risking the life of the leader of my
men.

TINA

How brave you are!

EBBA

How brave!

CHRISTINA

How insufferable!

CHARLES

Now it's your turn, Christina.

TINA

My greatest fault is my overwhelming desire for perfection,
and my inability to reach it often enough.
   *(*CHRIS *suddenly appears behind* TINA*)*

CHRIS

Rubbish! Why don't you tell them how you're afraid of the
dark? About your nightmares!

TINA

I don't have nightmares!

CHRIS

Liar! Why don't you tell them how you're afraid to sleep
without someone being near?

TINA

The game is over!

CHRISTINA

The game is over!

CHRIS

The hell it is! *(She whips out a fencing sword and challenges*
EBBA*)* So you can't decide among those dancing partners. Is
that why you have to kiss them *all?* (EBBA *squeals and runs*
away from her. CHRIS *challenges* CHARLES*)* What's behind
those profound silences? Great thoughts? Or is your mind a
total blank? (CHARLES *backs away.* CHRIS *challenges* MAG-
NUS*)* And you! Are you as brave as you look, or is it just the
uniform? Confess! Confess!

CHRISTINA

(Dryly) I used to love confession . . .

MAGNUS

If you were a man, I'd *show* you if it's just the uniform.

CHRIS

(Whipping out a second sword) All right, then show me!

EBBA

Christina!

CHARLES

What are you doing?

TINA

Stop!

CHRIS

En garde!

MAGNUS

En garde! And then I have a few hard truths to ask *you,* my
lady!

CHRIS

You'll have to hit me first!

TINA, EBBA and CHARLES

Stop! Please! Stop!

367

(CHRIS and MAGNUS duel. He is confident at first, but she beats him several times and he hardens)

MAGNUS

I'll damn well run you through!

CHRIS

Oh, will you? I shouldn't count on it, Magnus— *(She manages a strategic hit)*

AZZOLINO

You were good!

CHRISTINA

The best!

(OXENSTIERNA enters)

OXENSTIERNA

Children! Children! You're waking the entire household!

TINA

I'm sorry, Oxenstierna. We'll be quiet—

CHRIS

We will *not* be quiet! I am Queen! I will make as much noise as I like! *(She lets out a loud, long, savage bellow)*

TINA

(Over CHRIS's sustained cry) I don't see how you can act like that!

(TINA runs out sobbing, followed by OXENSTIERNA. CHRIS laughs)

CHRIS

(To MAGNUS, still fencing) Had enough?

MAGNUS

No!

AZZOLINO

I must say you were strong—

CHRISTINA

You have to be strong to rule a country. You must be the center, the absolute *power!*

AZZOLINO

Power! But surely that's not—

CHRISTINA

Not like a woman?

MAGNUS

(Winded) Hey! You're almost as good as a man!

CHRIS

"Almost"! *(With one deft thrust* CHRIS *flips the sword from* MAGNUS*'s hand and points her sword at his throat)* Say I'm better!

MAGNUS

All right! . . . All right! . . . You're better!
(CHRIS *lets him up)*

CHRIS

Come back tomorrow. I'll beat you again!

MAGNUS

(Ironically) I'll look forward to it.
(MAGNUS *exits.* CHRIS *continues practicing triumphantly)*

CHRISTINA

There! Didn't I show him?

AZZOLINO

Did you really enjoy winning?

CHRISTINA

Of course!

AZZOLINO

Wouldn't it have been better the other way around?

CHRISTINA

How do you mean?
(CHRIS *disappears)*

AZZOLINO

No man likes being beaten by a woman. It's human nature.

CHRISTINA

Then human nature will have to change!

AZZOLINO

Even yours, Christina?
(Pause. CHRISTINA *looks up, suddenly fully aware of him again)*

CHRISTINA

I'm saying no more. I'd forgotten how skilled you people are at drawing out admissions. Inquisitor!

AZZOLINO

Confessor.

CHRISTINA

Are the instruments of torture ready, "confessor"? Or is confession the greatest torture of all?

(Before AZZOLINO *has a chance to respond, there are sounds outside, and* BIRGITO *runs in and starts gesticulating excitedly to* CHRISTINA. *He is followed by* DOMINIC, *who is also very agitated)*

AZZOLINO

What's the matter?

DOMINIC

I can't understand it! He won't accept any of the rooms I show him.

*(*BIRGITO *pantomimes something to* CHRISTINA*)*

AZZOLINO

How many has he seen?

DOMINIC

Twelve.

AZZOLINO

You've shown him twelve rooms and none are satisfactory?

*(*BIRGITO *gestures to* CHRISTINA*)*

CHRISTINA

They are satisfactory, but they are not sufficient.

AZZOLINO

How many rooms do you require?

CHRISTINA

Twenty.

AZZOLINO

For your attendants?

CHRISTINA

For myself.

DOMINIC

(Aside to AZZOLINO*)* I thought the fellow was mad. He gets it from his mistress.

CHRISTINA

Birgito and I get restless at night, so we prowl from room to room.

Whenever I find a bed I like, I lie down. Birgito pulls along his pile of bedding and sleeps on the floor beside me.

DOMINIC

I never heard of such a thing. We can't possibly—
    (AZZOLINO *silences him with a gesture*)

AZZOLINO

(*To* CHRISTINA, *a new tone in his voice*) We will do our best to accommodate you. (DOMINIC *looks at him questioningly*) See that their needs are taken care of.

DOMINIC

Twenty rooms?

AZZOLINO

More, if necessary.

DOMINIC

Very well, Father.

AZZOLINO

And make sure that every room has fresh flowers.

DOMINIC

I'll do my best.
    (DOMINIC *exits in consternation, followed by a triumphant*
    BIRGITO)

CHRISTINA

Thank you.

AZZOLINO

Why do you sleep in twenty rooms?

CHRISTINA

It's more restful—

AZZOLINO

Why are you afraid of the dark?

CHRISTINA

That was long ago—

AZZOLINO

Why did you become a Catholic?

CHRISTINA

To cure me of insomnia!
    (*Ominous lights whirl out of the darkness in the back-*
    ground)

AZZOLINO

I can assure you of beds, but not of sleep.

CHRISTINA

I thought this was the house of miracles.

AZZOLINO

For some it is.

CHRISTINA

Then it will have to be for me . . .

AZZOLINO

Why can't you sleep, Christina?

(She covers her face with her hands, overwhelmed by the nightmare which is growing around her. TINA *appears out of the whirling lights and cries out)*

TINA

Mama! Mama! Mama!

(CHRIS enters from the darkness in a black shawl, playing at being CHRISTINA's *mother)*

CHRIS

Yes, child?

TINA

Mother, what is that big black box beside your bed?

CHRIS

Your father.

TINA

Mother, it's a box!

CHRIS

He is inside.

TINA

He can't breathe!

CHRIS

The dead don't breathe. The dead don't speak. The dead don't see. The dead don't— *(CHRIS suddenly breaks off and shouts at* CHRISTINA*)* I refuse to play this part! I hate Mother!

CHRISTINA

(With steel in her voice) You must ask Christina to sleep beside you.

372

CHRIS

No! She has Father in the box! She refuses to bury him!

CHRISTINA

You must order Tina to sleep next to the big black box.

CHRIS

I won't! It's mad! *You* do it!

(CHRIS *throws the black shawl at* CHRISTINA, *then stands back, watching her.* CHRISTINA *stares at it)*

AZZOLINO

Afraid, Christina?

(*For a moment,* CHRISTINA *fingers the shawl, then, meeting his eyes, she steels herself, and taking the challenge, puts it over her head and walks into the nightmare)*

CHRISTINA

(As her own mother, to TINA) Your father . . . has disappointed me . . . very much, Christina.

TINA

How?

CHRISTINA

By dying.

TINA

Oh.

CHRISTINA

Do you know what you learn by that? . . . You can't trust men. They make you promises and then—they leave you! *(She watches the box being carried out)* Come back! Come back! Now I have nothing!

(CHRIS *holds up a small golden casket)*

CHRIS

You have this.

(*She throws it at* CHRISTINA)

CHRISTINA

Oh, God!

(*She forgets herself. She can hardly go on.* TINA *calls her back into the scene)*

TINA

Mama! What a pretty golden casket! What's inside it?

373

CHRISTINA

Your father's heart . . .

TINA

My father's heart . . . Give it to me! He loved me!

CHRISTINA

He loved *me!* He loved *me!* And now I have no friend!

TINA

I'll be your friend . . .

CHRISTINA

(Looking at TINA *scornfully)* You? You? *(Her eyes breathe hate)* A child is no friend! A child is nothing! I need someone to understand me. Someone to keep me company, to make me smile . . .
> *(Suddenly* BIRGITO *appears, wearing an exaggerated court costume)*

TINA

Oh, Mama! Who is that awful man behind you?

CHRISTINA

It's Gonzago.

TINA

Why is he here?

CHRISTINA

To make us laugh! Dance, Gonzago, dance!
> *(He dances with grotesque and malformed steps)*

TINA

But he's so ugly! How can you bear to have him near you?

CHRISTINA

Dwarfs bring you luck! They keep out evil spirits. Have one with you always when you are with child. Or else you may bring forth a creature with skin like scales, or charred, or hairy. Or one with a giant head, but no eyes or mouth. Or one—*(*CHRISTINA *breaks off. She tears off the shawl)* I won't go on! She's a hysterical female! I despise everything about her! Why wasn't *she* the one who died? *(She moves violently away, as the dwarf grabs* TINA *and whirls her off.* CHRISTINA *wakens from the nightmare)* Oh, God, I didn't mean to say that!

374

AZZOLINO

(Giving her the mercy of a response, yet knowing she does mean it) Of course . . .

CHRISTINA

I don't mean it . . . I don't mean it . . .

AZZOLINO

Perhaps you'd like to rest—

CHRISTINA

No! *(She pulls herself together)* I can face my own nightmares, Cardinal Azzolino. I am not my mother.

AZZOLINO

Is she still alive?

CHRISTINA

Not to me.

AZZOLINO

Why not to you?

CHRISTINA

You should ask her that. She despised me from the moment I was born. I soon learned to return the affection—in kind.

AZZOLINO

And yet you keep a dwarf, like she did—

CHRISTINA

It's the same one. She gave him to me as a farewell present. I think she thought I would throw him back in her face. I wouldn't give her the satisfaction.

AZZOLINO

Do you keep him to bring you luck as well?

CHRISTINA

No.

AZZOLINO

Why, then?

CHRISTINA

To remind me of my inner self.

AZZOLINO

You see your inner self—like that?

375

CHRISTINA

How do you see your self? *(He looks at her for a moment. He doesn't answer. She bursts out with)* Thank God I have no daughter! I couldn't bear anyone to feel about me as I felt about her!

AZZOLINO

She made you hate all women—

CHRISTINA

Hate women! *(She laughs.* EBBA *and* CHRIS *enter, hand in hand)* You've read every line of that book, haven't you, Azzolino? Surely you know the worst thing I'm accused of isn't hating women! *(She laughs again, then she looks back at* CHRIS *and* EBBA*)* Have you ever found a woman of such beauty, such intelligence, that she was, in every form, in every gesture, exactly what a woman ought to be?

AZZOLINO

Yes. The Virgin Mary.

CHRISTINA

I'll match my Ebba to her any day!

EBBA

(Laughing) Christina, you must give up hunting!

CHRIS

Why, Ebba?

EBBA

It's making you into a lean young boy! You look like a fellow who is just about to have to shave!

CHRIS

I know.

EBBA

You must come boating with us tomorrow. And let the *men* handle the oars. You and I will just sit still.

CHRIS

I'll copy you.

EBBA

I'll come and choose your dress.

CHRIS

And will you comb my hair for me?

EBBA

Of course I will. But you can't do much with it until it grows! Why did you slice it all off?

CHRISTINA

Because I'll never be like you!

EBBA

What?

CHRIS

I'll never be like you, Ebba.

EBBA

Dear Christina . . .

CHRIS

Isn't it ironic that I should have the crown and you have everything else?

EBBA

I haven't so much.

CHRIS

Oxenstierna said that when I fell in love, I would feel beautiful . . .

EBBA

And so you will . . .

(CHRISTINA *moves toward* EBBA)

CHRISTINA

But I love you—

CHRIS

And when I think of you, I feel so ugly. *(She retreats, and eventually disappears)*

CHRISTINA

Knowing your beauty makes me know my ugliness the more. Watching you walk, with such grace, I realize how awkward I am, how clumsy—

EBBA

It's not true, Christina . . .

CHRISTINA

I ought by rights to hate you, but I can't.

EBBA

And I don't want you to—

CHRISTINA

Exploring myself . . . is such a barren country. Exploring you—
what natural wonders! When I touch you, I realize what a woman
should be.

EBBA

So I was born . . .

CHRISTINA

Aren't men's bodies strange, Ebba? So oddly made! How can we
ever know what they're feeling? When I touch you, I know your
body's secrets. Know how it echoes me. When you share my
bed—

AZZOLINO

This is mortal sin!

CHRISTINA

I love you, Ebba.

AZZOLINO

Stop! (CHRISTINA *looks up) Stop.* (EBBA *disappears)* What is this
blasphemous scene?

CHRISTINA

You said you wanted to know everything about me—

AZZOLINO

How can you tell me this?

CHRISTINA

Do you want to hear the truth, or only what you want to hear?

AZZOLINO

The truth.

CHRISTINA

I loved that woman more than I have ever loved a man.

AZZOLINO

Have you ever tried to love a man?

CHRISTINA

I've found none worthy.

AZZOLINO

Perhaps you didn't look hard enough.

CHRISTINA

Well, get out your lantern, Cardinal, and let's go search! Perhaps there's one waiting just around the corner! Tell me, have *you* ever found a man you could love as I loved Ebba?

AZZOLINO

I cannot allow any more of this—

CHRISTINA

Love is so rare! Must we deny it when we find it? Is it to be called hideous just because the object is the same sex? Don't you love the Pope?

AZZOLINO

You will not go on!

CHRISTINA

(Furiously) Indeed, I will not go on, Azzolino! . . . I thought you wanted to hear my life. But you only want the pale acceptable edges of it. I thought I was to be received by the Church. Instead, I find myself on trial for my life! I do not regret my life, Azzolino —except for the last few hours of it. I have had enough of standing in this antechamber, denied the courtesies that would be granted an ordinary kitchen maid! You can take your drafty corridor and save it for the next Queen who happens to come your way. Am I pure enough to be let in? I refuse to answer! But see how the world will laugh when they find out *I* walked out on the Pope! *(She strides toward the exit)*

AZZOLINO

(Calmly) That is an extremely brave gesture—for a woman who has nowhere to go.

(She exits. DOMINIC *enters from another direction)*

DOMINIC

Your voices could be heard all the way from the chapel!

AZZOLINO

Have the choir sing louder.

DOMINIC

Isn't it going well, Father?

AZZOLINO

I wouldn't exactly say so. No.

DOMINIC

Word seems to have leaked out that she's here. There's quite a crowd gathering in the square.

AZZOLINO

Friendly or hostile?

DOMINIC

Mostly, I think, they have come to stare.

AZZOLINO

How is His Holiness?

DOMINIC

Resting . . . *(AZZOLINO paces, troubled)* Is she anything like what they say?

AZZOLINO

She is an extremely complex woman.

DOMINIC

Why did she give up the throne?

AZZOLINO

I don't know yet.

DOMINIC

Why did she become a Catholic?

AZZOLINO

Dominic, would you like to take over the questioning?

DOMINIC

No, Father. No—but the Cardinals are very anxious for your decision. I've been sent to find out what's happening.

AZZOLINO

Crowds in the square always make them nervous.

DOMINIC

How long do you think it will take?

AZZOLINO

I'm not a soothsayer, Dominic!

DOMINIC

Have you any idea what you will say?

AZZOLINO

None whatsoever. I don't even know if she'll come back!
    (Pause)

DOMINIC

(Suddenly bursting out) I think it's unfair of His Holiness to test you this way!

380

AZZOLINO

What do you mean?

DOMINIC

You're as much on trial here as she is!

AZZOLINO

So you've realized that too, have you?

DOMINIC

It isn't right for you to be put in this position. Your whole career in the Church could hinge on what you decide.

AZZOLINO

What's the matter, Dominic? Don't you think I'm up to the challenge?

DOMINIC

Of course you are, Father—

AZZOLINO

Then show your faith in me by calming down.

DOMINIC

How can I be calm? The entire Holy City is in turmoil! The Cardinals say they must have your answer—

AZZOLINO

So that they can serve her up to the crowd, neatly labeled "saint" or "sinner"—

DOMINIC

Father—

AZZOLINO

(Sharply) When I have an answer, they will get it!

DOMINIC

I don't think they'll wait much longer—

AZZOLINO

They will wait as long as it takes! The woman has spent her entire life on display to the public. Now, for a few hours she is alone with herself. She is no longer a Queen, or a freak, or a heathen, or a candidate for canonization, she is a human being. A very troubled human being—

DOMINIC

But you owe them a decision—

AZZOLINO

Hang what we owe them! What about what we owe to *her?*
(CHRISTINA *reenters*)

CHRISTINA

I cannot find Birgito—
(At this moment BIRGITO *rushes in as if being chased)*

DOMINIC

What were you doing in the Pope's private quarters?

CHRISTINA

Do not touch him! Come here, Birgito. *(*BIRGITO *runs to her and gestures excitedly)* Quietly now! Quietly! Begin again. What have you found?
(She watches his gestures intently)

AZZOLINO

(To DOMINIC*)* Go. Keep everyone patient, if you can. I depend on you.
*(*DOMINIC *exits.* CHRISTINA *begins to react to* BIRGITO *with increasing surprise and concern)*

CHRISTINA

No! No! It can't be! *(To* AZZOLINO*)* Is this true?

AZZOLINO

I don't know what he's saying.

CHRISTINA

He says . . . the Pope is ill. Is it true?

AZZOLINO

Yes.

CHRISTINA

How long has he been ill?

AZZOLINO

Several months now.

CHRISTINA

Is it serious?

AZZOLINO

Extremely.

CHRISTINA

Do you mean . . . he's not expected to recover?

AZZOLINO

It is in the hands of God . . .
  (Pause)

CHRISTINA

(Shaking her head in disbelief, near tears) To come all this way and
find him dying—it can't be true.

AZZOLINO

Christina—

CHRISTINA

I need him to *live!*

AZZOLINO

Whatever happens to His Holiness, the *Church* remains.

CHRISTINA

(Collecting herself) Why wasn't I told of this?

AZZOLINO

No one was told. The enemies of the Church are only too ready
to take advantage of such circumstances.

CHRISTINA

Am I considered an enemy?

AZZOLINO

He must be protected—

CHRISTINA

From me? How lovely!

AZZOLINO

I didn't mean—

CHRISTINA

In the event that he should die, who will succeed him? *(AZZOLINO
is silent. After a moment, she repeats)* I said, who will succeed him?
*(He turns toward her and looks her directly in the eye. She looks
at* BIRGITO, *who confirms her suspicion by pointing at* AZZOLINO
and nodding) Aha! *(AZZOLINO turns his back)* Go and pack our
bags, Birgito. It is obvious we came to Rome at the wrong time.
(BIRGITO exits) So you have ambitions! *(AZZOLINO turns to her but
does not answer)* Ambition is an evil demon, Cardinal. You must
guard against it.

AZZOLINO

I am not ambitious. I am simply one of those best qualified to lead.

CHRISTINA

And you are vain, too!

AZZOLINO

No. Merely honest.

CHRISTINA

And what is your greatest fault?

AZZOLINO

My overwhelming desire for perfection.

CHRISTINA

How often do you reach it?

AZZOLINO

Probably no oftener than you.

(CHRISTINA *laughs*)

CHRISTINA

Well, you'll have to reach it now if you plan to become the Holy of Holies. Or possibly you could leave it all to your sister-in-law.

AZZOLINO

I have no sister-in-law.

CHRISTINA

What a pity! I understand the Pope before this found *his* indispensable. What was her name? Olympia Maidalchini? They say that half the red hats in the College of Cardinals were earned in her bed!

AZZOLINO

How dare you!

CHRISTINA

I dare, dear possible Pope, because I am leaving. Do you think I don't know what's happening in this corridor?

AZZOLINO

What is happening?

CHRISTINA

A bid for the papal crown, with me as a pawn.

AZZOLINO

That isn't so!

CHRISTINA

What's the matter, Cardinal? Don't you like the truth game? (*Mockingly, she makes the fencing gesture of touché*)

384

AZZOLINO

You are mistaken.

CHRISTINA

Am I? You forget, I've played these power games myself. I know exactly what you need to assure your election.

AZZOLINO

And what is that?

CHRISTINA

An extraordinary feat. A demonstration of your remarkable powers. And by amazing good fortune the perfect opportunity has fallen right into your lap. You can confront the most spectacular convert the Church has ever known—and keep her out!

AZZOLINO

This is absurd—

CHRISTINA

Think what they'll all say: "What a holy man he is, this Cardinal! Unimpressed by titles and earthly vanities! Interested only in preserving the purity of the Church! Hosannah to Azzolino! He must be Pope!"

AZZOLINO

So that is what you think . . . *(Pause)* Very well, go to him. Go in to His Holiness.

CHRISTINA

What?

AZZOLINO

He's there. At the end of that corridor. *(He gestures to his right)*

CHRISTINA

But—

AZZOLINO

Go. His door's unlocked. There's nothing on this earth to stop you. *(She turns toward the Pope's quarters, but hesitates)* Don't be frightened. He's an old man, and very frail. I am sure you can put your case to him most convincingly. It's very possible he will press you to his heart. *(She turns again toward the exit, but still, for some reason, makes no move to leave)* Why do you hesitate?

CHRISTINA

I don't know . . .

AZZOLINO

You've been waiting a long time for this moment. Go on—

CHRISTINA

What will happen when I've been received by him?

AZZOLINO

Your life in Rome will begin.

CHRISTINA

My life in Rome . . .

AZZOLINO

Concerts . . . balls . . .

CHRISTINA

Entertainments . . . fireworks . . .

AZZOLINO

Music . . . laughter . . .

CHRISTINA

Music! Laughter! Yes! Oh, yes!

AZZOLINO

And you will have lost your chance forever—

CHRISTINA

My chance?

AZZOLINO

To find out why you came. *(CHRISTINA does not speak)* Stay, Christina. Stay and talk with me. *(CHRISTINA looks at him)* I think you need us very much . . .

> *(This reaches CHRISTINA. She turns to him. From the distance comes the sound of vespers, gentle and stirring. She pauses to listen)*

CHRISTINA

Father, if you only knew— *(She breaks off)*

AZZOLINO

What is it?

CHRISTINA

It seems so strange—to call somebody "Father."

AZZOLINO

You don't remember yours?

CHRISTINA

Oh, yes. I do! We used to go walking together, my hand in his.

AZZOLINO

And you missed him when he died?

CHRISTINA

I would sometimes walk, like this . . . *(She extends her hand, as if holding the hand of a taller, unseen person)* . . . as if he were still there. I do it even now sometimes. *(She closes her hand on air. Her face expresses the memory of loss—of holding nothing)*

AZZOLINO

I lost my father, too, when I was young.

CHRISTINA

Strange. I never thought of Cardinals having fathers.

AZZOLINO

We do. And brothers and sisters and even aunts and uncles.

CHRISTINA

But no sons.

AZZOLINO

No. No sons. At least—not officially.

(CHRISTINA *laughs)*

CHRISTINA

What a shame! Then, holiness could be hereditary.

AZZOLINO

Like royalty.

CHRISTINA

Like royalty.

(TINA *appears in the background, slowly removes a crown from her head, and disappears)*

AZZOLINO

You sigh whenever I mention it. Was it all so difficult?

CHRISTINA

You ask that only because you haven't yet had power yourself.

AZZOLINO

That's why I want so very much to know how you could give it up.

CHRISTINA

How I could give it up . . . *(CHRIS appears briefly, slowly removes a crown from her head, and disappears)* . . . The crown . . . It is so little . . . Do you know, Azzolino, I once gave up the sun?

387

(Music begins. An extraordinary golden headdress of the sun appears, dimly approaching from the distance. It is being borne by BIRGITO *as the court page. But it is so big, he cannot be seen.* TINA *runs in and, amazed, watches the sun as it comes closer and closer, growing brighter and brighter)*

TINA

Oh! What is it? *(It comes nearer)* How beautiful it is!

CHRISTINA

How beautiful . . .

TINA

I've never seen anything like it! *(*BIRGITO *puts it on her head)* Oh, who could have sent me such a gift?

*(*MAGNUS *enters)*

MAGNUS

I did.

TINA

Magnus! Magnus Gabriel de la Gardie! *(*BIRGITO *exits)* I didn't know you were back from France! No one told me!

MAGNUS

I'm my surprise for you.

TINA

(Touching the headdress) And this . . .

MAGNUS

I wanted to bring something worthy of you. So there was only one thing to bring: the sun.

TINA

Thank you, Magnus. I'll treasure it forever! . . . You know, I expected nothing from you. And at the same time—

CHRISTINA

I expected nothing less.

MAGNUS

Masques and balls are all the rage in Paris. The headdresses are unbelievable. Everybody tries to outdo everybody else. The Prince of Navarre wore a headdress so tall he fell over backwards! It took ten men to put him back on his feet!

TINA

Tell me all about the court of France . . .

MAGNUS

It's said that Louis has *three* mistresses!

TINA

(Blushing) I mean, tell me what they wear.

MAGNUS

The men wear ruffles and breeches. They're always competing about who has the shapeliest legs!

(TINA *laughs, slightly embarrassed)*

TINA

And what about the women? Do they dress the same as we do?

MAGNUS

Far more elaborately. Brocades and silks. Bright colors. And a new style—

TINA

What new style?

MAGNUS

—with what they do in front.

TINA

What do they do?

MAGNUS

They wear tight laces that pull their waists in very small down here— *(He demonstrates, touching her waist)* —and push the rest way out in front up here, like this . . . *(He cups his hands beneath her breasts lightly)*

TINA

Oh? *(She stands stock still, not daring to move as his hands remain touching her)*

MAGNUS

Their necklines are cut straight across like this, to here. *(He traces a line across her bosom)* Sometimes so low their nipples pop out! *(Demonstrating, he touches the points of her breasts, and she pulls back involuntarily)* What's the matter?

TINA

Nothing . . .

MAGNUS

(With a grin) I was only trying to show you—

TINA

Yes, I know—

MAGNUS

Do you mind?

TINA

Of course not. It's just . . . that I'm Queen. And so I have
to do . . . I have to be . . . Everything I do must be . . .

MAGNUS

I understand perfectly.

TINA

But I want you to know—

MAGNUS

Don't think another thing about it. I understand.
(He goes. TINA *dances alone, pretending to be the Goddess
of the Sun in her headdress)*

CHRISTINA

He "understood." I was sure *I* "understood." I was beside myself
with joy!

*(*OXENSTIERNA *enters as* TINA *is dancing)*

OXENSTIERNA

Your Majesty—

TINA

You may tell me how I look.

OXENSTIERNA

Like the Goddess of the Sun, Christina.

TINA

You may tell me if I look happy.

OXENSTIERNA

Radiant.

TINA

Not the costume—*me.*

OXENSTIERNA

Yes. You.

TINA

I have a surprise for you . . . I am going to make him my husband.

OXENSTIERNA

Who?

TINA

Magnus Gabriel de la Gardie!

OXENSTIERNA

(Shocked) . . . de la Gardie!

TINA

Hasn't he a beautiful name? I love to say it.

OXENSTIERNA

But—

TINA

I'm announcing it tonight.

OXENSTIERNA

But you can't!

TINA

His name and his blood are the best. There can be no objections.

OXENSTIERNA

You have to consult—

TINA

I have consulted with my heart. My heart knows best.

OXENSTIERNA

That's unlike you to say.

TINA

I know. I am not like myself. I begin to think there is some hope for me.

(CHARLES enters)

CHARLES

Christina, you look . . .

(He can't think of a word. TINA fills in for him)

TINA

Radiant?

391

CHARLES

Yes, radiant, Christina.

TINA

Thank you, Charles.

CHARLES

Would you like to hear my new flute?

TINA

No, not just now—I've got to see Magnus. Where is he?

CHARLES

I don't know—

TINA

I must find him! *(Calling)* Magnus! *(She runs off)*

CHRISTINA

Magnus!

(CHARLES and OXENSTIERNA exit)

AZZOLINO

Did you find him?

CHRISTINA

(A strange note in her voice) Yes, I found him.

AZZOLINO

Where was he?

CHRISTINA

In the garden—educating Ebba Sparre with exactly the same lesson! *(MAGNUS appears with EBBA in the distance. TINA comes upon them. They do not see her. MAGNUS traces on EBBA the same lines he traced on TINA. But EBBA, laughing, reacts warmly and sensuously to his touch. TINA watches, extremely disturbed)* With the very same caresses I was ready to share a *throne* for, he was proposing to Ebba Sparre!

(EBBA and MAGNUS kiss and joyously run off. TINA tears off the headdress of the sun and runs out)

AZZOLINO

What did you do?

CHRISTINA

(Defiantly) I made him my commanding officer!

(CHRIS and MAGNUS enter from opposite sides. CHRIS gives him orders coldly)

CHRIS

Have you inspected the troops?

MAGNUS

Yes, Your Majesty.

CHRIS

Is all in order?

MAGNUS

Yes, Your Majesty. It is.

CHRIS

Very well. *(She turns to go)*

MAGNUS

Your Majesty—

CHRIS

(Coldly) Yes?

MAGNUS

You never call me by my name any more.

CHRISTINA

(Under her breath) Magnus Gabriel de la Gardie . . .

MAGNUS

And . . . you never . . . speak to me as a friend.

CHRIS

(After a moment, like a glacier) How is your lovely wife?

MAGNUS

Coming along nicely, thank you.

CHRIS

(Bitterly) Tell her she must come see me—after she has calved.

(MAGNUS goes out)

AZZOLINO

(Almost to himself) And you still feel the pain . . .

CHRISTINA

(Emotionally) Not in the least. It is healed. Scar tissue. *(EBBA, big with child, walks in slowly, sewing)* It's her affair, isn't it, if she wants to turn herself into a cow?

CHRIS

My God, is there nobody left who can keep their legs together? I said I didn't want to see you that way!
(She turns her back on EBBA*).*

EBBA

We can't go on not talking to each other—

CHRIS

How can you bear to look like that?

EBBA

Like what?

CHRIS

Like a stuck pig.

EBBA

What's wrong?

CHRIS

You've spoiled yourself. You've been ruined. And you go
around like that—for everyone to see?

EBBA

Christina, I'm married!

CHRIS

(Tortured) So you are.

EBBA

When you're married, you'll do the same—and with the
same result.

CHRIS

I never want to look that way. Never! *(She exits)*

EBBA

Christina!

CHRISTINA

(To AZZOLINO*)* Do you know how many times my mother blew
up like a whale and then blew down again? Again and again and
again! And I'm her only living child! . . . Some were washed away
before they formed. Some were formed and never had a heartbeat.
Some came out and saw the world—and died. *(She confronts*
EBBA*)* How can you sit there sewing?

EBBA

What would you have me do?

CHRISTINA

Why don't you get up and scream?

EBBA

Why?

CHRISTINA

For the pain on your baby's birthday.

EBBA

Women have managed it before.

CHRISTINA

The creatures are so large. Those solid heads. And such a small place to come out of.

EBBA

Nature's with you at the proper moment.

CHRISTINA

Is she? Always?

EBBA

Well, I suppose that one can't guarantee it—

CHRISTINA

How do you know it won't be born a dwarf, or an idiot? How do you know it won't come out a monster—like me?

EBBA

Christina! What are you saying?

CHRISTINA

How do you know it won't come out like me—a monster?

EBBA

You're talking nonsense! I won't listen to you! *(She disappears)*

AZZOLINO

Why do you call yourself a monster?

CHRISTINA

I came here to forget!

AZZOLINO

I thought you came to understand—

CHRISTINA

No! I won't go on! What tricks are you using to make me say these things? Things I have never spoken to a soul before!

Words I thought never to say come pouring out—
(TINA *runs in, distraught*)

TINA

Oh, what shall I do? Oxenstierna!

CHRISTINA

No! There will be no more telling!
(OXENSTIERNA *enters*)

TINA

I'm bleeding!

OXENSTIERNA

Bleeding . . .

CHRISTINA

I said that we will not go on!
(But TINA *is not to be stopped*)

TINA

I wasn't doing anything and suddenly—there's blood!

OXENSTIERNA

Your Majesty—

TINA

Oh, why do I feel so terrible? So strange? I'm bleeding!

OXENSTIERNA

Christina . . . you're supposed to.

TINA

Supposed to?

OXENSTIERNA

When you reach a certain age.

TINA

The age that I am now?

OXENSTIERNA

It means—that you can have a baby.

TINA

I'm going to have a baby!

OXENSTIERNA

No, no. You *can* have a baby. Your body is grown up enough
to make a baby. But you won't have one for many years. First
you must get married.

TINA

I see. That's right. Every child should have a father, shouldn't
it? I will marry, and God will hear about it and send me down
a baby.

OXENSTIERNA

Well, that's not exactly how it is—

TINA

How *is* it?

OXENSTIERNA

I will send someone to explain it to you.
(He exits. TINA *waits)*

CHRISTINA

He never did . . . And one day I came upon it in a book.
*(*CHRIS *enters)*

CHRIS

(Grimly) Look!
(She slaps an open book down in front of TINA*)*

CHRISTINA

The Act.

TINA

What are they doing?

CHRISTINA

That Act.

CHRIS

It's obvious, isn't it?

CHRISTINA

I couldn't believe it!

TINA

(Looking at the page) Is that the way it's done? That awful
method? Is *that* how it happens?

CHRIS

Apparently.

TINA

It must hurt.

CHRIS

I really don't know.

TINA

It must be terrible!

CHRIS

No wonder nobody speaks about it.

TINA

It terrifies me! Terrifies me!

CHRIS

Don't be a coward!

TINA

You mean—you'd do it?

CHRIS

Me? Submit to that from a man? The Sovereign Queen of Sweden go down on her back and be ploughed like a field? Never!

(EBBA *enters*)

EBBA

(Quietly) It can be . . . quite nice, you know.

TINA

That—violence?

EBBA

It actually can be . . . very enjoyable.

CHRIS

But you married a man you *chose!*

CHRISTINA

(Involuntarily getting involved in the scene) They want me to marry Charles. It would be like going to bed with a mongoose!

AZZOLINO

Surely you could have tried to like him?

(CHRISTINA *turns on him.* CHRIS, EBBA *and* TINA *disappear*)

CHRISTINA

What do you know about these things? Such questions are resolved for you. You escaped from it all the day you took your vow of celibacy.

AZZOLINO

Even celibacy involves a decision.

CHRISTINA

And what about when it's simply a fact? When virginity hangs upon you like a lead weight and you long to push it off, but you're too frightened of what you'll find when it's gone?

AZZOLINO

Do you think young priests just put on a cassock one day and all earthly longings vanish in the air?

CHRISTINA

Then how do they bear it?

AZZOLINO

They devote themselves to good works and cold baths.

CHRISTINA

You're mocking me.

AZZOLINO

A little. I'm sorry.

CHRISTINA

How do *you* bear it? *(He doesn't reply.* CHRISTINA *continues mischievously)* Or is it no trouble for you?

AZZOLINO

(Harshly) I pray!

CHRISTINA

(After a moment, seriously) Yes. Forgive me. *(She looks into his eyes)* You must need to pray harder than most . . . *(Pause)* How old were you when you decided to become a priest?

AZZOLINO

Fifteen.

CHRISTINA

It seems such a waste, somehow—

AZZOLINO

A waste!

CHRISTINA

A man with your strength, your capacity for life. Now *Charles* should have been a priest!

AZZOLINO

Don't you think I have a talent for it?

CHRISTINA

An almost frightening talent.

AZZOLINO

Frightening?

CHRISTINA

(Staring at him) You have such power . . . to make me open doors in my mind that I thought were locked forever. I thought giving words to these thoughts would kill me, and yet you make me go deeper and deeper . . .

AZZOLINO

For your sake, not for mine—

CHRISTINA

(A cry of pain) How much further must I go? *(He does not answer, but looks steadily at her. She turns away and moves about restlessly)* Since you became a priest, have you ever imagined things you shouldn't imagine? Or wanted to see . . . things you should never see?

AZZOLINO

What sort of things?

CHRISTINA

Because of your vows . . . Have you never thought of what you might be missing?

AZZOLINO

One cannot allow oneself to think.

CHRISTINA

I think . . . I think all the time . . .

AZZOLINO

That is why you must speak . . . You need to tell me more, don't you?

CHRISTINA

(Bursting out) Oh, why do you make me go on?

AZZOLINO

Tell me, Christina—

CHRISTINA

No!

(EBBA *appears in the darkness)*

EBBA

No!

AZZOLINO

You must tell me *all*—

400

CHRISTINA

I can't!

EBBA

Christina, I can't! I can't!

CHRISTINA

There are terrible things, things you should never hear . . .

AZZOLINO

I must hear.

EBBA

Christina, it's impossible!

CHRISTINA

Even the most terrible thing of all?

AZZOLINO

Yes.

EBBA

No! How can you ask such a thing?

CHRISTINA

(To EBBA*)* Who else could I ask?

EBBA

Not me!

CHRISTINA

Who else could I turn to?

AZZOLINO

Tell *me!*
        (Pause)

CHRISTINA

I want to know what it's like . . .
        (Pause)

EBBA

Find out for yourself!

CHRISTINA

But then it will be too late!

EBBA

For what?

CHRISTINA

To know if it's what I want. How can I know unless I can watch?

EBBA

Dear God . . .

CHRISTINA

For the friendship I have given you. For the love I've felt for you. Help me, Ebba. I beg you. Help me.

EBBA

My poor Christina!

CHRISTINA

I will be quiet. I will hide in a corner in the dark. Magnus will never know. Please . . .

AZZOLINO

And she let you watch?

CHRISTINA

She took pity on me. If only she knew what I really felt—! As if to be there, hidden, was what I wanted! To watch . . . him . . .

AZZOLINO

Magnus Gabriel de la Gardie . . .

CHRISTINA

To watch him enter and begin to caress his wife . . . *(Night.* MAGNUS *enters to* EBBA *and begins to make love to her. In the shadows,* CHRISTINA *watches)* How that sight went through me! *(As* MAGNUS *and* EBBA *are about to consummate their union,* CHRISTINA *cries out)* Aah!

*(*MAGNUS *thrusts* EBBA *away)*

MAGNUS

Who's there? *(Silence)* I said who is it?

*(*CHRISTINA *steps forward into the light)*

CHRISTINA

Christina.

MAGNUS

Christina! *(Coming toward her threateningly)* What are you doing here?

EBBA

Magnus, please! I let her!

MAGNUS

What was this to be? A public demonstration?

(He comes closer to CHRISTINA*)*

CHRISTINA

(*Retreating*) Magnus, please, I'm sorry.

MAGNUS

Don't be sorry.

EBBA

What are you going to do?

MAGNUS

Why, exactly what she wants. (*He takes* CHRISTINA *by the hand. She tries to pull away, but he holds her firmly*) I've enough for two. Come on, Christina. Come to bed with us—

CHRISTINA

No! No!

MAGNUS

You want to find out what it's like? Well, I'll show you!

EBBA

Magnus, stop it!

MAGNUS

Come lie between us—or wouldn't you know which way you'd want to turn? Well, what's the difference? Left side, right side—you're game for anything, aren't you? Come, Christina! Here's a space for you.

CHRISTINA

Let me go!

EBBA

She is the *Queen*.

MAGNUS

I know what she is. And *Queen* says all of it. She isn't *woman*, that is sure. (*He thrusts her away*)

EBBA

Please, stop.

MAGNUS

Poor ignorant Christina. Wants to learn. Won't someone teach her? Teach her but not touch her, eh, Christina? Teach her from a distance. Why not for real? (CHRISTINA *stands mute, as if in shock*) Why hasn't any man ever wanted her? Why couldn't she attract even a stableboy? Why does everyone hold back from her—even Charles?

403

EBBA

Because she's *Queen.*

MAGNUS

Most Queens end up bedded. She never will. *(To* CHRISTINA*)*
Do you know why? *(She pulls back)* You're cold inside . . .

CHRISTINA

(As if remembering) Cold . . .

MAGNUS

. . , like the frozen tundra. Even when you wear the golden
headdress of the sun, it shines with the ice of the northern
lights.

CHRISTINA

(Remembering) Ice . . .

MAGNUS

You pretend to be in love with me. But when I touch you,
you feel nothing, do you? *(He is holding her)* Nothing gives
way inside you. Nothing cries out to be surrendered, to be
taken. You were born without the quality of woman. You
couldn't get it now, not for all your kingdom or your wealth.
(He thrusts her away) I don't care where you go, how hard
you look or who they pair you up with, no one will ever love
you. No one will ever love you, Christina. You don't know
how to love!

CHRISTINA

You can't say such a thing! *(*MAGNUS *kisses* EBBA *passionately,
defiantly. To* AZZOLINO*)* How could he say such a thing? *(*MAGNUS
takes* EBBA *brusquely and strides out)* I love. I *do* love!

AZZOLINO

Whom do you love, Christina?
*(She looks at him for a moment, confused, upset, unable to
answer. Then she cries out after* MAGNUS*)*

CHRISTINA

You are relieved of your command, Magnus Gabriel de la Gardie!
You are made *nothing!* *(She covers her face with her hands. She
is extremely agitated)*

AZZOLINO

(With great compassion) Go on. Don't stop. Tell me the rest . . .

404

CHRISTINA

I dismissed De la Gardie from his post.

(OXENSTIERNA *enters*)

CHRISTINA

Do you think I did right?

AZZOLINO

It was your prerogative.

CHRISTINA

I didn't ask what was my prerogative. I asked if I did right.

OXENSTIERNA

Your Majesty . . .

(CHRIS *enters. Her scene with* OXENSTIERNA *parallels*
CHRISTINA's *scene with* AZZOLINO)

AZZOLINO

Well, I—

CHRIS

I was wrong!

OXENSTIERNA

What?

CHRISTINA

I was at fault.

CHRIS

I was at fault, do you hear me?

OXENSTIERNA

Yes, I hear you.

CHRISTINA

I didn't know what I was doing!

CHRIS

I let my emotions carry me away!

OXENSTIERNA

It can happen.

CHRIS

I don't want it to happen!

OXENSTIERNA

As you grow older, you will grow more sure.

CHRISTINA

You mean more like a stone.

405

OXENSTIERNA

I mean the unformed heart and mind often waver.

CHRIS

In men as well as women?

OXENSTIERNA

Well, perhaps less in a man.

CHRISTINA

I didn't ask to be this sex!

CHRIS

Why does God will it on me and then punish me for it?

OXENSTIERNA

You can acquire the firmness of a man.

CHRIS

How?

OXENSTIERNA

By acquiring a husband.

CHRIS

A husband . . .

CHRISTINA

A husband. A mate. The solution to everything!

OXENSTIERNA

For the sake of the State, you must begin to think about an heir.

CHRISTINA

Make sons, make daughters; make sons, make daughters . . .

OXENSTIERNA

What joy you'd bring to all the people if you would take a husband.

CHRIS

Would I, Oxenstierna? And what joy would I bring to myself? *(She runs out)*

CHRISTINA

They kept insisting that I marry Charles.

AZZOLINO

He was no match for you.

CHRISTINA

Who on God's earth could be a match for me?

AZZOLINO

He would have to be a man—quite rare.

(They look at each other for a moment, their eyes holding)

OXENSTIERNA

Christina, Charles admires you deeply.

CHRISTINA

He's never mentioned it.

OXENSTIERNA

He becomes tongue-tied in front of you.

CHRISTINA

And in front of everyone else, does he suddenly become the court wit?

OXENSTIERNA

There are customs, differences of rank. He is afraid to speak.

CHRISTINA

I see. And if I were a woman without title, would he come charging in and sweep me off my feet?

OXENSTIERNA

You know he cannot ask you for your hand.

CHRISTINA

I know. But I will tell you a secret, Oxenstierna. If he did, I would gladly give it to him.

OXENSTIERNA

You would?

CHRISTINA

I would have it cut off at the wrist and sent to him in a velvet box . . . But as for giving him one more inch of my body—no! No! I will never do it!

OXENSTIERNA

What are you saying?

CHRISTINA

I am Queen of Sweden. By reason of my exalted rank and privilege, I am allowed anything I want. I am allowed to marry a man I do not love. I am allowed, by night, to submit to God-knows-what idiotic fumblings and horrors, and by day to rule the fumbler and the entire world. I am allowed, after these exquisite nocturnal pleasures, to blow up like a cow, and stumble around—fingers, face, breasts and paunch enormous. And after months of this comic self-entertainment I am allowed to bring forth, in unimaginable pain, a dwarf, a monster, a vegetable, or, if by chance I am supremely fortunate—another creature like myself.

OXENSTIERNA

Ordinary women do this daily.

CHRISTINA

I am not ordinary! If there is one thing you have taught me since I could hear, it is the specialness of me. Kings rule and indulge between the sheets in every sort of pleasure. And then they go off to battle and joyfully await news of the arrivals of their sons. I would be happy to be a King and do all those things. But I will not submit to being boarded by a jackass in order to blow up like a mountain and erupt again and again in excruciating torment for the State! Find me a man who will bear my children!

OXENSTIERNA

Christina—

CHRISTINA

Find me a battalion of men who will each let me have my way with them and watch me ride out of their lives forever at the dawn. Find me a chance encounter on a hill where *I* pursue and *he* takes the consequences.

OXENSTIERNA

Christina, you're asking the impossible.

CHRISTINA

I am a Queen! I can have anything I want! And I tell you I will not submit my body and my mind to what is asked of me.

OXENSTIERNA

But if you love—

CHRISTINA

I loved once. I was betrayed.

OXENSTIERNA

You will again.

CHRISTINA

I will never give myself to a man. Never! I will never give myself to a man—*(Suddenly she turns and faces* AZZOLINO *squarely)*— unless it be to you.

> (AZZOLINO *looks at her. Their eyes hold)*
> *(Blackout)*

Act Two

A brilliant midmorning. The bells are beginning to chime the hour.

By the second chime, BIRGITO *enters from upstage, carrying a richly brocaded box tied with a golden ribbon. He is excited about its contents and waits expectantly for* AZZOLINO, *who arrives with* DOMINIC *from stage right just as the clock strikes ten.*

AZZOLINO

Where is your mistress?

(BIRGITO *gestures that she has sent him to deliver this present. He holds it up for* AZZOLINO *to untie it.* AZZOLINO *undoes the ribbon. The sides of the box fall away, revealing an exquisitely carved ivory goblet.* AZZOLINO *admires it coolly. It is very beautiful, but it does not explain why* CHRISTINA *is not here.* DOMINIC *takes the goblet and inspects it with admiration. Then suddenly, as he examines it closely, his eyes open wide with shock. He thrusts the goblet back at* AZZOLINO, *who now examines it again—and sees exactly what it is that* DOMINIC *is scandalized about. He is turning to* BIRGITO *to demand some kind of explanation, when, from upstage,* CHRISTINA *appears.* AZZOLINO *and* DOMINIC *stare at her in astonishment. No longer is she wearing the clothes of a man. She is dressed, instead, in a beautiful gown—whose décolletage leaves no doubt as to her gender)*

CHRISTINA

(Delighted at the effect she is making) I have come to continue my confession. *(Seeing that* DOMINIC *is staring at her open-mouthed,* AZZOLINO *makes a gesture that dismisses him.* DOMINIC *exits. Following* AZZOLINO's *example,* CHRISTINA *sends* BIRGITO *away. Now only* AZZOLINO *is left staring)* What's the matter?

AZZOLINO

That dress . . .

CHRISTINA

You protested about my other clothing. I wanted to show you that my heart is in the right place.

AZZOLINO

So I see . . .

CHRISTINA

Are you aware that all Rome is talking about our sessions together?

AZZOLINO

Yes, I am aware of it.

CHRISTINA

Christina and the Cardinal, alone, day after day. Doesn't the gossip disturb you?

AZZOLINO

Not at all.

CHRISTINA

How thoroughly self-possessed you are, Cardinal.

AZZOLINO

(Wryly) It comes with the hat.

CHRISTINA

I thought you might feel you were being compromised.

AZZOLINO

No.

CHRISTINA

Then why haven't you thanked me for my gift?

AZZOLINO

If I were choosing a gift for the Vatican, I don't think I'd pick "The Rape of the Sabine Women."

CHRISTINA

But, Azzolino, think of all those converts!

AZZOLINO

Most of our converts wear clothes!

CHRISTINA

I'll have them painted on! Bring the goblet to my apartments tonight, after eleven.

AZZOLINO

What are you doing?

CHRISTINA

Courting you.

AZZOLINO

I am serious.

CHRISTINA

So am I. Quite.

AZZOLINO

You are misbehaving.

CHRISTINA

Yes, Cardinal.

AZZOLINO

You are going beyond the bounds of decency!

CHRISTINA

Yes, Cardinal. I am.

AZZOLINO

Do you know what that means?

CHRISTINA

A passport to hell? I thought I'd earned that already.

AZZOLINO

There are degrees in hell.

CHRISTINA

Well, I've always wanted nothing but the best.

AZZOLINO

You are incorrigible!

CHRISTINA

I am like a child.

AZZOLINO

You are playing a game.

CHRISTINA

To be honest, I'm not sure whether I am or not . . . Do you refuse
my gift?

AZZOLINO

Of course!

CHRISTINA

You could sell it and feed several thousand starving orphans.

AZZOLINO

You sell it, then, and bring me the gold.

411

CHRISTINA

I see. Gold is holy and flesh is not.

AZZOLINO

That wasn't flesh you gave me, it was ivory.

CHRISTINA

Well, then, between flesh and ivory, which is more holy?

AZZOLINO

Why did you never marry?

CHRISTINA

The Inquisition continues!

AZZOLINO

Why did you never marry?

CHRISTINA

Why didn't *you?*

AZZOLINO

Christina, you are driving me out of all patience.

CHRISTINA

Most people take marriage for granted. What was there about you and me that we did not?

AZZOLINO

You and I—

CHRISTINA

Is marriage a natural state—or the most unnatural?
　(OXENSTIERNA *appears*)

OXENSTIERNA

Marriage is the natural state.
　(CHRIS *appears*)

CHRIS

Not to me.

OXENSTIERNA

It is God's way of renewing the generations.

CHRIS

My pig "renewed the generations" yesterday. And as far as I know, she was never a bride.

OXENSTIERNA

Christina, by your refusal to marry you are making the entire country uneasy.

CHRIS

Why? Because they are deprived of their vicarious enjoyment of my wedding night?

OXENSTIERNA

They are anxious about the succession! They want you to have children.

(Enter CHARLES*)*

CHRIS

(Grimly) Do they, indeed?

OXENSTIERNA

Your Majesty, Charles is here.

CHRIS

(Not looking at him) Ah, yes, Charles . . .

OXENSTIERNA

Will you see him?

CHRIS

If you insist.

*(*OXENSTIERNA *smiles encouragingly at* CHARLES *and backs out discreetly, leaving them alone. Pause.* CHARLES *clears his throat. He is awkward and cannot get out what he has to say)*

CHARLES

Have you noticed . . . that all our friends are married?

CHRIS

(Distantly) Are they?

CHARLES

They all seem . . . very happy.

CHRIS

Oh? They do?

CHARLES

With all of them married, doesn't it make you . . . want anything?

CHRIS

It makes me want to widen my circle of acquaintances.

CHARLES

(Putting his fingertips lightly on her arm) Christina—

413

CHRIS

(Crying out) Don't touch me! *(Then, collecting herself, coldly)* I have not given you leave to touch me.

CHARLES

Forgive me. What permission do I have?

CHRIS

To speak.

CHARLES

I . . . *(He can't go on)*

CHRIS

I have given you leave to speak. What do you have to say?

CHARLES

(He sputters; he starts; he can't get it out) Nothing! *(He flees from her presence)*

CHRISTINA

Poor Charlie . . .

(CHRIS *goes out the other way)*

AZZOLINO

You should have helped him.

CHRISTINA

Tell me, Azzolino, if you were he, would you have blundered like that?

AZZOLINO

I hope not!

CHRISTINA

When I said I hadn't given you leave to touch me, would you have snatched your hand away?

AZZOLINO

No . . . If one wants something badly enough, then— *(He breaks off)*

CHRISTINA

(Steadily) Then what?

AZZOLINO

(Quietly) Then one lets nothing stand in one's way.

CHRISTINA

My mind exactly.

CHRIS

(Enters, calling out) Oxenstierna! Oxenstierna!
(OXENSTIERNA *comes running)*

OXENSTIERNA

(Eagerly) Yes, Your Majesty!

CHRIS

I have some good news for you.

OXENSTIERNA

Ah, at last!

CHRIS

You said the people wanted me to ensure the succession.

OXENSTIERNA

Yes.

CHRIS

Well, tell them their sovereign is happy to oblige them. I want you to be the first to know: I am going to have a son.

OXENSTIERNA

God in heaven!

CHRIS

Next Tuesday.

OXENSTIERNA

What are you saying?

CHRIS

I am going to present the country with my heir! *(*CHARLES *enters)* Here he is!

CHRISTINA

How do you like that for immaculate conception?

CHRIS

It was an extremely easy delivery. I'm quite surprised.

OXENSTIERNA

Christina, what the country wants—

CHRIS

—is a King if I should die. Hereby I provide one.

OXENSTIERNA

By decree!

CHRIS

The perfect way. Then we all know what we're getting.

Congratulate me! I am the first woman in history to have a
son two years older than herself!

CHARLES

I don't want to be your son! I want to be your husband!

CHRIS

How bold he is this morning.
(TINA *runs in with a baby's bib*)

TINA

Let's play house! You can be my baby son. *(She puts the bib
around* CHARLES*'s neck)*

CHARLES

I don't want to be anybody's son!

CHRIS

Ungrateful boy!

CHARLES

What shall I do?
(OXENSTIERNA *throws up his hands and exits.* TINA *puts*
CHARLES*'s head in her lap)*

TINA

There, there, don't cry. Drink your milk, now. *(She feeds him
from an imaginary cup)*

CHARLES

Oh, God, what shall I do?

CHRISTINA

He was a lovely baby. Except, poor boy, he was always drunk.

AZZOLINO

Perhaps you drove him to it.

CHRISTINA

As a matter of fact, he's turned out quite well in spite of everything.

CHRIS

You are going to be the bravest and strongest of all sons.

CHARLES

In the name of God, Christina!

CHRIS

You will ride into battle close beside me. And when I die—

416

CHARLES

I don't want to profit from your death!

CHRIS

Of course you do. That's what it means to be a son.

CHARLES

I want to have a son *with* you. *Our* son. Someone who will love us and live on after us—

CHRISTINA

Azzolino, are you ever sorry that you have no son?

AZZOLINO

Are you?

CHARLES

I want to marry you, Christina.

CHRIS

What's gotten into you? I've never seen you so audacious.

CHARLES

I'm at my wits' end, Christina. I don't know what to do—

AZZOLINO

Why did you abdicate?

CHRISTINA

Oh, God.

CHRIS

I don't mean to hurt you, Charlie. I'm very fond of you.

CHARLES

But not enough to marry me?

AZZOLINO

Why did you abdicate?

CHRISTINA

To become a Catholic!

AZZOLINO

Why did you become a Catholic?

CHRISTINA

To find you.

CHRIS

You'd be much better off as my heir.

AZZOLINO

I am charged with the salvation of your soul—

417

CHRISTINA

(Suggestively) I know a way that you could save it—

AZZOLINO

I am not your suitor, I'm your priest!

CHARLES

I don't want to be your heir, I want to be your husband!
(At this show of strength, TINA *exits)*

CHRISTINA

You men just will not fit yourselves into the proper categories!

CHARLES

(To CHRIS*)* I want to be a father too.

CHRIS

Then do it with somebody else. How many times do I have
to repeat: I have no intention of bearing children! *(*OXEN-
STIERNA *and* MAGNUS *enter)* What are *they* doing here?

CHARLES

I asked them to come and second me.

OXENSTIERNA

Tell us frankly, Christina . . .

MAGNUS

Is it simply that you don't like Charles?

OXENSTIERNA

Shall we look for other candidates?

CHRIS

I tell you no!

AZZOLINO

Why did you abdicate?

CHRISTINA

They kept trying to get me married.

AZZOLINO

There have been virgin queens. Why did you abdicate?

MAGNUS

Why won't you marry?

CHRIS

The matter is settled. Am I never to hear the end of this?

AZZOLINO

Why did you abdicate?

CHARLES

Why won't you marry?

CHRIS

Let me be, I tell you!

OXENSTIERNA

Why won't you marry?

MAGNUS

Why?

CHRIS

Stop it! *(She clasps her hands to her ears and runs out)*

CHRISTINA

Stop it!

AZZOLINO

Why won't you marry?

CHRISTINA

Stop it! Stop it!

(There is a blinding flash of light. TINA *appears, dressed all in white, wearing a halo and looking like the Virgin Mary)*

TINA

(Speaking in beatific tones) I am dedicating my maidenhead to God.

CHRISTINA

It was the only thing I could say that would get them to stop pestering me.

MAGNUS

What are you talking about?

TINA

I am dedicating my maidenhead to God.

CHARLES

It's a joke!

OXENSTIERNA

She's only joking!

MAGNUS

Tina, you really are absurd—

(They burst out laughing at her, and exit, leaving her standing alone in a holy glow)

419

CHRISTINA

They're Protestants, you see. To them, virginity has no value. It never occurred to them I'd find a place where it has.

AZZOLINO

So that's why you wanted to become a Catholic. To justify your desire not to marry.

CHRISTINA

Nuns don't marry, and nuns are praised in the Church.

AZZOLINO

And so are mothers.

CHRISTINA

And yet the greatest mother of them all produced her child *without* fornication. Is it possible the idea was as repellent to her as it was to me?

AZZOLINO

You can't compare yourself to the Blessed Virgin.

CHRISTINA

Mary understands me. No matter how bizarre I may seem to the rest of the world, Mary understands.

AZZOLINO

You used the Church!

CHRISTINA

Oh, no—the Church used me. It was delighted to think it might catch such a great fish in its net. All I had to do was whisper, and it sent emissaries—to tempt me into the one true faith. It sent me priests, disguised as strolling fiddlers. Didn't they tell you how it was?

AZZOLINO

Yes. They told me.

CHRISTINA

No one but me knew who they were. *(Upstage,* CHRIS *pantomimes greeting an unseen fiddler)* In public, we talked of worldly things . . .

CHRIS

(As if to the fiddler) Tell me, fiddler, where do you come from?
(Silence. There is no answer)

420

CHRISTINA

(To AZZOLINO*)* Do you remember where he came from?

AZZOLINO

. . . Tuscany.

CHRIS

(To the unseen fiddler) How is the weather in Tuscany?
*(*CHRISTINA *looks at* AZZOLINO, *waiting for an answer)*

AZZOLINO

(After a moment's pause) Warm.

CHRIS

Do you know the newest music of Lully? You must teach my
court musicians.

*(*CHRIS *freezes, waiting for an answer.* AZZOLINO *realizes
that if he does not provide the answers, the scene will not
go on)*

AZZOLINO

Gladly.

CHRIS

But first, you must show me the latest innovations in the
dance.

*(*MUSIC *begins.* CHRIS *raises her hand and begins dancing
with her unseen partner)*

CHRISTINA

In private, we talked of God.

CHRIS

(As she dances) Tell me about the sacraments . . .

CHRISTINA

Tell me about the sacraments . . .

AZZOLINO

There are seven: eucharist, baptism, confirmation, penance, extreme unction, marriage, holy orders.

CHRIS

Tell me about baptism . . .
(As in a dream, CHRISTINA *begins to dance, like* CHRIS*)*

CHRISTINA

. . . about baptism . . .

421

AZZOLINO

Baptism brings grace, removing all previous sin from the soul.

CHRIS

Tell me about the catechism.

CHRISTINA

. . . the catechism . . .

AZZOLINO

In it are the answers to all questions of the heart.

(CHRISTINA *approaches* AZZOLINO *and begins to dance with him.* CHRIS *moves into the shadows and eventually disappears*)

CHRISTINA

Tell me about mortal and venial sin.

AZZOLINO

Venial sin is committed without knowing it is sin. Mortal sin is sin committed knowingly.

CHRISTINA

(Moving closer to him, feeling his presence) Tell me about the peace to be found in religion.

AZZOLINO

It is infinite.

CHRISTINA

(Holding him closer and closer) Tell me about the visions of the saints. *(More and more aroused)* Tell me about joy! Love! God! Tell me about ecstasy! *(Holding him, she throws her head back in rapture)* Oh, I do want to convert! Yes! Yes!

(TINA *enters, kneels and says joyfully as* CHRISTINA *continues to embrace* AZZOLINO)

TINA

I am in love with God! I accept the body and the blood of Christ, I accept the body and the blood, I accept the body . . .

(CHRISTINA *whispers these words along with* TINA, *all the while holding* AZZOLINO, *caressing him*)

AZZOLINO

(Quietly) Let me go. (CHRISTINA *looks at him, as if wakening. He repeats it steadily) Let me go. (She allows him to pull back.* TINA *disappears. Pause)* What in the world possessed you?

CHRISTINA

I was having visions.

AZZOLINO

You were being carried away by God-knows-what illicit fantasy!

CHRISTINA

Illicit fantasy! It was God, you know, who invented the sense of touch.

AZZOLINO

Not for the way you were using it!

CHRISTINA

Azzolino, do not play the innocent.

AZZOLINO

I am extremely displeased with you.

CHRISTINA

I see. And did Olympia Maidalchini please you more? *(He is stopped)* You see, I know. I have spies, too. They tell me things.

AZZOLINO

What do they tell you?

CHRISTINA

Enough to make your pretense of purity look a little thin.

AZZOLINO

What do they say?

CHRISTINA

They say you shared her bed. Often. They say that's where you earned your bright red hat.

AZZOLINO

Do you believe them?

CHRISTINA

Yes, I believe them. And I rejoice in that belief! *(She moves closer to him)* I think you have known the pleasures of the flesh—and I envy you your knowledge.

AZZOLINO

Christina, I am put here in this corridor to judge you.

CHRISTINA

I am jealous of you, Cardinal Azzolino! Jealous of you for what you have had and I have not.

423

AZZOLINO

Your future in Rome rests in my hands alone.

CHRISTINA

I am jealous of what you know.

AZZOLINO

I am trying to judge you fairly. But you're making it impossible.

CHRISTINA

What about you? What about your eyes, the way they look right through me. What about your voice—

AZZOLINO

I am not responsible for those!

CHRISTINA

Are you not, dear Azzolino? On the contrary, I think you know exactly what you're doing. You know very well the effect your presence here is having on me. It's what you want. Admit it!

(Pause)

AZZOLINO

Christina, you are not the first to think you are in love with your confessor.

CHRISTINA

And what about the confessor? Does he never fall . . .?

AZZOLINO

You must try and keep your mind on the matters we're discussing.

CHRISTINA

Us! That's what we're discussing.

AZZOLINO

I mean serious matters.

CHRISTINA

(Laughing) Serious matters!

(CHRIS appears, carrying a silver bowl heaped with snow, and a bottle of wine. She pours the wine onto the snow, then scoops up handfuls and devours it. OXENSTIERNA enters urgently, followed by MAGNUS and CHARLES, as if at court in a Council of State)

OXENSTIERNA

Serious news, Your Majesty—France and Spain are going to war!

424

CHRIS

Oxenstierna, have you ever eaten snow drenched in wine?
(She offers him the bowl. He pushes it aside)

MAGNUS

We must strengthen our armed forces.

CHRIS

You swallow it by handfuls. It can cure any fever, any pain.

CHARLES

Should we give priority to the Army or the Navy?

CHRIS

I like the sailors' uniforms the best.

OXENSTIERNA

Christina—

CHRIS

Let's put the Army into Navy uniforms!

OXENSTIERNA

Christina, please! There are important decisions to be made.

CHARLES

Should we support France or Spain?

CHRIS

(Dreamily, looking at her hand) The Spanish ambassador
kissed the *inside* of my hand . . .

MAGNUS

The French Army is stronger.

CHRIS

I shall give the French ambassador another chance. *(She
holds out her other palm to be kissed)*

CHARLES

We *must* seek an alliance with one or the other.

CHRIS

Which are the better lovers?

OXENSTIERNA

You don't seem to understand. The country is in danger!

CHRIS

Listen! *(They draw near her. She confides)* In another hundred years—we'll all be dead!

OXENSTIERNA

Christina . . .

CHRIS

I don't hear music.

CHARLES

You must come to a decision.

CHRIS

We must have music!

OXENSTIERNA

A responsible decision!

CHRIS

Have you heard that bawdy song they're singing about me in
the taverns?

(BIRGITO *enters as a page, with a guitar*)

MAGNUS

This is no time for songs.

CHRIS

It goes like this—

OXENSTIERNA

We are on the brink of *war!*

CHRIS

(Singing)
The Queen of Sweden sleeps alone
And swears she'll never marry.
Is she a monster, dame or man,
Oh, which sex does she carry?
Come tarry,
Come tarry,
Come board the monster, dame or man,
And see which sex she'll carry.

(CHRISTINA *suddenly cries out*)

CHRISTINA

I'll tell you what sex Christina is! She isn't *any!*

(Pause)

OXENSTIERNA

Christina, the country must be governed. We are here to
help you. Tell us what you want.

426

CHRISTINA

To be loved.

OXENSTIERNA

Your people love you.

CHRISTINA

Send them to my bedroom.

OXENSTIERNA

Christina . . .

CHRISTINA

The contact of another human being—that comfort—that's all that's wanted. And if one has it, all problems, everywhere, are solved. It's being left apart, alone, singular, that causes all the world's worst troubles. We should send our armies out to embrace each other! *There's* the way to peace.

CHARLES

How can this come from you, who wanted no one!

CHRISTINA

No one or *any*one. What's the difference?

OXENSTIERNA

Christina, the nation is waiting. This won't solve our problems of State!

CHRISTINA

The biggest problem of the State is *my* problem.

OXENSTIERNA

You must be responsible!

CHRISTINA

To the State, or to myself?

OXENSTIERNA

You are Queen!

CHRISTINA

So you've been telling me for over twenty years. But if only, just for once, I could *not* be Queen!

CHARLES

What would you be?

CHRISTINA

A woman of the streets! A gypsy! A sorcerer! I could become a highwayman, a gambler, a fusilier! I could run away to sea, become a vagabond, a pirate! I could be anything—anything! *(OXEN-STIERNA, CHARLES and MAGNUS disappear)* I could be the Queen of Rome!

> *(A burst of organ music. Bright golden light.* TINA *and* CHRIS *run in with a papal crown and a golden cloak)*

TINA

Make way!

CHRIS

Make way!

TINA and CHRIS

Excelsior!

TINA

To the Glory of God, Christina the Pope!

CHRIS

Pop*ess*.

> *(They crown* CHRISTINA *and plunge to their knees beside her)*

TINA and CHRIS

Bless us, Father.

CHRISTINA

(Dispensing blessings in singsong litany) Pax vobiscum . . .

CHRIS

What is your title?

CHRISTINA

I am the Virgin Christina!

TINA

What is your kingdom?

CHRISTINA

I am the Queen of masques and pageants. I am High Priestess of the Happy Holy Days. Where people celebrate, I reign.

CHRIS

What is your congregation?

CHRISTINA

All those who search for joy. All those who cry each moment of the day, "I cannot bear the life I'm living!" I am the patron saint of the confused and lonely, the priestess of the weeping and afraid, the shepherdess of the unwillingly wanton. I am Christina! High Pontifess of Joy!

CHRIS

Hosanna!
(TINA *flees in horror*)

AZZOLINO

Exactly as I thought—

CHRISTINA

If you want pain and penance, worship at *his* altar. But if you look for laughter, follow me!
(CHRIS *exists triumphantly, carrying the papal crown*)

AZZOLINO

You *are* here under false colors! You came to Rome to set up a separate kingdom for yourself!

CHRISTINA

(Waking from her visions) What?

AZZOLINO

You saw yourself on a raised dais, sitting next to the Pope on an equal throne.

CHRISTINA

I didn't mean—

AZZOLINO

You *did* expect to be the Queen of Rome. You still expect it! Once that door is opened to you, you expect to reign along with him.
(She looks at him, her eyes widening in horror and self-realization)

CHRISTINA

(Suddenly blurting out) Yes! It's true!

AZZOLINO

You came to Rome because there's no Queen here to rival you.

CHRISTINA

It's true! It's true!

AZZOLINO

You joined the Catholic Church because—

CHRISTINA

(Crying out helplessly) I didn't know what else to do!

AZZOLINO

The accusations in this book—are they false or true, Christina?

429

CHRISTINA

(Wildly) All false! All true! What do they say? I gave myself to men? Women? Dogs? *(Suddenly she looks at him directly and says deeply)* I gave myself to no one! I have—never—loved! Not even God. *(She falls to the floor in deep contrition)* Oh, help me to come to Him. No one has ever loved me. Can He love me? Help me, Azzolino. I don't know what to do. *(She sobs, face to the ground in deep humility)*

AZZOLINO

You have come to Him. You have confessed to Him. He will not turn away. *(He puts his hand over her head in benediction)* God, grant peace of soul to your daughter, Christina. Look upon her with compassion, absolve her from all sin, bring her to Thy light. *(He touches her head)* May the Lord bless you and keep you, may He cause His countenance to shine upon you and be gracious unto you, may He lift his countenance upon you, and give you peace. Amen.

> *(She rises, as if a great weight has been removed. After a long time, she speaks)*

CHRISTINA

In this place, I have told you things I have never told another human being.

AZZOLINO

You were speaking *through* me to God.

CHRISTINA

What will you say when they ask you if Christina is worthy of being received into the Church?

> *(A long silence)*

AZZOLINO

I will answer—yes.

CHRISTINA

Do you really believe I am?

AZZOLINO

Sometimes God reveals His wonders slowly. If you are not a true believer now, belief may come—

CHRISTINA

"May come"!

AZZOLINO

It *will* come. I am certain.

CHRISTINA

In other words, you plan to lie for my sake.

AZZOLINO

No . . . to give you the benefit of the doubt.

CHRISTINA

Because you have come to *care!*

AZZOLINO

I care for your *soul!*

CHRISTINA

Never mind. I need no further declaration.

AZZOLINO

Please listen to me—

CHRISTINA

Oh, this *is* the house of miracles! You needn't say another word!

AZZOLINO

Christina! Stop!

CHRISTINA

(With joy) I give you my full attention. My full mind. My full heart.

AZZOLINO

I want to admit you to the Church, but you must help me.

CHRISTINA

In every way I can.

AZZOLINO

You must study the laws of the Church.

CHRISTINA

If you will teach me.

AZZOLINO

You must do your best to live by them.

CHRISTINA

With all my heart.

AZZOLINO

Not flaunting them, not going against them.

CHRISTINA

Of course not.

431

AZZOLINO

Not asking others to go against them.

CHRISTINA

Azzolino, what are you trying to say?

AZZOLINO

Christina, this is very hard for me . . .

CHRISTINA

Go on.

> *(Pause)*

AZZOLINO

(With great difficulty) You know the laws under which I live .

CHRISTINA

Some of them.

AZZOLINO

You know I have vowed to consecrate my life to the service of God.

CHRISTINA

I know.

AZZOLINO

Then you must realize that my thoughts—must always be with Him. That it is impossible for me to feel towards any other—the devotion that I owe to Him, or to accept from any other—such feelings towards me.

CHRISTINA

(Appalled) What are you saying?

AZZOLINO

(With gentleness and sympathy) You must promise me, Christina, that if I admit you here you will never again allow yourself to display to me—or to behave towards me—as you have been doing.

CHRISTINA

(Anguished) You dare propose such a bargain?

AZZOLINO

Christina—

CHRISTINA

You want me to stifle what I feel?

AZZOLINO

There is no other way.

CHRISTINA

(A despairing cry) But I have found my happiness in you!

AZZOLINO

You must find it in God. If you love the Church—

CHRISTINA

I love the Church because you brought me to it!

AZZOLINO

You cannot say that!

CHRISTINA

But it's true! Has nothing happened between us during these hours? Have you no feelings for *me?*

AZZOLINO

You cannot ask that of a priest!

CHRISTINA

I ask it of *you.* I feel for *you.*

AZZOLINO

You cannot love me *and* the Church!

CHRISTINA

But I do!

AZZOLINO

Then you must stop. Or if you cannot, then at least you must keep silent.

CHRISTINA

You want me to stop up my brain, my eyes, my mouth? Become once more the Doll Queen?

AZZOLINO

You must never speak of these things again!

CHRISTINA

You may find safety in lies, Azzolino. I do not.

AZZOLINO

Christina, if I vouch for you, will you behave?

CHRISTINA

What will you do if I don't? Excommunicate me?

AZZOLINO

The Church demands obedience!

CHRISTINA

The old war cry!

433

AZZOLINO

You know if you are not accepted here, no place will take you.

CHRISTINA

I know that.

AZZOLINO

You know your only chance for a life of dignity is here.

CHRISTINA

I know, I know!

AZZOLINO

Then in the name of heaven, help me to help you. Promise me that you will obey the laws of the Church.

CHRISTINA

They ask too much!

AZZOLINO

If you want the Church to bring you to God—

CHRISTINA

I don't need the Church to bring me to God. I was *born* with Him within me!

AZZOLINO

If you want to be within the Church—

CHRISTINA

Let it receive me as I am or reject me!

AZZOLINO

—you must submit to its will!

CHRISTINA

I will not! I will love you if I choose! I defy the Pope and the Church and Heaven!

AZZOLINO

You will not be admitted! Ever! As God is my witness, you will never be let in!

(AZZOLINO *exits in a fury.* CHRISTINA *manages to hold herself proudly erect until he has gone. Then she begins to sway —and collapses on the floor. Above her unconscious form,* TINA *appears, as in a vision)*

TINA

I am the most wonderful Queen that Sweden has ever had! For one thing, I am extremely pretty. All the mothers of the kingdom want their daughters to look exactly like me. My blond hair, my blue eyes, my gentle disposition. I am the example of goodness for the entire world to follow. I rule my people with a gentle hand, and the country lives in peace and joy, held together by sheer love of me!

(CHRIS appears)

CHRIS

I am the best Queen who ever lived. Kings included. Everyone's amazed when they see me review the troops. I am the country's finest soldier. I rule with a firmness and dispatch that makes me the equal of any man living. In fact, I challenge you to find a man as reasonable and clear-headed as I. There is none extant. Last week I was paid the highest compliment ever. Parliament is thinking of declaring me King!

(CHRISTINA stirs, tortured by these visions. She raises herself and mutters)

CHRISTINA

I am going to give up the crown . . .

TINA

What did she say?

CHRIS

(In amazement) She wants to give up the crown!

TINA

How can you consider such a thing?

CHRIS

You must be mad!

CHRISTINA

I'm lonely.

TINA

You're *supposed* to be lonely. It's the privilege of your station.

CHRISTINA

And I'm tired.

CHRIS

You don't get enough fresh air.

CHRISTINA

I have too much to do.

TINA

You should leave it all to Oxenstierna. All you have to do is
sign.

CHRISTINA

I'd rather be no Queen at all than a Doll Queen!

TINA

But to be Queen is to be everything!

CHRISTINA

I'd rather be nothing and be at peace!

CHRIS

You'd give up the power?

CHRISTINA

Gladly.

TINA

The glory?

CHRISTINA

Oh, God, yes!

CHRIS

You're a coward! A weakling!

CHRISTINA

I don't care.

TINA

What will people say?

CHRISTINA

I don't care.

TINA

You're only thinking of your personal pleasure.

CHRISTINA

"Pleasure"! Oh, my God!

CHRIS

A Queen must sacrifice her life for her duty.

CHRISTINA

And what if she tries to do her duty and always, always fails!

TINA

That's not true!

CHRIS

Of course it isn't true!

CHRISTINA

I am unfit for this occupation. The months go by. I don't know where they're going. In the days, I face one crisis after the next. In the nights, I scream out with dreams whose horrors multiply when I awaken. Shall I choose the hard way or the soft way? Shall I rule with a hand of iron or a heart of love? I think of love. I want to break into the male servants' bedrooms. Treaties are read to me, I hear only the voices of the speakers. I am asked to choose emissaries, I choose them by the color of their eyes.

CHRIS

You must be manly—

CHRISTINA

I feel that Nature is setting traps for me—and I shall not escape!

TINA

You are a woman—

CHRISTINA

Sometimes I've prayed to turn into a man. And then for a moment I feel strong and able. I stride through events and move them. I am Power. I am Strength. And then I fade. The moon is in an unfavorable quadrant. The tides are out of phase. My will seems to wither, like decaying flowers. I cry out to be loved and loving, but if it were to happen, I'd be all the more confused. *(She turns to them)* Look at me! I am a grotesque! A freak! Look at my man-woman brain, my man-woman heart, my man-woman body! Look at me! Two sexes! Both at once and neither! I'm being torn apart! I must give up the crown—

CHRIS

No!

TINA

No!

CHRISTINA

I *must!*

CHRIS

But what is it you want?

CHRISTINA

I want . . . not to be a woman. I want to tear out the feminine parts of me!

437

CHRIS

(Roughly) Control yourself!

TINA

(Soothingly) Be calm.

CHRISTINA

Or if I must still be a woman, make me not a Queen.

TINA

But if you're not a Queen, what are you?

CHRISTINA

Myself! Oh, God, set me free! Let me out of me!

CHRIS

Pull yourself together!

TINA

Compose yourself!
(Sounds are heard in the distance, growing closer. Cheering crowds, martial music, marching feet)

CHRISTINA

Oh, God, let me be not a Queen or not a woman! *(She pulls off the royal sash, tears at her clothes)*

CHRIS

You are both!

TINA

Both!

CHRISTINA

No!

CHRIS and TINA

You must be both!

CHRISTINA

I *can't!*
(The sounds grow louder; they are overwhelming. TINA *curtsies.* CHRIS *makes a military salute. Between them,* CHRISTINA *tears at her hair with both hands, as if she would rip herself apart. The sounds grow to a deafening crescendo.* CHRISTINA *screams. Sudden silence. Everything blacks out. The lights change. It is several days later.* AZZOLINO *is pacing the corridor. After a moment,* DOMINIC *enters from upstage)*

AZZOLINO

What is her condition?

DOMINIC

Feverish.

AZZOLINO

Have you sent physicians to her?

DOMINIC

Yes. But she sends them away.

AZZOLINO

Who is attending her, then?

DOMINIC

Only her dwarf.

AZZOLINO

Why doesn't she send for me?

DOMINIC

I don't know, Father.

AZZOLINO

She ought to send for me.

DOMINIC

As you have said, she is very proud.

AZZOLINO

Well, I can't wait any longer. It's essential that I see her. *(He starts to leave upstage)*

DOMINIC

Father . . .

AZZOLINO

Yes?

DOMINIC

His Holiness thinks it best if you don't. I was asked to tell you.

AZZOLINO

But I am her confessor. She may need me.

DOMINIC

Still, it is his . . . wish that you not go.

AZZOLINO

Are you telling me the Pope has *forbidden* me to see Christina?

DOMINIC

Yes, Father. I'm sorry.

AZZOLINO

I can't obey. *(He starts to go)*

DOMINIC

Please, Father, don't. He's doing it for your sake. He is concerned about the rumors.

AZZOLINO

What rumors?

DOMINIC

Haven't you heard?

AZZOLINO

For heaven's sake, Dominic, speak out!

DOMINIC

Stories, Father. Stories. They're circulating all over Rome. About how you and she . . . How she and you—

AZZOLINO

By God, I must give credit to the people of small imagination! How quickly their limited minds outstrip the facts. A Queen comes to the Vatican. I am sent to question her. And all at once we are together not in a corridor, but in a bed. Is there no other possible encounter between a man and woman except the sexual? In spite of centuries of learning, of cultivation of spirit, mind and soul, does it always come down to that one animal fact? How dare they say we are that much—or that little—to each other? What do they know? Imbeciles! Cretins! God save me from the common mind! *(He dismisses* DOMINIC, *who exits. Alone,* AZZOLINO *takes the ivory goblet and contemplates it. Then suddenly he puts it aside)* God save me from myself. . . .

> *(He falls on his knees in prayer. Moments pass. He is still on his knees in fervent devotions, when* CHRISTINA *enters behind him. She moves slowly, risen from the sickbed. She is wearing a long cape which covers her from shoulders to the floor)*

CHRISTINA

Why didn't you come to me? *(*AZZOLINO *rises)* I waited.

AZZOLINO

But you did not send for me.

CHRISTINA

No . . . I came to you instead.
(Pause)

AZZOLINO

How do you feel?

CHRISTINA

I'm still breathing, thank you.

AZZOLINO

Prayers were said for you.

CHRISTINA

(With a half smile) On your instructions?

AZZOLINO

Yes.

CHRISTINA

(With irony) I am touched by your concern.

AZZOLINO

(In the same vein) I am not quite as cruel as you make me out to be. Although I was perhaps a little severe at our last meeting. I'm sorry.

CHRISTINA

Well! An apology. That's more than I expected.

AZZOLINO

I shouldn't have forced the questioning beyond your endurance.

CHRISTINA

Oh, is that how you think you were severe with me?

AZZOLINO

Wasn't it?

CHRISTINA

Oh, no.

AZZOLINO

How, then?

CHRISTINA

. . . Tell me, have you informed the powers-that-be of your decision yet?

AZZOLINO

I haven't made a decision.

CHRISTINA

Ah . . . then let me help you.

AZZOLINO

You?

CHRISTINA

Why not? Fever clears the head.

AZZOLINO

But—

CHRISTINA

You said I couldn't enter the Church and go on loving you.

AZZOLINO

Yes.

CHRISTINA

Bitter alternatives. Because I want them both. But if I must choose one, as you have made it clear I must, then, Azzolino— I choose you.

AZZOLINO

Christina!

CHRISTINA

What are you going to do? Order your guards to throw me out?

AZZOLINO

I don't know what I'm going to do with you!

CHRISTINA

Do what you like! I have made my decision!

AZZOLINO

Christina! What do you expect of me?

CHRISTINA

I expect you to go on and on hiding yourself behind your crimson robes! *(She throws off the cape and reveals herself to be fully dressed in a crimson Cardinal's costume)* I expect you to keep hitching up your skirts as if I were a mouse nipping at your heels. "Go away! Oh, go away! How can you say these shocking things to me? After all, I am a Cardinal!"

AZZOLINO

What is this exhibition?

CHRISTINA

I'm showing you yourself.

AZZOLINO

This is—

CHRISTINA

Sacrilege! Of course it is! That's your first line of defense, isn't it? "Sacrilege! Blasphemy! This is mortal sin!" Go, wrap your red robe tighter.

AZZOLINO

Christina—

CHRISTINA

I wouldn't mind if the phrases were yours. But they aren't. They come with the costume!

AZZOLINO

These robes are a symbol—

CHRISTINA

Yes. Of Azzolino the Father. But, tell me, where is the symbol of Azzolino the *man? (He starts to leave)* Go on! Walk out! Are you so afraid of me? *(He turns back)* You wanted the truth. Well, there's more to hear yet!

AZZOLINO

I beg you not to say things we will *both* have to do penance for afterwards.

CHRISTINA

I cannot tell you how grateful I would be if *you* had any cause for penance! I would go from here to Jerusalem on my knees if I could get you to admit to one guilty thought.

AZZOLINO

Christina, don't—

CHRISTINA

You refused my nude carvings. I don't blame you. They are lascivious. But do you know what I lay in bed imagining this evening?

AZZOLINO

No.

CHRISTINA

The most lewd sculpture in the world . . . You and I, made of spun sugar, and fully clothed, standing three inches high on a cake. Wouldn't it be obscene, that sculpture?

443

AZZOLINO

Why obscene?

CHRISTINA

Because we'd be two, then. Two together. And two together is a couple, and a couple is coupling and that, of course, between a Queen and a Cardinal, is obscene.

AZZOLINO

It is not as obscene for the Queen as it is for the Cardinal.

CHRISTINA

And yet, the Queen is a virgin—and the Cardinal is not.

AZZOLINO

That is not the issue! You and I—

CHRISTINA

Why not you and I? Why not? Why not? Are we so despised by God that we are to be denied what others take with ease? Is there some mystery about us? And if so, are we something more in His eyes? Or something less?

AZZOLINO

(Increasingly disturbed by her) Christina, I beg you—

CHRISTINA

If God sent me this love, can it be wrong for me to feel it and express it? . . . Through my confession, you know me as no human being on earth has ever known me. There is only one kind of knowing left. Know me that way! *(She falls to her knees)*

AZZOLINO

Get up, in the name of heaven!

CHRISTINA

Look how low I have been brought by you, I who said I never could be humbled! Here I am on my knees—and happy to be here!

AZZOLINO

I beg you to rise. *(He turns away)*

CHRISTINA

What is it? Do you hate me so much? Can't you bear to look at me? To touch me? Am I that much of a monster?

AZZOLINO

Get up!

444

CHRISTINA

Never, unless you raise me!

(AZZOLINO *raises her to her feet. They face each other in silence, nearly touching. There is a pause, then* AZZOLINO *speaks with quiet intensity*)

AZZOLINO

You think because I wear these robes that I am inhuman. You think that I am something removed from the world. Suspended. Serene. Insulated against "ordinary" cravings and desires.

CHRISTINA

You forget. I know about Olympia.

AZZOLINO

Oh, yes. Olympia. How do you see the episode with her? A youthful aberration? A coldly cynical affair? I strayed once, confessed, was absolved—and am forever beyond that? ... Would you like to hear the truth of it?

CHRISTINA

No—

AZZOLINO

Are you afraid you might find out what I really am, beneath the drapery? *(He goes on his knees to her)*

CHRISTINA

What are you doing?

AZZOLINO

I have listened to your confession. Now, "Cardinal Christina," you will listen to mine! *(He grasps the hem of her gown)*

CHRISTINA

Let go!

AZZOLINO

Bless me, Father, for I have sinned.

CHRISTINA

Get up! Get up! Let go of me!

AZZOLINO

(He tightens his grip on her) You *will* listen! *(Half in horror, half in terror, she stands still)* Bless me, Father, for I have sinned. I have possessed a woman. I have given myself to the pleasures of the flesh. I have been consumed by lust. I am a fallen priest. *(She*

445

turns away. He holds her fast) For a priest to have a woman, that is not uncommon, is it? It is *how* he has her, isn't it, that determines the degree of sin? A whore for a sudden need—that isn't pretty, perhaps, but it might be pardonable. A long-continuing alliance with a woman—that is not sanctioned, but surely it must find *some* approbation in the eyes of God. But neither of these is the way I loved . . . *(He tightens his grip on her as his tone becomes more impassioned)* The way I had a woman was to be had *by* her. My love wasn't love, it was a consuming fire. An unconquerable obsession! A need for her—beyond my need for God. That was my experience of love: I was debased, my mind and spirit enslaved. I was possessed by living demons! While I loved, I was no use to God; the Church, myself or anyone! To be with her, embraced by her, within her, I would even have surrendered up my life. *(She starts to speak. He interrupts her)* I am not finished! I prayed to God for some deliverance. I lived on bread and water for a thousand days. I did not allow myself to sleep. I scourged myself. And after *years* of self-inflicted penance, I was cured. And I vowed never again to let myself fall. *(He tears off his Cardinal's robe and reveals himself to be wearing a hair shirt)* To keep my thoughts within their necessary borders, to remind myself of those days in hell, I would submit myself to any torture.

CHRISTINA

Azzolino!

AZZOLINO

God is here, I want to be able to serve Him! I want to feel His call again, in innocence, as I did when I was a boy. I do not want to lose myself again, Christina.

> *(He tears off the hair shirt and reveals his flesh, swollen and bleeding.* CHRISTINA *pulls back for a moment, horrified. Then, slowly, with great gentleness and pity, she reaches out and touches his wounds)*

CHRISTINA

God have mercy! How long have you been wearing this? Since that time long ago?

AZZOLINO

(After a long pause) No. Since you. *(She is stunned. He rises)* I

446

knew, even before you knew, how much there could be between us.

CHRISTINA

And you never told me . . .

AZZOLINO

I thought I had made myself impervious. I had kept my vows for ten long years. And then you came. You—strange, tormented creature. Confused, courageous, brilliant creature. Fearing what I feared, loving what I loved. You set up in me such echoes—

CHRISTINA

Azzolino—

AZZOLINO

You asked me once what was my greatest fault. Now I will tell you. My greatest fault is, in spite of years on my knees, in spite of all the teachings of the Church, in spite of the sacred trust of this uniform—in spite of all these things—I love. And worse than this, I do not think it is a sin. I do not even think it is a weakness. I glory in it! I do love! I do want! I do desire!

CHRISTINA

Do you desire—me?

AZZOLINO

(After a very long time) Yes. I do.
> *(They face each other, overwhelmed at their mutual confession)*

CHRISTINA

(After a long silence, overcome) Dear merciful God!
> *(She takes off her Cardinal's robe and begins to put it on* AZZOLINO. EBBA *appears)*

EBBA

Can you imagine? They say you love me!
> *(*CHARLES *appears)*

CHARLES

Why can't you love me, Christina? Why? Why?
> *(*MAGNUS *appears)*

MAGNUS

You'll never love anyone. And no one will ever love you. You don't know how to love!
> *(*EBBA, CHARLES *and* MAGNUS *disappear)*

447

CHRISTINA

I never meant to cause you pain—

AZZOLINO

I know that.

CHRISTINA

If only I had known what you were suffering, for me . . .

AZZOLINO

Part of penance is to suffer in silence.

CHRISTINA

My dear Azzolino—

AZZOLINO

Tears?

CHRISTINA

(Through them) No. Oh, no.

AZZOLINO

And you the woman I love most for her courage!

CHRISTINA

Azzolino—if we loved—it would be a love of equals—taking nothing, giving all.

AZZOLINO

I know . . . *(He touches her face)*

CHRISTINA

(After a long pause) I want to give myself to you.

AZZOLINO

Christina, we would be damned—

CHRISTINA

And if we were? We'd float through hell together forever, like Paolo and Francesca. What an exquisite punishment! Eternally joined together in the act of love!

AZZOLINO

Christina—

CHRISTINA

If I don't have you, I will have no one . . . Once! Just once!

AZZOLINO

It is never *once*. Once is always only the beginning.

CHRISTINA

Then let's begin and give ourselves to love. Let's enjoy all that God

448

has given humans to enjoy. Let's celebrate Him. Let's fulfill
His commands. Say *yes*—to Him, to Life, to Love, to Everything!

AZZOLINO

How magnificent you are!
(Suddenly he comes to her. They kiss)

CHRISTINA

God, oh, God. I love you, Azzolino.

AZZOLINO

Christina, dear Christina . . .
(A moment. BIRGITO *bursts in)*

CHRISTINA

What is it, Birgito? *(*BIRGITO *pantomimes swiftly, seriously)* I don't
understand. *(Then, beginning to comprehend what he is telling her,
she looks stunned)* No. It isn't possible. *(*BIRGITO *continues. She
cries out)* It can't be happening *now!* Not *now!* *(He continues to
pantomime)* I don't want to hear! Go away! Go away!
(She rushes at BIRGITO. AZZOLINO *stops her.* BIRGITO *runs
out)*

AZZOLINO

What is it? What did he say?

CHRISTINA

Is God so jealous of me?

AZZOLINO

(Strongly) What did Birgito say?

CHRISTINA

Nothing! It was a dance! A meaningless pantomime!
(Agitated, CHRISTINA *buries her head in her hands.* OXEN-
STIERNA *enters)*

OXENSTIERNA

The King is dying.

CHRISTINA

(Under her breath) The King is dying.

AZZOLINO

What?
*(*CHRISTINA *looks at* AZZOLINO*)*

449

CHRISTINA

(Slowly, carefully) The Pope is dying . . .
    *(*DOMINIC *enters, highly disturbed)*

DOMINIC

(Urgently) Father—

AZZOLINO

I am coming.

DOMINIC

The Pope is dying.

OXENSTIERNA

    The King is dying.

CHRISTINA

(Crying out defiantly as AZZOLINO *and* DOMINIC *exit)* Everybody
dies!

    (Once they have gone, CHRISTINA*'s thoughts erupt into
    bizarre, unearthly visions, part memory, part nightmare)*

OXENSTIERNA

Your father's dead. You must get ready for the coronation.

CHRISTINA

No, I don't want to!

OXENSTIERNA

You must get ready for the coronation.
    *(*TINA *and* CHRIS *enter, carrying the symbols of office)*

CHRISTINA

I don't want it! I don't want the crown! *(*TINA *and* CHRIS *chase
her, trying to put the crown on her head)* Take it away! Take it
away! *(They finally crown her, pinning her down forcefully as she
struggles to escape)* You're killing me!
    (A blast of trumpets rings out)

OXENSTIERNA

God save her sovereign majesty—Christina, Queen of Sweden!
    *(*CHARLES *enters and kneels to her)*

CHRISTINA

(Struggling in the grip of CHRIS *and* TINA*)* Charlie, dear Charlie!
Save me! Take the crown! *(She tries to give the crown to him, but
cannot reach him. She shouts at* CHRIS *and* TINA*)* Let me go! *(They*

hold her fast) Let me go! *(Suddenly she breaks away.* CHRIS *and* TINA *exit.* CHRISTINA *instantly takes the crown off her head and crowns* CHARLES*)* Thank you! Thank you for setting me free!

OXENSTIERNA

You must get ready for the abdication.

CHRISTINA

(Triumphant) I've done it!

OXENSTIERNA

You must get ready for the abdication.

CHRISTINA

It's finished! Now I'm going to live!

OXENSTIERNA

You must get ready for the abdication.

CHRISTINA

The abdication is over! I did it, Oxenstierna! And look what was in store for me! I fell in love! I found a man! *The* man—

OXENSTIERNA

(Sternly) You must get ready for the abdication.
(He exits. Suddenly, the meaning of his words comes through to her)

CHRISTINA

(Murmurs) No, no . . . *(She looks around. She is alone. She cries out)* Birgito! *(Instantly, he appears)* Birgito, I am being asked to give him up. I can feel it. Worlds out there that suddenly need him. And I am being asked to let him go. What must I do? Renounce him for the sake of God? Is this the purpose of my life? To abdicate everything? I won't! I won't! I can't! *(Wildly, she clutches* AZZOLINO*'s discarded robe. Gently,* BIRGITO *takes it from her. Impulsively she throws her arms about him)* How can I bear it, Birgito? How am I to bear it?
(For a moment, they cling to each other. AZZOLINO *enters.* BIRGITO *exits.* AZZOLINO *stands for a long time in silence)*

AZZOLINO

The Pope has asked to see you. *(*CHRISTINA *looks at him)* You swore you'd take communion only from his hand. There is still time.

451

CHRISTINA

He wishes, then, to give it?

AZZOLINO

With all his heart, Christina.

CHRISTINA

Because of what you told him of me?

AZZOLINO

Because of what you are.

(Pause. Their eyes hold)

CHRISTINA

Did he speak to you—about yourself?

AZZOLINO

Yes. He blessed me . . . spoke of the kingdom I would inherit . . . urged me to consecrate my life anew to God.

CHRISTINA

Renouncing me for Him—like rival lovers.

AZZOLINO

Christina—

CHRISTINA

(Crying out) I hate your God! He's nothing but a trickster! Gives with the right hand just to have the pleasure of taking away with the left! *(Intensely)* Moments ago I thought my life had meaning. I thought I understood why I gave up all I had, why I came. For love—for the solution of that final mystery! But that was not God's plan, was it? His plan—His great wide cosmic plan—was to snatch you away just before the mystery is solved! *(At the end of her being)* What kind of God is that? Are we His playthings? Does He throw us happy moments just to snatch them all away? Is that why we exist? So He can taunt, tease, torture, *murder* us?

AZZOLINO

Christina, I can't bear to see you this way—

CHRISTINA

Go blind, then, and thank your God for another miracle!

AZZOLINO

(Angrily) That we breathe, think, feel, hear, see, is enough of a

miracle! That He continues to let us do so when we squander most of His gifts most of the time is the greatest miracle of which I can conceive!

(Pause)

CHRISTINA

Azzolino, what are we going to do?

AZZOLINO

What can I say to comfort you?

CHRISTINA

You let me go so easily!

AZZOLINO

(Struggling within himself) If you think that, you have understood nothing of me.

CHRISTINA

Then how can this happen—to us?

(Pause)

AZZOLINO

(Gently, and with great pain) All lovers feel . . . that they are exceptions. That they make their own rules, create their own laws. That they live—as you and I have lived in this corridor—in their own special universe. But God's kingdom is greater—and, in the end, it must be served.

(A long silence)

CHRISTINA

Are we not the earth's strangest couple? Saying no to each other —and having that the greatest gift we each can give?

AZZOLINO

I have one more: just one last time to say . . . I love you. *(She looks at him as if he had given her the universe. Slowly,* AZZOLINO *raises his hand and makes a cross above her, in benediction. In response,* CHRISTINA *makes a cross of benediction over him. For a moment, their fingertips touch, communicating all desire, all passion, all holiness. Then they slowly lower their hands)* Won't you go in and receive the Pope's blessing?

CHRISTINA

Do you think I'm worthy of it?

453

AZZOLINO

I think you are. I think you've been through enough of a trial to enter heaven.

CHRISTINA

Have I? Well, if ever I *do* get there, I must ask God a question.

AZZOLINO

What question?

CHRISTINA

(After a long pause, a tortured cry from the heart) Why?
> *(She looks at* AZZOLINO *once more, searching for answers.*
> *Their eyes hold, communicating for the last time the depth*
> *of their feeling. Then* CHRISTINA *turns and exits toward the*
> *Pope.* AZZOLINO *watches her go)*
> *(Blackout)*

The Ice Wolf

A Tale of the Eskimos

A Play for Young People
in Three Acts

by
JOANNA HALPERT KRAUS

"I was working one summer in children's drama near Ottawa in Canada, and one of my staff brought me an Eskimo print on rice paper, which showed the body of a wolf and the face of a girl." The story on which *The Ice Wolf* is based is not an Eskimo legend, Joanna Kraus explains, but "a tale the artist told to explain that print." The image haunted her, and as her master's thesis in theatre at UCLA, she wrote the play, based on the artist's tale, immersing herself first in Canadian Eskimo culture. "I wanted every detail as authentic as possible." *The Ice Wolf* has had nearly a hundred productions in the United States, Canada and England and has been translated into Spanish. "Some people say it's not a play for children because it deals with serious issues. When it gets put on, it's by people who say, 'I don't care if they fire me, I'm going to do this play.' "

Kraus grew up in Portland, Maine, and saw there, as a little girl, productions of the children's theatre company she joined at the age of thirteen. She worked with them for five years, touring rural Maine, giving performances in firehouses and vacant lots, "anywhere we could—many of the children had never seen live actors before. I made a private vow to try to bring theatre, which had been so important to me, to other children." Kraus is an assistant professor at State University College in New Paltz, New York, where she teaches drama and trains prospective teachers of language arts to use "sound and motion" and other theatre techniques. She has published many articles about children's theatre and three other plays—one about Harriet Tubman—which are distributed by *New Plays for Children*. In 1971 she won the Charlotte B. Chorpenning Cup for achievement in playwrighting (awarded by the Children's Theatre Conference) and, in 1976, a CAPS Fellowship in playwrighting from the New York State Council on the Arts. She lives in Poughkeepsie with her husband and adopted Korean son.

CHARACTERS

STORYTELLER

ANATOU, a girl born to Eskimo parents. Her skin is pale and her hair blond—a phenomenon in the village.

KARVIK, her father

ARNARQIK, her mother

TARTO, her best friend, a village boy

KIVIOG, Tarto's father

ATATA, an old man of the village but a good hunter

SHIKIKANAQ, a village girl

MOTOMIAK, a village boy

VILLAGER 1, a woman

VILLAGER 2, a man

WOOD GOD, the God of the Forest

A BEAVER

A FOX

AN ERMINE

PLACE AND TIME

The entire action of the play takes place in a small, isolated Eskimo village, Little Whale River, and the forest, a few days inland. It is located in the Hudson Bay area of Canada.

The time is long before the missionaries established their settlements, long before white man had been seen, a time when the spirits and the shaman, or the wise man, ruled.

PROLOGUE

It is the end of January. In the foreground we see an expanse of white spread out. It is broken in a few places by hillocks which rise up like seals' heads from the plains. There is an atmosphere of cold beauty and awesome space.

The STORYTELLER *enters on the apron of the stage. He is dressed, as are all the Eskimos, in the attire of the Hudson Bay Eskimos, but somehow there is the quality about him of excitement. He is no ordinary hunter.*

STORYTELLER

Far beyond the world you know—
Of sun, rushing rivers, and trees
Is the Northland
Where the winter snow is gray,
There is no sound of birds
Nothing but the stillness of space
Of endless snow
And endless cold.
There, the child Anatou was born
In the village of Little Whale River
It was small, beside the sea
But the search for food never ended.

(Lights up on igloo, Eskimos in circle, one beating a drum, chanting) Aja, I remember. It was one of the coldest nights of the year, so cold the dog team had buried themselves in the snow.

ATATA .

And the seal-oil lamps trembled before the Great North wind.

KARVIK

Just before dawn, when the baby came, Karvik had to go out and repair their home. His fingers seemed to freeze at once. Never had there been such a storm in Little Whale River.

(Lights up on KARVIK, *who is cutting a snow block and fitting it into dome)*

459

ARNARQIK

Inside, Arnarqik sewed the caribou skins she had chewed. She was making new clothes for Karvik. Only once did she dare to look at the small child beside her wrapped in skins. It was strangely still, strangely quiet. It was unlike any child Arnarqik had ever seen.

STORYTELLER

Atata was by the seal's breathing hole . . . *(Lights up on* ATATA *crouched by breathing hole, poised, ready with harpoon)* . . . waiting . . . waiting . . . waiting until the seal came up for air. For days there had been no food in Little Whale River. He thought the birth of a new child might bring him luck! Then . . . he struck with his harpoon!

*(*ATATA *harpoons seal)*

ATATA

Aja, Nuliayuk, now everyone will eat!

STORYTELLER

He took the choice bit of meat, the seal's liver, to return to the Seal Goddess, Nuliayuk. The shaman, the wise man, had told him to do this so she would feast on it and then remember to send more seals to the hunters of Little Whale River. Atata rushed back. Now there was something to celebrate. A new child, a fresh-caught seal. There would be drum chants and dancing and stories in the long white night. *(Drum chants begin. They break off abruptly)* But there was no singing or dancing.

KARVIK

It was long ago . . .

ARNARQIK

Just about this time.

STORYTELLER

It was a pale dawn . . .

ATATA

Like this one . . .

STORYTELLER

When Anatou was born.

Act One

SCENE 1

The interior of KARVIK *and* ARNARQIK'*s home in Little Whale River. Masses of thick, heavy caribou skins are spread about. Seal-oil lamps, made of soapstone, light the home.*

At curtain rise, the sound of Eskimo dogs howling. A strong wind is blowing. Dressed in their customary furs, villagers come in from all sides. They crawl through the passageway, and lights come up in the interior of the igloo. KARVIK *and* ARNARQIK *are seated. Their new child is beside* ARNARQIK *on a caribou skin not visible from the entrance.*

KARVIK

Welcome! Welcome all of you!

VILLAGER 2

Aja! Your first child. Of course we'd come. *(To others)* We must sing many songs to welcome it.

KIVIOG

And if it's a man child, Karvik will already have made him a harpoon, a sled and a whip.

VILLAGER 1

By the next moon he will be able to use them. Wait and see!
(They laugh)

VILLAGER 2

Good, he can hunt a seal with us this winter and the caribou next fall. If he's as good a hunter as Karvik, we'll get twice as much.

KIVIOG

And he'll be a companion for my son, Tarto, born under the same moon.
(They all laugh except KARVIK *and* ARNARQIK, *who are strangely quiet)*

VILLAGER 1

Karvik! Arnarqik! You are silent. Show us the man child. We've come a long way to see him.
*(*ARNARQIK *moves slowly)*

461

ARNARQIK

It is a girl child . . . but we are glad.

KARVIK

She will be good.

ARNARQIK

It is true. There is joy in feeling new life come to the great world.

VILLAGER 1

A girl! Ah-ah. That means more care.

VILLAGER 2

And more attention.

KIVIOG

She cannot hunt.

VILLAGERS

(Politely) But let us see her anyway.

(Troubled, ARNARQIK *moves away, then points to the caribou skin)*

ARNARQIK

There, look for yourself.

*(*KARVIK *has turned away. Villagers crowd around the child, move back abruptly, and then whirl on* KARVIK *and* ARNARQIK*)*

VILLAGER 1

(In low horror) Her hair is white!

VILLAGER 2

Her face is pale.

KIVIOG

She cannot be an Eskimo.

VILLAGER 1

She cannot be one of us!

KARVIK

Of course she is. Her hair will get darker. Wait.

VILLAGER 2

But her face. Look at it. No Eskimo child was ever born as pale as that.

VILLAGER 1

She's a devil.

462

ARNARQIK

No!

VILLAGER 1

She will not live one moon.

ARNARQIK

She will live.

VILLAGER 1

She will bring bad luck.

ARNARQIK

She's only a baby.

KIVIOG

Put her out in the snow now, before she turns the gods against us.

VILLAGER 2

And our stomachs shrink.

VILLAGER 1

And our dishes are empty.

VILLAGER 2

It's happened before. We all know it. Get rid of the child before it's too late.

KIVIOG

She will offend Nuliayuk, the goddess of the seals. Nuliayuk will stay at the bottom of the sea and keep the seals beside her, and we will all go hungry. Put the child out into the snow or we will die of famine!

ARNARQIK

No! She will be a good Eskimo.

VILLAGER 2

Then let her grow up in another village. We don't want her here.

KIVIOG

She doesn't look like us. She won't think like us.

VILLAGER 1

She doesn't belong here.

KARVIK

Then where does she belong? Where should she go?

VILLAGER 1

Put her out in the snow. *(Starts to grab her)*

ARNARQIK

No! No! No, I can't. Don't you understand? She is our child.

VILLAGER 2

Then leave our village in peace. Don't anger the spirits of Little
Whale River.

KARVIK

But this is our village and you are our people. How can we leave
it? Wait! She will be like the others. You'll see. She'll sew and cook
just as well as any Eskimo girl. Better! Arnarqik will teach her.

KIVIOG

(Holds up his hands) Very well. We will watch and wait. Perhaps
you are right, and we will see her hair and cheeks grow darker. But
we have no gifts or good wishes to welcome a white-faced child
—a white-faced girl child!

(Villagers exit. ARNARQIK *tries to run after them)*

ARNARQIK

Come back! Wait! Please wait. Don't go yet. Oh, Karvik, what will
we do?

KARVIK

(Slowly) Her hair should be as dark as the raven's wing.

ARNARQIK

It is as white as the caribou's belly. Karvik, what if they are right?
She is different. Karvik, why is her hair pale? Why doesn't she cry?
She is so still! It's not natural.

KARVIK

She is frightened already. The Fair One will have a hard journey.
(Looks out the passageway) Arnarqik, the villagers spoke wisely.
(Looks for a long time at his wife) She would never know. It would
not hurt if we put her in the snow now.

ARNARQIK

No, Karvik! You mustn't ask me to.

KARVIK

But if we leave, will the next village think she looks more like an
Eskimo?

ARNARQIK

(Shakes her head) No, she is Anatou, the Fair One—she will not

464

change. But I will teach her, Karvik. She will be a good Eskimo girl!

KARVIK

But will they ever think she is like the others?

ARNARQIK

Yes. Yes. Of course they will. Let us stay here. Who knows what is beyond the snow?

KARVIK

Then we must be strong. We must teach Anatou to be strong. Only then will our home be her home and our friends her friends. It won't be easy, Arnarqik.

(ARNARQIK *is beside the baby*)

ARNARQIK

Oh, Karvik, I couldn't leave her. Not like that! *(Abruptly she changes)* Look, Karvik . . . she is smiling. *(Picks her up)* Oh, Karvik, we mustn't let them hurt her. We must protect her.

KARVIK

Sing, Arnarqik, sing the morning song. Bring Anatou luck. She will have a hard journey.

ARNARQIK

(Sits and sings or chants)
    I rise up from rest
    Moving swiftly as the raven's wing
    I rise up to greet the day
    Wo-wa
    My face is turned from dark of night
    My gaze toward the dawn
    Toward the whitening dawn.
    (Lights fade)

STORYTELLER

But her hair did not grow dark as the raven's wing. Instead, each day she grew fairer. They called her the "different one," and when the blinding snow swept across the North or when the hunters returned with empty sleds, the villagers whispered, "It's Anatou. She's the one."

465

SCENE 2

The village. TARTO, SHIKIKANAQ *and* MOTOMIAK *are playing an Eskimo game, a combination of Hide-and-Seek and Touch.* MOTO-MIAK *is just dashing for the goal pursued by* SHIKIKANAQ. TARTO *is at the goal watching and laughing.*

TARTO

Hurry up, Motomiak. She's right behind you. Shikikanaq is right behind you!

> (MOTOMIAK *turns to look, still running.* ANATOU *enters. She sees the race but moves out of the way too late and they collide.* MOTOMIAK *falls and* SHIKIKANAQ *tags him)*

SHIKIKANAQ

There! I won!

MOTOMIAK

That wasn't fair. You made me lose the game, Anatou. I've never lost before—not to a girl! See what you made me do. Clumsy!

ANATOU

I'm sorry. I tried to get out of the way. I didn't see you in time.

SHIKIKANAQ

(Whispering) You better not say anything more, Motomiak, or Anatou will put a spell on you—the way she did the seals.

TARTO

What are you talking about? You know that isn't true.

ANATOU

Oh, I'm sorry I spoiled your game, Motomiak, but couldn't you start again?

SHIKIKANAQ

No. I won. Tarto saw. Didn't you, Tarto?

> (TARTO *nods)*

MOTOMIAK

Beside, we don't want to play in front of a freak.

> (ANATOU *gasps)*

TARTO

Who's a freak?

MOTOMIAK

She is. The whole village says so.

ANATOU

(Furious) No, I'm not! I'm an Eskimo just like you.

SHIKIKANAQ

(Doubtfully) Ohh . . .

MOTOMIAK

Well, her face is different enough.

(ANATOU *touches it)*

TARTO

Why, what's wrong with it? It has two eyes, a nose and a mouth just like everyone else's.

SHIKIKANAQ

But it's white, Tarto—like snow. I bet if you put her in the sun she'll melt, and that's why she stays inside all the time.

TARTO

You're just jealous because she's prettier than you, Shikikanaq.

ANATOU

Stop it. Stop it, all of you. *(She is crying)* Leave me alone. *(Starts to go)*

TARTO

(Furious) Now see what you've done. If she were made of snow, Shikikanaq, she couldn't cry. *(Crosses to her)* Come on, Anatou. They didn't mean it. Please come back. *(To others)* Let's have another game—all four of us.

SHIKIKANAQ

Well . . . all right . . . if she'll tell us why she looks that way.

TARTO

(Sharply) What way?

SHIKIKANAQ

I mean her eyes and her hair. They're such funny colors. There must be a reason.

ANATOU

(Desperate) I don't know. Each time you've asked me I said I didn't know.

467

SHIKIKANAQ

I bet if you asked your mother and father they'd know. It must be something terrible or they'd tell you.

MOTOMIAK

Maybe the Wood God from the forest put a spell on an animal and sent it back here. No one else in Little Whale River looks like you. Maybe that's why you look so funny. They say he has the power to make an animal appear like a human.

SHIKIKANAQ

And he can make people look like animals too . . . just by saying a spell! My father says that's why no Eskimo should go into the forest.

ANATOU

No! No! It's not true. I'm just like you are!

MOTOMIAK

Then, maybe, some devil spirit looked at you and it took all the color away.

SHIKIKANAQ

Yes, that's it. And why do you always sit inside and sew?

ANATOU

(Lying) There's a lot of work. It has to get done.

TARTO

(Quickly) She can sew better than any woman in the whole village! Show them, Anatou.

> *(He points to her dress, which is carefully and beautifully stitched.* SHIKIKANAQ *examines it)*

SHIKIKANAQ

It is beautiful. There aren't any mistakes at all.

ANATOU

(Can't believe her praise) My mother taught me and she is very good and careful.

SHIKIKANAQ

Can you make anything else?

ANATOU

Two snows ago, I made warm boots for my father. Very special boots, and he's worn them ever since.

MOTOMIAK

Then how come he's lost in the snow right now, if the boots you made were so special?

ANATOU

He went to look for food. Both my mother and father did. That's all I know.

MOTOMIAK

There's barely any food left in the village. For three days the hunters have returned with empty sleds.

ANATOU

Famine is everywhere. Not just here. I heard my father say so before he left. That is why he said he was going far away to look.

MOTOMIAK

You made those boots your father wore. I bet you put a charm on them. Shikikanaq and I saw you talking to them once and blowing on them.

ANATOU

No! That's not true. I was cleaning them.

MOTOMIAK

But you were talking too, you were putting a charm on them, weren't you?

· ANATOU

Don't you see? If I did have any magic powers, I'd bring them back. They're my parents. I love them. They're the only ones who've been good to me. *(Softly)* I couldn't stay in Little Whale River if it weren't for them.

SHIKIKANAQ

(Cruelly) Well, they're gone now. So you can go too.

ANATOU

What do you mean? They're coming back. I know they are.

MOTOMIAK

Maybe. But my father says you killed your own parents.

ANATOU

(With a cry) No!

TARTO

(Challenging MOTOMIAK *and pinning his arm back)* Take that back or else!

MOTOMIAK

(Stubbornly) That's what my father said.

TARTO

(Knocking him down) Well, he's wrong.

> *(A fight starts.* SHIKIKANAQ *shrieks and* ANATOU *watches,
> horrified. Three villagers rush in)*

SHIKIKANAW

(Quickly) She started it. It's all her fault. Anatou's fault!

KIVIOG

(To ANATOU*)* Get away from our children.

> *(*VILLAGER 2 *has separated the boys)*

TARTO

Anatou wasn't doing anything.

KIVIOG

Be still!

VILLAGER 1

She's brought nothing but trouble since the day she was born.

TARTO

(To KIVIOG*)* But it's not fair, Father, she—

KIVIOG

Silence! For days we have searched for Karvik and Arnarqik. They
are good people. Karvik was the best hunter we had. But no man
can fight off charmed boots.

VILLAGER 2

No wonder they got lost in the blizzard.

VILLAGER 1

Look at her. She doesn't care her parents are gone.

ANATOU

(Suddenly) I don't understand. Do you mean they're . . . they're
dead? *(*KIVIOG *nods)* How can you be sure?

KIVIOG

If they haven't frozen, they have starved. We cannot find them
anywhere.

VILLAGER 1

You're to blame. You and your witchcraft.

VILLAGER 2

Look, she doesn't even care.

ANATOU

Don't you think I want them here? Don't you think the fire is colder without my mother's face and lonesome without my father's singing? They went to look for food . . . for all of us. I'm hungry too . . . just like the rest of you.

VILLAGER 1

Then why do you anger the Seal Goddess? We used to have days of feasting.

VILLAGER 2

Pots boiling . . .

KIVIOG

But since the same day you were born, the hunters have had to work twice as hard—twice as hard for the same amount!

VILLAGER 2

We used to thank the Seal Goddess, bow down to her and give her seal liver. Now there is none to give her and she is angry— at the bottom of the sea. Our harpoons break in our hands.

ANATOU

It is the bitter cold.

VILLAGER 2

Why is there blizzard after blizzard if the gods aren't angry?

VILLAGER 1

Why is there a famine if the gods aren't angry?

KIVIOG

It's your fault.

VILLAGER 2

You're to blame.

KIVIOG

We have kept silent for the sake of Karvik and Arnarqik, but now they are no longer here.

VILLAGER 1

They took care of you and see what it brought them to!

ANATOU

(Sobbing) But I am all alone too.

VILLAGER 2

There is no more to eat.

471

VILLAGER 1

No oil to burn.

VILLAGER 2

We fear sickness.

KIVIOG

And the souls of the dead.

VILLAGER 1

The souls of animals and men.

VILLAGER 2

We know the spirits of the earth and the air are angry with us.

ANATOU

What am I to do? What do you want of me?

KIVIOG

Leave here. Leave us!

ANATOU

But I haven't done anything. Where will I go? I'll never find my way alone.

KIVIOG

If you stay, you will get no help or protection from us, Anatou. From now on, find your own food and eat with the dogs. No one else will eat with you.

VILLAGER 2

And from now on, speak to yourself. No one else will listen.
    (Adults start off)

VILLAGER 1

Go home, children, all of you. Go home quickly.

KIVIOG

Don't talk to that one. That one is evil. Leave her alone.
    (They leave. ANATOU *has turned away.* TARTO *looks back before exiting but she doesn't see it.* ANATOU *sinks down, unable to bear it)*

ANATOU

It isn't true! I loved my parents. Even Tarto believed them. He didn't say a word—he didn't even say goodbye. Oh, Moon God, is there nothing I can do?
    (She is crying. TARTO *reappears, puts his hand out to touch her hair, then in fear withdraws it)*

472

TARTO

(Gently) What are you going to do? Where will you go?

ANATOU

(Jerks her head up abruptly but doesn't turn around) All right! All right! I'm leaving. Are you satisfied now?

TARTO

But it's me, Anatou—Tarto. I wanted to say goodbye.

ANATOU

(Turns around) Tarto, you came back!

TARTO

But I can't stay. If they catch me . . . I'll . . . I'll get into trouble. I brought you some food, Anatou. It's just a little, but I thought . . .

ANATOU

Thank you, Tarto. *(Suddenly she takes off an amulet that she is wearing)* Tarto, you're the only friend I have now. I want you to keep this to remember me. The Shaman gave it to my mother before I was born. It's to bring good luck, but it was really always meant for a boy child, not a girl. *(He takes it)* Tarto, I wish I had something special to give you, but it's all I have.

TARTO

Then it is special, Anatou. I'll always keep it. I won't forget you. I promise. And when I am older, Anatou, I'll harpoon my own seal. I'll be the best hunter in the village and the men will do anything I say because I'll know all the hiding places of the seals. Then they'll listen to me and . . . *(Breaks off and slowly asks what he has always wondered)* Anatou, why is your hair so light?

ANATOU

(Pierced by the question) Tarto, why is the sky gray in the winter? I don't know. All I want is to be like the others, to play with you and sing with you, and I want to see my mother and father again. I love them. Do you believe me? *(He nods)* I want to be friends with the villagers, but they won't let me. You're the only one who tries to understand. I used to wake up and say, "Today will be different." My mother said, "Anatou, every day is the beginning of some new wonderful thing." But it wasn't true! Each day ended the same way and each dawn I was frightened again. And then today . . . today it was the worst of all.

TARTO

I'm sorry, Anatou.

ANATOU

Tarto, you were brave to come back here. You know they'll be angry if they find you here.

TARTO

I know.

ANATOU

You will be a fine hunter, Tarto . . . the finest of the whole village one day. Tarto, why did you come back?

TARTO

I am your friend, Anatou. I always will be even if . . .

ANATOU

Even if what, Tarto?

TARTO

Anatou, listen. My father said . . . that . . . well, he said . . . *(Gulps)* . . . He said you put spells on the seals so they couldn't come out of the water. Anatou, couldn't you say another spell so we could all eat? Then it would be all right again, Anatou.

ANATOU

(Horrified) Do you believe that, Tarto?

TARTO

(Miserably) Well, first I said it wasn't true! But today . . .

ANATOU

Tarto, listen. There's nothing I can do. I can't make a spell like a shaman, like the wise man. I'm hungry, too, just like you. Even if I wanted to, there is nothing I can do.

TARTO

(Slowly) Don't you want to? Don't you want to help us, Anatou?

ANATOU

Don't you believe me either, Tarto? Doesn't anyone? I'm not any different. I don't have any magic powers. I'm just like anyone else.

TARTO

Your skin is white, mine is brown. Your hair is pale like the dawn, mine is dark like the night. *(He is colder now)* You're not like anyone I've seen.

(A long pause)

474

ANATOU

I've never heard you say that before. Everyone else, but not you!
You never seemed to care. You made up for all the others.
(Sound of Eskimo dogs)

TARTO

(Uncomfortably) I have to go, Anatou . . . it's late. What will you
do?

ANATOU

(With a horrible realization) I know I can't stay here now. Tarto,
when you lose everything at once, your choice has been made. You
can only follow it.

TARTO

But where will you go? What will you do?

ANATOU

(Pauses, making a difficult decision) The forest, Tarto. It's only a
few days from here. I've heard about it from the old men and the
shaman.

TARTO

(Impulsively) But you can't. Don't you know about it? It's a place
of whispers in the night, of strange whines. They say the trees are
living beings but they can't speak. It's not safe for an Eskimo to
spend a night in the forest. What if the Wood God changes you
into a wolf or another animal?

ANATOU

(Slowly) Yes . . . what if he changes me into a wolf?

TARTO

(Continuing without hearing her) It's dark and mysterious, Anatou. It's a place where Eskimos never go.

ANATOU

But, don't you see? That's just why. There is no place else!
(Pauses) Maybe the Wood God won't care if my hair is pale
. . . like the dawn!

Act Two

SCENE 1

Outside the forest at night. Late March. The opening of this scene is mimed and the audience sees only ANATOU's *silhouette.*

STORYTELLER

Anatou ran. It was dark and frightening. The only sound she heard was the wind whipping the snow around her.

*(*ANATOU *drops from exhaustion. She is crying, but she must continue)*

ANATOU

Where shall I go?

STORYTELLER

No one could hear her cry. There was no one but the wind. Anatou knew if she stopped too long she would freeze in the fierce cold. Then suddenly she saw the place where no one had ever been.

(Part of the forest appears stage right. ANATOU *stops stage left)*

ANATOU

The forest! I remember the old men used to tell each other tales by the fire. What did they say? No Eskimo must ever go into the forest. You must never spend the night there. But that's where the Wood God lives. *(She starts to move toward the forest)* I must go. I must ask him. *(Rest of forest scrim appears as* ANATOU *runs first to stage right, then to stage left, stopping at center stage. Exhausted, she sinks to the ground. She is trembling with fear and slowly rises to her knees. Softly)* Wood God! *(Louder)* Wood God! *(Looks all around her)* Wood God . . . help me.

(The WOOD GOD *enters. He appears, as the spirits are reputed to, in the shape of an animal. He has chosen the shape of an awesome owl that is white in color)*

WOOD GOD

Who dares to come into my forest where the wind and snow cry into the darkness?

476

ANATOU

(Draws back) Are you the Wood God?

WOOD GOD

I am! And will be till the end of time! Who said you could enter my forest?

ANATOU

(Terrified) No one.

WOOD GOD

Where do you come from?

ANATOU

I come from Little Whale River.

WOOD GOD

Are you an Eskimo? *(She nods)* Then why did you come here? Don't you know no Eskimo comes into the middle of the forest and dares to disturb my sleep? Leave my kingdom now and be glad you still have your life.

ANATOU

(Pleading) No! You don't understand. Please don't send me away.
(Crying. The WOOD GOD *comes closer, and as he approaches, moonlight shines around them both)*

WOOD GOD

Ah-ah. Even in the darkness your hair shines. Is it the moon, child?

ANATOU

(Desperate) Wood God. Wood God, can't you see? Even hidden here it shines and glitters. If I were to crawl into a cave it would be the same.

WOOD GOD

(Lifts her face and peers into it) Your face is as pale as ice. *(Softer)* And your eyes are red from crying. *(Shakes his head)* That's too bad. It means you're human.

ANATOU

I am an Eskimo. But they don't believe me. Nobody does. Help me. Wood God, help me!

WOOD GOD

How can I help you? Are you hungry, child? Is that why you came here?

477

ANATOU

(Nods) We all are . . . no one has eaten in days. But it is not my fault . . . they blame me because my hair shines, because it isn't like the raven's wing. But I am hungry too. I can't go any further . . . I can't.

WOOD GOD

We have no food to give you, child. You must leave. Your people will be worried. *(He starts to exit)*

ANATOU

Wait! Wait and hear me, Wood God. It is not food I want. It is not food that made me wake the great spirit of the Wood God.

WOOD GOD

What, then?

ANATOU

(Slowly) I want what only your powers can grant. But first, Wood God, hear my story.

WOOD GOD

Begin. Quickly, child. You mustn't savor what tastes bitter.

ANATOU

Aja. It is true. You do see much.

WOOD GOD

Begin from the beginning; when you were born.

ANATOU

Even though I was a girl, my parents were happy, or at least they seemed to be. Even though I couldn't hunt . . . even though . . . even though I was different.

WOOD GOD

Why? You have two arms, two legs, and a face with two eyes and a mouth.

ANATOU

But a face that people were afraid of and hair that grew lighter instead of darker. They named me Anatou, the Fair One.

WOOD GOD

So you are Anatou. Then not all the spirits of the earth and air can help you. You are as you are.

ANATOU

But you can help me, Wood God. Please. You must.

478

WOOD GOD

Go home, fair child. I can do nothing. I cannot turn your pale hair
to the dark of the night or your fair skin brown. I cannot teach
them to like you. You must do that yourself. Go home to your
parents. Go home where you belong.

ANATOU

(Blurts out) I can't. They'll kill me if I do.

WOOD GOD

(Puzzled) Who will? Your parents, too?

ANATOU

No, they are spirits now. They were the only good people I ever
knew. I did love them, Wood God. Some people say that I am a
witch and that I cursed my parents, that the Seal Goddess is angry
with me. They say that is why there is no food. But it isn't true,
Wood God! It isn't true!

WOOD GOD

My power would only hurt you, Anatou. You are young. Go back.

ANATOU

I've heard you can make a seal seem like a man or a girl seem like
a wolf. Is that true?

WOOD GOD

I can.

ANATOU

Then, Wood God . . .

WOOD GOD

(Interrupts) Think, Anatou. Is it so terrible to be an Eskimo girl,
to learn to laugh and sing, to sew and cook.

ANATOU

Wood God, my father and mother taught me to sew and cook,
but not to laugh and sing. I don't know what that is.

WOOD GOD

But what about the villagers?

ANATOU

They only taught me one thing—to hate. When my parents were
gone, they wanted me to eat in the passageway with the dogs.
They would not give me a skin to sew. Everywhere I went they
turned away. *(Softly)* Even Tarto.

479

WOOD GOD

Tarto?

ANATOU

My best friend.

WOOD GOD

Where is he?

ANATOU

Wood God, they all say I'm planning evil, and now even Tarto thinks so, too. Wood God, Wood God, there are more ways of killing than with a harpoon!

WOOD GOD

(Pauses before he speaks) What do you wish, Anatou?

ANATOU

I don't want to be human any more. It hurts too much. I want you to turn me into a wolf. Then they'll be afraid of me. Then they'll leave me alone.

WOOD GOD

Think, Anatou, think! An animal cannot . . .

ANATOU

Is a wolf's face white like mine?

WOOD GOD

You know it is not.

ANATOU

Then quickly change me into a beast.

WOOD GOD

An animal is hungry.

ANATOU

I am used to that.

WOOD GOD

He tears with his teeth to eat. A wolf is alone.

ANATOU

I am alone now.

WOOD GOD

Anatou, there is no return. What if you miss your village?

ANATOU

Miss them! When you take a thorn out of an animal's paw, does it miss it? When you fill an empty stomach, does it miss the ache?

When you cannot remember pain, do you miss the tears? What would I miss, Wood God, but all of these things.

WOOD GOD

Once it is done, you cannot change your mind.

ANATOU

I will not want to.

WOOD GOD

You will never be an Eskimo girl again, not until you are about to die. Not till then. Are you sure? Are you sure, Anatou?

ANATOU

Will I forget everything? I want to forget everything. Now.

WOOD GOD

No, Anatou. Not at first. As time goes by, you'll forget more and more and only remember your life here.

ANATOU

No! I want to forget everything now. Everything, Wood God. I want to forget I was ever Anatou, the Fair One.

WOOD GOD

But you can't escape pain, Anatou. Even a wolf can't escape that. *(She pauses to think, she looks up. He watches her closely)* Are you ready?

ANATOU

Yes. *(Suddenly frightened)* Wood God, will it hurt much?

WOOD GOD

Listen to my words. Hear them well. *(Lifts his arms so it appears as though his spirit, in the shape of a white owl, were commanding the universe. Drumbeat begins)*

Come, spirits of earth and sky.
Rise through the snow.
Speed over the ice.
Encircle this child in a coat of thick fur.
(Three forest animals appear—a FOX, *a* BEAVER, *and an* ERMINE—*and form a circle around* ANATOU*)*

FOX

Night protect it.

BEAVER

Forest watch it.

481

ERMINE

Nothing harm it.

WOOD GOD

As long as it remembers . . .

FOX

As long as it remembers . . .

BEAVER

As long as it remembers . . .

WOOD GOD

To stay in the forest far from man.

ERMINE

Far from man.

FOX

(Echoes) . . . from man.

> *(There is more dancing. Animals close in. Their movements become more intense, then with a cry, they disappear and we see the wolf)*

FOX

It is done!

ERMINE

Now you are a wolf!

BEAVER

A wolf!

> *(This should not be a realistic representation, but rather done with masks in a costume, lean and sleek, that would be worn under the Eskimo dress, removed and disposed of at the end of the enchantment with a momentary darkening of the stage and more intense beating of the drum. There should be a marked difference in the movement once ANA-*
> *TOU has been changed into a wolf)*

SCENE 2

STORYTELLER

All that winter Anatou lived with the animals enjoying the forest. She made friends with the beaver, fox and ermine. She forgot she had ever been Anatou, the Fair One—an Eskimo. Then one morning she woke up to a spring sun. It warmed the air and touched her fur.

(Spring in the forest. Early dawn. ANATOU *wakes,* stretches, and smells the air with curiosity)

ANATOU

Whorlberries. That's what I smell. And sunlight! Even the forest can't shut it out. *(She puts a paw down on a patch of melting snow)* Beaver! Fox! Wake up. The snow's melting.

(They enter)

FOX

Did you have to wake me up to tell me that? It happens every spring.

ANATOU

(With growing excitement) But there are at least a thousand things to see and smell and hear. Come on. I'll race you through the forest and we'll explore the other side.

BEAVER

(Slowly) What do you mean by "the other side"? We've never gone beyond the edge.

ANATOU

Oh, that was all right in the wintertime. But now it's spring. I want to leave the forest today, see what else there is.

FOX

(Sharply) No, Anatou.

BEAVER

I thought you liked it here in the forest.

ANATOU

Of course I do, but . . . *(reluctant to speak of it)* but last night I had a strange dream. I can't remember it now. But it was something out there. There's something I have to see.

483

BEAVER

Outside the forest?

FOX

Don't go there, Anatou.

ANATOU

Why not?

FOX

Don't go or you'll be sorry.

ANATOU

I just want to look. It's a beautiful day. I want to run in the sunlight and explore.

FOX

If you leave, the Wood God will be furious.

ANATOU

The Wood God? Why? I'll be back tonight, I promise. What's there to be afraid of?

FOX

(Quietly) Danger.

BEAVER

Danger.

ANATOU

Maybe there's something dangerous for little animals like you, but I'm strong. I've got sharp teeth and claws. *(Boasting)* Nothing can hurt me.

FOX

You're a fool!

ANATOU

(Angry) Wait and see. I'll be back without a scratch on me. I'm not afraid like the rest of you.

BEAVER

Listen to her! We'll let her go if she wants to.

FOX

For the last time. We're warning you. Don't go. There'll be trouble if you do.

ANATOU

I must go. I don't know why, but I must. Don't try to stop me.

484

FOX

Remember, we warned you!

BEAVER

You wouldn't listen.

ANATOU

I can't help it. It's something inside. *(Lights fade, the animals exit. Forest scrim rises and* ANATOU *mimes her journey through the forest. She stops at the edge. The hilltops are brown, and there are black willow twigs with new buds)* Willow trees! And sunlight everywhere. Wood God, what a beautiful world outside your forest.

> *(Her journey continues in dance movement. The lights fade to indicate twilight. She stops, worn out)*

ANATOU

Loons on the water. It's so peaceful here. *(Enjoying it)* I'm all alone in the world. *(She prepares to settle down when lights begin to come up on a summer village tent and we hear the sharp sound of an Eskimo dog howling.* ANATOU *peers at the tent and moves in cautiously, closer and closer. The tent should be a movable unit that glides on. As* ANATOU *gets closer, we hear the sound of Eskimo singing or chanting.* ANATOU *realizes what it is and cries out)* Eskimos! Wood God! Wood God! Wood God! I'd forgotten. Oh, I should never have left the forest. *(As she watches,* KIVIOG *and* TARTO *cross stage to tent)* Tarto. And he still has the charm I gave him. He still has it.

KIVIOG

Tarto, we'll never have to worry with you as a hunter. All the pots of the village will boil this spring. Aja, since Anatou left, there's been plenty to eat.

TARTO

There'd be enough for her, too, if she were here.

KIVIOG

Forget about her, Tarto.

> *(They go inside)*

ANATOU

(Creeping closer) Look at them eating, laughing and singing. "Let her die in the snow." That's what they said. I'll show them. I'm

485

strong now. I'll get even. If it's the last thing I do, I'll get even. *(She moves nearer the tent and sees a piece of meat outside)* I'll take some back to the forest. *(But the dogs hear her and they start howling. The singing stops and a* VILLAGER *runs out with his bow and arrow.* ANATOU *sees him and runs, but not before he shoots an arrow at her.* ANATOU *falls and the man disappears into the tent.* ANATOU *is hurt but gets up, limping to the side of the tent)* That one! That one used to call me names. He hurt my mother and father. *(In pain)* I'm remembering. His arrow cut through my heart! *(*VILLAGER *comes out to check whether the animal is dead or not, and he carries another weapon. He looks about)* He'll kill me! Unless . . . *(*ANATOU *springs. There is a short struggle and the man falls without a sound)* Who is stronger now, Eskimo? Who's stronger now?

> *(*ANATOU *leaves)*
>
> *(Curtain)*

SCENE 3

In the forest. ANATOU *goes toward* FOX. FOX *retreats.* ANATOU *approaches* BEAVER. *He moves away in fear.*

WOOD GOD

You must leave man alone.

ANATOU

He did not leave me alone. Why should I?

WOOD GOD

Man has a bow, harpoons, knives, spears. You will see, Anatou. He will hunt you out. Stay away! Do not hurt another human.

ANATOU

But he wounded me.

FOX

You shouldn't have gone near his tent.

BEAVER

You don't deserve to stay in the forest with us.

486

ANATOU

But the wound hurt. *(Softly)* And then . . . I saw his face. I remembered. I remembered everything before then!

WOOD GOD

That wound will heal, Anatou. But will this new wound heal? Your hatred is more chilling than the ice caves near the sea. It will grow if you don't kill it now, Anatou. It will grow and freeze your heart.

FOX

You are a disgrace to the animals.

BEAVER

Animals kill because they must eat.

FOX

They must survive.

WOOD GOD

It's the law of the forest. But you, Anatou, killed out of hate. Men do that, not the animals!

ANATOU

(With awful realization) Wood God . . . when I saw him, and I saw the tent, and I remembered how they made me leave the village, and the arrow pierced me . . . I felt something . . . something I had forgotten. I had to get even!

WOOD GOD

(Sternly) Live in peace with man, Anatou, or leave the forest forever. *(He sweeps off with the animals)*

(Curtain)

SCENE 4

The interior of a snow house. Drums are beating. Three village hunters are assembled in a circle. In the distance there is the piercing cry of a wolf. They shudder.

KIVIOG

(Rises) We must try again. The wolf must be stopped.

ATATA

Never was a wolf spirit so hungry for men's souls.

VILLAGER 2

Hunter after hunter has gone and not returned. What can we do?

ATATA

Aja! But what good is a bow and arrow?

VILLAGER 2

What good are knives if we live in terror in our own houses?

KIVIOG

The great North is no longer safe. We mustn't let the wolf escape this time. Since spring, he has not let us alone. At night he always disappears into the forest . . . where no Eskimo ever goes.

VILLAGER 2

Even if it does go into the forest, we must find it and put an end to this.

ATATA

But if we go into the forest, we'll be trapped.

KIVIOG

We are trapped in our own homes now!

ALL

Aja! Aja!

ATATA

Never has there been a wolf like this. Its howl makes the fire die and the seal-oil lamp tremble.

VILLAGER 2

We must hunt till we find it.

ATATA

We have lost many good hunters.

VILLAGER 2

They have all failed.

KIVIOG

But we must find it.

TARTO

(Has been sitting there all the time unnoticed by the others) I have hunted before. Let me go, Father.

KIVIOG

Tarto! This is a council for our best hunters. Go outside. You should not be here. You're too young.

VILLAGER 2

He is so small that we don't notice him. It's all right, Kiviog.

ATATA

Perhaps he is so small that he could creep up on the wolf and he wouldn't notice him either.

(They all laugh)

TARTO

Please, Father. Please, I'm strong.

KIVIOG

No. We go too far. You will be tired.

TARTO

I won't. Wait and see.

KIVIOG

The men of Little Whale River are going to the forest, Tarto. It's dangerous.

TARTO

Then I will find the wolf's hiding place.

VILLAGER 2

He is swift, Kiviog. His eyes are sharp. He is as good a hunter as the men. If he wishes, let him come. *(*KIVIOG *thinks, then nods to* TARTO. TARTO *beams)*

KIVIOG

We must cover the great North and not stop till the snow is free of the wolf's tracks.

VILLAGERS

Aja! Aja!

VILLAGER 2

We must hunt towards the great plains.

KIVIOG

And hunt towards the forest.

ATATA

And by the caves along the sea.

KIVIOG

We've no time to waste. Harness the dogs!

(Drums increase. Men leave to get dog teams and begin the hunt. Interior fades)

489

Act Three

SCENE 1

The forest. There is snow on the ground and a rock unit has been added left center. There is a group of tangled trees that have been blown down in the winter near the right center. ANATOU *sleepily comes from behind the rock. She sniffs the air casually; then her body tenses.*

ANATOU

(Calling with increasing alarm) Wood God! Wood God! Wood God! I smell danger.

(BEAVER and FOX *appear)*

FOX

The hunters are here.

BEAVER

The hunters.

ANATOU

But the Eskimos are afraid of the forest. Why do they come here?

FOX

They hunt the wolf.

BEAVER

They hunt you.

FOX

Anatou.

WOOD GOD

(Entering) I warned you, Anatou. You have hurt too many of them. They are angry, angry enough to enter the forest and to hunt you out.

ANATOU

I'm frightened, Wood God. Please help me.

WOOD GOD

You hate and so you killed. You deliberately disobeyed me after I first sheltered you. I cannot protect you now.

490

ANATOU

Was I wrong to defend myself, Wood God, to wound when I was wounded?

WOOD GOD

You've been cruel, Anatou, and hate is like a disease spreading through your heart. If you strike an Eskimo, how does the Beaver know that you won't strike him, too, when he sleeps in the night?

ANATOU

No! I'd never do that. You know that, Wood God.

WOOD GOD

How do I know? I only see what you do. That speaks for itself.

ANATOU

(Ashamed) I won't leave the forest again, Wood God. I have been wrong.

WOOD GOD

(Angry) It's too late for that, Anatou. The hunters are here.

FOX

They're coming closer.

BEAVER

Closer.

ANATOU

(Panicked) Wood God, what should I do?

WOOD GOD

(Harshly) Replace the hunters you made them lose. Erase the terror you've caused them. Anatou, even the animals have been frightened of you.

ANATOU

But I didn't mean to hurt them. They've been good to me. I didn't want to hurt the animals.

WOOD GOD

(Watching her intently) If you cannot live in peace with man, Anatou, then one day you will have to face his bow and arrow. There is no law of the forest that can protect you from that time.

ANATOU

Wood God, why didn't you warn me? Why did you not stop me? I have worn a coat of thick hate—so thick it stopped my feeling or seeing anything else.

491

WOOD GOD

We tried, Anatou, but before you weren't ready to hear our words.

ANATOU

I am now, Wood God. Please, please, animals.

FOX

Hurry, Anatou. They are closer.

ANATOU

What should I do?

WOOD GOD

Run, Anatou. There is no time. If the hunters find you . . .

ANATOU

I know.

WOOD GOD

But remember this: if you are truly sorry, if you know what understanding means, if you can show me your heart is empty of all its dark hate and cruelty, no matter what happens, your spirit will not die. It will live forever and teach others. Remember that.

ANATOU

Thank you, Wood God.

WOOD GOD

Now run, Anatou.

ANIMALS

Run, Anatou, run.

> (ANATOU *exits across the stage. Village hunters enter. They are frightened. Suddenly a wind comes up*)

VILLAGER 2

Aja! The wind is alive.

ATATA

Let's leave. No Eskimo should be here.

KIVIOG

No! We have promised our village.

TARTO

We cannot return till the wolf is found.

KIVIOG

Look! His tracks are here.

VILLAGER 2

Follow them!

KIVIOG

Sh-h-h-h. Fresh tracks. Quickly, carefully.

(There is silence as they begin the serious search)

ANIMALS

(Whispering) Hurry, Anatou. Hurry.

(ANATOU streaks across the stage. They see her)

VILLAGER 1

Follow it! Follow it!

(They rush off left. TARTO, who is behind them, gets trapped in the fallen trees; his bow and arrow fly to the side. He tries to escape, but is caught fast)

TARTO

I can't get out! *(Trying to free himself)* I'm trapped! *(There is deathly silence around him)* Where did they go? I can't even hear them. *(Shouting)* Father! Father, come back. Hurry! *(Sees his bow and arrow, but he can't reach it. ANATOU runs on right. She stumbles on bow and arrow and in so doing kicks it to other side. TARTO is terrified. He whispers, horrified)* The wolf. What'll I do?

(He tries to struggle out, but he can't. ANATOU comes closer. TARTO is wearing the charm she gave him. She half turns away)

ANATOU

It's Tarto! I've got to help him.

(ANATOU moves in. TARTO thinks she is going to attack him. He becomes more and more terrified)

TARTO

No! No! Father! Help! Help! *(He covers his face instinctively, afraid to watch, but then forces himself to look. ANATOU pushes with all her might and finally the pressure is released and TARTO is out of the trap. He is amazed and does not understand what happened. As soon as TARTO is free, ANATOU starts to run, but it is too late. Just as she is passing the rock unit, we hear the whiz of an arrow and ANATOU falls behind the rock unit)* No! He set me free. Don't kill him. He set me free.

(KIVIOG, ATATA and VILLAGER 2 rush in)

KIVIOG

Tarto, what happened?

TARTO

I got trapped over there in the logs . . . and then the wolf . . . he set me free.

KIVIOG

What?

TARTO

The wolf, Father, the wolf. That's the truth. He pulled the log away so I could get out. I thought he was going to kill me.

KIVIOG

Where is your bow and arrow?

TARTO

There! I couldn't reach them. But, Father, he saved my life. He pushed the log away.

ATATA

Aja. The forest is alive with things we can't understand.

KIVIOG

Where is he now?

TARTO

The arrow hit him near the rock . . . but . . . *(They look. She is not there)* He's not there. Where did he go?

ATATA

It may be a trick.

VILLAGER 2

(Advancing cautiously) Here's a fresh footprint.

ATATA

Watch out.

(They move cautiously)

TARTO

(With a cry) It's . . . *(Turns to* KIVIOG*)* Anatou. It's Anatou, Father. We've hurt her.

(They all stare, amazed by the sight of the girl. TARTO *kneels down by the rock unit.* ANATOU's *spirit appears above. This can be done by seeing her through a scrim on a higher level so that she looks the same but paler, as though in a dream)*

ANATOU

Tarto . . . don't cry

TARTO

(To himself) Anatou. You were my best friend. *(To her)* I didn't mean to hurt you. Do you understand. We didn't mean . . . *(He can't say it. He tries to hold back the anguish inside)*

ANATOU

I do, Tarto, I do. Oh, Wood God, they can't hear me.

TARTO

She could have killed me, Father, but she didn't. She saved my life instead.

VILLAGER 2

Aja. She was brave.

KIVIOG

Braver than all the hunters of Little Whale River. None of us would have done what she did. *(He puts his hand on* TARTO*'s shoulder, but he can't say what he'd like to)*

VILLAGER 2

But why did she run into the forest?

TARTO

Don't you see? She had no place else to go. We chased her here. *(This is the most painful of all)* Anatou, even I chased you away.

KIVIOG

We would not speak or smile at the different one, remember. Our silence was worse than a hundred harpoons.

TARTO

Will she forgive me, Father?

KIVIOG

The spirits of the dead know our hearts, Tarto. You cannot keep a secret from them.

TARTO

But will she forgive me?

KIVIOG

We are all to blame.

TARTO

But I want to know! I have to know! She saved me, Father, and then the hunters shot an arrow when she finished.

KIVIOG

She had a bigger heart than you or I, Tarto, but if she is angry

we'll be trapped by the snow and the wind and lose our way. No
Eskimo should ever enter the realm of the forest. If she forgives
us, our way will be safe.

(They prepare to leave)

ANATOU

Wood God! Please let me help them.

WOOD GOD

(Pleased) Till the end of the forest, and then I will guide them.

ANATOU

Do they understand, Wood God? How will they remember?

WOOD GOD

Tarto will tell your story tonight, the first time, and they will tell
it for many nights. They will remember, for someone will always
tell the story of Anatou, the Fair One.

VILLAGER 2

(Goes over slowly and picks up the arrow, holds it thoughtfully)
I shot it! I killed her!

KIVIOG

No, we all killed her. But when? Today or long ago?

(Curtain)

I Lost a Pair of Gloves Yesterday

(A Monologue Play)

by
MYRNA LAMB

Myrna Lamb has written, "Sometimes we lose/The line between our own invention/And what is true/Because we have made things true/So often . . ." She began making things true in the theatre at the age of eight when she wrote her first play. At twelve, she wrote, produced and directed her third play, "about a rotten little girl named Violet" at her New Jersey junior high school. She was "engaged at sixteen, married at seventeen, pregnant at eighteen and a mother at nineteen." At twenty, Lamb began an acting career in New Jersey, which quickly led to New York and the Actors' Mobile Theatre. Most often, during her twenties, she held jobs as a bookkeeper, secretary or editor and was simultaneously a political activist (in the peace and civil rights movements), a student (in writing at the New School), an actress, a mother (to two daughters) and a wife.

During her thirties, she gave up acting and "decided to invest in myself." She joined NOW and was instrumental in developing its play-reading group into the New Feminist Repertory Theatre. The NFRT produced her one-acts *But What Have You Done for Me Lately, The Serving Girl and the Lady* and *In the Shadow of the Crematorium,* which were the first breakthroughs in feminist theatre. *Mod Donna,* her "space-age soap opera" (with music by Susan Hulsman Bingham), was produced at the Public Theatre in 1970. A collection of these plays, under the title *The Mod Donna and Scyklon Z,* was published a year later. Lamb and composer Nicholas Meyers began work on an opera, *Apple Pie,* in late 1970, and it was produced—"after a long struggle"—in 1975 and 1976, also at the Public Theatre. She wrote *I Lost a Pair of Gloves Yesterday* after her father died and has performed it several times herself.

Myrna Lamb has received fellowships from the Rockefeller and John Simon Guggenheim Foundations, and two National Endowment for the Arts grants, one for work on *Mother Ann,* the opera about the founder of the Shaker religion she and Meyers are currently completing. She lives in New York City.

CHARACTERS

AN ACTRESS

The actress walks on. Looks at audience. Shuffles through her papers. Finds her place. Begins to read.

ACTRESS

I lost a pair of goddamn leather furlined gloves yesterday. *(Pause)* And a pair of big round sunglasses. *(Loses her place. Finds it again)* A year ago I lost a pair of leather furlined gloves. Probably the same kind of place. A phone booth. Yesterday, the phone booth was in the Commodore Hotel, at the second level. Last year, the phone booth was in Boston. One of those big tall buildings. Prudential, I think. With banks of phone booths and banks of elevators that make you sick. *(Pause)*

I had to call Paris. A year ago in Boston. A very important call. It seemed very important. It was very cold outside. And it had taken me *years* to get around to buying a pair of gloves. Leather and furlined! When you consider that for *years* I had gone around! In gloves with holes! In the fingers. Some kind of wool. Mostly driving gloves. The kind with leather, some kind of leather . . . on the palms. And there was one pair in particular. Red. They didn't go with anything, but I wore them. When anyone looked at me, I pulled the hole up around my finger or fingers whichever it was. And the leather or whatever it was cracking around the palm. And the red didn't go with anything.

(Actress reshuffles papers. Begins again)

I don't know. I go in phases. Probably when I had these gloves with holes in the fingers . . . I had a whole bunch of new underwear. I had decided that I was beautiful for a while after I was thirty. I lost a lot of weight. About forty pounds. And I decided I was too beautiful now for all those old torn nightgowns and pajamas and things and I didn't need those all-in-ones any more and nobody was wearing shirtwaists so who needed waistcinchers. And padded bras made my breasts very sort of hot underneath and achy and my shoulders would get sore and even the skin would rub through and the underpants had some of them gone through two pregnancies six years apart and they were stretched out of shape and this millionaire meatpacker wanted to sleep with me. Had wanted to for years since I was sixteen. So I decided that I would buy all new underwear and nightgowns and I fixed up the drawers with them so the drawers looked like a work of art. Anybody could have opened them up and I would've been proud. But there's nobody left to look. My grandmother and my mother-in-law are dead and my mother isn't interested any more . . .

(Actress drops papers. Picks some of them up. Begins again)

But for some reason I didn't buy new gloves. I kept meaning to, but the idea was kind of foreign to me. I had all these sort of old gloves. Probably my mother had bought most of them. I don't really remember buying any of them. But maybe I did someplace cheap. Here and there when the weather would turn cold and I needed them. Maybe a five-and-dime or a supermarket. I'm an impulse buyer. Not a shopper. And also when I need things, I try to buy them if I'm somewhere where they're on sale. My coats were kind of old too. The ones I wore all the time. I never could throw anything away. If it looked like it ever could be used. I was very poor. As a child and teenager. And I never had my own clothes. I had to wear castoffs. My aunt's spectator shoes. Too old for me. *(Pause)* Once I added up what I was wearing and nothing I had on was mine. I mean bought for *me.* Except my underpants. Just white cotton. But they were mine. *(Pause)* But you didn't get elected Row Monitor for that. Row Monitor was supposed to be the child in the row that looked nice because it was clean. The child, I mean. But it really was the child who had nice clothes and looked pretty or handsome because of the clothes. Which I never did. Cotton underpants wouldn't have impressed them. They probably all had them. *(Long pause. Staring into audience)*

Of course, one time I took them off. We kids thought it was really exciting. We were just a little bunch of little kids. Girls actually. And we wanted to do something to . . . well . . . excite isn't the word for then. It's the word for *now.* But something daring. You know. And it was probably my idea. Although why I should want to take off the only thing that was mine, I don't know. We all took off our underpants. You understand we had dresses on. But they were probably pretty short. And we carried the underpants in our hands. Like handkerchiefs. I remember thinking if not saying.

(Actress looks through papers in a rather frantic manner)

We got into some kind of trouble. I was always doing that. I remember that there were kind of sympathetic people. Somebody's parents who lived in an apartment instead of a flat. And I got out of the trouble. Because it *was* probably my idea. But I took their mind off it by telling them how my father beat me which he did. But telling them about it made them feel very superior and gave them a reason to understand me and forgive me. I knew about those things instinctively when I was a little kid. I knew how to take the curse off when a grownup found out what a little bastard I was. Although I don't think I ever thought of myself as anything but daring and brave and smarter than they were if I wanted to be.

(Actress throws papers all over the stage. Some fall into the audience)

Oh, I'm tired of the way I remember things. What's the use of it all anyway. What should I do? Put it to music and sing it? I lost my gloves, goddamn it. Last year first and now this year. That isn't all I lost. I lost . . . I lost my father. He died. A couple of weeks ago. And we buried him in his new tuxedo. He didn't have any studs or maroon carnation or cummerbund. And I don't know where they are. My mother won't tell me. Maybe she doesn't know or maybe she threw them out. And she won't give me his sterling silver flute either. She probably wants to sell it. Oh God. I didn't know I loved him this much. Although I knew I wanted . . . No. I didn't want to sleep with him. But I did have this kind of feeling about him. Very romantic. And more. Long after I should have. It was Palmolive Aftershave. That's what he used to wear. And much later a guy I used to work for wore it too. At the time, I didn't know *why* I was so crazy for *him*. I figured it out later. Palmolive Aftershave. It was the way he smelled. I used to love the way he smelled, this guy. I didn't really think about my father that way. Not really. Not deliberately. At least, I tried not to . . .

(Actress picks up papers throughout next speech, retrieving even those that have fallen into audience)

It's hard to believe all that now. I said they should make him look nice. They did. But they didn't make him look like him which is just as well. And there was this peculiar sickly sweet smell on my hands after I touched him. Everybody around me smelled of it. Even afterwards. In the limousine.

For a couple of weeks after that I thought I would never feel sexual again. I thought it was all gone. No life force, I thought. And anyway I wanted to believe he was alive somewhere. Somewhere having a good time. The kind of good time he never allowed himself when he was alive. Free. Spending money. Well, he did try to do that toward the end. But then my mother wouldn't let him. Because I guess she saw it as her money then. As soon as he was dead, it would be her money. And if she let him spend it, not in the way that she wanted to spend it . . . well . . . it wouldn't be there for *her*. She doesn't want to admit that that's what she felt, but then he wanted this color television set. He kept talking about it. She didn't want him to get it. Or at least such an expensive one.

(Pause. Actress says last line to herself. Walks off clutching papers to her breast)

Anyway, I did lose. This pair of gloves. Yesterday. Yesterday.

Out of Our Fathers' House

Based on Eve Merriam's Growing Up Female in America: Ten Lives

Arranged for the stage by EVE MERRIAM, PAULA WAGNER and JACK HOFSISS

Music by Ruth Crawford Seeger

Adapted by Daniel Schrier

With additional music by
Daniel Schrier and Marjorie Lipari

The text of *Out of Our Fathers' House* is taken entirely from the diaries, journals and letters of the characters portrayed.

Out of Our Fathers' House, by Eve Merriam, Paula Wagner and Jack Hofsiss, was first produced in July 1975 at the Lenox Arts Center in western Massachusetts, directed by Hofsiss.

"I feel, acting certain roles, that I have to deny parts of myself," Paula Wagner says, "like my intelligence. *Out of Our Fathers' House* allowed me to use all of myself as an actress—my mind, my talent, my feelings . . ."

"I suggested Paula do a one-woman show based on the anthology of women's journals and letters I'd done, *Growing Up Female in America,*" Eve Merriam says. "Later we went through the book together," Wagner says, "choosing the women and the events we thought were the most theatrical. When I went to Jack with the book, he suggested we do it as a full piece, with three actresses."

"What struck me at once," Jack Hofsiss says, "was how eminently theatrical these extraordinary women's lives were."

All three collaborators speak enthusiastically of how rewarding work on the piece was. "It's amazing," Wagner says, "the difference it makes when people really believe in what they're doing." Wagner tells a story of going to an exhibit about Maria Mitchell at the New York Planetarium. "I stayed there for hours looking at pictures of her, how she sat, and practiced looking through a telescope just like she did."

Eve Merriam wrote book and lyrics for the Broadway musical *Inner City* (music by Helen Miller); her latest musical theatre piece, *The Club*, was produced in late 1976, off-Broadway at The Circle in the Square, directed by Tommy Tune. Paula Wagner has acted leading roles at the New York Shakespeare Festival and the Yale Repertory Company and appeared on Broadway in *Lenny*. Jack Hofsiss was educated at Georgetown University, began working in the theatre in Washington, D.C. (The Arena Stage, The Folger Library Theatre), and has directed major productions for the New York Shakespeare Festival.

507

CHARACTERS

ELIZA SOUTHGATE (1783–1809) Schoolgirl

ELIZABETH CADY STANTON (1815–1902) Founder of the
Women's Suffrage Movement

MARIA MITCHELL (1818–1889) Astronomer

"MOTHER" MARY JONES (1830–1930) Labor organizer

DR. ANNA HOWARD SHAW (1847–1919) Minister and doctor

ELIZABETH GERTRUDE STERN (1890–1954) In the Jewish ghetto

Three actresses play all six women and the minor characters.
Musicians perform the songs (number of singers and instruments
used are at the discretion of the director). ACTRESS #1 plays ELIZA
SOUTHGATE and GERTRUDE STERN; ACTRESS #2 plays MARIA
MITCHELL and ANNA HOWARD SHAW; ACTRESS #3 plays ELIZABETH
CADY STANTON and MOTHER MARY JONES. *Out of Our Fathers'
House* may also be performed by six actresses.

AUTHORS' NOTE
Out of Our Fathers' House, while taken from the actual writings
of the characters portrayed, takes the theatrical form of a hypothetical conversation among the different woman characters. This
is historically impossible, since these women could never have had
such a conversation, but it is valid for the purposes of the piece.
This is a timeless interaction in which these women act out for
both themselves and each other the stories of their lives—in particular the accounts of their emergence "out of their fathers'
house." It is essential that the piece be personal and conversa-
tional. The characters are not retelling but rather reliving their
experiences. Both together and alone they make the journey into
a world of self-sufficiency and the "solitude of self."

The stage is an abandoned summerhouse; there is a carousel horse, battered and broken, upstage right; a wicker table upstage center, or possibly an old coatrack, and another coatrack upstage left. Down center are three chairs placed in a semicircle in which musicians sit playing as the audience enters. The mood should be warm and comfortable. This is the secret place where one would run off to think and be alone.

As the lights dim, the musicians begin to sing.

Song: "Built My Lady a Fine Brick House"
I built my lady a fine brick house,
I built it in a garden.
I put her in, but she jumped out,
Oh, fare thee well, my darling.

I built my lady a high stone wall,
I built it in a garden.
I put her in, but she jumped out,
Oh, fare thee well, my darling.

I built my lady a gate with a lock,
I built it in a garden.
I put her in, but she jumped out,
So fare thee well, my darling.

> (ACTRESS #1 *has entered during the last part of the song and states the first of the rules of etiquette for young ladies of the late eighteenth century in America. Others follow and take lines in sequence. The actresses carry with them lanterns and large wicker baskets which contain any props and costumes they might need for the show. It has the effect of running away from home. Rules of etiquette:)*

ACTRESS #1

Bite not thy bread, but break it.

ACTRESS #2

Look not earnestly at any other that is eating.

ACTRESS #3

Never sit down at the table until asked, and after the blessing.

ACTRESS #1

When moderately satisfied, leave the table.

ACTRESS #2

Sing not, hum not, wriggle not.

ACTRESS #3

When any speak to thee, stand up.

ACTRESS #2

Say not "I have heard it before."

ACTRESS #1

Never endeavor to help him out if he tell it not right.

ACTRESS #3

Snigger not. Never question the truth of it.

ACTRESS #2

Do not remove the gloves.

ACTRESS #3

Do not make a call of ceremony on a wet day . . . Always have an umbrella beside you and overshoes.

ACTRESS #1

Getting wet seldom fails to produce a cold.

ACTRESS #2

To lose your dinner is not half so dangerous.

ACTRESS #3

Wet feet and wet clothes have sent thousands to eternity before their time.

ACTRESS #1

Avoid unnecessary exposure to the evening air.

ACTRESS #2

Do not touch the piano unless asked.

ACTRESS #3

Do not call upon a gentleman unless he is a confirmed invalid.
(The musicians are offstage by now)

Song: "Little Bird" (Theme for Gertrude Stern)
I'm as free a little bird as I can be
I'm as free a little bird as I can be

I will build my nest in the sour apple tree
Where those bad boys will never bother me.

VOICE

Elizabeth Gertrude Stern, born in 1890 in a Jewish ghetto of a
large Midwestern city, growing up to obey her father's commandments.

Oh, who will shoe your little foot?
And who will glove your little hand?

(Pause)

GERTRUDE

(Sings)
Oh, it's papa will shoe my little foot
And it's mama will glove my little hand
(Spoken)
. . . I remember looking down at the face of my father, beautiful
and still in death, and for a brief moment, feeling my heart rise
up . . . Surely it was in a strange suffocating relief . . . Now I am
free!

(Sings)
And it's you who'll kiss my red-rosy cheek
When you come from that far-distant land.

Song: "Molly Hare" (Theme for Mother Jones)
Old Molly Hare, what are you doing there?
Running through a cotton patch as fast as I can tear.
Riding of a goat, leading of a sheep,
I won't be back till the middle of the week.

VOICE

Mary Harris Jones, born in 1830, lived to be one hundred years
old and became known to children and adults alike as "Mother
Jones."

MARY

I asked a man in prison once how he happened to be there, and
he said that he had stolen a pair of shoes. I told him if he had
stolen a railroad he would be a United States Senator.

Song: "My Horses Ain't Hungry" (Theme for Anna Shaw)
My horses ain't hungry, they won't eat your hay,
So I'll get on my pony, I'm going away.

With all our belongings we'll ride till we come
To a lonely little cabin, we'll call it our home.

VOICE

Anna Howard Shaw, at age twelve, moved from a manufacturing town in Massachusetts to the wild woods of Michigan in 1859.

ANNA

Once when I was fourteen, I had been in the woods all day, buried in my books, and when I returned home at night, still in the dream world these books had opened to me, Father was awaiting my coming, dark with disapproval . . . *I was an idler who wasted time.* He ended a long arraignment by predicting that with such tendencies I would make nothing of my life.

Song: "What'll We Do with the Baby?"
(Theme for Elizabeth)

What'll we do with the baby?
What'll we do with the baby?
What'll we do with the baby-o?
We'll wrap it up in calico!
Wrap it up in calico and send it to its pappy-o.

VOICE

Elizabeth Cady Stanton, born in New York State in 1815 . . . The same year her father was elected to Congress.

ELIZABETH

The custom of calling women Mrs. John This and Mrs. Tom That, and colored men Sambo and Zip-coon, is founded on the principle that white men are the lords of all. I cannot acknowledge this principle, and therefore I cannot bear the name of another. If the nineteenth century is to be governed by the opinions of the eighteenth, and the twentieth by the nineteenth, then the world will always be governed by dead men. I would rather make a few slanders from a superabundance of life than to have all the proprieties of a well-embalmed mummy.

Song: "Rose, Rose and Up She Rises"
(Theme for Maria Mitchell)

Rose, rose and up she rises,
Rose, rose and up she rises,

512

Rose, rose and up she rises
So early in the morning.
I wonder where Maria's gone?
I wonder where Maria's gone?
I wonder where Maria's gone
So early in the morning?

VOICE

Maria Mitchell, born on Nantucket Island in 1818. Her father was
devoted to astronomy, and all the children were drafted into the
service of counting seconds by the chronometer during his obser-
vations.

MARIA

Once a lady asked me if I told fortunes, and when I replied in the
negative, she asked me if I weren't an astronomer. I admitted that
I made efforts in that direction. She then asked me what could I
tell if not fortunes. I told her that I could tell when the moon
would rise, and when the sun would set. She said, "Oh," in a tone
which plainly implied "Is that all?"

Song: "Young Maid" (Theme for Eliza Southgate)
When I was a young maid, young maid,
When I was a young maid, then oh then
It was ha, ha, this-a-way, ha, ha, that-a-way
This-a-way, that-a-way, then.

VOICE

Eliza Southgate, born in 1783 in Scarborough, Maine . . . sent by
her parents to finishing school near Boston when she was fourteen.

ELIZA

You may justly say, my best of fathers, that every letter of mine
is one which is asking for something more; never contented
. . . I only ask. If you refuse me, I know you do what you think
best, and I am sure I ought not to complain, for you have never
yet refused me anything that I have asked, my best of parents, how
shall I repay you?

Song: "Listen to the Voices"
Listen to the voices
Out of darkness into daybreak
Making their lives.

(At this point, the actresses sit in the chairs that are placed center, and begin to knit, and write and comb their hair. A musician sings. The song is "Monday Morning")

MUSICIAN

How old are you, my fair young maid?
I'm going to be sixteen next Monday morning.

ELIZA

Such a frolic! Such a chain of adventures I never before met with. For two days it had been storming so much that the snow drifts were very large; however, as it was the last assembly, I could not resist the temptation of going, as I knew all the world would be there. About seven I went downstairs and immediately slipt on my socks and coat, and met Mr. Motley in the entry. The snow was deep, but Mr. Motley took me up in his arms, and sat me in the carriage without difficulty. I found a full assembly, many married ladies, and every one disposed to end the winter in good spirits. At one we left dancing. It stormed dreadfully, we could not get a coach until three o'clock. There were now twenty in waiting, the gentlemen scolding and fretting, the ladies murmuring and complaining as they all flocked to engage a seat. Luckily I was one of the first. Mr. Motley took me up in his arms and carried me till my weight pressed him so far into the snow that he had no power to move his feet. I rolled out of his arms and wallowed till I reached the gate; then rising to shake off the snow, I turned and beheld my beau fixed and immovable; he could not get his feet out to take another step! At length, making a great exertion to spring his whole length forward, he made out to reach the poor horse, who lay in a worse condition than his master. By this time all the family had gathered to the window. Indeed they saw the whole frolic. I was perfectly convulsed with laughter.

MARIA

I was up before six, made the fire in the kitchen and made coffee. Then I set the table in the dining room, and made the fire there. Toasted the bread and trimmed the lamps. Rang the breakfast bell at seven. After breakfast, made my bed, and "put up" the room. Then I came down to the library and looked over my comet computations till noon. I am just beginning to notice the different colors of the stars. I wonder that I have been so long insensible to this charm in the skies. The tints of different stars are so delicate in their variety . . . Before dinner I did some tatting, and made seven button-holes for K. I dressed and then dined.

ELIZABETH

The first event engraved on my memory was the birth of a sister when I was four years old. I heard so many friends remark, "What a pity it is she is a girl!" that I felt a kind of compassion for the little baby. True, our family consisted of five girls and only one boy, but I did not understand at the time that girls were considered an inferior order of beings.

ELIZA

Mother dear: You mentioned in yours of the sixteenth that it was a long time since you had received a letter from me; but it was owing to my studies. Now, Mama, what do you think I am going to ask you for? A wig. Eleanor Coffin has got a new one just like my hair, and it's only five dollars. I must either cut my hair or have one—I cannot dress it at all stylish. How much time it will save. In one year's time we could save it in pins and paper, besides the trouble. At the assembly I was quite ashamed of my head, for nobody has long hair. If you will consent to my having one, do send me a five-dollar bill by the post immediately after you receive this, for I am in hopes to have it for the next assembly.

MARIA

Came back again to the library at one-thirty . . . and looked over nother set of computations, which took me until four o'clock. I was pretty tired by that time, and rested by reading "Cosmos." Lizzie E. came in, and I gossiped for half an hour. I went home to tea, and that over, I made a loaf of bread. Then I went up to my room and read through—partly writing—two exercises in German, which took me thirty-five minutes. It was stormy, and I had no observing to do, so I sat down to my tatting. Lizzie E. came in and I took a new lesson in tatting, so as to make the pearl-edge. I made about half a yard during the evening. What a pity that we cannot take dye stuff from the stars, so as to create a new brilliancy in fashion . . . At a little after nine I went home with Lizzie, and

515

carried to the post office. I had kept steadily at work for sixteen hours when I went to bed.

(At this point, the actresses begin to act out what they are saying. They can move around the stage, showing us and themselves just what they have gone through. They also play parts in each other's stories, gently aiding each other in their growth)

ELIZABETH

A student in my father's office told me one day, after conning my features carefully, that I had one defect that he could remedy. "Your eyebrows should be darker and heavier," he said, "and if you will let me shave them once or twice, you will be much improved." I consented, and slight as my eyebrows were, they seemed to have a handsome expression, for the loss of them had a most singular effect on my appearance. Everybody, including the shaver, laughed at my odd-looking face, and I was in the depths of humiliation while my eyebrows were growing out again. Needless to say, I never permitted the young man to repeat the experiment, although strongly urged to do so.

MARIA

I swept the sky two hours last night. Not a fringe of a cloud, all clear, all beautiful. I really enjoy that kind of work, but my back soon becomes tired, long before the cold chills me. I saw two nebulae in Leo with which I was not familiar, and that repaid me for the time . . . There will come with the greater love of science greater love to one another. We cannot see how impartially Nature gives of her riches to all without loving all, and helping all.

ELIZABETH

When I was eleven years old, my only brother, who had just graduated from Union College, came home to die. A young man of great talent and promise, he was the pride of my father's heart. I recall going into the large darkened parlor and finding the casket, mirrors and pictures all draped in white, and my father seated, pale and immovable as he took no notice of me. After standing a long while, I climbed upon his knee, when he mechanically put his arm about me, and with my head resting against his beating heart, we both sat in silence, he thinking of the wreck of all his hopes in the loss of a dear son—and I wondering what could be said or done to fill the void in his breast. At length he heaved a deep sigh and said, "Oh, my daughter, I wish you were a boy!" Throwing my arms about his neck, I replied, "I will try to be all my brother was." All that day, and far into the night I pondered the problems of boyhood. I thought that the chief thing to be done in order to equal boys was to be learned and courageous. So I decided to study Greek and learn to manage a horse. I learned to leap a fence on horseback. I began to study Latin, Greek and mathematics with a class of boys in the Academy, many of whom were much older than I. For three years one boy kept his place at the head of the class, and I always stood next. Two prizes were offered in Greek. I strove for one and took the second. One thought alone filled my mind. "Now," said I, "my father will be satisfied with me." I rushed into his office, laid the new Greek testament, which was my prize, on his table, and exclaimed: "I got it!" He took up the book, asked me some questions about the class, and evidently pleased, handed it back to me. Then he kissed me on the forehead and exclaimed with a sigh, "You should have been a boy!"

ELIZA

I thank heaven I was born a woman. I have now only patiently to wait till some clever fellow shall take a fancy to me and place me in a situation, I am determined to make the best of it, let it be what it will. We ladies, you know, possess that "sweet pliability of temper." But remember, I desire to be thankful I am not a man—I should not be content with mediocrity in any thing, but as a woman I am equal to the generality of my sex, and I do not feel that great desire of fame I think I should if I was a man. Were I a man, the law would be my choice. When I might hope to arrive at an eminence which would be gratifying to my feelings, I should then hope to be a public character, respected and admired. To be an eloquent speaker would be the delight of my heart.

ELIZABETH

As my father's office joined the house, I spent much of my time there, when out of school, talking with the students, and reading the laws in regard to women. One Christmas morning I went into the office to show them, among others of my presents, a new coral necklace and bracelets. They all admired the jewelry and then began to tease me with hypothetical cases of future ownership. "Now," said one, "if in due time you should be my wife, those ornaments would be mine. I could take them and lock them up, and you could never wear them except with my permission. I could even exchange them for a box of cigars, and you could watch them evaporate in smoke." When my attention was called to these odious laws, I would mark them in my father's books with a pencil, and I resolved to seize the first opportunity, when alone in the office, to cut every one of them out of the books; supposing my father and his library were the beginning and end of the law . . . However, this mutilation of his volumes was never accomplished. He explained to me one evening how laws were made, and that if his library should burn up it would make no difference in woman's condition. "When you are grown up, and able to prepare a speech," said he, "you must go down to Albany and talk to the legislators; tell them all you have seen in this office: the sufferings of women, robbed of their inheritance and left dependent on their unworthy sons, and if you can persuade them to pass new laws, the old ones will be a dead letter." Thus was the future object of my life foreshadowed and my duty plainly outlined by him who was most opposed to my public career when, in due time, I entered upon it.

MARIA

It seems to me that the needle is the chain of woman and has fettered her more than the laws of the country.

ELIZABETH

Sewing as an amusement is contemptible. It should be the study of every woman to do as little of it as possible.

MARIA

Once you emancipate her from the stitch-stitch-stitch, she would have time for studies which engross as never the needle can. I have a hunger of the mind which longs for knowledge of all around. Astronomy seems to me particularly fitted to women. A girl's eye is trained from early childhood to be keen, trained to the nicety of color. The eye that directs a needle in the delicate meshes of embroidery will equally bisect a star with the spider web of the micrometer.

ELIZABETH

When a woman pulls a cotton washrag from her pocket and begins to knit with a bowed head, fixing her eyes and concentrating her thoughts on a rag one foot square, it is impossible for conversation to rise above the washrag level. Think of the optic nerves being concentrated on a cotton rag. One can buy a whole dozen of these useful appliances with red borders and fringed for twenty-five cents. I beseech you, knit no more!

VOICE

Anna Howard Shaw, at age twelve, moved from a manufacturing town in Massachusetts to the wild woods of Michigan in 1859.

ANNA

Like most men, my dear father should have never married. In practical matters he remained a child. To him, an acorn was not an acorn, but a forest of young oaks; thus when he took up his claim of three hundred and sixty acres of land in the wilderness of northern Michigan, and sent my mother and five young children to live there alone until he could join us, he gave no thought to the matter in which we were to make the struggle and survive the hardships before us. From his viewpoint, he was doing a man's duty. He had furnished us with land and the four walls of a log cabin. Some day, he reasoned, the place would be a fine estate which his sons would inherit, and in the course of time pass on to their sons. But to the present, we were one hundred miles from a railroad, forty miles from the nearest post office, and half a dozen miles from any neighbors, save Indians, wolves and wildcats; we were wholly unlearned in the ways of the woods, yet we faced our situation with clear and unalarmed eyes the morning after our arrival. We held a family council after breakfast and in this, though I was only twelve, I took an eager and determined part. I loved work—it has always been my favorite form of recreation —and my spirit rose to the opportunities of it which smiled on us from every side. You see, I knew I was doing my share for the family, and already too, I had begun to feel the call of my career. For some reason I wanted to preach . . . to talk to people, to tell them things. Just why, just what, I did not yet know, but I had begun to preach in the silent woods—to stand upon tree stumps and address the unresponsive trees—to feel the stir of aspiration within me. Some day I am going to college. And before I die I shall be worth ten thousand dollars.

GERTRUDE

The first clear impression of my childhood is a summer day.

VOICE

Elizabeth Gertrude Stern, born in 1890 in a Jewish ghetto of a large Midwestern city, growing up to obey her father's commandments.

GERTRUDE

My mother, in her puffed sleeves and tight-fitting dress, walked near my father, in his long coat and high hat: for he was assistant to the rabbi in our city. We children trudged behind. We came at last to the river's edge. Our father stood, waited a moment, and then prayed that his sins should be washed away by the river. I looked into the muddy waters below us, and at my father. All my life I had believed that, even when I resisted him, he was right. But today it seemed to me childish and perhaps even silly to be standing there, chanting that beautiful old tongue, the Hebrew, that I too had been taught, and asking that our sins be washed away. Most of the people who lived near us were Catholics. They believed that if you told the priest what you had done, you would not be punished for your misdeeds. When I told my father one day of the Catholics, he looked down at me from his tall height, and said, "You can see how foolish and childish ignorant people are. A priest tells them that if they go to him, and confess, he can forgive them. Can a sin be undone by a confession?" And yet here was my father, grave and pleading, sending our own sins down the waters of the Ohio. I looked at him, opened my mouth, but did not speak. I knew he would be angry. From that day, however, I did not accept anything he told me about our faith until I analyzed it myself.

MARIA

How can we dispute authority which has come down to us all established for ages? We cannot accept anything as granted beyond the first mathematical formula. Question everything else.

MARY

My husband was an iron moulder and a staunch member of the Iron Moulders' Union. We were living in Memphis when a yellow fever epidemic swept the city. Its victims were mainly among the poor and the workers. The rich and the well-to-do fled the city. Schools and churches were closed. People were not permitted to enter the house of a yellow fever victim without permits. The poor could not afford nurses. Across the street from me, ten persons lay dead from the plague. The dead surrounded us. They were buried at night, quickly and without ceremony. All about my house I could hear weeping and the cries of delirium. One by one, my four little children sickened and died. I washed their little bodies and got them ready for burial.

My husband caught the fever and died. I sat alone through nights of grief. No one came to me. No one could. Other homes were as stricken as mine. All day long, all night long, I heard the grating of the wheels of the death cart.

After the union had buried my husband I got a permit to nurse the sufferers. This I did until the plague was stamped out. I returned to Chicago and went again into the dress-making business. I became more and more engrossed with the labor struggle and I decided to take an active part in the efforts of the working people to better the conditions under which they worked and lived. I became a member of the Knights of Labor. From that time on, I became wholly engrossed in the labor movement.

GERTRUDE

My father did not approve of my continuing high school. It was time for me to think of marrying a pious man. He and Mother disagreed about it—their one quarrel. It was perhaps due to my going to high school, Mother said, gently and dubiously, that I wanted something new. I wanted to dance, to play, to have fun. I didn't mean to go to work at fourteen or fifteen, marry at sixteen, be a mother at eighteen, and an old woman at thirty. My mother drew her fine dark brows together. She took my face in her little hands, round and soft, in spite of her constant work. "You shall

learn to dance, my daughter." And dance I did. I learned to dance
in what, I suppose, was a dreadful public dance hall, for I paid a
quarter a lesson there once every Wednesday night, and I danced
with the lady instructor whenever she thought of me. But I faith-
fully put my foot out . . . one-two-three and turn . . . as the long
line of men and women learned the steps of the waltz. I learned
to two-step, and to Schottische, and even—wild days those—to do
the barn dance. I wanted a new thing: happiness.

ELIZABETH

"What to do with a baby!" Though motherhood is the most
important of all the professions, requiring more knowledge than
any other department in human affairs, there was no attention
given to preparation for this office. When my baby was four days
old, we discovered that his collarbone was bent. The physician,
wishing to get a pressure on the shoulder, braced the bandage
round the wrist.

FIRST DOCTOR

Leave that ten days, and then it will be all right.

ELIZABETH

Soon after he left, I noticed that the baby's hand was blue, showing that the circulation had been impeded. This will never do.
Nurse, take it off.

NURSE

No, indeed. I shall never interfere with the doctor.

ELIZABETH

So I took it on myself to send for another doctor. He expressed
great surprise that the first should have put on so severe a bandage.

SECOND DOCTOR

That would do for a grown man, but ten days of it on a child would
make him a cripple.

ELIZABETH

However, he did nearly the same thing, only fastening it round the
hand, instead of the wrist. I soon saw that the ends of the fingers
were all purple. So I took it off. What we want is a little pressure
on that bone; that is what both those men have aimed at. How
can we get it without involving the arm is the question.

NURSE

I'm sure I don't know.

ELIZABETH

Well, bring me three strips of linen rolled double. I then folded one, wet in arnica and water, and laid it on the collarbone. I put two other bands, like a pair of suspenders, over the shoulders, crossing them both in front and behind, pinning the ends to the diaper, which gave the needed pressure without impeding the circulation anywhere. Several times night and day, we wet the compress and readjusted the bands, until the inflammation had subsided. At the end of ten days, the doctors appeared and made their examination. All was right. Whereupon I told them how badly their bandages worked, and what I had done myself. They smiled at each other and said:

FIRST DOCTOR

Well . . .

SECOND DOCTOR

Well . . .

FIRST DOCTOR

Well . . .

SECOND DOCTOR

Well . . .

FIRST DOCTOR

After all, a mother's instinct . . .

SECOND DOCTOR

. . . is better than a man's reason.

ELIZABETH

Thank you, gentlemen, there was no instinct about it. I did some hard thinking before I saw how I could get pressure on the shoulder without impeding the circulation, as you did . . . I trusted neither men nor books completely after this, either in regard to the heavens above or the earth below, but continued to use my "mother's instinct," if "reason" is too dignified a term to apply to a woman's thoughts.

MARIA

People have to learn sometimes not only how much the heart, but how much the head can bear.

ANNA

As an aid to public speaking I was taught to "elocute," and I remember in every mournful detail the occasion on which I gave my first recitation. We were having our monthly "public exhibition night," and the audience included not only my classmates, but their parents and friends as well. The selection I intended to recite was a poem entitled "No Sects in Heaven." But, when I faced my audience, I was so appalled by its size and by the sudden realization of my own temerity, that I fainted during the delivery of the first verse. Sympathetic classmates carried me into an anteroom and revived me, after which they naturally assumed that the entertainment I furnished was over for the evening. I, however, felt that if I let that failure stand against me I could never afterward speak in public; and within ten minutes, notwithstanding the protests of my friends, I was back in the hall and beginning my recitation a second time. The audience gave me its eager attention. Possibly it hoped to see me topple off the platform again, but nothing of the sort occurred. I went through the recitation with self-possession and even received some friendly applause at the end.

MARY

I organized an army of women housekeepers. On a given day they were to bring their mops and brooms and "the Army" would charge the scabs up at the mines. The general manager, the sheriff, and the corporation hirelings heard of our plans and were on hand. The day came and the women came with the mops and brooms and pails of water. I decided not to go up to the drip mouth myself, for I knew they would arrest me and that might rout the Army. I selected as leader an Irish woman who had a most picturesque appearance. She had slept late and her husband had told her to hurry up and get into the Army. She had grabbed a red petticoat and slipped it over a thick cotton nightgown. She wore a black stocking and a white one. She had tied a little red fringed shawl over her wild red hair. Her face was red and her eyes were mad. I looked at her and felt that she could raise a rumpus. I said, "You lead the Army up to the drip mouth, take that tin dishpan you have with you and your hammer, and when the scabs and the mules come up, begin to hammer and howl. Then all of you hammer and howl and be ready to chase the scabs with your mops and brooms. Don't be afraid of anyone!" Up the mountainside, yelling and hollering, she led the women, and when the mules came up with the scabs and the coal, she began beating on the dishpan and hollering, and all the Army joined in with her. The sheriff tapped her on the shoulder. "My dear lady," said he, "remember the mules. Don't frighten them." She took the old tin pan and she hit him with it and she hollered, "To hell with you and the mules!" He fell over and dropped into the creek. Then the mules began to rebel against scabbing. They bucked and kicked the scab drivers and started off for the barn. The scabs started running down the hill, followed by the army of women with their mops and pails and brooms. A poll parrot in a nearby shack screamed at the superintendent, "Ya got hell, did you? Ya got hell?" There was a great big doctor in the crowd, a company lap dog. He had a little satchel in his hand, and he said to me, "Mrs. Jones, I have a warrant for your arrest." "All right," said I, "keep it in your pill bag until I call for it. I am going to hold a meeting now." From that day on the women kept continual watch of the mines to see that the company did not bring in scabs. Every day women with brooms or mops in one hand and babies in the other arm, wrapped in little blankets, went to the mines and watched that no one went in. And all night long they kept watch.

There had been no bloodshed. There had been no riots. And the victory was due to the army of women with their mops and their brooms.

GERTRUDE

I had known for months that I loved Dr. Morton. That was why I could speak to him of those things I felt most deeply, and why I felt the peace of my work. We were young, and we were well. We were mysterious and beautiful to one another. I had, all my life, thought of the womanhood in me as something to be deprecated. I knew that a man of my faith must absent himself from his wife, as from defilement at certain holy times of his life. And always she must humbly beg God to pardon her that she is a woman. Had I not read in the prayer book the words my brothers and my father spoke daily . . . thanking God they were not women?

But my husband was modern. He said I must do anything I wanted to do, just as he did what he chose. Only, he must earn our living. Whatever I did I could do without thinking whether it was successful or not, only whether it made me happy. I took his hands in mine. I kissed him. But as I did, I know I wished he had said that my work was as practical a need to me as his. He thought I might do social work as a volunteer, without pay. I was, however, determined not to be an amateur. I wanted to work just as he did. I would not be happy otherwise. "So you want a career," he smiled, "and a husband tacked on?" "Haven't you one with me tacked on?" He kissed me then and laughed very tenderly indeed. "I like to work," I then said quietly, "I enjoy being important." He laughed then, relieved. He was delighted that I spoke like a child about my work. He kissed me and held me close.

MARIA

I put some wires into my telescope this morning. I dreaded it so much when I found yesterday that it must be done, that it disturbed my sleep. It was much easier than I expected. I took out the little collimating screws first, then I drew out the tube, and in that I found a brass plate which contained the lines . . . I was at first a little puzzled to know which screws held this in its place, and as I was very anxious not to unscrew the wrong ones, I took time to consider and found I need turn only two. Then out slipped the little plate with its three wires where five should have been, two having been broken. I took the hairs from my own head, taking care to pick out white ones because I have no dark ones to spare. I put in the two, by sticking them with sealing wax dissolved in alcohol into the little grooved lines which I had found. When I had, with great labor, adjusted these, as I thought, firmly, I perceived that some of the wax was still on the hairs and would make them yet coarser, and they were already too coarse: so I washed them with clear alcohol. Almost at once I washed out another wire and soon another. I went to work patiently and put in the five perpendicular ones besides the horizontal one, which like the others, had frizzled up and appeared to melt away. With another hour's labor I got in the five, when a rude motion raised them all again and I began over.

ELIZABETH

When I married Mr. Stanton, he announced to me that his business would occupy all his time, and that I must take charge of the housekeeping.

It is a proud moment in a woman's life to reign supreme within four walls. I studied up everything pertaining to housekeeping. Even washing day had its charms for me. The clean clothes on the lines and on the grass looked so white and smelled so sweet. I inspired my laundress with an ambition to get the clothes out earlier than our neighbors, and to have them ironed and put away sooner. I also felt the same ambition to excel in all departments of the culinary arts that I did at school in the different branches of learning. My love of order and cleanliness was carried throughout, from parlor to kitchen, from front door to back. I even gave the man an extra shilling to pile the logs of firewood with their smooth ends outward.

MARIA

There is an article on the study of medicine by women that states it would be better for the husband always to be superior to the wife. Why? And if so, doesn't this condemn the ablest of women to a single life? It is sad to see a woman sacrificing the ties of affection, even to do good.

GERTRUDE

During the influenza epidemic of 1917 my husband came down with the sickness. We already had two children. I knew that I must get work. Not, now, work to fill the time, or to express myself, but to earn the living of my family. What could I do?

One day it came to me. A big store needed a personnel director. The store manager spoke to me, smiled to hear I was a college woman, was interested but not antagonistic when he heard I was married. "Now, if you prove to be what we're looking for, there is a big job ahead of you, but first, you must know the work. First you must be a saleswoman." I was sent to the linen department,

527

then to the dress department. From there I was promoted to hats, and then to jewelry and books.

I had a problem not different from those many others were facing. I learned how to adjust things a bit. I prepared breakfast the night before. I taught my young daughter how to feed her little brother. I arranged for lunches for my children with a woman who lived near the school. Sometimes, I would run out to my home at noon, missing my own lunch, but having the peace of seeing that everything went well with my husband. He was tired and lonely, but he said nothing. He would sit, waiting till the children came home. After months I was promoted to the position of personnel director. I was a woman with a career for certain now. I was shown to my office. A pretty little thing with a real desk, a telephone, and a tray . . . for what? . . . for business letters. It looked just like the wire tray in which I drained dishes.

MARIA

Just at one o'clock I had got them all back in again. I attempted to put the plate back into its place. The sealing wax was not dry, and with a sudden motion I sent the wires all agog . . .

ELIZABETH

My second son was born, and a *third*. We moved from Boston to Seneca Falls, where our residence was on the outskirts of town . . . roads often muddy and no sidewalks most of the way. Mr. Stanton was frequently away from home. I had poor servants, and a fourth son was born. I have so much care with all these boys on my hands. How much I long to be free from housekeeping and children so as to have some time to read and think and write.

MARIA

Endow the already established institution with money. Endow the woman who shows genius with time.

Song: "Housewife's Lament"
With grease and with grime from corner to corner,
Forever at war and forever alert,
No rest for a day lest the enemy enter,
I spend my whole life in a struggle with dirt.

Oh, life is a toil and love is a trouble,
Beauty will fade and riches will flee,
Pleasures they dwindle and prices they double,
And nothing is as I would wish it to be.

This time they did not come out of the little grooved lines into which they were put, and I hastened to set them in parallel lines. I gave up then for the day, but, as they looked well and were certainly in firmly, I did not consider that I had made an entire failure.

I thought it nice ladylike work to manage such slight threads and turn such delicate screws; but fine as are the hairs on one's head, I shall seek something finer, for I can see how clumsy they will appear when I get on with the eyepiece and magnify their imperfections. They look parallel to the eye, but with a little magnifying power a very little crook will seem a billowy wave, and a faint star will hide itself in one of the yawning abysses.

I remembered at once that I had seen some cocoons in the library which I had carefully refrained from disturbing. I found them perfect, and unrolled them. I made the perpendicular wires of the spider's web, breaking them and doing the work over again a great many times.

GERTRUDE

My husband got well. Well enough to go to work again. I believed in my equal rights as a woman, but I was happy that day because he was head of our life and of our home. That was something I yielded to him. As I gave my love to him. I left the store. I was thirty-eight years old. More than half of my life had been lived. I was doing nothing: I went to my desk, and there, like an old friend, stood a typewriter. I could write . . . Sometimes it seemed to me my fingers burned with the need to write. I realized that all that I had been living through all these years—the years of my work, of my past, were a mine on which I could draw. I went to see a magazine editor. I received a first assignment, and then another. At the end of the first year, I had earned almost three thousand dollars. I earned it so easily it seemed criminal to be so successful, for I was so happy in this work.

MARIA

I at length got all the wires in—crossing the five perpendicular ones with a horizontal one . . . After twenty-four hours' exposure to the weather, I looked at them. The spider webs had not changed. They were plainly used to a chill and made to endure changes of temperature.

ELIZA

Among the many gentlemen I have become acquainted with and who have been attentive, one I believe is serious. I know not how to introduce this subject, yet, as I fear you may hear it from others and feel anxious for my welfare, I consider it a duty to tell you all. I felt cautious of encouraging his attentions tho' I did not wish to *discourage* them . . . He is a man of business, uniform in his conduct and *very much respected*. He is a man in whom I could place the most unbounded confidence. Nothing rash or impetuous in his disposition, but weighs maturely every circumstance: He appeared as solicitous that I should act with strict propriety as one of my most disinterested friends. He advises me like a friend and would not discourage his addresses till he had an opportunity of making known to my parents his character and wishes—this I promised, but the decision must rest with my parents, their wishes were my law. He insisted upon coming on immediately: that I refused to consent to. He is coming in October. And now, my dearest mother, I submit myself wholly to the wishes of my father and you, convinced that my happiness is your warmest wish, and to promote it has ever been your study. That I feel deeply interested in Mr. Bowne I candidly acknowledge. He is a firm, steady, serious man, there is nothing light or trifling in his character.

Song: "Monday Morning"
And now I am determined to have my own way and I'm Going to be married next Monday morning.

Here we are at Mrs. Carter's boarding house, and though we have endeavored to keep ourselves as much out of the way as possible, a great many people have called to pay their respects to Mr. and Mrs. Bowne. When I hear an old acquaintance call me Mrs. Bowne, it really makes me stare at first, it sounds so very odd.

I am enraptured with New York. You cannot imagine anything half so beautiful as Broadway. Mr. Bowne brings me a pocket full of fruit every day he comes home. I eat as many as I want, and I'm thinking how much I would give to get them to you. But this early fruit won't keep at all. As to news, New York is not so gay as last winter, few balls, but a great many tea parties. The city air has not stolen my country bloom yet, for everyone says, "I need not ask how you do, Mrs. Bowne, you look in such fine health."

ELIZABETH

My fifth child is a girl. The particulars I must give you. On Wednesday morning at six I awoke with a little pain which I well understood. Thereupon I jumped up, bathed and dressed myself, hurried the breakfast, eating none myself, of course, and got the house and all things in order, working bravely between the pains. I neither sat down nor lay down until half past nine, when I gave up all my vocations and avocations, secular and domestic, and devoted myself wholly to the one matter then brought before my mind. At ten o'clock the whole work was completed—the nurse and Amelia our housekeeper alone officiating. I had no doctor, and Mr. Stanton was away on business. When the baby was twenty-four hours old, I got up, bathed, making a sponge and sitz bath, put on my wet bandage, dressed, ate my breakfast, walked on the piazza, and the day being beautiful, I took a ride of three miles on the old plank road. Then I came home, rested an hour or so, read the newspaper and wrote a long letter to Mama . . . My joy in being the mother of a precious little girl is more than I can tell you. The baby is very large and plump, and her head is covered with black curly hair. Oh, how I do rejoice in her!

ELIZA

Walter Bowne, *Junior.* He is so hearty and well, he has not had a day's sickness. I am just starting to leave off his caps, I want his hair to grow before his grandmama sees him. He won't look so pretty without his caps. He creeps so much I find it hard to keep him so nice as I used to.

ANNA

The first notice of me ever printed in the newspaper: This was instigated by my brother-in-law, and was brief, but pointed. It

531

read, "A young girl named Anna Shaw preached her first sermon at Ashton yesterday. Her real friends deprecate the course she is pursuing."

The members of my family, meeting in solemn conclave, sent for me. They had a proposition to make. If I gave up my preaching, they would send me to college and pay for the entire course. We had a long evening together, and it was a very unhappy one. At the end of it, I was given twenty-four hours in which to decide whether I would choose my people and college, or my pulpit and the Arctic loneliness of a life that held no family circle. It did not take me twenty-four hours of reflection to convince me that I must go my solitary way.

ELIZA

You are anxious, my dear mother, to hear from my own hand how I am. My cough is extremely obstinate, I have occasionally a little fever, tho' quite irregular and sometimes a week without any. I have a new physician to attend me: he keeps me on a milk diet, but allows me to eat eggs and oysters. I am much better already, my cough seems to be my only disorder, he thinks he can cure that. Indeed he speaks with perfect confidence and says he has no doubt that as soon as I leave this severe New York winter and get to warmer weather in South Carolina, my cough will soon leave me. You will hear from me often, my dear mother. At present my mind seems so occupied: leaving my children, preparing to go, making arrangements to shut up my house. 'Tis quite a trial to leave my little ones . . . My little Mary has a wet nurse, she is a fine lively child . . . Adieu, my dear mother, I did not think I could have written half so much. Love to all my friends.

MARY

I went to Kensington, Pennsylvania, where seventy-five thousand textile workers were on strike. Of this number, more than ten thousand were little children. They were all stooped little things, round shouldered and skinny, some with their fingers off at the knuckles. Many of them were not yet ten years of age. I asked the newspapermen why they hadn't published the facts about child labor in Pennsylvania. They said that they couldn't because all ten mill owners had stock in the papers. "Well, I've got stock in these little children, and I'll arrange a little publicity." I decided that the children and I would go on a tour. I asked some of the parents if they'd let me have their little boys and girls for a week or ten days. I promised to bring them back safe and sound. They consented. The children carried knapsacks on their backs. They each had a knife and fork, a tin cup and plate. One little girl had a fife, and her brother had a drum. That was our band. The children were very happy, having plenty to eat, taking baths in the streams and rivers every day. I thought, When this strike is over and they go back to the mills, they will never have another holiday like this one. We marched to Jersey City, Hoboken, Princeton and into New York. Our march was doing its work. We were bringing to the attention of the nation the crime of child labor. In Coney Island, after the wild animal show, I put my little children into the empty iron cages and they clung to the bars while I talked. "You see those monkeys in those cages over there? The professors are trying to teach them to talk. The monkeys are too smart, for they fear that the manufacturers would buy them for slaves in their factories. And you see those little boys in those cages? Well, we are told that every American boy has the chance of being President. I tell you that those little boys would sell their chances any day for good square meals and a chance to play."

MARIA

A few evenings ago a meteor flashed upon me suddenly, very bright, very short-lived. It seemed to me that it was sent just for me especially, for it greeted me almost the first instant I looked up and was gone in a second, fleeting and beautiful. I am but a woman. For women there are, undoubtedly, great difficulties in the path, but so much the more to overcome. First, no woman should say, "I am but a woman." *But a woman*—what more can you ask to be?

ELIZA

I send a little pair of shoes for Mary, a little cuckoo toy for Walter, and a tumbler of orange marmalade. I have had only one letter from New York since I have been here . . . not one line from my husband. I can tell you nothing flattering of my health. I am very miserable at present. How are my dear little ones? I hope not too troublesome. I hardly trust myself to think of them, precious children—how they bind me to life. Adieu. I have a bad headache and am low-spirited today.

Song: "When the Train Comes Along"
When the train comes along, when the train comes along, I'm going to meet you at the station when the train comes along.

If my mother asks for me, tell her death doth summon me, I'm going to meet her at the station when the train comes along.

If my father asks for me, tell him death doth summon me, I'm going to meet him at the station when the train comes along.

VOICE UNDER MUSIC

Inscription on the monument in Archdale Churchyard, Charleston, South Carolina . . . "Sacred to the memory of Eliza Southgate Bowne, wife of Walter Bowne of New York, daughter of Robert Southgate Esquire of Scarborough, District of Maine, who departed this life on the nineteenth day of February, aged twenty-five years."

ANNA

The stagecoach took me within twenty-two miles of my destination. To my dismay, however, when I arrived Saturday evening, I found that the rest of the journey lay through a dense woods, and that I could reach my pulpit in time the next morning only by having some one drive me through the woods that night. It was not a pleasant prospect, for I had heard appalling tales of the stockades in this region and of the women who were kept prisoners there. But to miss the engagement was not to be thought of, and when, after I had made several vain efforts to find a driver, a man appeared in a two-seated wagon and offered to take me to my destination, I felt that I had to go with him, though I did not like his appearance. He was a huge, muscular person, with a protruding jaw and a singularly evasive eye; but I reflected that his forbidding expression might be due, in part at least, to the prospect of the long night drive through the woods, to which possibly he objected as much as I did. It was already growing dark when we started, and within a few moments we were out of the little settlement and entering the woods. With me I had a revolver I had long since learned to use, but which I very rarely carried. I had hesitated to bring it now—had even left home without it; and then, impelled by some impulse I never afterward ceased to bless, had returned for it and dropped it into my handbag. I sat on the back seat of the wagon, directly behind the driver, and for a time, as we entered the darkening woods, his great shoulders blotted out all perspective as he drove on in stolid silence. Soon the darkness folded around us like a garment. I could see neither the driver nor his horses. I could hear only the sibilant whisper of the trees and the creak of our slow wheels in the rough forest road. Suddenly the driver began to talk, and at first I was glad to hear the reassuring human tones, for the experience had begun to seem like a bad dream. I replied readily, and at once regretted that I had done so, for the man's choice of topics was most unpleasant. He began to tell me stories of the stockades—grim stories with horrible details, repeated so fully and with such gusto that I soon realized he was deliberately affronting my ears. I told him I could not listen to such talk. He replied with a series of oaths and shocking vulgarities, stopping his horses that he might turn and fling the words into my face. He ended by snarling that I must think him a fool to imagine he did not know the kind of woman I was. What was I doing in that rough country, and why was I alone with him in those dark woods at night? I tried to answer him calmly. "You know perfectly well who I am, and you understand that I am making this journey tonight because I am to preach tomorrow morning and there is no other way to keep my appointment." He uttered a laugh which was a most unpleasant sound. "Well," he said, coolly, "I'm damned if I'll take you. I've got you here, and I'm going to keep you here!" I slipped my hand into the satchel in my lap, and it touched my revolver. No touch of human fingers ever brought such comfort. With a deep breath of thanksgiving I drew it out and cocked it. "Here! What have you got there?" "I have a revolver," I replied, as steadily as I could. "And it is cocked and aimed straight at your back. Now, drive on. If you stop again, or speak, I'll shoot you." For an instant or two he blustered. "By God," he cried, "you wouldn't dare." "Wouldn't I?" I asked. "Try me by speaking just once more." Even as I spoke I felt my hair rise on my scalp with the horror of the moment, which seemed worse than any nightmare a woman could experience. But the man was conquered by the knowledge of the waiting, willing weapon just behind him. He laid his whip savagely on the backs of his horses, and they responded with a leap that almost knocked me out of the wagon. He did not speak again, nor stop, but I dared not relax my caution for an instant. Hour after hour crawled toward day, and still I sat in the unpierced darkness, the revolver ready. I knew he was inwardly raging, and that at any instant he might make a sudden jump and try to get the revolver away from me. I decided that at his slightest movement I must shoot. But dawn came at last, and just as its bluish light touched the dark tips of the pines we drove up to the log hotel in the settlement that was our destination. Here my driver spoke. "Get down," he said gruffly. "This is the place." I sat still. Even yet I dared not trust him. Moreover, I was so stiff after my vigil that I was not sure I could move. "You get down, and wake up the landlord. Bring him out here." He sullenly obeyed and aroused the hotel owner, and when the latter appeared I climbed out of the wagon with some effort but without explanation. That morning I preached in my friend's pulpit as I had promised to do, and the rough building was packed with lumber men who had come in from the neighboring camp. Their appearance caused a great stir. There were forty or fifty of them, and when we took up our collection it was the largest that had ever been taken in the history of the settlement, but I soon learned that it wasn't spiritual comfort that I offered which appealed to the men. My driver of the night before, who was one of their number, had told his pals of his experience, and the whole camp had poured into town to see the woman minister who carried a revolver. "Her sermon?" I overheard one of them say. "I dunno what she preached. But, sure don't make no mistake about one thing, the little lady preacher has sure got grit!"

(All the characters alternate the lines of "Solitude of Self")

ALL

(Alternating) We must make the voyage of life alone.

It matters not whether the solitary voyager be a man or a woman.

We come into the world alone, unlike all who have gone before us: we leave it alone under circumstances peculiar to ourselves.

No mortal ever has been, no mortal ever will be like the soul just launched on the sea of life.

Nature never repeats herself, and the possibilities of one human soul will never be found in another.

The same individual is not the same at all times. Each individual has a middle self, which is not the one of today, nor of yesterday, nor of tomorrow, but among these different selves.

In youth our most bitter disappointments, our brightest hopes and ambitions are known only to ourselves. Even our friendship and love we never fully share with another.

The solitude of individual life: its pains, its penalties, its responsibilities.

The solitude of self. It is the height of cruelty to rob the individual of a single natural right.

Our inner being, which we call our self, no eye nor touch has ever pierced.

Such is individual life. Who can take/. . . dare take/. . . on himself/herself/the rights,/the responsibilities, the duties/of another human soul?

> *(During the course of the preceding section, the actresses have moved their chairs into a close-knit semicircle downstage center: They place their lanterns on the floor in front of them. When they are done speaking, they stare out at the audience for the first time, seemingly to ask the audience to make its own choice. They stay looking at the audience as the lights dim slowly to darkness)*

537